1800 & 18/85

Owner's Workshop Manual

by J.H.Haynes

Associate Member of the Guild of Motoring Writers

and B.L.Chalmers-Hunt

A.M.I.M.I., A.M.I.R.T.E., A.M.V.B.R.A.

Models Covered

1798 c.c.	Austin 1800 Mk I De - Luxe - Saloon	October 1964 to May 1968
	Austin 1800 Mk II De - Luxe - Saloon	May 1968 on
	Austin 1800 S Model De - Luxe - Saloon	September 1969 on
1798 c.c.	Morris 1800 Mk I De - Luxe - Saloon	March 1966 to May 1968
	Morris 1800 Mk II De - Luxe - Saloon	May 1968 on
	Morris 1800 S Model De - Luxe - Saloon	October 1968 on
1798 c.c.	Wolseley 18/85 Mk I De - Luxe - Saloon	March 1967 to August 1969
	Wolseley 18/85 Mk II De - Luxe - Saloon	August 1969 on
	Wolseley 18/85 S Model De - Luxe - Saloon	August 1969 on

 J.H. HAYNES & CO. LTD. 1971

ABCDE 027
FGHIJ
KLMNO
PQRST

SBN 900550 27 9

HAYNES PUBLISHING GROUP
SPARKFORD YEOVIL SOMERSET ENGLAND
distributed in the USA by
HAYNES PUBLICATIONS INC
861 LAWRENCE DRIVE
NEWBURY PARK
CALIFORNIA, 91320
USA

Acknowledgements

Thanks are due to BLMC Ltd for their assistance with regard to the use of technical material and illustrations; to Castrol Ltd, for lubrication chart information; to the 'Autocar' for permission to use the cutaway illustration on the cover; and to Champion Ltd, for the sparking plug photographs.

Thanks are especially due to J R S Hall and L Tooze for their assistance when working on the engine and gearbox.

Whilst every care is taken to ensure that the information in this manual is correct, bearing in mind the changes in design and specification which are a continuous process, even within a model range, no liability can be accepted by the authors and publishers for any loss, damage or injury caused by any errors or omissions in the information given.

Photographic Captions & Cross References

For the ease of reference this book is divided into numbered chapters, sections and paragraphs. The title of each chapter is self explanatory. The sections comprise the main headings within the chapter. The paragraphs appear within each section.

The captions to the majority of photographs are given with the paragraphs of the relevant section to avoid repetition. These photographs bear the same number as the sections and paragraphs to which they refer. The photograph always appears in the same chapter as its paragraph. For example if looking through chapter ten it is wished to find the caption for photograph 9:4 refer to section 9 and then read paragraph 4.

To avoid repetition once a procedure has been described it is not normally repeated. If it is necessary to refer to a procedure already given this is done by quoting the original chapter, section and sometimes paragraph number.

The reference is given thus: Chapter No./Section No. Paragraph No. For example chapter 3, section 6 would be given as: Chapter 2/6. Chapter 2, Section 6, Paragraph 5 would be given as Chapter 2/6:5. If more than one section is involved the reference would be written: Chapter 2/6 to 7 or where the section is not consecutive 2/6 and 9. To refer to several paragraphs within a section the reference is given thus: Chapter 2/6.2 and 4.

To refer to a section within the same chapter the chapter number is usually dropped. Thus a reference in a chapter merely reads 'see Section 8', this refers to Section 8 in that same chapter.

All references to components on the right or left-hand side are made as if looking forward to the bonnet from the rear of the car.

2

AUSTIN 1800 MK I - An excellent family car combining a spacious interior with lively performance from a transverse engine

Introduction

This is a manual for the do-it-yourself minded Austin/Morris 1800 and Wolseley 18/85 motoring enthusiasts. It shows how to maintain these cars in first class condition, and how to carry out repairs when components become worn or break. By doing all maintenance and repair work themselves owners will gain three ways: they will know the job has been done properly; they will have had the satisfaction of doing the job themselves; and they will have saved garage labour charges which, although quite fair bearing in mind the high cost of capital equipment and skilled men, can be as high as 40/- an hour. Regular and careful maintenance is essential if maximum reliability and minimum wear are to be achieved.

The author has stripped, overhauled, and rebuilt all the major mechanical and electrical assemblies and most of the minor ones as well. Only through working in this way can solutions be found to the sort of problems facing private owners. Other hints and tips are also given which can only be obtained through practical experience.

The step-by-step photographic strip and rebuild sequences show how each of the major components was removed, taken apart, and rebuilt. In conjunction with the text and exploded illustrations this should make all the work quite clear - even to the novice who has never previously attempted the more complex job.

Although the 1800 and 18/85 range of cars are hard-wearing and robust it is inevitable that their reliability and performance will decrease as they become older. Repairs and general reconditioning will become necessary if the car is to remain roadworthy. Early models requiring attention are frequently bought by the more impecunious motorist who just cannot afford the repair prices charged in garages. It is in these circumstances that the manual will prove to be of maximum help, as it is the ONLY workshop manual written from practical experience especially for owners of cars covered in this manual (as opposed to service operators and garage proprietors).

Manufacturers official manuals are usually splendid publications which contain a wealth of technical information. Because they are issued primarily to help the manufacturers' authorised dealers and distributors they tend to be written in very technical language, and tend to skip details of certain jobs which are common knowledge to garage mechanics. Owner's workshop manuals are different as they are intended primarily to help the owner, and therefore contain details of all sorts of jobs not normally found in official manuals.

Owners who intend to do their own maintenance and repairs should have a reasonably comprehensive tool kit. Some jobs require special service tools, but in many instances it is possible to get round their use with a little care and ingenuity. For example a $3\frac{1}{2}$ inch diameter jubilee clip makes a most efficient and cheap piston ring compressor.

Throughout this manual ingenious ways of avoiding the use of special equipment and tools are shown. In some cases the proper tool must be used. Where this is the case a description of the tool and its correct use is included, and details are given of where it can usually be borrowed or hired.

When a component malfunctions garage repairs are becoming more and more a case of replacing the defective item with an exchange rebuilt unit. This is excellent practice when a component is thoroughly worn out, but it is a waste of good money when overall the component is only half worn, and requires the replacement of but a single small item to effect a complete repair. As an example, a non-functioning dynamo can frequently be repaired quite satisfactorily just by fitting new brushes.

A further function of this manual is to show the owner how to examine malfunctioning parts; determine what is wrong; then how to make the repair.

Although every care has been taken to ensure all the information in this manual is correct, bearing in mind current manufacturers' practice to make small alterations and design changes without re-classifying the model, no liability can be accepted for damage, loss or injury caused by any errors or omissions in the information given.

Given the time, mechanical do-it-yourself aptitude, and a reasonable collection of tools this manual will show the enthusiastic owner how to maintain and repair his car really economically with minimum recourse to professional assistance and expensive tools and equipment.

Contents

Routine Maintenance

The maintenance instructions listed below are basically those recommended by the manufacturer. They are supplemented by additional maintenance tasks which, through practical experience, the author recommends should be carried out at the intervals suggested.

The additional tasks are indicated by an asterisk, and are primarily of a preventative nature in that they will assist in eliminating the unexpected failure of a component due to fair wear and tear.

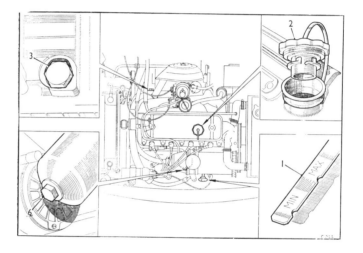

LUBRICATION SYSTEM - ROUTINE MAINTENANCE

1 Oil level markings in dipstick   2 Oil filler cap   3 Oil drain plug   6 Oil filter bowl

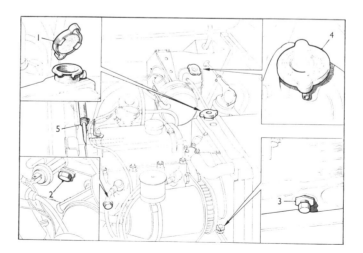

COOLING SYSTEM - ROUTINE MAINTENANCE

1 Radiator filler cap   3 Radiator drain plug   5 Heater return (outlet) hose
2 Block drain plug   4 Expansion tank pressure re-lief cap

Weekly or before a long journey

1. Check oil level in engine/transmission unit and top up if necessary, (see page 18).
2. Check battery level and top up to correct level if necessary.
3. Check tyre pressures and adjust as necessary. (See page 180).
4. Check coolant level in radiator and top up if necessary.
5. Top up windscreen washer bottle.

Every 3,000 miles (5,000Km) or 3 months

Complete all weekly service items plus:
6. Top up carburettor piston damper/s.
7. Check level of fluid in hydraulic clutch reservoir and top up if necessary. (See page 87).
8. Check fluid level in power steering reservoir and top up if necessary. (See page 196).
9. Check tightness of steering column clamp bolt. (Access to the bolt is not easy and it is recommended that your Distributor should carry out this check).
10. Check brake pedal travel and adjust rear brakes if necessary. (See page 131).
11. Check level of fluid in brake master cylinder reservoir and top up if necessary. (See page 131).
12. Check headlamp alignment. (See page 168).
13. Check automatic transmission fluid level and top up if necessary. (See page 118).

Every 6,000 miles (10,000Km) or 6 months

Complete all service items in 3,000 miles service plus:
14. Check valve rocker clearances and adjust if necessary. (See page 43).
15. Check fan belt tension and adjust if necessary. (See page 53).
16. Check correct operation of automatic advance/retard system. (See page 82).
17. Lubricate distributor parts as necessary. (See page 80).
18. Check distributor contact breaker points, clean and adjust. (See page 79).
19. Clean and adjust spark plugs. (See page 82).
20. Check front and rear wheel alignment and adjust if necessary.
21. Inspect front disc brake pads. (See page 137).
22. Check tightness of nuts and bolts on suspension and universal joints.
23. Check battery cell specific gravity readings. (See page 154).
24. Check correct operation of all lamps.
25. Drain oil from engine/transmission unit and refill with fresh oil. (See pages 10 and 18).
26. Fit new oil filter element. (See page 32).
27. Lubricate door locks and hinges.
28. Check selector operation and parking push engagement on automatic transmission.

Every 12,000 miles (20,000Km) or 12 months

Complete all service items in 6,000 mile service, less item 19, plus:
29. Fit new oil filler cap and filler assembly.

Topping up carburettor piston damper.

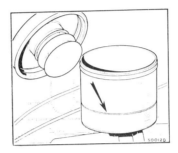

Topping up power steering fluid reservoir.

(1) Brake and (2) Clutch master cylinders (3) Vent holes

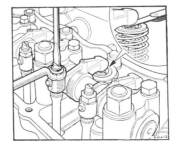

Adjusting rocker/valve stem clearances.

7

30. Test and clean breather control valve – not 'S' type.
31. Fit new air cleaner elements. (See page 57).
32. Clean mechanical pump filter.
33. Fit new spark plugs.
34. Check steering and suspension moving parts for wear.
35. Inspect and clean out rear brake linings and drums.

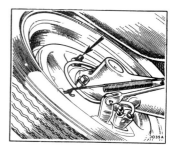

Rear Brake adjuster

Every 24,000 miles (40,000Km) or 18 months

---

36. Completely change brake fluid.

Every 36,000 miles (60,000Km) or 30 months

---

37. Fit new brake servo unit filter.

Every 40,000 miles (65,000Km) or 3 years

---

38. Fit new seals and preferably flexible hoses on braking system.
39. Inspect cylinders and metal pipes.

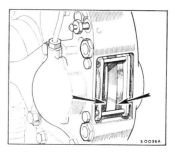

Checking brake pads for wear

Additional service items not covered by manufacturers service schedule

---

*   Every 3,000 miles (5,000Km) or 3 months
1. Adjust brakes. Inspect pads and hoses.
2. Inspect all rubber boots on steering or transmission.
3. Wash bodywork and chrome fittings. Clean interior of car.
4. Check all lights for correct operation.
5. Lubricate all locks and hinges.
6. Lubricate dynamo bearing.
7. Lubricate all controls.

*   Every 6,000 miles (10,000Km) or 6 months
8. Check condition of all cooling system and heater hoses.
9. Lubricate clutch and brake pedal pivots.
10. Check fuel lines and union joints for leaks.
11. Adjust carburettor slow running and tune if necessary.
12. Examine exhaust system for leaks or holes.
13. Wax polish body and chrome plating.
14. Change over tyres to equalise wear.
15. Balance front wheels.

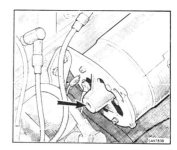

Generator rear bearing.

*   Every 12,000 miles (20,000Km) or 12 months
16. Steam clean underside of body, engine compartment and engine.
17. Inspect ignition leads for cracking or perishing.
18. Fit new windscreen wiper blades.
19. Fit new contact breaker points.

*   Every 24,000 miles (40,000Km) or 18 months
20. Check and adjust any loose play in rack and pinion steering.
21. Examine ball joints and hub bearings for wear and replace as necessary.
22. Check tightness of battery earth lead on bodywork.
23. Renew condenser in distributor.
24. Test engine cylinder compressions, if low determine cause and rectify as necessary.

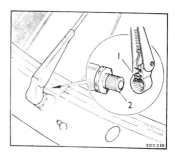

Windscreen wiper arm (1) release clip
(2) splined drive shaft

LUBRICATION CHART
EXPLANATION OF SYMBOLS

 CASTROL XL, 20W-50. A high-quality balanced, multi-grade oil with 'liquid tungsten' recommended for the engine transmission unit in both summer and winter.

 CASTROLEASE LM GREASE. A lithium based, high-melting point grease for use wherever indicated on the chart.

If oil consumption presents a problem after your car has covered a considerable mileage, then it is advisable to use the next heavier Castrol grade in summer.

 Weekly

ENGINE. Check oil level and, if necessary, refill to the correct level with **CASTROL XL**.

After the first 500 miles, and thereafter every 6,000 miles, drain off the old oil while warm, clean and replace magnetic drain plug, and refill with fresh **CASTROL XL**.

NOTE: Owners are advised that more frequent sump-draining periods are desirable if the operation of the car involves:
  (1) Frequent stop/start driving.
  (2) Operation during cold weather, especially when appreciable engine idling is involved.
  (3) Where much driving is done under dusty conditions.

Sump capacity:—8¾ pints plus 1¼ pints filter.
  Models previous to July 1966—11½ pints + 1¼ pints filter.

OVERSEAS

Above —12°C (10°F)	CASTROL XL
Below —12°C (10°F)	CASTROL Z

Every 6,000 miles

DYNAMO. With the oil can add two or three drops of **CASTROLITE** through the central hole in the rear end bearing plate. Do not over-lubricate.

Every 6,000 miles

DISTRIBUTOR. Remove distributor cover and rotor arm and lightly smear the cam with **CASTROLITE**. At the same time place a spot of **CASTROLITE** on the contact breaker pivot. Apply a few drops of **CASTROLITE** to the automatic advance weights and to the screw in the centre of the cam spindle. Do not over-lubricate.

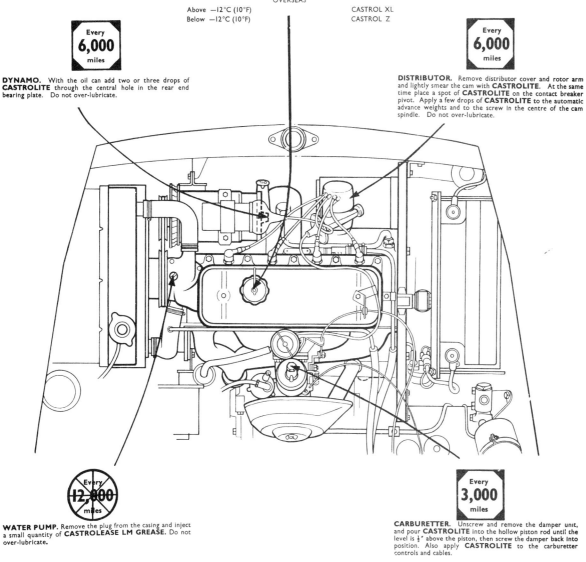

Every 12,800 miles

WATER PUMP. Remove the plug from the casing and inject a small quantity of **CASTROLEASE LM GREASE**. Do not over-lubricate.

Every 3,000 miles

CARBURETTER. Unscrew and remove the damper unit, and pour **CASTROLITE** into the hollow piston rod until the level is ½" above the piston, then screw the damper back into position. Also apply **CASTROLITE** to the carburetter controls and cables.

Recommended Lubricants

COMPONENT	CLIMATIC CONDITIONS PREDOMINATING	CORRECT CASTROL PRODUCTS
ENGINE & TRANSMISSION	All temperatures above −12°C (10°F)	Castrol XL (20W/50) or Castrol GTX
DISTRIBUTOR, CARBURETTOR, DASHPOT, OIL CAN ..	Temperatures −18°C to −7°C (0° to 20°F) ..	Castrolite or Castrol Super 10W/40
	All temperatures below −18°C (0°F)	Castrol CR 5W/20
STEERING RACK (STANDARD)	All conditions	Castrol Hypoy
(POWER STEERING)	All conditions	Castrol XL (20W/50) or Castrol GTX
ALL GREASE POINTS	All conditions	Castrolease L. M
UPPER CYLINDER LUBRICANT...	All conditions	Castrollo
AUTOMATIC TRANSMISSION AND POWER STEERING	All conditions	Castrol TQ

Additionally Castrol 'Everyman' oil can be used to lubricate door, boot and bonnet hinges, and locks, pivots etc.

Ordering Spare Parts

Always order Genuine British Leyland and Unipart spare parts from your nearest BLMC dealers or local garage. BLMC authorised dealers carry a comprehensive stock of GENUINE PARTS and can supply most items 'over the counter'.

When ordering spare parts it is essential to give full details of your car to the storeman. He will want to know the commission, car, and engine numbers. When ordering parts for the transmission unit or body it is also necessary to quote the transmission casing and body numbers.

Commission number: Located on a plate mounted on the right-hand wing valance.

Car number: As above, or on the bonnet lock platform.

Engine number: Stamped on the block or a metal plate fixed centrally to the front of the cylinder block. The letter 'H' or 'L' preceding the engine number denotes either a High or Low compression engine.

Transmission casing assembly: Stamped on a facing provided on the casing just below the starter motor.

Automatic transmission assembly: Stamped on metal plate attached to the torque converter housing above the starter motor.

Body number: Stamped on a plate fixed to the right-hand wing valance.

If you want to retouch the paintwork you can obtain an exact match (providing the original paint has not faded). When obtaining new parts remember that many assemblies can be exchanged. This is very much cheaper than buying them outright and throwing away the old part.

Genuine parts are supplied in cartons bearing one or both of these symbols:

Chapter 1/Engine

Contents

Specifications

Engine Specifications & Data – 1800 Mark I. (October 1964 – April 1968)

Type	18 AMW, 18C, 18WB
Number of cylinders	4
Bore	3.160 inch
Stroke	3.5 inch
Compression ratio...	8.2 :1
Capacity	109.75 cu. inch
Combustion chamber volume (valve fitted)	2.59 to 2.65 cu. inch
Valve operation	Overhead by push rod
Oversize bores	+.010, +.020, +.030, +.040 inch

Crankshaft

Main journal diameter	2.1265 to 2.127 inch
Min. regrind diameter	2.0865 inch
Crankpin journal diameter	1.8759 to 1.8764 inch
Min. regrind diameter	1.836 inch
Crankshaft end thrust	Taken on thrust washer at centre main bearing.
Crankshaft end float	.002 to .003 inch

Main bearings

Number and type	5 thin wall type
Material	Steel backed copper lead or reticular tin.
Length: front, centre and rear	1 1/8 inch
Intermediate	7/8 inch
Diametrical clearance	.001 to .0027 inch
Undersizes	.010, .020, .030, .040 inch

Connecting rods

Type	Angular split big end, bushed small end.
Length between centres	6.5 inch

Big End Bearings

Type and material	Steel backed copper lead or VP3
Length	.775 to .785 inch
Diametrical clearance	.0015 to .0032 inch
End float on crankpin (normal)	.008 to .012 inch
Undersizes	.010 inch, .020 inch, .030 inch, .040 inch.

Pistons

Type	Aluminium solid skirt
Clearance of skirt in cylinder: Top	.0036 to .0045 inch
Bottom	.0018 to .0024 inch
Number of rings	4 (3 compression, 1 oil control)
Width of ring grooves: Top)	
Second)	.064 to .065 inch
Third)	
Oil control	.1578 to .1588 inch
Gudgeon pin bore	.8128 to .813 inch

Piston rings

Compression

Type : Top)...	Plain
Second and third)...	Tapered Cast iron molybdenum filled.
Width: Top)	
Second and third)	.0615 to .0625 inch
Fitted gap : Top)	
Second)	.012 to .017 inch
Ring to groove clearance : Top)	
Second and third) ...	.0015 to .0035 inch

Oil Control

Type	Slotted scraper
Width	.1552 to .1562 inch
Fitted gap	.012 to .017 inch
Ring groove clearance	.0015 to .0036 inch

Gudgeon pin

Type	fully floating
Fit in piston	Hand push fit at 16°C (60°F)

Camshaft
    Journal diameters : Front   ... ...   1.78875 to 1.78925 inch
                         Centre   ... ...   1.72875 to 1.72925 inch
                         Rear   ... ...   1.62275 to 1.62325 inch
    Bearing liner inside diameter (reamed after
        fitting) : Front... ... ...   1.79025 to 1.79075 inch
                Centre   ... ...   1.73025 to 1.73075 inch
                Rear ... ...   1.62425 to 1.62475 inch
    Bearings : Type   ... ...   White metal lined, steel backed
    Diametrical clearance ... ...   .001 to .002 inch
    End thrust   ... ...   Taken on locating plate
    End float... ... ...   .003 to .007 inch
    Drive   ... ...   Chain and sprocket from crankshaft.
    Timing chain ... ...   3/8 pitch x 52 pitches
Tappets
    Type   ... ...   Barrel with flat base
    Outside diameter ... ...   13/16 inch
    Length   ... ...   2.293 to 2.303 inch
Rocker Gear
    Rocker shaft
        Length   ... ...   14 $1/32$ inch
        Diameter... ... ...   .624 to .625 inch
    Rocker arm
        Bore... ... ...   .7485 to .7495 inch
    Rocker arm bush inside diameter... ... ...   .6255 to .626 inch
Valves
    Seat angle ; Inlet and exhaust... ... ... $45\frac{1}{2}°$
    Head diameter : Inlet   ... ...   1.562 to 1.567 inch
                Exhaust   ... ...   1.343 to 1.348 inch
    Stem diameter : Inlet   ... ...   .3422 to .3427 inch
                Exhaust   ... ...   .3417 to .3422 inch
    Stem to guide clearance : Inlet   ... ...   .0015 to .0025 inch
                       Exhaust... ... ...   .002 to .003 inch
    Valve lift : Inlet and exhaust... ... ...   .360[2] and [3]
                                 .320 inch [1]

Valve guides
    Length : Inlet... ... ...   1 $7/8$ inch
          Exhaust   ... ...   2 $13/64$ inch
    Outside diameter : Inlet and exhaust ... ...   .5635 to .5640 inch
    Fitted height above head : Exhaust   ... ... $5/8$ inch
                      Inlet   ... ... $3/4$ inch
    Interference fit in head : Inlet and Exhaust ... ...   .0005 to .00175 inch

Valve springs   Double spring

	Outer	Inner
Free length	2 9/64 inch	1 31/32 inch
Fitted length	1 9/16 inch	1 7/16 inch
Load at fitted length	60.5 lb	30 lb
Load at top of lift	105 lb	50 lb
Valve crash speed	5,700 r.p.m.	

Valve timing
    Timing marks... ... ...   Dimples on camshaft and crankshaft wheels

	1	2	3
Rocker clearance : Running cold	.015 inch	.018 inch	.015 inch
Timing	.020 inch	.020 inch	.020 inch
Inlet valve : Opens	T.D.C.	5°B.T.D.C.	5°B.T.D.C.
Closes...	50°A.B.D.C.	45°A.B.D.C.	45°A.B.D.C.
Exhaust valve : Opens	35°B.B.D.C.	51°B.B.D.C.	40°B.B.D.C.
Closes	15°A.T.D.C.	21°A.T.D.C.	10°A.T.D.C.

1.   Between 18AMW/U/H27523 to H97273, and L20547 to L97811.
2.   Up to 18AMW/U/H27272, L20546; and between 18AMW/U/H9724 to H101630, and L97811 to 97850. Up to 18WB/SB/U/H3063, A/H3936.
3.   From 18AMW/U/H101631, L97851 and 18WB/SB/U/H3064, A/H3937. Camshaft identified by three grooves on end of shaft.

Lubrication
    System   ... ...   Wet sump, pressure fed
    System pressure : Running ... ...   50 to 75 lb/sq inch.
                Idling   ... ...   15 to 25 lb/sq inch.
    Oil pump... ... ...   Hobourn - Eaton rotor

Capacity	3¼ gal. /min at 1,000 r.p.m.
Oil filter...	Tecalemit full flow felt element
By pass valve opens	13 to 17 lb/sq inch
Oil pressure relief valve	70 lb/sq inch
Relief valve spring : Free length	3 inch
Fitted length	2 5/32 inch
Load at fitted length	15. 5 to 16. 5 lb.

Torque Wrench settings (lb. ft.)

Main bearing nuts	70
Flywheel set screws	40
Big end bolts	35
Big end nuts (12 sided)	33 ± 2
Cylinder head nuts...	45 to 50
Cylinder head nuts (up to 18AMW/U/H95775, L94704)	40
Rocker bracket nuts	25
Oil pump to crankcase	14
Transmission case to crankcase	25
Cylinder side cover screws	2
Cylinder side cover screws (later type with deep pressed cover from 18AMW/U/H37052, L20578)	5
Timing cover 1/4 inch screws	6
Timing cover 5/16 inch screws	14
Crankshaft pulley nut	70
Front plate 5/16 inch screws...	20
Water pump to crankcase	17
Water outlet elbow nuts...	8
Rocker cover nuts	4
Manifold nuts	15
Oil filter centre bolt	15
Clutch to flywheel	25 to 30
Carburettor - stud nuts	15
Carburettor - float chamber securing bolt	7. 5
Distributor clamp nut (bolt trapped)	2. 5
Spark plugs	30

Engine Specifications & Data - 1800 MkII, 18/85 MkII and 18/85 with 18H engine (May 1968 on).
   The engine specifications are identical to the 1800 MkI except for the differences listed below:

Type	18H
Compression ratio...	9. 0:1
Combustion chamber volume (valve fitted)	2. 32 to 2. 38 cu. inch.

Connecting rods

Type	Horizontal split big end, solid small end, multi-side nut locking big end bolts.

Pistons

Clearance of skirt in cylinder : Top	0. 0021 to 0. 0033 inch
Bottom	0. 0006 to 0. 0012 inch
Number of rings	3 (2 compression, 1 oil control)

Piston rings

Compression

Type : Top	plain sintered alloy
Second and third...	Tapered, sintered alloy 'Top' marked.
Fitted gap : Top)	
Second)	0. 012 to 0. 022 inch.

Oil Control

Type	Two chrome-faced rings with expander
Width	0. 152 to 0. 158 inch
Fitted gap	0. 015 to 0. 045

Gudgeon pin

Type	Press fit in connecting rod
Fit in piston	Hand push fit at 16°C. (60°F)

Valves

Head diameter : Inlet	1. 625 to 1. 630 inch

Engine Specifications & Data – 1800 MkII 'S' and 18/85 MkII 'S' (Oct. 1968 on)
The engine specifications are identical to the 1800 MkI except for the differences listed below:

Type	18H
Compression ratio...	9. 5:1
Combustion chamber volume (valve fitted)	2. 22 to 2. 28 cu. inch.
Connecting rods	
Type	Horizontal split big end, bushed small end.
Valves	
Head diameter : Inlet	1. 625 to 1. 630 inch.
Valve timing	
Rocker clearance : Running cold	0. 015 inch
Timing	0. 020 inch
Inlet valve : Opens...	16°B. T. D. C.
Closes...	56°A. B. D. C.
Exhaust valve : Opens	51°B. B. D. C.
Closes	21°A. T. D. C.

Engine Specifications & Data 1800 MkII 'S' with 18H engine.
The engine specifications are identical to the 1800 MkI except for the differences listed below:

Type	18H219
Compression ratio...	9. 5:1
Combustion chamber volume (valve fitted)	2. 22 to 2. 28 cu. inch.
Connecting rods	
Type	Horizontal split big end, bushed small end.
Valves	
Head diameter : Inlet	1. 625 to 1. 630 inch
Valve timing	
Rocker clearance : Running cold	0. 015 inch
Timing	0. 020 inch
Inlet valve : Opens...	16°B. T. D. C.
Closes...	56°A. B. D. C.
Exhaust valve : Opens	51°B. B. D. C.
Closes	21°A. T. D. C.

1.   General description

The 1798cc engine is a four cylinder overhead valve type fitted with single or twin S. U. carburettors depending on the model. It is transversely mounted in the car and supported by rubber mountings which reduce both noise and vibrations.

Two valves per cylinder are mounted vertically in the cast iron cylinder head and run in pressed in valve guides. They are operated by rocker arms and pushrods from the camshaft which is located at the base of the cylinder bores in the left hand side of the engine when viewed from the clutch end.

The cylinder head has all five inlet and exhaust ports on the left hand side. Cylinders 1 and 2 share a siamised inlet port and also cylinders 3 and 4. Cylinders 1 and 4 have individual exhaust ports and cylinders 2 and 3 share a siamised exhaust port.

The cylinder block and upper half of the crankcase are cast together. The bottom half of the crankcase consists of a combined transmission casing and oil sump except for the automatic transmission models when the automatic transmission is self contained.

The pistons are made from anodised aluminium with solid skirts. Three compression rings and an oil control ring are fitted on all models. The oil control ring is of the slotted design but on the Mk II 'S' engines a 3 part oil control ring is fitted. The fully floating gudgeon pin is retained in the piston by a circlip

at each end of the hole. Renewable steel backed copper lead or reticular tin shell bearings are fitted to the big ends.

At the front of the engine is a double row chain driving the camshaft via the camshaft and crankshaft chain wheels. The chain is tensioned by a spring loaded slipper type tensioner which automatically adjusts to accommodate chain stretch. The camshaft is supported by three steel backed white metal bearings. If these are replaced it is necessary to ream the bearings in position.

The overhead valves are operated by means of rocker arms mounted on the rocker shaft running along the top of the cylinder head. The rocker arms are activated by pushrods and tappets which in turn rise and fall in accordance with the cams on the camshaft. The valves are held closed by small double valve springs.

The statically and dynamically balanced forged steel crankshaft is supported by five renewable main bearings. Crankshaft end float is controlled by four semi-circular thrust washers two of which are located on either side of the centre bearing.

The centrifugal water pump and radiator cooling fan are driven, together with the dynamo or alternator, from the crankshaft pulley wheel by a rubber/fabric belt. The distributor is mounted towards the rear of the right hand side of the cylinder block and advances and retards the ignition timing by mechanical and vacuum means. The distributor is driven at half crankshaft speed by a short shaft and skew gear from a skew gear on the camshaft. The oil pump is driven from the camshaft skew gear and

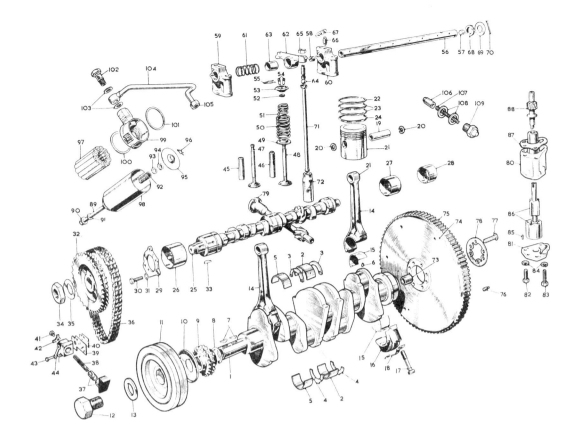

Fig. 1.1. EXPLODED VIEW OF ENGINE INTERNAL PARTS

No.	Description
1	Crankshaft
2	Crankshaft main bearing (Nos. 1, 3, and 5)
3	Upper thrust washer
4	Lower thrust washer
5	Crankshaft main bearing (Nos. 2 and 4)
6	Oil restrictor
7	Key for gear and pulley
8	Gear packing washer(s)
9	Timing gear
10	Oil thrower (First type illustrated)
11	Pulley
12	Nut for crankshaft
13	Locking washer
14	Connecting rod
15	Bearing - big-end
16	Big-end - bearing cap
17	Set screw for cap
18	Tab washer
19	Gudgeon pin
20	Circlip
21	Piston
22	Compression ring - top
23	Compression ring - second and third
24	Scraper ring
25	Camshaft
26	Camshaft bearing liner - front

No.	Description
27	Camshaft bearing liner - centre
28	Camshaft bearing liner - rear
29	Locking plate
30	Screw - plate to block
31	Shakeproof washer
32	Timing gear
33	Key for gear
34	Nut for camshaft
35	Locking washer
36	Timing chain
37	Slipper head and cylinder
38	Spring
39	Body back plate
40	Joint
41	Plug for body
42	Lockwasher for plug
43	Bolt tensioner to block
44	Lock washer
45	Exhaust valve guide
46	Inlet valve guide*
47	Exhaust valve*
48	Inlet valve*
49	Valve spring collar
50	Valve spring - outer*
51	Valve spring - inner*
52	Packing ring
53	Spring cap
54	Valve cotters*

No.	Description
55	Circlip for cotter*
56	Valve rocker shaft
57	Plain plug
58	Screwed plug
59	Bracket with tapped hole
60	Plain bracket
61	Spring
62	Valve rocker
63	Rocker bush
64	Adjusting screw
65	Locknut for screw
66	Locking screw
67	Screw locating plate
68	Spring washer (D/C)
69	Washer for rocker
70	Split pin
71	Push-rod
72	Tappet
73	Clutch shaft bush
74	Flywheel
75	Starter ring
76	Dowel for clutch
77	Bolt crankshaft to flywheel
78	Locking plate
79	Distributor drive spindle
80	Oil pump body
81	Cover
82	Screw - cover to body (short)
83	Screw - cover to body

No.	Description
	(long)
84	Spring washer
85	Dowel for pump body
86	Shaft with rotors
87	Joint to block
88	Driving spindle
89	Centre bolt
90	Washer
91	Sealing washer
92	Spring
93	Steel washer
94	Felt washer
95	Pressure plate
96	Circlip
97	Element
98	Container
99	Oil filter head assembly
100	Joint washer - container to filter head
101	Joint washer - filter head to block
102	Screw for banjo union
103	Washer for screw
104	Oil pipe
105	Nut for nipple
106	Oil relief valve
107	Spring
108	Washer(s) - 1 off copper
109	Cup nut - spring

*First type valve assembly

located beside the crankshaft.

2. Routine maintenance

1. Once a week, or more frequently if necessary, remove the dipstick and check the engine oil level which should be at the 'MAX' mark. Top up the oil in the sump with the recommended grade of oil (see page 10 for details). On no account allow the oil to fall below the 'MIN' mark on the dipstick.

2. Every 6,000 miles run the engine until it is hot, place a container with a capacity of at least 13 pints under the drain plug in the transmission case, undo and remove the drain plug, and allow the oil to drain for at least ten minutes. At the same time renew the oil filter element as described in section 25.

3. Clean the drain plug, ensure the washer is in place, and return the plug to the transmission case. Tighten the plug firmly. Refill the sump with the correct amount of recommended oil (see technical data for the correct capacity).

4. In very hot or dusty conditions, or in cold weather with a great deal of stop/start driving, with considerable use of the choke control, it is beneficial to change the engine oil every 3,000 miles.

5. Check and adjust the valve rocker clearance as described in section 55.

3. Major operations with engine in place

Not many major operations can be carried out on the 1800 engine with it in place because it is not possible to drop the sump as can be done with most conventional cars. The following operations are possible however:

(a) Removal and replacement of the cylinder head assembly.
(b) Removal and replacement of the timing chain and gears.
(c) Removal and replacement of the engine mountings.

4. Major operations with engine removed

The following major operations can be carried out with the engine out of the body and on the bench or floor:

(a) Removal and replacement of the clutch/flywheel.
(b) Removal and replacement of the main bearings.
(c) Removal and replacement of the crankshaft.
(d) Removal and replacement of the oil pump.
(e) Removal and replacement of the big end bearings.
(f) Removal and replacement of the pistons and connecting rods.
(g) Removal and replacement of the camshaft.

5. Engine and manual transmission - removal

The sequence of operations listed in this section is not critical, as the position of the person undertaking the work or the tool in his hand will determine to a certain extent the order in which the work is tackled. Obviously the power unit cannot be removed until everything is disconnected from it, and following the sequence listed will ensure nothing is forgotten.

1. Turn the water drain tap on the side of the cylinder block and also remove the drain plug at the bottom of the radiator. N.B. Do not drain the water in your garage or the place where you will remove the engine transmission unit if receptacles are not available to catch the water. Remove the radiator filler cap.

2. Disconnect the battery by undoing the terminal nuts and screws which hold the terminal leads to the terminal posts (photo A) and then remove the battery from the carrier (photo B).

3. With a suitable container in position, unscrew the drain plug from the underside of the transmission casing and drain all the oil. When the oil has all drained out screw the plug back in tightly to ensure that it is not mislaid (photo).

4. With the assistance of a second person to take the weight of the bonnet, undo the lower stay retaining bolt. Replace the bolt to ensure that it is not lost (photo).

5. Using a soft pencil, mark the outline position of both the hinges at the bonnet to act as a datum for refitting, and remove the bonnet hinge retaining bolts (photo).

6. With the assistance of the second person lift away the bonnet and put in a safe place so that it will not be scratched (photo).

7. Undo the air cleaner retaining wing nut and lift away the air cleaner (photo).

8. Disconnect the choke control cable (photo A), and the throttle control cable, (photo B) from the carburettor linkage.

9. Make a note of the colour coding of the two low tension cables at the ignition coil and disconnect the two cables (photo).

10. Mark the high tension cables relative to the spark plugs for correct refitting and disconnect the four leads (photo).

11. Remove the high tension cable from the centre of the ignition coil. Release the two distributor cap retaining clips and lift away the distributor cap.

12. Disconnect the electric cable connector to the oil pressure warning light switch (photo).

13. Disconnect the low tension cable from the side of the distributor body (photo).

14. Make a note of the position of the two heater hoses at the rear of the engine to ensure that they are refitted the correct way round. Slacken the two clips and separate the hoses from the metal pipes (photo).

15. Release the radiator overflow hose from the filler cap neck. Slacken the top hose clips and remove the radiator top hose.

16. Refer to Chapter 2, Section 5 and remove the radiator and surround. Remove the four fan mounting bolts and lift away the fan (photo).

17. Disconnect the heavy duty cable from the rear end of the starter motor (photo).

18. Make a note of the colour coding and positioning of the cables to the rear of the generator or alternator and release these electrical connections. Locate and slacken the generator or alternator mounting bolts and push the unit towards the engine. Lift the fan belt from the generator or alternator pulley, then from the crankshaft pulley and finally from the water pump pulley. Remove the mounting bolts and lift away the generator or alternator.

19. Lift the rotor arm from the distributor spindle and put in a safe place (photo).

20. Disconnect the water temperature gauge sender unit electric cable (photo).

21. Disconnect the fuel feed pipe to the carburettor (electric pump installation), (photo), or the fuel feed pipe to the fuel pump (mechanical pump installation) and plug

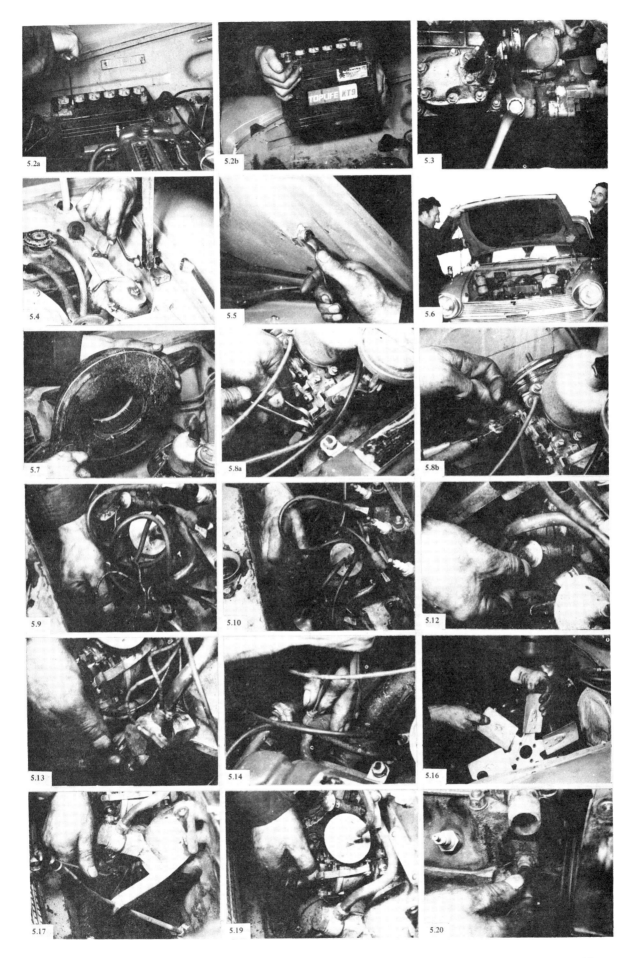

5.2a

5.2b

5.3

5.4

5.5

5.6

5.7

5.8a

5.8b

5.9

5.10

5.12

5.13

5.14

5.16

5.17

5.19

5.20

the end of the pipe with a pencil to stop the entry of dirt or loss of petrol.

22. Remove the bolts securing the horn in place and disconnect the electrical wires at the snap connectors. Place the horn on one side.

23. Undo the clamp holding the exhaust manifold to the downpipe and lift away the clamp.

24. Remove the bolt holding the earthing strap to the power unit at the clutch cover.

25. Remove the clutch slave cylinder clevis pin by extracting the split pin (photo A) and lifting out the cotter pin (photo B).

26. Remove the two clutch slave cylinder mounting bolts to the flywheel housing (photo) detach the tension spring, and tie the cylinder back out of the way. ON NO ACCOUNT DEPRESS THE CLUTCH PEDAL AFTER THIS HAS BEEN DONE.

27. Make a note of the location of the starter motor solenoid low tension cable connections and release the cable connections, (photo A). Remove the solenoid mounting screw and tie the solenoid back out of the way (photo B).

28. Remove the nuts and washers on the 'U' bolts holding the drive shaft inner universal joints to the differential shaft flanges (photo).

29. Disconnect the lower engine tie-rod at the transmission casing and carefully swing down (photo).

30. Extract the 'U' bolts from the drive shaft universal joints using a screwdriver to lever out if tight (photo).

31. Place the gear change lever in the neutral position. Unscrew the six nuts and spring washers from the gear change cable housing (photo).

32. Pull the cable housing back from the transmission unit (photo A) and allow to hang down well away from the unit (photo B).

33. Disconnect the exhaust pipe from the flexible rubber mounting (photo).

34. Release the exhaust tail pipe from its mounting (photo) and also from the support bracket from the differential housing and lift away the complete exhaust system.

35. Release the speedometer drive cable at the drive gear adaptor on the transmission case and cover (photo).

36. Using a tyre lever between the exhaust pipe bracket and the universal joint carefully push each flange inwards so as to clear each joint (photo).

37. Carefully lift out each drive shaft coupling (photo).

38. Remove the mounting nut and bolt on the top of the engine damper (photo).

39. Remove the mounting nut and bolt on the bottom of the engine damper (photo).

40. Disconnect the brake vacuum hose (photo) from the inlet manifold take off pipe (arrowed).

41. Place a rope sling around the front of the engine just behind the timing cover and a further sling immediately in front of the engine rear plate, or alternatively fit lifting brackets.

42. Take the weight of the power unit and remove the two nuts and bolts on left hand front mounting bracket (photo).

43. Remove the two nuts and bolts on the right hand front power unit mounting brackets (photo).

44. Remove the two remaining nuts and bolts from each of the mounting brackets and lift away the two brackets (photo A and B).

45. Remove the bolts securing the mounting channel to the vertical mounting support (photo).

46. Remove the bolts securing the vertical mounting

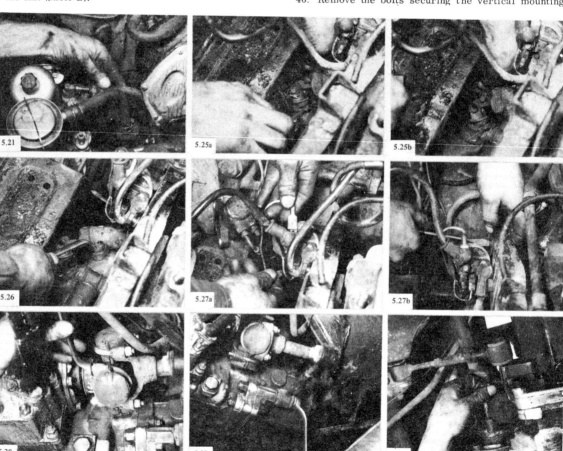

5.21   5.25a   5.25b
5.26   5.27a   5.27b
5.28   5.29   5.30

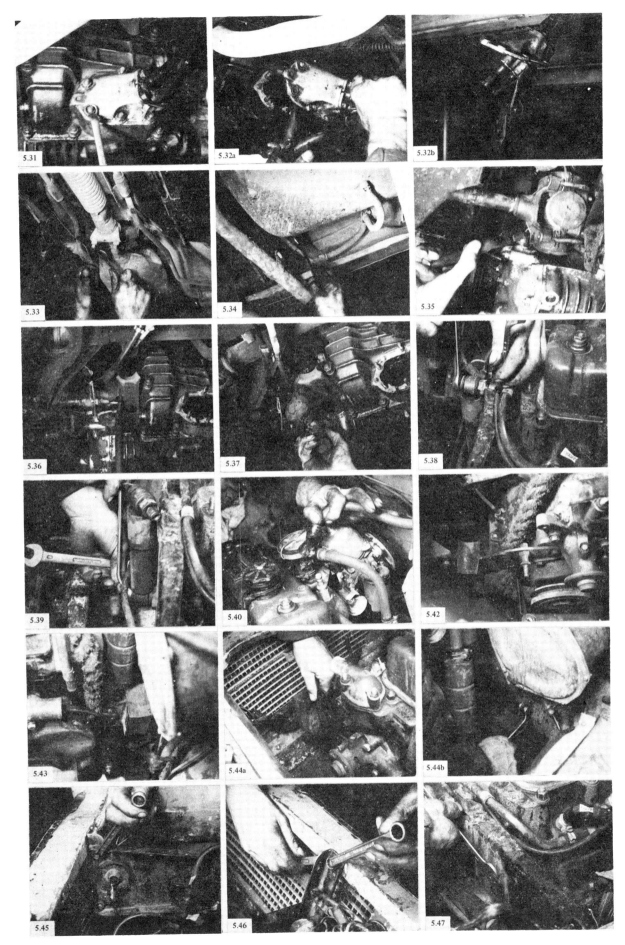

support to the front grille crossmember (photo).

47. Disconnect the rubber mounting from the mounting channel (photo).

48. Tilt the power unit and lift away the mounting channel (photo). Make special note that there is an electrical cable passing through a rubber grommet in the mounting channel. Feed the cable through the grommet to avoid damage to the cable. (Location of cable shown in photo).

the location of the cables and bracket.

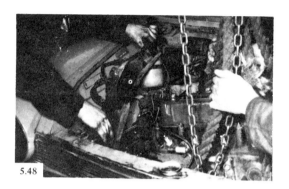

5.48

49. Raise the power unit and pull on the front to bring the front end forward as far as possible (photo).

50. Recheck that no electrical connection, fuel pipe connection or control cable has been left attached to the power unit.

51. Carefully manipulate the power unit from the engine compartment. To assist it is recommended that a second person be called upon to help at this stage (photo).

52. Lift the power unit away from the engine compartment, take care not to scratch the wing panels or wing mirrors. Old blankets over the paintwork will assist in preventing damage to the paintwork (photo).

53. With the unit suspended but away from the car thoroughly wash the exterior with paraffin or grease solvent such as 'Gunk'. Wash off with a strong water jet and dry thoroughly. The unit is now ready for dismantling.

---

6. Engine and automatic transmission - removal

1. The procedure for removal of an engine fitted to an automatic gearbox is identical except that instead of removing the gear cable housing from the transmission unit it is necessary to move the gear selector to the 'P' position.

2. Release the selector and park cable clevis pins located at the bulkhead side of the bracket next to the screen wash bottle bracket. Also disconnect the two cables from the bracket. Reference to photo will show

---

7. Engine - separating from manual transmission unit

Full details of this operation are given in Chapter 7, Section 2.

---

8. Engine - separating from automatic transmission unit

Full details of this operation are given in Chapter 8, Section 11.

---

9. Engine - dismantling - general

1. It is best to mount the engine on a dismantling stand, but if this is not available, stand the engine on a strong bench so as to be at a comfortable working height. Failing this, it can be stripped down to the floor.

2. During the dismantling process the greatest care should be taken to keep the exposed parts free from dirt. As an aid to achieving this aim, it is a very sound scheme to thoroughly clean down the outside of the engine, removing all traces of oil and congealed dirt.

3. A good grease solvent such as 'Gunk' will make the job much easier, as, after the solvent has been applied and allowed to stand for a time, a vigorous jet of water will wash off all the solvent and the grease and filth. If the dirt is thick and deeply embedded, work the solvent into it with a strong stiff paintbrush.

4. Finally wipe down the exterior of the engine with a rag and only then, when it is quite clean should the dismantling process begin. As the engine is stripped, clean each part in a bath of paraffin or petrol

5. Never immerse parts with oilways in paraffin, i.e. the crankshaft, but to clean wipe down carefully with a petrol dampened rag. Oilways can be cleaned out with pipe cleaners. If an air line is present all parts can be

5.49

5.51

5.52

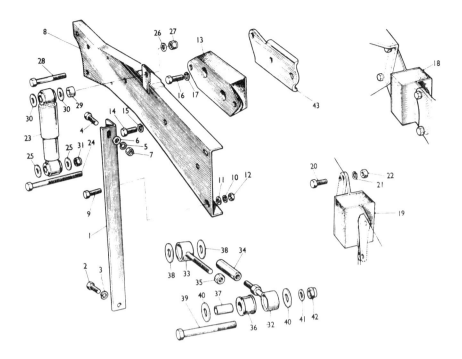

Fig. 1. 2. ENGINE MOUNTINGS

No.	Description	No.	Description	No.	Description	No.	Description
1	Mounting support	13	Rubber mounting	23	Shock absorber	34	Sleeve - rod
2	Screw - support to body	14	Screw - mounting to channel	24	Bolt - absorber to engine	35	Nut - rod
3	Spring washer	15	Spring washer	25	Plain washer - large	36	Rubber bush
4	Screw - support to body	16	Screw - mounting to engine	26	Plain washer - small	37	Spacer tube
5	Spring washer	17	Spring washer	27	Locknut - bolt	38	Plain washer - rod to R. H. sus-
6	Plain washer	18	Rubber mounting - rear	28	Bolt - absorber to support		pension bolt
7	Nut - screw	19	Rubber mounting - front	29	Distance piece - bolt	39	Bolt - rod to flywheel housing
8	Mounting channel	20	Screw - mounting to engine/	30	Plain washer	40	Plain washer
9	Screw - support to mounting		body	31	Locknut - bolt	41	Plain washer
10	Spring washer	21	Spring washer	32	Engine tie-rod	42	Locknut - bolt
11	Plain washer	22	Nut - screw	33	Engine tie-rod	43	Tie-rod bracket
12	Nut - screw						

blown dry and the oilways blown through as an added precaution.

6. Re-use of old gaskets is a false economy and can give rise to oil and water leaks, if nothing worse. To avoid the possibility of trouble after the engine has been re-assembled always use new gaskets throughout.

7. Do not throw the old gaskets away as it sometimes happens that an immediate replacement cannot be found and the old gasket is then very useful as a template. Hang up the gaskets as they are removed on a suitable hook or nail.

8. To strip the engine it is best to work from the top down. The crankcase provides a firm base on which the engine can be supported in an upright position. When the stage where the crankshaft must be removed is reached, the engine can be turned on its side and all other work carried out with it in this position.

9. Wherever possible, replace nuts, bolts and washers finger-tight from wherever they were removed. This helps avoid later loss and muddle. If they cannot be replaced then lay them out in such a fashion that it is clear from where they came.

10. Engine - removing ancilliary components

Before basic engine dismantling begins it is necessary to strip it of ancilliary components and these are as follows:

> Closed circuit breathing system;
> Exhaust emission control equipment;
> Dynamo or alternator;
> Distributor;
> Thermostat;
> Inlet manifold and carburation;
> Exhaust manifold;
> Starter motor.

It is possible to strip all these items with the engine in the car if it is merely the individual items that require attention. Presuming the engine to be out of the car on the bench, starting on the right-hand side of the unit, follow the procedure described below:

1. Remove the closed circuit breather (photo A) by undoing the three retaining clips, and undo the bolt which secures the breather pipe/tappet cover in place (photo B). Remove the exhaust emission control equipment where fitted.

10.1a

10.1b

2. Slacken off the dynamo or alternator retaining bolts and remove the unit with its support brackets.
3. To remove the distributor first disconnect the manifold vacuum advance/retard pipe which leads from the small securing clip on the cylinder head. Unscrew the clamp bolt at the base of the distributor and lift the distributor away from its base plate and drive shaft.
4. Remove the thermostat cover by releasing the three nuts and spring washers which hold it in position and then remove the gasket and thermostat unit.
5. Moving to the left hand side of the engine, remove the carburettor if still in place (photo).
6. Then remove the inlet and exhaust manifolds (photo) after unscrewing the brass nuts and washers holding the manifolds to the cylinder head.
7. If still fitted undo the two bolts which hold the starter motor in place and lift the motor away (photo).
8. The engine is now stripped of all ancilliary components and is ready for major dismantling to begin.

---

11. Cylinder head removal - engine on bench

---

1. With the engine out of the car and standing upright on the bench or on the floor remove the cylinder head as follows:
2. Unscrew the two rocker cover bolts and lift the rocker cover and gasket away.
3. Unscrew the rocker pedestal nuts (four) and the eleven main cylinder head nuts half a turn at a time in the order shown in FIG 1:3. When all the nuts are no longer under tension they may be screwed off the cylinder head one at a time.

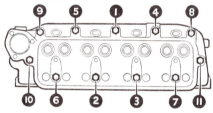

Fig. 1.3. Cylinder head nut tightening sequence.

4. Remove the rocker assembly complete, and place it on one side.
5. Remove the push rods, keeping them in the relative order in which they were removed. The easiest way to do this is to push them through a sheet of thick paper or thin card in the correct sequence.
6. The cylinder head can be removed by lifting upwards.

10.5

10.6

10.7

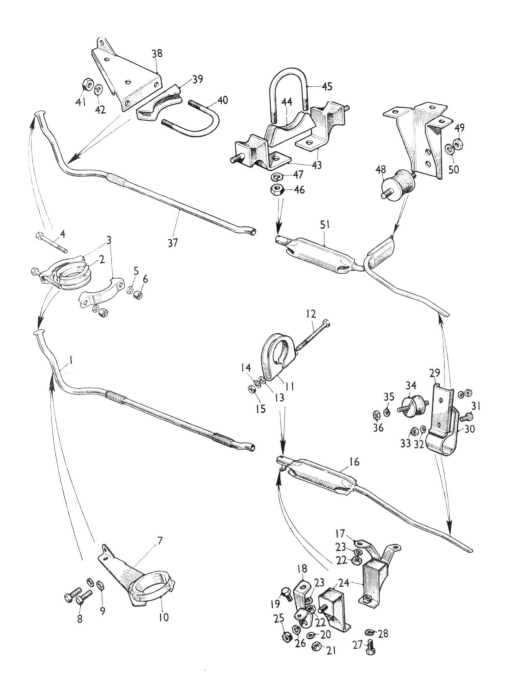

Fig. 1.4. EXHAUST SYSTEM COMPONENTS - ALL MODELS EXCEPT MK II 'S'

No.	Description	No.	Description	No.	Description	No.	Description
1	Front pipe	13	Plain washer	25	Nut - mounting to bracket	37	Front pipe*
2	Inner clamp - pipe to manifold	14	Spring washer	26	Spring washer	38	Bracket pipe to transmission*
		15	Nut	27	Screw - mounting to silencer	39	Support bracket*
3	Outer clamp - pipe to manifold	16	Silencer and tail pipe (rear)	28	Spring washer - mounting to silencer	40	'U' bolt - pipe to bracket*
4	Bolt for clamp	17	Silencer mounting bracket - R. H.	29	Strap - tail pipe support	41	Nut*
5	Plain washer			30	Clip - tail pipe to strap	42	Spring washer*
6	Nut	18	Silencer mounting bracket - L. H.	31	Screw - clip	43	Silencer mounting*
7	Bracket - pipe to transmission	19	Screw - bracket to body	32	Spring washer	44	Support bracket*
8	Screw - bracket to transmission	20	Spring washer	33	Nut	46	Nut*
9	Spring washer	21	Nut - bracket to body	34	Tail pipe mounting	47	Spring washer*
10	Clip - pipe to bracket	22	Nut - bracket to body	35	Nut - mounting to strap/body	48	Tail pipe mounting* ≁
11	Clip - front to rear pipe	23	Spring washer - bracket to body	36	Spring washer	49	Nut* ≁
12	Screw - clip	24	Silencer mounting			50	Spring washer* ≁
						51	Twin silencer and tail pipe* ≁

*From A17S-54318A
M17S-9937A
W17S-101A

≁ Germany from commencement

25

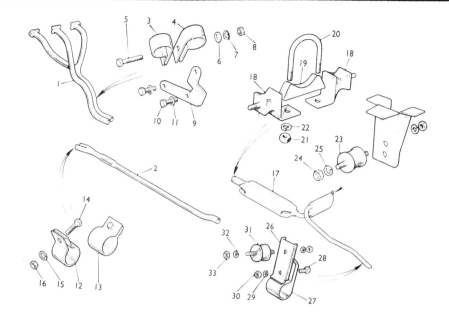

Fig. 1.5. EXHAUST SYSTEM COMPONENTS - MK II 'S' MODELS

No.	Description	No.	Description	No.	Description	No.	Description
1	Exhaust manifold	10	Screw - bracket to transmission	16	Nut	25	Spring washer
2	Front pipe			17	Twin silencer and tail pipe	26	Strap - tail pipe support
3	Clip - manifold to bracket	11	Spring washer	18	Silencer mounting	27	Clip - tail pipe to strap
4	Clip - manifold to bracket	12	Clip - front pipe to manifold	19	Support bracket	28	Screw
5	Bolt - clips to bracket	13	Clip - front pipe to manifold	20	'U' bolt	29	Spring washer
6	Plain washer	14	Screw	21	Nut	30	Nut
7	Spring washer	15	Spring washer	22	Spring washer	31	Tail pipe mounting
8	Nut			23	Tail pipe mounting	32	Spring washer
9	Bracket			24	Nut	33	Nut

If the head is jammed, try to rock it to break the seal. Under no circumstances try to prise it apart from the block with a screwdriver or cold chisel as damage may be done to the faces of the head of the block. If the head will not readily free, turn the engine over by the flywheel as the compression in the cylinders will often break the cylinder head joint. If this fails to work, strike the head sharply with a plastic headed hammer, or with a wooden hammer, or with a metal hammer with an interposed piece of wood to cushion the blows. Under no circumstances hit the head directly with a metal hammer as this may cause the iron casting to fracture. Several sharp taps with the hammer, at the same time pulling upwards, should free the head. Lift the head off and place on one side.

12. Cylinder head removal - engine in car

To remove the cylinder head with the engine still in the car the following additional procedures to the above must be followed (these procedures should be carried out before those listed in the previous section):

1. Disconnect the battery by removing the lead from the positive terminal. (Negative terminal on later cars).

2. Drain the water by turning the taps at the base of the radiator, and at the bottom left hand corner of the cylinder block.

3. Loosen the clip at the thermostat housing end on the top water hose, and pull the hose from the thermostat pipe.

4. Remove the heater/demister unit inlet hose by releasing the clip securing it to the cylinder head (on cars fitted with heater/demister units).

5. Remove the air cleaner/s, the S.U. carburettor/s and the heat shield, as described in Chapter 3, and undo the clamp holding the exhaust manifold to the exhaust down pipe. Leave the inlet and exhaust manifolds in place as they provide useful leverage when removing the cylinder head.

6. The procedure is now the same as for removing the cylinder head when on the bench. One tip worth noting is that should the cylinder head refuse to free easily, the battery can be reconnected up, and the engine turned over on the solenoid switch. Under no circumstances turn the ignition on unless the wire to the electric pump (if fitted) is disconnected, and ensure that the distributor cap is removed as otherwise the engine might fire.

13. Valve removal

1. The valves can be removed from the cylinder head by the following method: With a pair of pliers remove the spring circlips holding the two halves of the split tapered collets together. Compress each spring in turn with a valve spring compressor until the two halves of the collets can be removed. Release the compressor and remove the spring, shroud and valve.

2. If, when the valve spring compressor is screwed down, the valve spring retaining cap refuses to free and expose the split collet, do not continue to screw down on the compressor as there is a likelihood of damaging it.

3. Gently tap the top of the tool directly over the cap with a light hammer. This will free the cap. To avoid the compressor jumping off the valve retaining cap when it is tapped, hold the compressor firmly in position with one hand.

4. Slide the rubber oil control seal off the top of each valve stem and then drop out each valve through the combustion chamber.

5. It is essential that the valves are kept in their correct sequence unless they are so badly worn that they are to be renewed. If they are going to be kept and used again, place them in a sheet of card having eight holes numbered 1 to 8 corresponding with the relative positions the valves were in when fitted. Also keep the valve springs, washers etc., in correct order.

14. Valve guide - removal

If it is wished to remove the valve guides they can be removed from the cylinder head in the following manner: Place the cylinder head with the gasket face on the bench and with a suitable hard steel punch drift the guides out of the cylinder head.

15. Rocker assembly - dismantling

1. To dismantle the rocker assembly, release the rocker shaft locating screw, remove the split pins, flat washers, and spring washers from each end of the shaft and slide from the shaft the pedestals, rocker arms, and rocker spacing rings.

2. From the end of the shaft undo the plug which gives access to the inside of the rocker which can now be cleaned of sludge etc. Ensure the rocker arm lubricating holes are clear.

16. Timing cover, gears and chain - removal

The timing cover, gears and chain can be removed with the engine in the car providing the radiator, radiator surround and fan belt are removed. The procedure for removing the timing cover, gears and chain is otherwise the same irrespective of whether the engine is in the car or on the bench, and is as follows:

1. Bend back the locking tab of the crankshaft pulley locking washer under the crankshaft pulley retaining bolt, and with a large spanner remove the bolts and locking washers.

2. Placing two large screwdrivers behind the crankshaft pulley wheel at 180° to each other, carefully lever off the wheel. It is preferable to use a proper extractor if this is available, but large screwdrivers or tyre levers are quite suitable, providing care is taken not to damage

the pulley flange.

3. Remove the woodruff key from the crankshaft nose with a pair of pliers and note how the channel in the pulley is designed to fit over it. Place the woodruff key in a glass jam jar as it is very small part and can easily become lost.

4. Unscrew the bolts holding the timing cover to the block. NOTE that three different sizes of bolt are used, and that each bolt makes use of a large flat washer as well as a spring washer.

5. Pull off the timing cover and gasket.

6. With the timing cover off, take off the oil thrower. NOTE: The concave side faces forward. Take out the bottom plug from the chain tensioner, fit a 1/8 inch Allen key in the cylinder and turn the key clockwise until the slipper head is pulled right back and locked behind the limit head.

7. Bend back the locking tab on the washer under the camshaft retaining nut noting how the locking tag fits in the camshaft gearwheel keyway. Remove the nut as shown in Fig. 1:6.

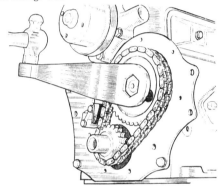

Fig. 1.6. Camshaft chainwheel securing nut removal.

8. To remove the camshaft and crankshaft timing wheel complete with chain, ease each wheel forward a little at a time levering behind each gearwheel in turn with two large screwdrivers at 180° to each other. If the gearwheels are locked solid then it will be necessary to use a proper gearwheel and pulley extractor, and if one is available this should be used anyway in preference to screwdrivers. With both gearwheels safely off, remove the woodruff keys from the crankshaft and camshaft with a pair of pliers and place them in a jam jar for safe keeping. Note the number of very thin packing washers behind the crankshaft gearwheel and remove them very carefully.

17. Camshaft - removal

The camshaft cannot be removed with the engine in place in the car. With the engine on the bench remove the timing cover gears and chain, as described in Section 16. Then remove the distributor drive gear as described in Section 18. With the drive gear out of the way, proceed in the following manner:

1. Remove the three bolts and spring washers which

hold the camshaft locating plate to the block. The bolts are normally covered by the camshaft gearwheel.

2. Remove the plate. The camshaft can now be withdrawn. Take great care to remove the camshaft gently, and in particular ensure that the cam peaks do not damage the camshaft bearings as the shaft is pulled forward.

18. Distributor drive - removal

To remove the distributor drive with the transmission unit still in position it is first necessary to remove one of the tappet cover bolts. With the distributor and the distributor clamp plate already removed, this is achieved as follows:

1. Unscrew the single retaining bolt and locking washer to release the distributor housing.

2. With the distributor housing removed, screw into the end of the distributor drive shaft a 5/16 inch U.N.F. bolt. A tappet cover bolt is ideal for this purpose. The drive shaft can then be lifted out, the shaft being turned slightly in the process to free the shaft skew gear from the camshaft skew gear. In this engine the gear shaft can only be removed when the crankshaft is at 90° before or after T.D.C. so the pistons are all halfway down their bores.

3. If the transmission unit has already been removed then it is a simple matter to push the drive shaft out from inside the crankcase.

19. Piston, connecting rod and big end bearing-removal

Unlike a conventional engine it is not possible to remove the pistons or connecting rods whilst the engine is still in the car as it is necessary to first remove the flywheel housing and primary drive gear cover and then separate the transmission unit as described in Chapter 7 (manual) or Chapter 8 (automatic). Then proceed as follows:

1. Knock back with a cold chisel the locking tabs on the big end retaining bolts, and remove the bolts and locking tabs. On Mk II and Mk II'S' models special bolts and multisided nuts are used instead of tab lock washers and bolts (see Fig. 1:7). Undo the nuts and place to one side. It is recommended that the bolts and multisided nuts are kept as matched sets.

2. Remove the big end caps one at a time, taking care to keep them in the right order and the correct way round. Also ensure that the shell bearings are also kept with their correct connecting rods and caps unless they are to be renewed. Normally, the numbers 1 - 4 are stamped on adjacent sides of the big end caps and connecting rods, indicating which cap fits on which rod and which way round the cap fits (see Fig. 1:8). If no numbers or lines can be found then with a sharp screwdriver scratch mating marks across the joint from the rod to the cap. One line for connecting rod No. 1, two for connecting rod No. 2 and so on. This will ensure that there is no confusion later as it is most important that

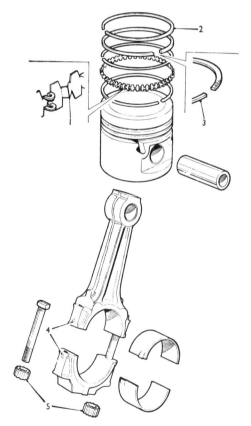

Fig. 1.7. PISTON & CONNECTING ROD ASSEMBLY
WITH PRESS FIT GUDGEON PIN

1 Expander rail must butt	4 Connecting rod and cap
2 Top compression ring	identification
3 Second compression ring	5 Multi-sided nut

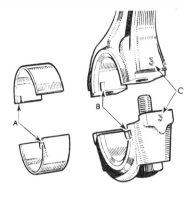

Fig. 1.8. The connecting rod big-end bearing locating tag (A) and grooves (B). The figures (C) indicate the cylinder from which the rod and cap were removed.

the caps go back in the correct position on the connecting rods from which they were removed.

3.   If the big end caps are difficult to remove they may be gently tapped with a soft hammer.

4.   To remove the shell bearings, press the bearing opposite the groove in both the connecting rod and the connecting rod caps and the bearings will slide out easily.

5.   Withdraw the pistons and connecting rods upwards and ensure they are kept in the correct order for replacement in the same bore.   Refit the connecting rod caps and bearings to the rods if the bearings do not require renewal, to minimise the risk of getting the caps and rods muddled.

20. Gudgeon pin

1.   Two types of gudgeon pin retention are employed on models covered by this manual. All models except Mk II 'S' models have fully floating gudgeon pins and these are retained by circlips at each end of the pin. To extract the pin remove the circlip at one end and push the pin out, immersing it in boiling water if it appears reluctant to move. Make sure the pins are kept with the same piston for ease of refitting.

2.   On Mk II 'S' models a press fit gudgeon pin is used and requires a special BLMC tool No. 18G1150 to remove and replace the pin. This tool is shown in Fig. 1:9 and must be used in the following manner:

(a)   Securely hold the hexagonal body in a firm vice and screw back the large nut until it is flush with the end of the main centre screw. Well lubricate the screw and large nut as they have to withstand high loading. Now push the centre screw in until the nut touches the thrust race.

(b)   Fit the adaptor No. 18G1150C onto the main centre screw with the piston ring cut away positioned uppermost. Then slide the parallel sleeve with the groove end first onto the centre screw.

(c)   Fit the piston with the 'FRONT' or 'A' mark on, towards the adaptor on the centre screw. This is important because the gudgeon pin bore is offset and irreparable damage will result if fitted the wrong way round. Next fit the remover/replacer bush on the centre screw with the flange end towards the gudgeon pin.

(d)   Screw the stop nut onto the main centre screw and adjust it until approximately 1/32 inch end play ('A' in Fig. 1:9) exists, and lock the stop nut securely with the lock screws. Now check that the remover/replacer bush and parallel sleeve are positioned correctly in the bore on both sides of the piston. Also check that the curved face of the adaptor is clean and slide the piston onto the

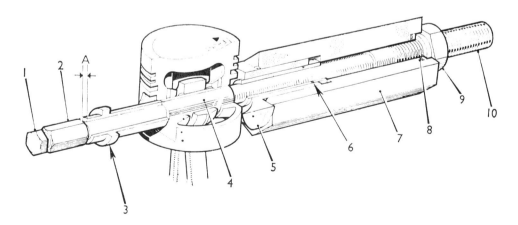

Fig. 1.9. GUDGEON PIN REMOVAL USING BLMC TOOL 18G 1150 AND ADAPTORS 18G 1150C

No.	Description	No.	Description	No.	Description	No.	Description
1	Lock screw		pin remover/replacer bush	6	Groove in sleeve away from	8	Thrust race
2	Stop nut	4	Gudgeon pin		gudgeon pin	9	Large nut
3	Flange away from gudgeon	5	Piston support adaptor	7	Service tool body	10	Centre screw

Dimension A = 1/32 inch

tool so it fits into the curved face of the adaptor with the piston rings over the cut away.

(e) Screw the large nut up to the thrust race and holding the lock screw turn the large nut with a ring spanner or long socket until the gudgeon pin is withdrawn from the piston.

21. Piston ring removal

1. To remove the piston rings, slide them carefully over the top of the piston, taking care not to scratch the aluminium alloy. Never slide them off the bottom of the piston skirt. It is very easy to break the cast iron piston rings if they are pulled off roughly so this operation should be done with extreme caution. It is helpful to make use of an old 0.020 inch feeler gauge.
2. Lift one end of the piston ring to be removed out of its groove and insert the end of the feeler gauge under it.
3. Turn the feeler gauge slowly round the piston and as the ring comes out of its groove apply slight upward pressure so that it rests on the land above. It can then be eased off the piston with the feeler gauge stopping it from slipping into an empty groove if it is any but the top piston ring that is being removed.

22. Flywheel and adaptor plate - removal and replacement

Full details of this operation are given in Chapter 7, Section 2.

23. Crankshaft and main bearing - removal

With the engine removed from the car and separated from the transmission, remove the timing gears, big end bearing, pistons, flywheel and engine adaptor. Removal of the crankshaft can be attempted only with the engine on the bench or clean floor.

1. Undo by one turn the nuts which hold the five main bearing caps.
2. Unscrew the nuts and remove them together with the washers. Mark the bearing end caps to ensure correct reassembly.
3. Remove the two bolts and tab washers which hold the front main bearing cap against the engine front plate.
4. Remove the main bearing caps and the bottom half of each bearing shell, taking care to keep the bearing shells in the right caps.
5. When removing the centre bearing cap note the bottom semi-circular halves of the thrust washers, one half lying on either side of the main bearing. Lay them with the centre bearing along the correct side.
6. Slightly rotate the crankshaft to free the upper halves of the bearing shells and thrust washers which can be extracted and placed over the correct bearing cap.
7. Remove the crankshaft by lifting it away from the crankcase.

24. Lubrication system - description

1. A forced feed system of lubrication, as shown in Fig. 1:11, is fitted with oil circulating round the engine from the transmission unit (manual) or sump (automatic) below the block. The level of engine oil is indicated on the dipstick which is fitted on the right hand side of the engine. It is marked to indicate the optimum level, which is the maximum mark.
2. The level of oil ideally, should not be above or below this line. Oil is replenished via the filler cap on the front of the rocker cover located as shown in Fig. 1:12.
3. The eccentric rotor type oil pump is bolted in the left hand side of the crankcase and is driven by a short shaft from the skew gear on the camshaft which also drives the distributor shaft.
4. The pump is the non-draining variety to allow rapid pressure build up when starting from cold.
5. Oil is drawn from the sump through a gauze screen in the oil strainer, this being shown in Fig. 1:10 and is sucked up the pickup pipe and drawn into the oil pump.

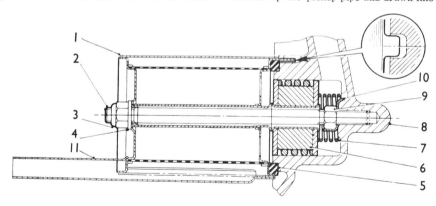

Fig. 1.10. OIL PICK-UP STRAINER (SECOND TYPE)

No. Description	No. Description	No. Description	No. Description
1 Oil strainer assembly	4 Plain washer	7 Spring for magnet	10 Lockwasher for nut
2 Shaft	5 Sealing ring	8 Front cover	11 Suction pipe
3 Nut for shaft	6 Filter magnet	9 Locknut - shaft	

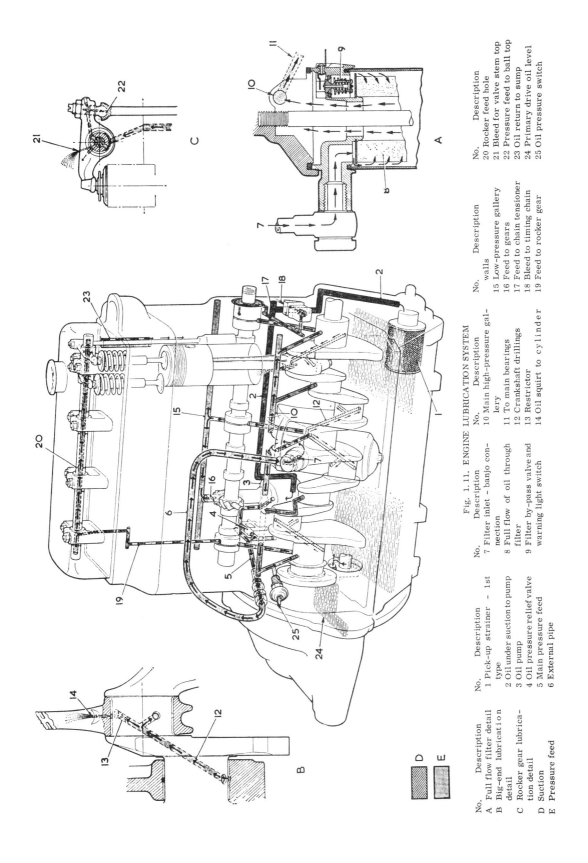

Fig. 1.11. ENGINE LUBRICATION SYSTEM

No.	Description	No.	Description	No.	Description
A	Full flow filter detail	1	Pick-up strainer – 1st type	7	Filter inlet – banjo connection
B	Big-end lubrication detail	2	Oil under suction to pump	8	Full flow of oil through filter
C	Rocker gear lubrication detail	3	Oil pump	9	Filter by-pass valve and warning light switch
D	Suction	4	Oil pressure relief valve		
E	Pressure feed	5	Main pressure feed		
		6	External pipe		

No.	Description	No.	Description
10	Main high-pressure gallery	15	Low-pressure gallery
11	To main bearings	16	Feed to gears
12	Crankshaft drillings	17	Feed to chain tensioner
13	Restrictor	18	Bleed to timing chain
14	Oil squirt to cylinder walls	19	Feed to rocker gear

No.	Description
20	Rocker feed hole
21	Bleed for valve stem top
22	Pressure feed to ball top
23	Oil return to sump
24	Primary drive oil level
25	Oil pressure switch

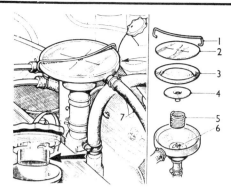

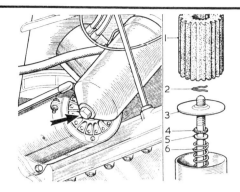

Fig. 1.12. ENGINE BREATHER CONTROL VALVE
(SECOND TYPE) AND OIL FILLER CAP FILTER (AR-
ROWED)

1 Spring clip	5 Spring
2 Cover	6 Cruciform guides
3 Diaphragm	7 Control valve to sepa-
4 Metering needle	rator hose

Fig. 1.14. ENGINE OIL FILTER COMPONENT PARTS
SHOWING RETAINING BOLT (ARROWED)

1 Filter element	4 Seating washer (felt)
2 Clip	5 Steel washer
3 Seating plate	6 Spring

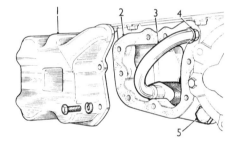

Fig. 1.13. OIL PICKUP STRAINER - AUTOMATIC
TRANSMISSION ONLY

1 Engine oil cover	4 'O' ring seal
2 Gasket	5 Drain plug - engine oil
3 Strainer and pick-up tube	

From the oil pump it is forced under pressure along a
gallery on the right hand side of the engine, and through
drillings to the big end, main and camshaft bearings. A
small hole in each connecting rod allows a jet of oil to
lubricate the cylinder wall with each revolution.
6.   From the camshaft front bearing oil is fed through
drilled passages in the cylinder block and head to the
front rocker pedestal where it enters the hollow rocker
shaft. Holes drilled in the shaft allow for the lubrication
of the rocker arms, and the valve stems and push rod
ends.
7.   This oil is at a reduced pressure to the oil delivered
to the crankshaft bearings. Oil from the front camshaft
bearing also lubricates the timing gears and the timing
chain. Oil returns to the sump by various passages, the
tappets being lubricated by oil returning via the push rod
drillings in the block.
8.   On all models a full-flow oil filter as shown in Fig.
1:14, is fitted, and all oil passes through this filter before it reaches the main oil gallery. The oil is passed

directly from the oil pump across the block to an external pipe on the right hand side of the engine which feeds
into the filter head.

25.   Oil filter removal and replacement

1.   The full flow oil filter fitted to all engines is located
three quarters of the way down the right hand side of the
engine towards the front.
2.   It is removed by unscrewing the long centre bolt
(photo) which holds the filter bowl in place. With the
bolt released (use a 9/16 A.F. spanner) carefully lift
away the filter bowl which contains the filter and will also
be full of oil. It is helpful to have a large basin under
the filter body to catch the oil which is bound to spill.

25.2

3.   Throw the old filter element away and thoroughly
clean down the filter bowl, the bolts and associated parts
with petrol and when perfectly clean wipe dry with a
non-fluffy rag.
4.   A rubber sealing ring is located in a groove round
the head of the oil filter and forms an effective leak
proof joint between the filter head and the filter bowl.
A new rubber sealing ring is supplied with each new
filter element.

5. Carefully prise out the oil sealing ring from the locating groove. If the ring has become hard and is difficult to move take great care not to damage the sides of the sealing ring groove.

6. With the old ring removed, fit the new ring in the groove at four equidistant points and press it home a segment at a time. Do not insert the ring at just one point and work round the groove pressing it home as, using this method, it is easy to stretch the ring and be left with a small loop of rubber which will not fit into the locating groove (photo).

7. Reassemble the oil filter assembly by first passing up the bolt through the hole in the bottom of the bowl, and with a steel washer under the bolt head, and a rubber or felt washer on top of the steel washer and next to the filter bowl (photo).

8. Slip the spring over the bolt inside the bowl (photo).

9. Then fit the other steel washer and the remaining rubber or felt washer to the centre bolt (photo).

10. Fit the sealing plate over the centre bolt with the concave side facing the bottom of the bowl (photo).

11. Then slide the new element into the oil filter bowl (photo).

12. With the bolt pressed hard up against the filter body (to avoid leakage) three quarter fill the bowl with engine oil.

13. Offer the bowl up to the rubber sealing ring and before finally tightening down the centre bolt, check that the lip of the filter bowl is resting squarely on the rubber sealing ring and is not offset and off the ring. If the bowl is not seating properly, rotate it until it is. Run the engine and check the bowl for leaks.

26. Oil pressure relief valve - removal and replacement

1. To prevent excessive oil pressure - for example, when the engine is cold, an oil pressure relief valve is built into the left hand side of the engine at the rear.

2. The relief valve is identified externally by a large 9/16 inch domed hexagon nut. To dismantle the unit unscrew the nut and remove it, complete with the two fibre or copper sealing washers. The relief spring and the relief spring cup can then be easily extracted.

3. In position, the metal cup fits over the opposite end of the relief valve spring resting in the dome of the hexagon nut, and bears against a machining in the block. When the oil pressure exceeds 70 lbs. sq. inch the cup is forced off its seat and the oil by-passes it and returns via a drilling directly to the sump.

4. Check the tension of the spring by measuring its length. If it is shorter than 3 inches it should be replaced by a new spring. Reassembly of the relief valve unit is a reversal of the above procedure.

27. Oil pump - removal and dismantling

1. Undo the nuts from the three studs which hold the oil pump to the crankcase and lift away the pump and its drive shaft, together with the pump gasket.

2. Undo the two bolts and spring washers holding the oil pump cover in place and pull the cover off the two dowels in the pump body which hold it in its correct position.

3. Pull out from the pump body the outer rotor and the inner rotor, together with the pump shaft.

28. Timing chain tensioner - removal and dismantling

1. Remove the cover from the timing gears as described in Section 16 and lock the rubber tensioner in its fully retracted position as described in Section 16, paragraph 6.

2. Knock back the tabs of the joint lockwasher and undo the two bolts which hold the tensioner and its backplate to the engine.

3. Pull the rubber slipper together with the spring and plunger from the tensioner body. Fit the Allen key to its socket in the cylinder and, holding the slipper and plunger firmly, turn the key clockwise to free the cylinder and spring from the plunger.

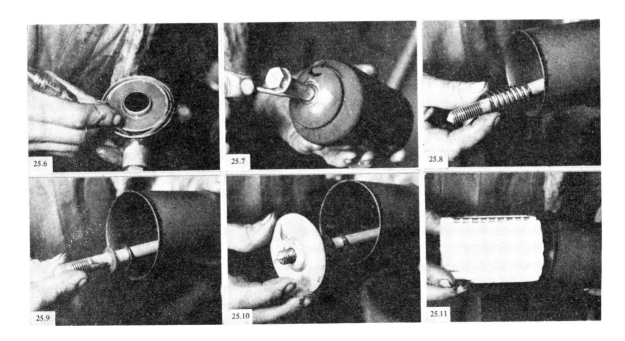

25.6   25.7   25.8
25.9   25.10   25.11

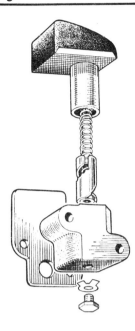

Fig. 1.15. Timing chain tensioner components.

knocking from the crankcase and a slight drop in oil pressure. Main bearing failure is accompanied by vibration which can be quite severe as the engine speed rises and falls, and a drop in oil pressure.

2. Bearings which have not broken up, but are badly worn will give rise to low oil pressure and some vibration. Inspect the big ends, main bearings and thrust washers for signs of general wear, scoring, pitting and scratches. The bearings should be matt grey in colour. With lead-indium bearings should a t r a c e of copper colour be noticed the bearings are badly worn as the lead bearing material has worn away to expose the indium underlay. Renew the bearings if they are in this condition or if there is any sign of scoring or pitting.

3. The undersizes available are designed to correspond with the regrind sizes, i.e. .010 bearings are correct for a crankshaft reground -.010 undersize. The bearings are in fact, slightly more than the stated undersize as running clearances have been allowed for during their manufacture.

4. Very long engine life can be achieved by changing big end bearings at intervals of 30,000 miles and main bearings at intervals of 50,000 miles, irrespective of bearing w e a r. Normally, crankshaft wear is infinitesimal a n d regular changes of bearings will ensure mileages of between 100,000 to 120,000 miles before crankshaft regrinding becomes necessary. Crankshafts normally have to be reground because of scoring due to bearing failure.

29. Engine - examination and renovation - general

1. With the engine stripped down and all parts thoroughly clean, it is now time to examine everything for wear. The following items should be checked and where necessary renewed o r renovated a s described in the following sections:

2. Examine the crankpin and main journal surfaces for signs of scoring or scratches. Check the ovality of the crankpins at different positions with a micrometer. If more than 0.001 inch out of round, the crankpins will have to be reground. They will also have to be reground if there are any scores or scratches present. Also check the journals in the same fashion. On highly tuned engines the centre main bearing has been known to break up. This is not always immediately apparent, but slight vibration in an otherwise normally smooth engine and a very slight drop in oil pressure under normal conditions are clues.

3. If the centre main bearing is suspected of failure it s h o u l d be immediately investigated by removing the power unit and separating the engine from the transmission, and then removing the centre main bearing cap. Failure to do this will result in a badly scored centre main journal. If it is necessary to regrind the crankshaft and fit new bearings your local BLMC garage or engineering works will be able to decide how much metal to grind off and the correct undersize shells to fit

30. Big end and main bearings - e x a m i n a t i o n and renovation

1. Big end bearing failure is accompanied by a noisy

31. Cylinder bores - examination and renovation

1. The cylinder bores must b e examined for taper, ovality, scoring and scratches. Start by carefully examining the top of the cylinder bores. If they are at all worn a very slight ridge will be found on the thrust side. This marks the top of the piston travel. The owner will have a good indication of the bore wear prior to dismantling the engine, or removing the cylinder head. Excessive oil consumption accompanied by b l u e smoke from the exhaust is a sure sign of worn cylinder bores and piston rings.

2. Measure the bore diameter just under the ridge with a micrometer and compare it with the diameter at the bottom of the bore, which is not subject to wear. If the difference between the two measurements is more than .006 inch then it will be necessary to fit special piston rings or to have the cylinders rebored and fit oversize pistons and rings. If no micrometer is available remove the rings from a piston and place the piston in each bore in turn about $\frac{3}{4}$ inch below the top of the bore. If an 0.010 inch feeler gauge can be slid between the piston and the cylinder wall on the thrust side of the bore then remedial action must be taken. Oversize pistons are available in the following sizes:-

+.010 inch (.254 mm),   +.020 inch (.508 mm)
+.030 inch (.762 mm),   +.040 inch (1.016 mm)

3. These are accurately machined to just below these measurements so as to provide correct running clearances in bores bored out to the exact oversize dimensions.

4. If the bores are slightly worn but not so badly worn as to justify reboring t h e m, special oil control rings can be fitted to the existing pistons which will restore compression and stop the engine burning oil. Several different types are available and the manufacturers instructions concerning their fitting must be followed closely.

32. Pistons and piston rings - examination and renovation

1. If the old pistons are to be refitted, carefully remove the piston rings and then thoroughly clean them. Take particular care to clean out the piston ring grooves. At the same time do not scratch the aluminium in any way. If new rings are to be fitted to the old pistons, then the top ring should be stepped so as to clear the ridge left above the previous top ring. If a normal but oversize new ring is fitted it will hit the ridge and break, because the new ring will not have worn in the same way as the old, which will have worn in unison with the ridge.

2. Before fitting the rings on the pistons each should be inserted approximately 3 inch down the cylinder bore and the gap measured with a feeler gauge as shown in Fig. 1:16. This should be between 0.012 in. and 0.017 in. or as detailed in the specifications at beginning of this chapter. It is essential that the gap is measured at the bottom of the ring travel, as if it is measured at the top of a worn bore and gives a perfect fit, it could easily seize at the bottom. If the ring gap is too small rub down the ends of the ring with a very fine file until the gap, when fitted, is correct. To keep the rings square in the bore for measurement, line each up in turn with an old piston in the bore upside down, and use the piston to push the ring down about 3 inches. Remove the piston and measure the piston ring gap.

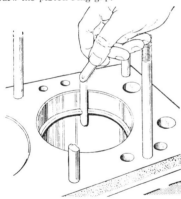

Fig. 1.16. Measuring piston ring gap in cylinder bore.

3. When fitting new pistons and rings to a rebored engine the ring gap can be measured at the top of the bore as the bore will now not taper. It is not necessary to measure the side clearance in the piston ring grooves with rings fitted, as the groove dimensions are accurately machined during manufacture. When fitting new oil pistons it may be necessary to have the grooves widened by machining to accept the new wider rings. In this instance the manufacturers representative will make this quite clear and will supply the address to which the pistons must be sent for machining.

4. When new pistons are fitted, take great care to fit the exact size best suited to the particular bore of your engine. BLMC go one stage further than merely specifying one size of piston for all standard bores. Because

Fig. 1.17. Measuring piston ring groove clearance.

of very slight differences in cylinder machining during production it is necessary to select just the right piston for the bore. A range of different sizes are available either from the piston manufacturers or from the dealer for the particular model of car being repaired.

5. Examination of the cylinder block face will show, adjacent to each bore, a small diamond shaped box with a number stamped in the metal. Careful examination of the piston crown will show a matching diamond and number. These are the standard piston sizes and will be the same for all four bores. If standard pistons are to be refitted or standard low compression pistons changed to standard high compression pistons, then it is essential that only pistons with the same number in the diamond are used. With larger pistons, the amount of oversize is stamped in an ellipse in the piston crown.

6. On engines with tapered second and third compression rings, the top narrow side of the ring is marked with a 'T'. Always fit this side uppermost and carefully examine all rings for this mark before fitting.

33. Camshaft and camshaft bearings - examination and renovation

1. Carefully examine the camshaft bearings for wear. If the bearings are obviously worn or pitted or the metal underlay just showing through, then they must be renewed. This is an operation for your local BLMC dealer or the local automobile engineering works as it demands the use of specialised equipment. The bearings are removed using a special drift after which the new bearings are pressed in, care bein taken that the oil holes in the bearings line up with those in the block. With another special tool the bearings are then reamed in position.

2. The camshaft itself should show no sign of wear, but, if very slight scoring marks on the cams are noticed, the score marks can be removed by very gentle rubbing down with very fine emery cloth or an oil stone. The greatest care should be taken to keep the cam profiles smooth.

34. Valves and seats - examination and renovation

1. Examine the heads of the valves for pitting and burning, especially the heads of the exhaust valves. The valve seatings should be examined at the same time. If the pitting on the valves and seats is very slight the marks can be removed by grinding the seats and valves together

with coarse, and then fine, valve grinding paste. Where bad pitting has occurred to the valve seats it will be necessary to recut them and fit new valves. If the valve seats are so worn that they cannot be recut, then it will be necessary to fit new valve seat inserts. These latter two jobs should be entrusted to the local BLMC agent or automobile engineering works. In practice it is very seldom that the seats are so badly worn that they require renewal. Normally, it is the valve that is too badly worn for replacement, and the owner can easily purchase a new set of valves and match them to the seats by valve grinding.

2.   Valve grinding is carried out as follows:

Place the cylinder head upside down on a bench, with a block of wood at each end to give clearance for the valve stems. Alternatively place the head at 45° to a wall with the combustion chambers facing away from the wall.

3.   Smear a trace of coarse carborundum paste on the seat face and apply a suction grinder tool to the valve head as shown in Fig. 1:18. With a semi-rotary action, grind the valve head to its seat, lifting the valve occasionally to redistribute the grinding paste. When a dull matt even surface finish is produced on both the valve seat and the valve, then wipe off the paste and repeat the process with fine carborundum paste, lifting and turning the valve to redistribute the paste as before. A light spring placed under the valve head will greatly ease this operation. When a smooth unbroken ring of light grey matt finish is produced, on both valve and valve seat faces, the grinding operation is complete.

Fig. 1. 18. Valve grinding using hand suction tool. Lift valve off seat occasionally to spread grinding paste evenly over seat and valve face.

4.   Scrape away all carbon from the valve head and the valve stem. Carefully clean away every trace of grinding compound, taking great care to leave none in the ports or in the valve guides. Clean the valves and valve seats with a paraffin soaked rag then clean with a clean rag, and finally, if an air line is available blow the valves, valve guides and valve ports clean.

35.   Timing gears and chain - examination and renovation

1.   Examine the teeth on both the crankshaft gear wheel and the camshaft gear wheel for wear. Each tooth forms an inverted 'V' with the gear wheel periphery and if worn, the side of each tooth under tension will be slightly concave in shape when compared with the other side of the tooth i. e. one side of the inverted 'V' will be concave when compared with the other. If any sign of wear is present the gear wheels must be renewed.

2.   Examine the links of the chain for side slackness and renew the chain if any slackness is noticeable when compared with a new chain. It is a sensible precaution to renew the chain at about 30, 000 miles and at a lesser mileage if the engine is stripped down for a major overhaul. The actual rollers on a very badly worn chain may be slightly grooved.

36.   Rockers and rocker shaft - examination and renovation

1.   Remove the threaded plug with a screwdriver from the end of the rocker shaft and thoroughly clean out the shaft. As it acts as the oil passages for the valve gear, clean out the oil holes and make sure they are quite clear. Check the shaft for straightness by rolling it on a flat surface. It is most unlikely that it will deviate from normal, but, if it does, then a judicious attempt must be made to straighten it. If this is not successful purchase a new shaft. The surface of the shaft should be free from any worn ridges caused by the rocker arms. If any wear is present, renew the rocker shaft. Wear is likely to have occurred only if the rocker shaft oil holes have become blocked.

2.   Check the rocker arms for wear of the rocker bushes, for wear at the rocker arm face which bears on the valve stem, and for wear of the adjusting ball ended screws. Wear in the rocker arm bush can be checked by gripping the rocker arm tip and holding the rocker arm in place on the shaft, noting if there is any lateral rocker arm shake. If any shake is present, and the arm is very loose on the shaft, remedial action must be taken. It is recommended that any worn rocker arm be taken to your local BLMC agent or automobile engineering works to have the old bush drawn out and a new bush fitted. The correct placement of the bush is shown in Fig. 1:19.

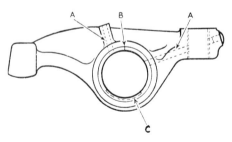

Fig. 1. 19. THE CORRECT POSITIONING OF VALVE ROCKER BUSH

A Oilways   C Oil groove
B Joint in rocker bush

3.   Check the tip of the rocker arm where it bears on the valve head, for cracking or serious wear on the case hardening. If none is present the rocker arm may be refitted. Check the pushrods for straightness by rolling them on a flat surface.

37. Tappets - examination and renovation

Examine the bearing surface of the tappets which lie on the camshaft. Any indentation in this surface or any cracks indicate serious wear and the tappets should be renewed. Thoroughly clean them out, removing all traces of sludge. It is most unlikely that the sides of the tappets will prove worn, but, if they are a very loose fit in their bores and can be readily rocked, they should be discarded and new tappets fitted. It is very unusual to find worn tappets and any wear present is likely to occur only at very high mileages.

38. Flywheel starter ring - examination and renovation

1. If the teeth on the flywheel starter ring gear are badly worn, or if some are missing, then it will be necessary to remove the ring. This is achieved by splitting the old ring using a cold chisel. The greatest care must be taken not to damage the flywheel during this process.
2. To fit a new ring gear, heat it gently and evenly with an oxyacetylene flame until a temperature of approximately $350^{0}C$ is reached. This is indicated by a light metallic blue surface colour. With the ring gear at this temperature, fit it to the flywheel with the front of the teeth facing the flywheel register. The ring gear should be either pressed or lightly tapped gently onto its register and left to cool naturally when the contraction of the metal on cooling will ensure that it is a secure and permanent fit. Great care must be taken not to overheat the ring gear, as if this happens the temper of the ring gear will be lost.
3. Alternatively, your local BLMC agent or local automobile engineering works may have a suitable oven in which the ring gear can be heated. The normal domestic oven will give a temperature of about $250^{0}C$ only, at the very least, except for the latest self cleaning type which will give a higher temperature. With the former it may just be possible to fit the ring gear with it at this temperature, but it is unlikely and no great force should have to be used.

39. Oil pump - examination and renovation

1. Thoroughly clean all the component parts in petrol and then check the rotor end float and lobe clearances in the following manner:
2. Position the rotors in the pump and place the straight edge of a steel rule across the joint face of the pump. Measure the gap between the bottom of the straight edge and the top of the rotors with a feeler gauge as shown in Fig. 1:20. If the measurement exceeds 0.005 inch then check the lobe clearances as described in the following paragraph. If the lobe clearances are correct then remove the dowels from the joint face of the pump body and lap joint the inner face on a sheet of plate glass.
3. Measure the gaps between the peaks of the lobes and the peaks in the pump body with a feeler gauge, and if the gap exceeds 0.010 inch then fit a replacement pump. This measurement is shown in Fig. 1:21.

40. Cylinder head - decarbonisation

1. This operation can be carried out with the engine either in or out of the car. With the cylinder head off, carefully remove with a wire brush and blunt scraper all

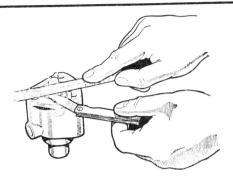

Fig. 1.20. Oil pump rotor end-float. This must not exceed 0.005 inch.

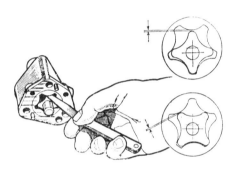

Fig. 1.21. Checking lobe clearance with the rotors positioned as shown in the illustration. Clearance must not exceed 0.010 inch.

traces of carbon deposits from the combustion spaces and the ports. The valve stems and valve guides should also be freed from any carbon deposits. Wash the combustion spaces and posts down with petrol and scrape the cylinder head surface free of any foreign matter with the side of a steel rule or a similar article. Take care not to scratch the surfaces.
2. Clean the pistons and top of the cylinder bores. If the pistons are still in the cylinder bores then it is essential that great care is taken to ensure that no carbon gets into the cylinder bores as this could scratch the cylinder walls or cause damage to the piston and rings. To ensure that this does not happen first turn the crankshaft so that two of the pistons are at the top of the bores. Place clean non fluffy rag into the other two bores or seal them off with paper and masking tape. The water ways and push rod holes should also be covered with a small piece of masking tape to prevent particles of carbon entering the cooling system and damaging the water pump, or entering the lubrication system and causing damage to a bearing surface.
3. There are two schools of thought as to how much carbon ought to be removed from the piston crown. One

is that a ring of carbon should be left around the edge of the piston and on the cylinder bore wall as an aid to keep oil consumption low. Although this is probably true for early engines with worn bores, on later engines however the tendency is to remove all traces of carbon during decarbonisation.

4. If all traces of carbon are to be removed, press a little grease into the gap between the cylinder walls and the two pistons which are to be worked on. With a blunt scraper carefully scrape away the carbon from the piston crown, taking care not to scratch the aluminium. Also scrape away the carbon from the surrounding lip of the cylinder wall. When all carbon has been removed, scrape away the grease which will now be contaminated with carbon particles, taking care not to press any into the bores. To assist prevention of carbon build-up the piston crown can be polished with a metal polish such as Brasso. Remove the rags or masking tape from the other two cylinders and turn the crankshaft so that the two pistons which were at the bottom are now at the top. Place non fluffy rag into the other two bores or seal them off with paper and masking tape. Do not forget the waterways and oilways as well. Proceed as previously described.

5. If a ring of carbon is going to be left round the piston then this can be helped by inserting an old piston ring into the top of the bore to rest on the piston and ensure that carbon is not accidently removed. Check that there are no particles of carbon in the cylinder bores. Decarbonising is now complete.

41. Valve guides - examination and renovation

Examine the valve guides internally for wear. If the valves are a very loose fit in the guides and there is the slightest suspicion of lateral rocking, then new guides will have to be fitted, their correct location being shown in Fig. 1:22. If the valve guides have been removed compare them internally by visual inspection with a new guide as well as testing them for rocking with the valves.

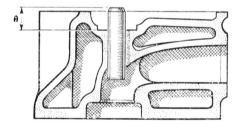

Fig. 1.22. CONNECT FITTING DIMENSIONS OF VALVE GUIDE ABOVE MACHINED FACE OF VALVE SPRING SEAT.
1. The exhaust valve guide dimension A = 5/8 inch.
2. The inlet valve guide dimension A = 3/8 inch.

42. Engine - reassembly - general

1. To ensure maximum life with minimum trouble from a rebuilt engine, not only must every part be correctly assembled, but everything must be spotlessly clean, all the oilways must be clear, locking washers and spring washers must always be fitted where indicated and all bearing and other working surfaces must be thoroughly lubricated during assembly. Before assembly begins renew any bolts or studs the threads of which are in any way damaged, and whenever possible use new spring washers.

2. Apart from your normal tools, a supply of non fluffy rag, an oil can filled with engine oil (an empty washing up fluid plastic bottle thoroughly cleaned and washed out will invariably do just as well), a supply of new spring washers, a set of new gaskets and a torque wrench should be collected together.

43. Crankshaft - replacement

Ensure that the crankcase is thoroughly clean and that all the oilways are clear. A thin twist drill is useful for cleaning them out. If possible, blow them out with compressed air. Treat the crankshaft in the same fashion, and then inject engine oil into the crankshaft oilways.

Commence work on rebuilding the engine by replacing the crankshaft and main bearings:

1. If the oil main bearing shells are to be replaced, (a false economy not to do so unless they are virtually new), fit the five upper halves of the main bearing shells to their location in the crankcase, after wiping the location clean.

2. Note that on the back of each bearing is a tab which engages in locating grooves in either the crankcase or the main bearing cap housings.

3. If new bearings are being fitted, carefully clean away all traces of the protective grease with which they are coated.

4. With the five upper bearing shells securely in place, wipe the lower bearing cap housings and fit the five lower shell bearings to their caps ensuring that the right shell goes into the right cap if the old bearings are being refitted.

5. Wipe the recesses either side of the centre main bearing which locate the upper halves of the thrust washers.

6. Generously lubricate the crankshaft journals and the upper and lower main bearing shells and carefully lower the crankshaft into position. Make sure that it is the right way round.

7. Introduce the upper halves of the thrust washers (the halves without tabs) into their grooves either side of the centre main bearing, rotating the crankshaft in the direction towards the main bearing tab (so that the main bearing shells do not slide out). At the same time feed the thrust washers into the locations with their oil grooves outwards away from the bearing.

8. Fit the main bearing caps into position ensuring that they locate properly. The mating surfaces must be spotlessly clean or the caps will not seat correctly.

9. When replacing the centre main bearing cap ensure that the thrust washers, generously lubricated, are fitted with their oil grooves facing outwards and the locating tab of each washer is in the slot in the bearing cap.

10. Replace the tab washers over the main bearing cap studs and replace the main bearing cap nuts and screw them up finger tight.

11. Test the crankshaft for freedom of rotation. Should it be very stiff to turn or possess high spots a most careful inspection must be made, preferably by a skilled mechanic with a micrometer to trace the cause of the trouble. It is very seldom that any trouble of this nature will be experienced when fitting the crankshaft.

12. Tighten the main bearing nuts using a torque wrench set to 70 lb. ft, and recheck the crankshaft for freedom

of rotation.

---

44. Piston and connecting rod - reassembly

If the same pistons are being used, then they must be mated to the same connecting rod with the same gudgeon pin. If new pistons are being fitted it does not matter which connecting rod they are used with, but the gudgeon pin should be fitted on the basis of selective assembly. To avoid any damage to the piston it is best to heat it in boiling water when the pin will slide in easily.

Lay the correct piston adjacent to each connecting rod and remember that the same rod and piston must go into the same bore. If new ones are being fitted it is necessary to ensure only that the right connecting rod is placed in each bore.

To assemble the piston and connecting rod, first fit a gudgeon pin circlip in position at one end of the gudgeon pin hole in the piston. Locate the connecting rod in the piston with the marking 'FRONT' on the piston crown towards the front of the engine, and the connecting rod caps towards the camshaft side of the engine. Slide the gudgeon pin in through the connecting rod little end until it rests against the previously fitted circlip. NOTE that the gudgeon pin should be a push fit. Finally fit the second circlip in position. Repeat this procedure for all four pistons and connecting rods.

The pistons and connecting rod assemblies on the Mk II 'S' models have a press fit gudgeon pin as opposed to the fully floating type. These are fully interchangeable in complete sets only. A special BLMC tool 18G1150 is required to fit the gudgeon pin as shown in Fig. 1:23 and should be used as follows:

1. Unscrew the large nut and withdraw the centre screw from the body a few inches. Well lubricate the screw thread and correctly locate the piston support adaptor.
2. Carefully slide the parallel sleeve with the groove end last onto the centre screw, up as far as the shoulder. Lubricate the gudgeon pin and its bores in the connecting rod and piston with Acheson's Colloids 'Oildag' graphite oil.
3. Fit the connecting rod and piston, side marked 'front' or △ to the tool with the connecting rod entered on the sleeve up to the groove. Fit the gudgeon pin into the piston bore up to the connecting rod. Next fit the remover/replacer bush flange end towards the gudgeon pin.
4. Screw the stop nut onto the centre screw and adjust the nut to give a 1/32 inch end play 'A' as shown in Fig 1:23. Lock the nut securely with the lock screw. Ensure that the curved face of the adaptor is clean and slide the piston on the tool so that it fits into the curved face of the adaptor with the piston rings over the adaptor cut-away.
5. Screw the large nut up to the thrust race. Adjust the torque wrench to a setting of 12lb. ft., which will represent the minimum load for an acceptable fit. Use the torque wrench previously set on the large nut, and a ring spanner on the lock screw. Pull the gudgeon pin into the piston until the flange of the remover/replacer bush is 0.04 inch from the piston skirt. It is critically important that the flange is NOT allowed to contact the piston. Finally withdraw the BLMC service tool.
6. Should the torque wrench not 'break' throughout the pull, the fit of the gudgeon pin in the connecting rod is not within limits and the parts must be renewed.
7. Ensure that the piston pivots freely on the gudgeon pin and it is free to slide sideways. Should stiffness exist wash the assembly in paraffin, lubricate the gudgeon pin with Acheson's Colloids 'Oildag' and recheck. Again if stiffness exists dismantle the assembly and check for signs of ingrained dirt or damage.

---

45. Piston ring - replacement

---

1. Check that the piston ring grooves and oilways are thoroughly clean and unblocked. Piston rings must always be fitted over the head of the piston and never from the bottom.

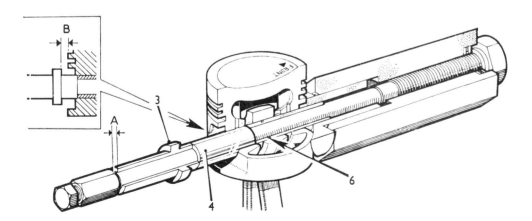

Fig. 1.23. GUDGEON PIN REFITTING USING BLMC SERVICE TOOL 18G 1150C
A = 1/32 inch end play
B = 0.04 inch from piston
3. Place flange towards gudgeon pin remover/replacer bush
4. Gudgeon pin
6. Groove in sleeve towards gudgeon pin

2. The easiest method to use when fitting rings is to wrap a 0.020 inch feeler gauge round the top of the piston and place the rings one at a time, starting from the bottom oil control ring, over the feeler gauge.

3. The feeler gauge, complete with ring, can then be slid down the piston over the other piston ring grooves until the groove is reached. The piston ring is then slid gently off the feeler gauge into the groove. Set all ring gaps 90° to each other.

4. An alternative method is to fit the rings by holding them slightly open with the thumbs and both of your index fingers. This method requires a steady hand and great care as it is easy to open the ring too much and break it. NOTE: On the Mk II 'S' engines a special oil control ring is fitted this being shown in Fig. 1:10.

30. To refit proceed as follows:

1. Fit the bottom rail of the oil control ring to the piston and position it below the bottom groove. Refit the oil control expander into the bottom groove and move the bottom oil control ring rail up into the bottom groove. Fit the top oil control rail into the bottom groove.

2. Inspect that the ends of the expander are butting out overlapping as shown in the insert in Fig. 1:10. Set the gaps of the rails and the expander at 90° to each other.

3. Refit the second compression ring with the side marked 'TOP' uppermost. Note that this ring is the thinner of the two compression rings. Finally refit the top compression ring.

46. Piston - replacement

The pistons, complete with connecting rods, can be fitted to the cylinder bores in the following sequence:

1. With a wad of clean non fluffy rag wipe the cylinder bores clean.

2. The pistons, complete with connecting rods, are fitted to their bores from above.

3. As each piston is inserted into its bore ensure that it is the correct piston/connecting rod assembly for that particular bore and that the connecting rod is the right way round, and that the front of the piston is towards the front of the bore i.e. towards the front of the engine. Lubricate the piston well with clean correct grade oil.

4. The piston will slide into the bore only as far as the oil control ring. It is then necessary to compress the piston rings into a clamp and to gently tap the piston into the cylinder bore with a wooden or plastic hammer. If a proper piston ring clamp is not available then a suitable jubilee clip does the job very well.

47. Connecting rod to crankshaft - reassembly

As the big ends on the connecting rods are offset it will be obvious if they have been inserted the wrong way

round as they will not fit over the crankpins. The centre two connecting rods should be fitted with the offset part of the rods facing outwards.

1. Wipe the connecting rod half of the big end bearing cap and the underside of the shell bearing clean, and fit the shell bearing in position with its locating tongue engaged with the corresponding groove in the connecting rod.

2. If the old bearings are nearly new and are being refitted then ensure they are replaced in their correct locations in the correct rods (photo).

47.2

3. Generously lubricate the crankpin journals with engine oil, and turn the crankshaft so that the crankpin is in the most advantageous position for the connecting rod to be drawn onto it.

4. Wipe the connecting rod bearing cap and back of the shell bearing clean and fit the shell bearing in position ensuring that the locating tongue at the back of the bearing engages with the locating groove in the connecting rod cap.

5. Generously lubricate the shell bearing and offer up the connecting rod bearing cap to the connecting rod (photo).

6. Fit the connecting rod bolts with the one piece locking tab under them and tighten the bolts using a torque wrench setting of 35 lb. ft. (photo). NOTE: From engine No. 18AMW/U/H37052. L20578 nuts having twelve sides are used in conjunction with the bolts. The nuts should be tightened using a torque wrench set to 33 ± 2 lb. ft, with the threads well lubricated. These are shown in Fig. 1:10.

7. Bend over the tab washers using a mole wrench (photo).

48. Oil pump and drive shaft - replacement

Invert the cylinder block and insert the oil pump drive shaft and its thrust washer the latter being placed on the oil pump side of the gear teeth. Fit a new oil

47.5

47.6

47.7

pump to crankcase gasket over the three studs followed by the oil pump. Ensure that the shaft dog correctly engages with the drive gear dog. Fit spring washers on the studs followed by the three nuts. Tighten the nuts using a torque wrench set to 14lb. ft.

---

49. Camshaft - replacement

1. Fit the engine front plate with a new gasket between the cylinder block and plate and tighten the three retaining bolts.
2. Wipe the camshaft bearing journals clean and lubricate them generously with engine oil. Check the camshaft end float as shown in Fig. 1:24.

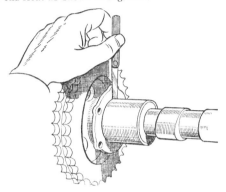

Fig. 1.24. Checking camshaft end-float.

3. Insert the camshaft into the crankcase gently, taking care not to damage the camshaft bearings, with the cams. Also take care when handling the camshaft as the edges of the lobes can be sharp.
4. With the camshaft inserted into the crankcase as far as it will go, rotate it slightly to ensure the skew gear has mated with the oil pump drive.
5. Replace the camshaft locating plate and tighten the three retaining bolts and washers.

---

50. Timing gears, chain tensioner, cover - replacement

1. Before reassembly begins check that the packing washers are in place on the crankshaft nose. If new gear wheels are being fitted it may be necessary to fit additional washers as detailed in paragraph 7. These washers ensure that the crankshaft gearwheel lines up correctly with the camshaft gearwheel.
2. Replace the woodruff keys in their respective slots in the crankshaft and camshaft and ensure that they are fully seated. If their edges are burred they must be cleaned with a fine file.
3. Lay the camshaft gearwheels on a clean surface so that the two timing dots are adjacent to each other. Slip the timing chain over them and pull the gearwheels back into mesh with the chain so that the timing dots, although further apart, are still adjacent to each other as shown in Fig. 1:25.
4. Rotate the crankshaft so that the woodruff key is at

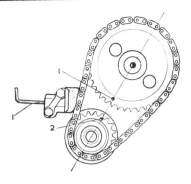

Fig. 1.25. Crank the engine until the timing dimples (1) and (2) are opposite each other before removing the timing chain and chain wheels. The chain tensioner is retracted into the unloaded position by turning the Allen key (3) in a clockwise direction.

top dead centre. (The engine should be in the upright position).
5. Rotate the camshaft so that when viewed from the front the woodruff key is at one o'clock position.
6. Fit the timing chain and gearwheel assembly onto the camshaft and crankshaft keeping the timing marks adjacent. If the camshaft and crankshaft have been positioned accurately it will be found that the keyways on the gearwheels will match the position of the keys, although it may be necessary to rotate the camshaft a fraction to ensure accurate lining up of the camshaft gear wheel (photo).

7. Press the gearwheels into position on the crankshaft and camshaft as far as they will go. NOTE: If new gearwheels are being fitted they should be checked for alignment before being finally fitted to the engine. Place the gearwheels in position without the timing chain and place the straight edge of a steel ruler from the side of the camshaft gear teeth to the crankshaft gearwheel and measure the gap between the steel rule and the gearwheel. Subtract 0.005 from the feeler gauge reading and add the resultant thickness of crankshaft gear packing washers (Fig. 1:26).
8. Next assemble the timing chain tensioner by inserting one end of the spring into the plunger and fit the other end of the spring into the cylinder as shown (photo).
9. Compress the spring until the cylinder enters the

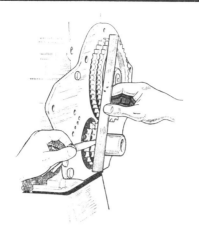

Fig. 1.26. Checking chain wheel alignment with a straight edge and feeler gauge.

50.8

plunger bore and ensure the peg in the plunger engages the helical slot. Insert and turn the Allen key clockwise until the end of the cylinder is below the peg and the spring is held compressed.

10. Fit the backplate and secure the assembly to the cylinder block with the two bolts. Turn the tabs of the lockwasher shown in Fig. 1:15 on page 34 and photo.

11. With the timing chain in position, the tensioner can now be relaxed. Insert the Allen key and turn it clockwise so the slipper head moves forward under spring pressure against the chain. Do not under any circumstances turn the key anti-clockwise or force the slipper head into the chain. Replace the bottom plug and lock with a tab washer.

12. On early engines fit the oil thrower to the crankshaft nose with the concave side forward. Later models make use of a modified timing cover and oil thrower with an 'F' on its front face, i.e. this face must be furthest from the engine. On no account use a later oil thrower with an early cover or vice-versa.

13. Fit the locking washer to the camshaft gearwheel with its locating tab in the gearwheel keyway as shown. (photo).

14. Screw on the camshaft gearwheel retaining nut and tighten securely (photo).

15. Bend up the locking tab of the locking washer to securely hold the camshaft retaining nut as shown (photo).

16. Generously oil the chain and gearwheels.

17. Ensure the interior of the timing cover and the timing cover flange is clean and generously lubricate the oil seal in the timing cover. Then with a new gasket in position, fit the timing cover to the block using the pulley to centralise the cover (photo).

18. Screw in the timing cover retaining bolts with the flat washer next to the cover flange and under the spring washer. The $\frac{1}{4}$ inch bolts should be tightened with a torque spanner to 6 lb. ft., and the 5/16 inch bolts to 14 lb. ft.

19. Fit the crankshaft pulley to the nose of the crankshaft ensuring that the keyway engages with the woodruff key as shown (photo).

20. Fit the crankshaft retaining bolt locking washer in position and screw on the crankshaft pulley retaining nut.

50.10　　　50.13　　　50.14

50.15　　　50.17　　　50.19

Tighten to a torque of 70lb. ft.

51. Valve and valve spring - reassembly

To refit the valves and valve springs to the cylinder head, proceed as follows:
1. Rest the cylinder head on its side, or if the manifold studs are fitted, with the gasket surface downwards.
2. Fit each valve and valve spring in turn, wiping down and lubricating each valve stem as it is inserted into the same valve guide from which it was removed.
3. As each valve is inserted slip the oil control rubber ring into place just under the bottom of the cotter groove (use a new rubber ring if at all possible).
4. Move the cylinder head towards the edge of the work bench if it is facing downwards and slide it partially over the edge of the bench so as to fit the bottom half of the valve spring compressor to the valve head.
5. Slip the valve springs and cap over the valve stem.
6. With the base of the valve compressor on the valve head, compress the valve spring until the cotters can be slipped into place in the cotter grooves. Gently release the compressor and fit the circlip in position in the grooves in the cotters.
7. Repeat this procedure until all eight valves and valve springs are fitted.

52. Rocker shaft - reassembly

1. To reassemble the rocker shaft fit the split pin, flat washer, and spring washer at the rear end of the shaft and then slide on the rocker arms, rocker shaft pedestals, and spacing springs in the same order in which they were removed.
2. With the front pedestal in position, screw in the rocker shaft locating screw and slip the locating plate into place. Finally, fit to the front of the shaft the spring washer, plain washer and split pin, in that order.

53. Tappet and pushrod - replacement

Generously lubricate the tappets internally and externally and insert them in the bores from which they were removed through the tappet chest.

With the cylinder head in position fit the pushrods in the same order in which they were removed. Ensure that they locate properly in the stems of the tappets, and lubricate the pushrod ends before fitment. Refit the two tappet covers with new cork gaskets and tighten the bolts using a torque wrench set to 2lb. ft.

54. Cylinder head - replacement

After checking that both the cylinder block and cylinder head mating surfaces are perfectly clean, generously lubricate each cylinder with engine oil.
1. Always use a new cylinder head gasket as the old gasket will be compressed and not capable of giving a good seal.
2. Never smear grease on either side of the gasket as when the engine heats up the grease will melt and may allow compression leaks to develop.
3. The cylinder head gasket is marked 'FRONT' and 'TOP' and should be fitted in position according to the markings. The copper side will in fact be uppermost.

4. With the gasket in position carefully lower the cylinder head onto the cylinder block.
5. With the head in position fit the cylinder head nuts and washers finger tight to the seven cylinder head holding down studs, which remain outside the rocker cover. It is not possible to fit the remaining nuts to the studs inside the rocker cover until the rocker assembly is in position.
6. Fit the pushrods as detailed in the previous section.
7. The rocker shaft assembly can now be lowered over its eight locating studs. Take care that the rocker arms are the right way round. Lubricate the ball joints, and insert the rocker arm ball joints in the pushrod cups. NOTE: Failure to place the ball joints in the cups can result in the ball joints seating on the edge of a pushrod or outside it when the head and rocker assembly is pulled down tight.
8. Fit the four rocker pedestal nuts and washers, and then the four cylinder head stud nuts and washers which also serve to hold down the rocker pedestals. Pull the nuts down evenly, but without tightening them right up.
9. When all is in position, the even cylinder head nuts and the four rocker pedestal nuts can be tightened down in the order shown in Fig. 1:3 page 24. Turn the nuts a quarter of a turn at a time and tighten the four rocker pedestal nuts to 25lb. ft., and the nine cylinder head nuts to 50lb. ft.

55. Rocker arm/valve - adjustment

1. The valve adjustments should be made with the engine cold. The importance of correct rocker arm/valve stem clearances cannot be overstressed as they vitally affect the performances of the engine.
2. If the clearances are set too open, the efficiency of the engine is reduced as the valves open late and close earlier than was intended. If, on the other hand the clearances are set too close there is a danger that the stem and pushrods will expand upon heating and not allow the valves to close properly which will cause burning of the valve head and possible warping.
3. If the engine is in the car, to get at the rockers it is merely necessary to remove the two holding down dome shaped nuts from the rocker cover, and then to lift the rocker cover and gasket away.
4. It is important that the clearance is set when the tappet of the valve being adjusted is on the heel of the cam (i.e. opposite the peak). This can be done by carrying out the adjustments in the following order, which also avoids turning the crankshaft more than necessary:

Valve fully open	Check and adjust
Valve No. 8	Valve No. 1
Valve No. 6	Valve No. 3
Valve No. 4	Valve No. 5
Valve No. 7	Valve No. 2
Valve No. 1	Valve No. 8
Valve No. 3	Valve No. 6
Valve No. 5	Valve No. 4
Valve No. 2	Valve No. 7

5. The correct valve clearance is given in technical data at the beginning of this chapter. It is obtained by slackening the hexagon locknut with a spanner while holding the ball pin against rotation with a screwdriver as shown in Fig 1:27. Then still pressing down with the screwdriver, insert a feeler gauge of the required thickness between the valve stem head and the rocker arm and adjust the ball pin until the feeler gauge will just move in and out without nipping. Then, still holding the

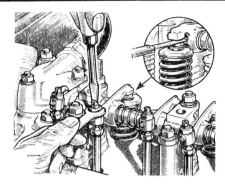

Fig. 1.27. Valve rocker clearance adjustment

ball pin in the correct position, tighten the locknut.
6.   An alternative method is to set the gaps with the engine running at idle speed. Although this method may be faster more practice is needed and it is no more reliable.

56.   Distributor and distributor drive - replacement

It is important to set the distributor drive correctly otherwise the ignition timing will be totally incorrect. It is easy to set the distributor drive in apparently the right position, but in fact exactly 180° out, by omitting to select the correct cylinder which must not only be at T. D. C. but must also be on its firing stroke with both valves closed. The distributor drive should therefore not be fitted until the cylinder head is in position and the valves can be observed. Alternatively, if the timing cover has not been replaced, the distributor drive can be replaced when the dots on the timing wheels are adjacent to each other.
1.   The distributor drive shaft can only be fitted with the pistons half way up or down their bores. Turn the crankshaft so that the pistons are in this position (90° before or after T. D. C.).
2.   Screw a 5/16 UNF bolt about 3½ in. (90mm) long into the threaded hole in the top end of the shaft and fit the shaft to the engine.
3.   Rotate the crankshaft so that No. 1 piston is at T. D. C. and on its firing stroke (the dots in the timing gears will be adjacent to each other). When No. 1 piston is at T. D. C. the inlet valve on No. 4 cylinder is just opening and the exhaust valve closing.
4.   With the pistons in the engine set at T. D. C. it will not be possible to remove the drive shaft, but it is possible to lift it sufficiently to bring it out of mesh with the drive gear on the camshaft. The drive shaft can then be turned to the correct timing position.
5.   When the marks '¼' on the flywheel are at T. D. C. or the groove on the crankshaft pulley wheel is in line with the T. D. C. pointer on the timing gear cover, then No. 1

and No. 4 piston are at T. D. C. (check that the No. 4 cylinder valves are just rocking to ensure correct stroke for No. 1 cylinder).
6.   Position the drive shaft so that the slot is just below the horizontal, and the larger of the two segments (one on each side of the slot) is at the top. As the gear on the shaft engages with the skew gear on the camshaft the drive shaft will turn anti-clockwise until the top of the slot is adjacent to the 2 o'clock position.
7.   Remove the bolt from the drive shaft.
8.   Replace the distributor housing and lock it in position with the single bolt and lock washer. It is important that the correct bolt is used so that the head does not protrude above the face of the housing.
9.   The distributor can now be replaced and the two screwing bolts and spring washers which hold the distributor clamping plate to the distributor housing tightened. If the clamp bolt on the clamping plate was not previously loosened and the distributor body was not turned in the clamping plate, then the ignition timing will be as previously set. If the clamping bolt has been loosened, then it will be necessary to retime the ignition as described in Chapter 5.

57.   Engine - Final assembly

1.   The rocker cover can now be fitted, using a new cork gasket. Fit the two tappet coverplates, using new gaskets, and tighten the tappet chest bolts to a torque of 2lb. ft. Do not exceed the figure or the covers will distort and cause an oil leak. Reconnect the ancilliary components to the engine in the reverse order to which they were removed.
2.   It should be noted that in all cases it is best to reassemble the engine and transmission unit as far as possible before fitting it to the car. This means that the inlet and exhaust manifolds, starter motor, water thermostat, oil filter, distributor, but not the carburettors or dynamo, should all be in position. Ensure that the oil filter is filled with engine oil, as otherwise there will be a delay in the oil reaching the bearings while the oil filter refills.
3.   Refit the transmission unit to the engine as described in Chapter 7, section 5 (manual gearbox) or Chapter 8, section 11 (automatic transmission).

58.   Engine - replacement

1.   Before installing into the car remove the filler plug on the primary drive cover and refill with 1½ pints of recommended grade engine oil.
2.   Ensure that all loose leads, cables etc. , are tucked out of the way. If not it is easy to trap one and so cause much additional work after the engine is replaced.
3.   Once the dynamo or alternator have been refitted it is recommended that a new fan belt is fitted.
4.   Where a vacuum servo unit is fitted do not forget to replace the vacuum pipe on the take off pipe from the inlet manifold.
5.   Finally, check that the drain taps are closed and refill the cooling system with water and the engine with the correct grade of oil. Start the engine and carefully check for oil or water leaks. There should be no oil or water leaks if the engine and transmission unit have been carefully reassembled, all nuts and bolts tightened down correctly, and new gaskets and joints used throughout.

FAULT FINDING CHART

Cause	Trouble	Remedy
SYMPTOM:	ENGINE FAILS TO TURN OVER WHEN STARTER BUTTON OPERATED	
No current at starter motor	Flat or defective battery Loose battery leads Defective starter solenoid or switch or broken wiring Engine earth strap disconnected	Charge or replace battery. Push-start car. Tighten both terminals and earth ends of earth lead. Run a wire direct from the battery to the starter motor or by-pass the solenoid. Check and retighten strap.
Current at starter motor	Jammed starter motor drive pinion Defective starter motor	Place car in gear and rock from side to side. Alternatively, free exposed square end of shaft with spanner. Remove and recondition.
SYMPTOM:	ENGINE TURNS OVER BUT WILL NOT START	
No spark at sparking plug	Ignition damp or wet Ignition leads to spark plugs loose Shorted or disconnected low tension leads Dirty, incorrectly set, or pitted contact breaker points Faulty condenser Defective ignition switch Ignition leads connected wrong way round Faulty coil Contact breaker point spring earthed or broken	Wipe dry the distributor cap and ignition leads Check and tighten at both spark plug and distributor cap ends. Check the wiring on the CB and SW terminals of the coil and to the distributor. Clean, file smooth, and adjust. Check contact breaker points for arcing, remove and fit new. By-pass switch with wire. Remove and replace leads to spark plugs in correct order. Remove and fit new coil. Check spring is not touching metal part of distributor. Check insulator washers are correctly placed. Renew points if the spring is broken.
No fuel at carburettor float chamber or at jets	No petrol in petrol tank Vapour lock in fuel line (In hot conditions or at high altitude) Blocked float chamber needle valve Fuel pump filter blocked Choked or blocked carburettor jets Faulty fuel pump	Refill tank! Blow into petrol tank, allow engine to cool, or apply a cold wet rag to the fuel line. Remove, clean, and replace. Remove, clean, and replace. Dismantle and clean. Remove, overhaul, and replace. Check CB points on S.U. pumps.
Excess of petrol in cylinder or carburettor flooding	Too much choke allowing too rich a mixture to wet plugs Float damaged or leaking or needle not seating Float lever incorrectly adjusted	Remove and dry sparking plugs or with wide open throttle, push-start the car. Remove, examine, clean and replace float and needle valve as necessary. Remove and adjust correctly.
SYMPTOM:	ENGINE STALLS & WILL NOT START	
No spark at sparking plug	Ignition failure - Sudden Ignition failure - Misfiring precludes total stoppage Ignition failure - In severe rain or after traversing water splash	Check over low and high tension circuits for breaks in wiring Check contact breaker points, clean and adjust. Renew condenser if faulty. Dry out ignition leads and distributor cap.
No fuel at jets	No petrol in petrol tank Petrol tank breather choked Sudden obstruction in carburettor(s) Water in fuel system	Refill tank. Remove petrol cap and clean out breather hole or pipe. Check jets, filter, and needle valve in float chamber for blockage Drain tank and blow out fuel lines

ENGINE FAULT FINDING CHART

Cause	Trouble	Remedy
SYMPTOM:	ENGINE MISFIRES OR IDLES UNEVENLY	
Intermittent sparking at sparking plug	Ignition leads loose	Check and tighten as necessary at spark plug and distributor cap ends.
	Battery leads loose on terminals	Check and tighten terminal leads.
	Battery earth strap loose on body attachment point	Check and tighten earth lead to body attachment point.
	Engine earth lead loose	Tighten lead.
	Low tension leads to SW and CB terminals on coil loose	Check and tighten leads if found loose.
	Low tension lead from CB terminal side to distributor loose	Check and tighten if found loose.
	Dirty, or incorrectly gapped plugs	Remove, clean, and regap.
	Dirty, incorrectly set, or pitted contact breaker points	Clean, file smooth, and adjust.
	Tracking across inside of distributor cover	Remove and fit new cover.
	Ignition too retarded	Check and adjust ignition timing.
	Faulty coil	Remove and fit new coil.
Fuel shortage at engine	Mixture too weak	Check jets, float chamber needle valve, and filters for obstruction. Clean as necessary. Carburettor(s) incorrectly adjusted.
	Air leak in carburettor(s)	Remove and overhaul carburettor.
	Air leak at inlet manifold to cylinder head, or inlet manifold to carburettor	Test by pouring oil along joints. Bubbles indicate leak. Renew manifold gasket as appropriate.
Mechanical wear	Incorrect valve clearances	Adjust rocker arms to take up wear.
	Burnt out exhaust valves	Remove cylinder head and renew defective valves.
	Sticking or leaking valves	Remove cylinder head, clean, check and renew valves as necessary.
	Weak or broken valve springs	Check and renew as necessary.
	Worn valve guides or stems	Renew valve guides and valves.
	Worn pistons and piston rings	Dismantle engine, renew pistons and rings.
SYMPTOM:	LACK OF POWER & POOR COMPRESSION	
Fuel/air mixture leaking from cylinder	Burnt out exhaust valves	Remove cylinder head, renew defective valves.
	Sticking or leaking valves	Remove cylinder head, clean, check, and renew valves as necessary.
	Worn valve guides and stems	Remove cylinder head and renew valves and valve guides.
	Weak or broken valve springs	Remove cylinder head, renew defective springs.
	Blown cylinder head gasket (Accompanied by increase in noise)	Remove cylinder head and fit new gasket.
	Worn pistons and piston rings	Dismantle engine, renew pistons and rings.
	Worn or scored cylinder bores	Dismantle engine, rebore, renew pistons & rings.
Incorrect Adjustments	Ignition timing wrongly set. Too advanced or retarded	Check and reset ignition timing.
	Contact breaker points incorrectly gapped	Check and reset contact breaker points.
	Incorrect valve clearances	Check and reset rocker arm to valve stem gap.
	Incorrectly set sparking plugs	Remove, clean and regap.
	Carburation too rich or too weak	Tune carburettor(s) for optimum performance.
Carburation and ignition faults	Dirty contact breaker points	Remove, clean, and replace.
	Fuel filters blocked causing top end fuel starvation	Dismantle, inspect, clean, and replace all fuel filters.
	Distributor automatic balance weights or vacuum advance and retard mechanisms not functioning correctly	Overhaul distributor.
	Faulty fuel pump giving top end fuel starvation	Remove, overhaul, or fit exchange reconditioned fuel pump.

ENGINE

Cause	Trouble	Remedy
SYMPTOM:	EXCESSIVE OIL CONSUMPTION	
Oil being burnt by engine	Badly worn, perished or missing valve stem oil seals Excessively worn valve stems and valve guides Worn piston rings Worn pistons and cylinder bores Excessive piston ring gap allowing blow-by Piston oil return holes choked	Remove, fit new oil seals to valve stems. Remove cylinder head and fit new valves and valve guides. Fit oil control rings to existing pistons or purchase new pistons. Fit new pistons and rings, rebore cylinders. Fit new piston rings and set gap correctly. Decarbonise engine and pistons.
Oil being lost due to leaks	Leaking oil filter gasket Leaking rocker cover gasket Leaking tappet chest gasket Leaking timing case gasket Leaking sump gasket Loose sump plug	Inspect and fit new gasket as necessary. " " " " " " " " " " " " " " " " " " " " " " " " " " " " Tighten, fit new gasket if necessary.
SYMPTOM:	UNUSUAL NOISES FROM ENGINE	
Excessive clearances due to mechanical wear	Worn valve gear (Noisy tapping from rocker box) Worn big end bearing (Regular heavy knocking) Worn timing chain and gears (Rattling from front of engine) Worn main bearings (Rumbling and vibration) Worn crankshaft (Knocking, rumbling and vibration)	Inspect and renew rocker shaft, rocker arms, and ball pins as necessary. Drop sump, if bearings broken up clean out oil pump and oilways, fit new bearings. If bearings not broken but worn fit bearing shells. Remove timing cover, fit new timing wheels and timing chain. Drop sump, remove crankshaft, if bearings worn but not broken up, renew. If broken up strip oil pump and clean out oilways. Regrind crankshaft, fit new main and big end bearings.

Chapter 2/Cooling System

Contents

Specifications

Type	Pressurised radiator. Thermo-siphon, pump assisted and fan cooled. Separate expansion tank
Thermostat Settings: Standard...	82°C (180°F)
Cold Climate	88°C (190°F)
Hot Climate	74°C (164°F)
Blow off pressure of Expansion Tank Cap	13 lb/sq in.
Cooling System Capacity	$8\frac{1}{2}$ pints ($9\frac{1}{2}$ pints with heater)

1. General description

The engine cooling water is circulated by a thermo-siphon, water pump assisted system, and the coolant is pressurised. This is primarily to prevent premature boiling in adverse conditions and also to allow the engine to operate at its most efficient running temperature, this being just under the boiling point of water. The overflow pipe from the radiator is connected to an expansion chamber which makes topping up unnecessary. The coolant expands when hot, and instead of being forced down the overflow pipe and lost, it flows into the expansion chamber. As the engine cools the coolant contracts and because of the pressure differential flows back into the top tank of the radiator.

The cap on the expansion chamber is set to a pressure of 12 lb/sq. in. which increases the boiling point of the coolant to 230°F. If the water temperature exceeds this figure and the water boils, the pressure in the system forces the internal valve of the cap off its seat thus exposing the expansion tank overflow pipe down which the steam from the boiling water escapes and so relieves the pressure. It is, therefore, important to check that the expansion chamber cap is in good condition and that the spring behind the sealing washers has not weakened. Check that the rubber seal has not perished and its seating in the neck is clean to ensure a good

seal. Also check the radiator filler cap rubber seal and neck to ensure a good seal. Most garages have a special tool which enables a radiator cap to be pressure tested.

The cooling system comprises the radiator, top and bottom hoses, heater hoses (if a heater/demister is fitted), the impeller water pump (mounted on the front of the engine it carries the fan blades and is driven by the fan belt), the thermostat and the two drain taps.

The system functions in the following manner: Cold water from the bottom of the radiator circulates up the lower radiator hose to the water pump where it is pushed round the water passages in the cylinder block, helping to keep the cylinder bores and pistons cool.

The water then travels up into the cylinder head and circulates round the combustion spaces and valve seats absorbing more heat. Then, when the engine is at its correct operating temperature, the water travels out of the cylinder head, past the open thermostat into the upper radiator hose, and so into the radiator header tank. The water travels down the radiator where it is rapidly cooled by the rush of cold air through the radiator core. As the radiator is mounted next to the wheel arch the fan PUSHES cold air through the radiator matrix. The water, now cool, reaches the bottom of the radiator, when the cycle is repeated.

When the engine is cold the thermostat (a valve able to open and close according to the temperature) maintains the circulation of the water in the engine by returning it via the by-pass hose to the cylinder block. Only when the correct minimum operating temperature has been reached, as shown in the specification, does the thermostat begin to open, allowing water to return to the radiator.

2. Cooling system - draining

1. If the engine is cold remove the filler cap from the radiator by turning the cap anti-clockwise, (See Fig. 2:1). If the engine is hot, having just been run, then turn the filler cap very slightly until the pressure in the system has had time to disperse. Use a rag over the cap to protect your hand from the escaping steam. If, with the engine very hot, the cap is released suddenly the drop in pressure can result in the water boiling. With the pressure released the cap can be removed.

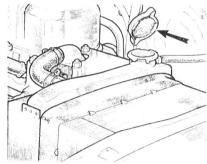

Fig. 2.1. Radiator filler cap removal.

2. If anti-freeze is used in the cooling system, drain it into a clean bowl of 10 pints capacity for re-use.
3. Remove the drain plug in the bottom of the radiator lower tank. When viewed from the side the plug is on the bottom right hand side of the radiator, (Fig. 2:2). Also open the engine drain tap which is halfway down the rear left hand side of the cylinder block, (Fig. 2:3).

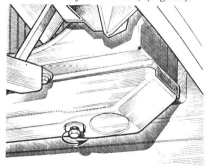

Fig. 2.2. Radiator drain plug removal.

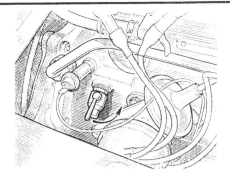

Fig. 2.3. Cylinder block drain tap.

4. When the water has finished running, probe the drain plug and tap orifices with a short piece of wire to dislodge any particles of rust or sediment which may be causing a blockage and preventing all the water running out.

3. Cooling system - flushing

With time, the cooling system will gradually lose its efficiency as the radiator becomes choked with rust, scale deposits from the water, and other sediment. To clean the system out, remove the radiator cap and drain plug and leave a hose running in the radiator cap neck for ten to fifteen minutes.

In very bad cases the radiator should be reverse flushed. This can be done with the radiator in position. The cylinder block tap is closed and a hose with a suitable tapered adaptor placed in the drain plug hole. Water under pressure is then forced through the radiator and out the header tank neck.

The hose is then removed and placed in the radiator filler cap neck and the radiator washed out in the usual manner.

4. Cooling system - filling

1. Close the engine drain tap and refit the radiator drain plug.
2. Fill the system slowly to ensure that no air locks develop. If a heater unit is fitted, check that the valve in the heater unit is open, otherwise an air lock may form in the heater. The best type of water to use in the cooling system is rain water, so use this whenever possible.
3. Completely fill the radiator, replace the cap, remove the expansion chamber cap and check that there is $2\frac{1}{2}$ inch of coolant (use a ruler or pencil) in the chamber.
4. If an anti-freeze mixture is to be used in the cooling system always use an anti-freeze with an ethylene glycol or glycerine base.
5. Replace the expansion chamber cap and turn firmly in a clockwise direction to lock it in position (Fig. 2:4).
6. Run the engine at a fast idle speed for approximately half a minute and remove the radiator filler cap slowly. Top up if necessary to the top of the filler neck and replace the cap.

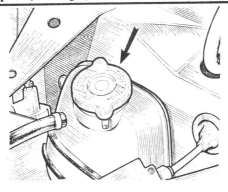

Fig. 2.4. Expansion tank cap (indicated by arrow).

5. Radiator - removal, inspection and cleaning

The radiator on all models is removed in the following manner:(All figures in brackets e.g. (6) refer to Fig. 2:5).
1. Drain the cooling system by removing the drain plug (2) from the bottom of the radiator and also by opening the tap situated at the rear left hand side of the cylinder block (Fig. 2:3).
2. Slacken the two bolts holding the radiator cowling upper support bracket (5) to the top cowl (26) (photo (A)), and carefully remove the bolts together with the plain washers (10), bracket distance pieces (8) and rubber grommets (7). Remove the two nuts and plain washers holding the upper support bracket to the thermostat housing and lift away the upper support bracket (photo (B)).

3. Remove the hose (16) connecting the radiator to the expansion tank. Release the hose from its clip on the cowling.
4. Slacken the upper hose clip (18) and disconnect the upper hose (15) from the radiator top tank (photo (A)). Also slacken the lower hose clip (17) at the lower radiator tank and disconnect the hose (13) from the radiator (photo (B)). Slacken the lower hose clip at the water pump and disconnect the hose from the water pump (photo (C)). If a heater is fitted slacken the clip securing the heater hose connection of the lower hose to the heater pipe and disconnect the joint. Remove the lower hose.
5. Remove the two bolts (9) and washers (10) securing the cowling lower support bracket (6) (photo (A)) and lift away the lower bracket distance pieces (8) and rubber grommets (7) (photo (B)).

5.5b

6. Remove the six screws (28) securing the upper cowling (26) to the radiator (photo) and lift away the upper cowling. Do not attempt to remove the lower cowling (27) at this stage.
7. Push the bottom of the radiator towards the rubber surround (4) and carefully lift away the radiator. If necessary lift away the lower cowling. With the radiator away from the car any leaks can be soldered or repaired

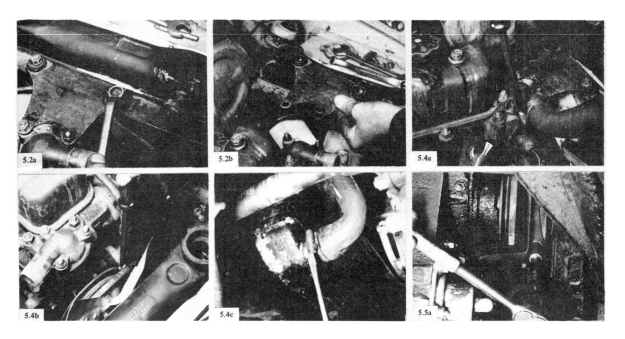

5.2a 5.2b 5.4a

5.4b 5.4c 5.5a

50

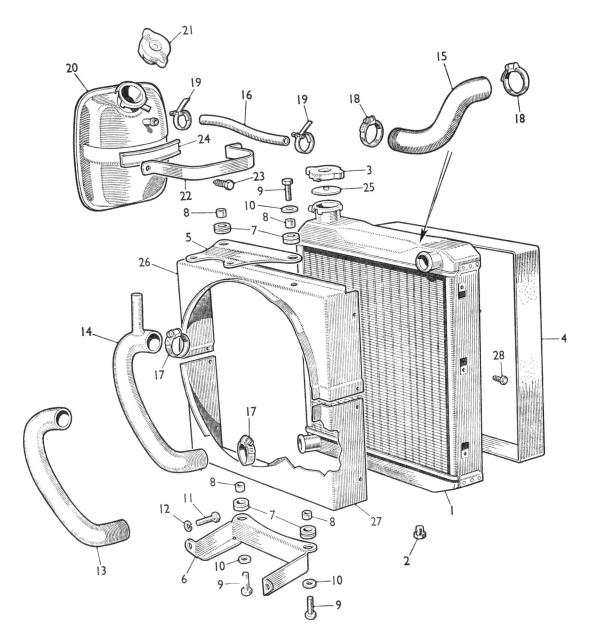

Fig. 2.5. EXPLODED VIEW OF THE RADIATOR AND EXPANSION TANK COMPONENTS

No.	Description	No.	Description	No.	Description	No.	Description
1	Radiator	7	Grommet – bracket		(heater fitted).	21	Expansion tank cap
2	Drain plug	8	Distance piece – bracket	15	Hose – radiator to cylinder	22	Clamp – tank to dash
3	Filler cap	9	Screw –bracket to radiator		head	23	Screw – clamp
4	Rubber surround – radiator	10	Plain washer – screw	16	Hose – radiator to expansion	24	Seating – clamp to tank
	cowl*	11	Screw – bottom bracket to		tank	25	Seal – filler cap
5	Radiator support bracket –		engine	17	Clip – hose to pump	26	Cowl – top
	top	12	Spring washer – screw	18	Clip – hose to cylinder head	27	Cowl – bottom
6	Radiator support bracket –	13	Hose – radiator to pump	19	Clip – hose to expansion tank	28	Screw – cowl to radiator
	bottom*	14	Hose – radiator to pump	20	Expansion tank*		

*1st type illustrated

5.6

with a suitable substance such as 'Cataloy'. Clean out the inside of the radiator by flushing as detailed earlier in this chapter. When the radiator is out of the car it is advantageous to turn it upside down and reverse flush. Clean the exterior of the radiator by carefully using a compressed air jet or a strong jet of water to clear away road dirt, flies etc.

Inspect the radiator hoses for cracks, internal or external perishing, and damage by overtightening of the securing clips. Replace the hoses if suspect. Examine the radiator hose securing clips and renew them if they are rusted or distorted. The drain tap or plug should be renewed if leaking or threads worn, but first ensure the leak is not caused by a faulty fibre washer behind the tap. If the tap is suspect try a new washer to see if this clears the trouble first.

---

6. Radiator - replacement

To replace the radiator proceed as follows:
1. Fit the drain plug (2) into the bottom of the radiator (1)
2. Replace the bottom cowl (27) in position but do not fix. Carefully lower the radiator into position easing the bottom part towards the rubber surround (4).
3. Replace the top cowl (26) and using the six screws (28) attach both cowls (26, 27) to the radiator.
4. Refit the two bolts (9) and plain washers (10) holding the lower cowling support bracket (6) to the radiator taking care to correctly position the bracket distance pieces (8) and grommets (7).
5. Refit the radiator bottom hose (13) to the water pump, the heater hose connection if applicable, and the bottom hose connection to the radiator lower tank. Secure all clips.
6. Reconnect the hose (16) to the radiator filler cap neck and tighten the clip (19).
7. Refit the upper hose (15) to the radiator top tank connection and tighten the clip (18).
8. Replace the top radiator support bracket (5) to the thermostat housing and secure using the nuts and plain washers. Also attach the top support bracket to the cowl using the two bolts (9), plain washers (10), bracket distance pieces (8) and grommets (7).
9. Close the tap situated at the rear left hand side of the cylinder block and refill the system with water or anti-freeze solution.
10. Start the engine and allow to run at a fast idle until the coolant reaches normal operating temperature. Check carefully for leaks especially at the hose joints which if evident are probably caused by loose clips. Finally check the coolant levels in expansion tank and radiator and top up as necessary.

---

7. Thermostat - removal, testing and replacement

To remove the thermostat, partially drain the cooling system (usually 4 pints are enough), loosen the upper radiator hose at the thermostat elbow end and ease it off the elbow. Unscrew the three nuts and lift away the washers from the thermostat housing. Slacken the two bolts (9) (Fig. 2:5) holding the radiator cowling upper support bracket (5) from the top cowl (26) and carefully remove the bolts together with the plain washers (10), bracket distance pieces (8) and rubber grommet (7). Lift away the thermostat elbow from the studs followed by the paper joint and finally the thermostat itself.

Test the thermostat for correct functioning by suspending it on a string in a saucepan of cold water together with a thermometer. Heat the water and note the temperature at which the thermostat begins to open. This should be 82°C (180°F). It is advantageous in winter to fit a thermostat that does not open until 88°C (190°F). Discard the thermostat if it opens too easily. Continue heating the water until the thermostat is fully open. Then let it cool down naturally. If the thermostat does not fully open in boiling water, or does not close down as the water cools, then it must be discarded and a new one fitted. If the thermostat is stuck open when cold this will be apparent when removing it from the housing.

Refitting the thermostat is the reverse procedure to removal. Always ensure that the cylinder head and thermostat housing elbow faces are clean and flat. If the thermostat elbow is badly corroded and eaten away fit a new elbow. A new paper joint must always be used.

If a new winter thermostat is fitted, provided the summer one is functioning correctly it can be placed on one side and refitted in the spring. Thermostats should last for two to three years at least between renewals.

---

8. Water pump - removal

---

1. Drain the cooling system.
2. Remove the radiator as previously described.
3. Loosen the dynamo securing bolts and the slotted link bolts and move the dynamo towards the engine. Lift the belt from the pulleys.
4. Undo the four bolts which bolt the fan and pulley to the water pump flange and carefully take off the fan and pulley. The easiest way to remove these bolts is to hold the head of a bolt with a spanner and then to rotate the fan clockwise (photo).

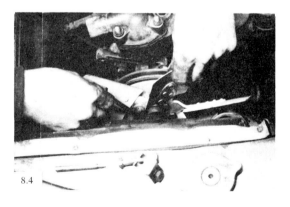

8.4

5. Slacken the clip on the water pump inlet hose and ease the hose off the pump inlet pipe.
6. Unscrew the four bolts which hold the pump to the front of the cylinder block and lift away the pump. Also remove the paper joint washer.

9. Water pump - dismantling and replacement

If the water pump starts to leak; shows signs of excessive movement of the spindle; or is noisy during operation, the pump can be dismantled and overhauled. Alternatively a service exchange reconditioned pump may be fitted. To dismantle the pump proceed as follows:
1. Remove the bearing locating wire, using a pair of pointed nosed pliers, through the hole in the pump body.
2. Using a suitable size two leg puller or a drift and a vice remove the fan pulley hub from the spindle. Take care not to damage or distort either the hub or spindle.
3. Carefully tap the spindle towards the rear, using a soft faced hammer, and withdraw it from the pump body together with impeller, oil seal and bearing assembly.
4. The impeller vane may be removed from the spindle by judicious tapping and levering, or preferably, if available, with an extractor. The oil seal assembly can then be slipped off. Reassembly of the water pump and refitting to the front of the cylinder block is the reverse procedure to the previous described sequence. There are however six important points to be noted:
(a) There is a small hole in the bearing body cover 'A', (Fig. 2:6), fitted to the water pump body with a grease plug and it is vital that when assembled this hole lines up with the lubrication hole in the pump body. To check that this is so, prior to reassembly remove the grease plug and check visually that the hole is in the correct position directly below the greasing aperture.
(b) Regrease the bearing by pushing a small amount of grease into the greaser and then screwing in the greasing plug. Under no circumstances should grease be applied under pressure as it could ruin the efficiency of the oil seals.
(c) Ensure that the pulley hub is a tight fit on the spindle

and that the face of the hub is flush with the end of the spindle, 'B' (Fig. 2:6).
(d) Very carefully inspect the seal for wear or damage and if suspect fit a new one. Refer to Fig. 2:6 and check the grease thrower to bearing clearance 'D'.
(e) When refitting the hub always ensure that there is a clearance 'C' of 0.020 to 0.030 inch between the impeller vanes and the body of the pump.
(f) Before refitting the water pump clean the mating faces of the water pump body and cylinder block and to ensure a good water tight joint always fit a new paper joint washer.

10. Fan belt - removal and replacement

If the fan belt is worn or has stretched unduly, it should be renewed. The most usual reason for replacement is that the belt has broken in service. It is therefore recommended that a spare belt is always carried in the car. Replacement is a reversal of the removal sequence, but as replacement due to breakage is the most usual operation it is detailed below.
1. Loosen the dynamo pivot and slotted link bolts and move the dynamo towards the engine.
2. Carefully manoeuvre the belt between each fan blade in turn, through the small gap at the top front side of the radiator.
3. Slip the belt over the crankshaft, water pump and dynamo pulleys.
4. Adjust the belt as detailed in the following section and tighten the dynamo mounting bolts. NOTE: After fitting a new belt it will require adjustment 250 miles later.

11. Fan belt - adjustment

It is important to keep the fan belt correctly adjusted and although not listed by the manufacturers, it is considered that this should be a regular maintenance task to be performed every 6,000 miles. If the belt is loose

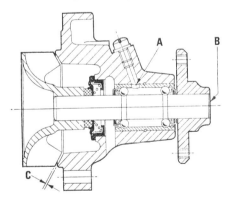 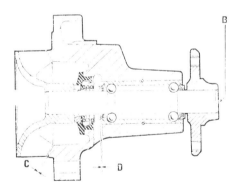

Fig. 2.6. SECTIONAL VIEW OF THE TWO WATER PUMPS SHOWING THE GREASE PLUG (LEFT) AND SEALED TYPE (RIGHT)
A Lubricating and bearing holes coincide   B Hub face flush with spindle end   C .020 to .030 in. clearance   D .042 to .062 in. clearance

it will slip, wear rapidly and cause the dynamo and water pump to malfunction. If the belt is too tight the dynamo and water pump bearings will wear rapidly causing premature failure of these components.

The fan belt tension is correct when there is $\frac{1}{2}$ inch of lateral movement at the mid point position of the belt run between the dynamo pulley and the water pump.

To adjust the fan belt, slacken the dynamo securing bolts and move the dynamo in or out until the correct tension is obtained. It is easier if the dynamo bolts are only slackened a little so it requires some force to move the dynamo. In this way the tension of the belt can be arrived at more quickly than by making frequent adjustments. If difficulty is experienced in moving the dynamo away from the engine a tyre lever placed behind the dynamo and resting against the block gives good control so that the dynamo can be held in position whilst the securing bolts are tightened.

12. Expansion tank

The radiator coolant expansion tank is mounted on the engine bulkhead and does not require any maintenance. It is important that the expansion tank pressure filler cap is not removed whilst the engine is hot (Fig2:6).

Should it be found necessary to remove the expansion tank, disconnect the radiator to expansion tank hose connection at the radiator filler neck having first slackened the clip. Release the hose from its clip on the side of the radiator cowling. Remove the expansion tank

bracket screws and carefully lift away the tank together with its bracket and hose.

Refitting is the reverse sequence to removal. Add either water or anti-freeze solution until it is 2.5 inch from the bottom of the tank.

13. Temperature gauge and thermal transmitter

The thermal transmitter is placed in the cylinder head just below the thermostat and is held in position by a special gland nut to ensure a water tight joint. It is connected to the gauge located on the instrument panel by a cable on the main ignition feed circuit and a special bi-metal voltage stabilizer.

If unsatisfactory gauge readings are being obtained the thermal transmitter may be tested by removing the cable connection on the transmitter and placing the metal cable end on a good earthing point, for example a paint free part of the cylinder head. Switch on the ignition and note movement of the gauge needle. If the needle moves to the hot sector a new thermal transmitter should be fitted. If the needle fails to move then a break in the wiring or a fault in the gauge (which is tested by substitution) will be the cause of the trouble.

To remove the thermal transmitter, partially drain the cooling system (usually 4 pints is enough) and unscrew the transmitter gland nut from the side of the cylinder head. Withdraw the thermal transmitter. Refitting is the reverse procedure to removal.

COOLING SYSTEM

FAULT FINDING CHART

Cause	Trouble	Remedy
SYMPTOM:	**OVERHEATING**	
Heat generated in cylinder not being successfully disposed of by radiator	Insufficient water in cooling system	Top up radiator
	Fan belt slipping (Accompanied by a shrieking noise on rapid engine acceleration)	Tighten fan belt to recommended tension or replace if worn.
	Radiator core blocked or radiator grill restricted	Reverse flush radiator, remove obstructions.
	Bottom water hose collapsed, impeding flow	Remove and fit new hose.
	Thermostat not opening properly	Remove and fit new thermostat.
	Ignition advance and retard incorrectly set (Accompanied by loss of power, and perhaps, misfiring)	Check and reset ignition timing.
	Carburettor(s) incorrectly adjusted (mixture too weak)	Tune carburettor(s).
	Exhaust system partially blocked	Check exhaust pipe for constrictive dents and blockages.
	Oil level in sump too low	Top up sump to full mark on dipstick.
	Blown cylinder head gasket (Water/ steam being forced down the radiator overflow pipe under pressure)	Remove cylinder head, fit new gasket.
	Engine not yet run-in	Run-in slowly and carefully.
	Brakes binding	Check and adjust brakes if necessary.
SYMPTOM:	**UNDERHEATING**	
Too much heat being dispersed by radiator	Thermostat jammed open	Remove and renew thermostat.
	Incorrect grade of thermostat fitted allowing premature opening of valve	Remove and replace with new thermostat which opens at a higher temperature.
	Thermostat missing	Check and fit correct thermostat.
SYMPTOM	**LOSS OF COOLING WATER**	
Leaks in system	Loose clips on water hoses	Check and tighten clips if necessary.
	Top, bottom, or by-pass water hoses perished and leaking	Check and replace any faulty hoses.
	Radiator core leaking	Remove radiator and repair.
	Thermostat gasket leaking	Inspect and renew gasket.
	Radiator pressure cap spring worn or seal ineffective	Renew radiator pressure cap.
	Blown cylinder head gasket (Pressure in system forcing water/steam down overflow pipe)	Remove cylinder head and fit new gasket.
	Cylinder wall or head cracked	Dismantle engine, dispatch to engineering works for repair.

Chapter 3/Fuel System and Carburation

Contents

Specifications

Air Cleaner

Type	Disposable single or twin paper element type with warm/cold air intake and silencer tube

Carburettor:

1800,   18/85
(1964-1968) (1967-1968)

Make and Type	S.U. HS6 at 30°
Diameter	1.750 ins (44.45mm)
Jet..	0.100 ins (2.54mm)
Needles: Standard	TW
Weak	CIW
Rich	SW
Piston Spring	Yellow

Fuel Pump:

1800

Make and Type	S.U. Electric AUF200 type (AUF209 or 215 model)
Delivery rate	56 pints per hour
Suction (minimum)	
Delivery Pressure (minimum)	2 to 3.8 lb/sq in. (0.14-0.27 kg/cm^2)
Fuel Tank Capacity	10½ Imp. gallons

Carburettor Specifications and Data:

1800 Mk II and 18/85
(1968 on)

The carburettor specification is identical to the 1800 Mk I except for the differences listed below.

Make and Type	S.U. HS6 at 20°
Needles: Standard	ZH
Rich	TW

Carburettor Specifications and Data:

1800 Mk II S
(1968 on)

The carburettor specification is identical to the 1800 Mk I except for the differences listed below.

Make and Type	Twin S.U. HS6 at 30°
Needles: Standard	TZ
Rich	CI
Piston Spring	Red

Fuel Pump Specifications and Data:

1800 Mk II, 1800 Mk II S and 18/85 with 18H engine

The fuel pump specification is as follows:

Make and Type	S.U. Mechanical: AUF 700 (AUF 704 model)
Suction (minimum)	6 in. (152mm) Hg.
Delivery pressure (minimum)	3 lb/sq. inch (.21 Kg/cm^2)

1. General description

The fuel system on all models covered by this manual comprises a fuel tank at the rear of the car, either an S.U. mechanical or electrical fuel pump and single or double S.U. HS6 variable choke semi-downdraft carburettors together with the necessary fuel lines between the tank, pump and carburettor/s.

All models are fitted with air cleaners which remove dust and dirt from the air before it reaches the carburettors. The single or double air cleaner elements are disposable and must be renewed at the recommended mileages.

2. Air Cleaners - removal, replacement and servicing

It is recommended that the element be renewed at 12,000 miles or 12 month intervals or earlier when the car is being used in dusty conditions.

SINGLE CARBURETTOR MODELS

To remove the filter element, unscrew the wing nut from the centre of the air cleaner cover (photo) and lift off the cover. Lift away the element. Thoroughly clean the container, fit a new element and replace the cover and wing nut. The element should not be disturbed at any other time.

2.1

TWIN CARBURETTOR MODELS

To remove the filter elements unscrew the two wing nuts from the cover on the top of the air cleaner and lift away the nuts, steel and rubber washers. Withdraw the two elements. Thoroughly clean the container, fit two new elements and replace the cover, rubber and steel washers and the wing nuts. The elements should not be disturbed at any other time.

The air cleaner intake should be positioned adjacent to the exhaust manifold in winter to reduce the possibility of carburettor icing causing fuel starvation. In warmer weather the intake should be moved away from the manifold. To gain access to the intake clip screw remove the two nuts and washers holding the air cleaner in the carburettor and lift away the air cleaner. The intake must not be set in between the two recommended positions.

3. Carburettor - description

1. The variable choke S.U. carburettor as shown in Fig. 3:1 is a relatively simple instrument and is basically the same irrespective of its size and type. It differs from most other carburettors in that instead of having a number of various sized fixed jets for different conditions, only one variable jet is fitted to deal with all possible conditions.
2. Air passing rapidly through the carburettor draws petrol from the jet so forming the petrol/air mixture. The amount of petrol drawn from the jet depends on the position of the tapered carburettor needle, which moves up and down the jet orifice according to the engine load and throttle opening, thus effectively altering the size of jet so that exactly the right amount of fuel is metered for the prevailing road conditions.
3. The position of the tapered needle in the jet is determined by engine vacuum. The shank of the needle is held at its top end in a piston which slides up and down the dashpot in response to the degree of manifold vacuum.
4. With the throttle fully open, the full effect of inlet manifold vacuum is felt by the piston which has an air bleed into the choke tube on the outside of the throttle. This causes the piston to rise fully, bringing the needle with it. With the accelerator partially closed only slight

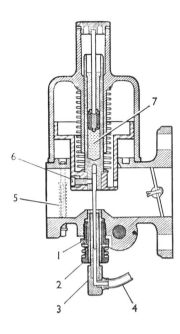

Fig. 3.1. SECTION THROUGH THE S.U. CARBUR-
ETTOR BODY

1 Jet locking nut   5 Piston lifting pin
2 Jet adjusting nut   6 Needle securing screw
3 Jet head   7 Piston damper oil well
4 Nylon feed pipe

inlet manifold vacuum is felt by the piston (although, of
course on the engine side of the throttle the vacuum is
greater), and the piston only rises a little, blocking
most of the jet orifice with the metering needle.

5. To prevent the piston fluttering, and giving a richer
mixture when the accelerator is suddenly depressed, an
oil damper and light spring are fitted inside the dashpot.

6. The only portion of the piston assembly to come into
contact with the piston chamber or dashpot is the actual
central piston rod. All the other parts of the piston assembly, including the lower choke portion, have sufficient
clearance to prevent any direct metal to metal contact
which is essential if the carburettor is to function correctly.

7. The correct level of the petrol in the carburettor is
determined by the level of the float chamber. When the
level is correct the float rises and by means of a lever
resting on top of it closes the needle valve in the cover
of the float chamber. This closes off the supply of fuel
from the pump. When the level in the float chamber drops
as fuel is used in the carburettor the float drops. As it
does, the float needle is unseated so allowing more fuel
to enter the float chamber and restore the correct level.

4. Carburettor (Single) - removal and replacement

1. Remove the carburettor to air cleaner retaining nuts

and spring washers from the two studs and lift away the
air cleaner.

2. Disconnect the mixture control and throttle control
cables from the carburettor linkages.

3. Unscrew the clip securing the fuel inlet pipe to the
float chamber and carefully pull away the flexible pipe.
Pull off the distributor vacuum control pipe from its
connection on the side of the carburettor body. Detach
the return spring from the throttle lever and the linkage
connecting the cam to the throttle lever at the cam end.

4. Remove the four nuts and spring washers holding
the carburettor to the inlet manifold. Carefully withdraw the carburettor away from the inlet manifold
together with the gasket, distance piece and progressive
throttle bracket (on early models the throttle bracket)
as shown in Fig. 3:2.

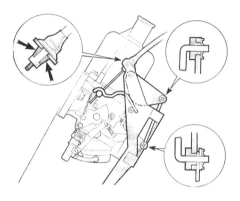

Fig. 3.2. The progressive throttle assembly.
The throttle link and cable fitments are shown
in inserts.

5. To release the throttle cable outer casing squeeze
the retaining lugs together and pull clear. The red diaphragm locates on the throttle bracket and the black
diaphragm on the bulkhead.

6. Refitting the carburettor is the reverse procedure
to removal. Always use new gaskets and Starlock washers when reconnecting the throttle link to the cam. Adjust the throttle cable at the trunnion so that the cam
lever holds against the cam face.

5. Carburettor - dismantling and reassembly

1. All reference numbers refer to Fig. 3:3. Unscrew
the piston damper (10) and lift away from the chamber
and piston assembly (8). Using a screw-driver or small
file scratch identification marks on the suction chamber
and carburettor body (2) so that they may be fitted together in their original position. Remove the three
suction chamber retaining screws (13) and lift the suction
chamber from the carburettor body leaving the piston in
situ.

2. Lift the piston spring (12) from the piston, noting
which way round it is fitted, and remove the piston. Invert it and allow the oil in the damper bore to drain out.
Place the piston in a safe place so that the needle will
not be touched or the piston roll onto the floor. It is recommended that the piston be placed on the neck of a
narrow jam jar with the needle inside so acting as a stand.

3. Mark the position of the float chamber lid relative

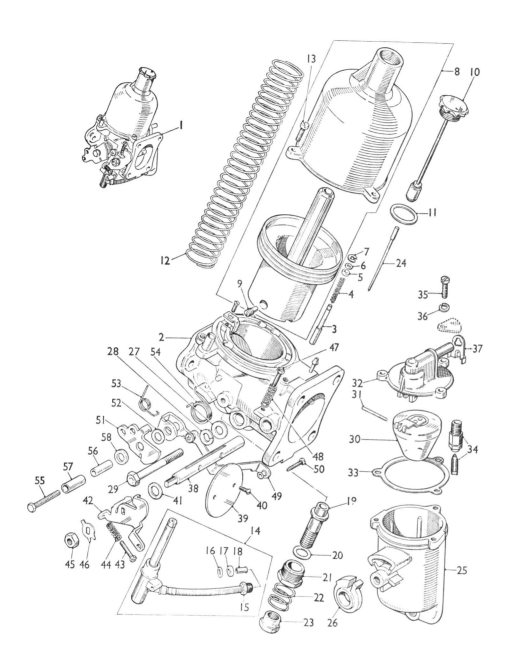

Fig. 3.3. EXPLODED VIEW OF THE S.U. CARBURETTOR

No.	Description	No.	Description	No.	Description	No.	Description
1	Carburettor assembly	16	Washer	31	Hinge pin – float to lid	45	Throttle spindle nut
2	Body	17	Gland	32	Float-chamber lid	46	Tab washer – nut
3	Piston lifting pin	18	Ferrule	33	Sealing washer	47	Throttle adjusting screw
4	Spring – pin	19	Jet bearing	34	Needle and seat	48	Spring – screw
5	Neoprene washer	20	Brass washer – jet bearing	35	Screw	49	Pick-up lever and link
6	Brass washer	21	Jet locking nut	36	Spring washer	50	Screw – link to jet
7	Circlip – pin	22	Jet locking spring	37	Baffle plate lid	51	Cam lever
8	Chamber and piston assembly	23	Jet adjusting screw	38	Throttle spindle	52	Washer – cam lever
9	Needle locking screw	24	Needle	39	Throttle disc	53	Cam lever spring
10	Piston damper	25	Float-chamber	40	Screw – disc to spindle	54	Pick-up lever spring
11	Fibre washer	26	Adaptor	41	Brass washer – spindle	55	Pivot bolt
12	Piston spring	27	Plain washer	42	Throttle return lever	56	Pivot bolt tube
13	Screw – chamber to body	28	Spring washer	43	Cam stop screw	57	Outer tube
14	Jet assembly	29	Bolt – float-chamber to body	44	Spring – screw	58	Distance washer
15	Nut	30	Float				

to the body and unscrew the three screws (35) holding the float chamber lid (32) to the float chamber body (25). Remove the lid and withdraw the pin (31) thereby releasing the float and float lever (30). Using a spanner or socket remove the needle valve assembly (34).

4. Disconnect the jet link from the base of the jet and unscrew the nut (15) holding the flexible nylon tube into the base of the float chamber (25). Carefully withdraw the jet and nylon connection tube.

5. Unscrew the jet adjustment nut (23) and lift away together with its locking spring (22). Also unscrew the jet locknut (21) and lift away together with the brass washer (20) and jet bearing (19).

6. Remove the bolt (29) securing the float chamber to the carburettor body and separate the two parts.

7. To remove the throttle and actuating spindle release the two screws (40) holding the throttle in position in the slot in the spindle (38), make a note of the tapered edges of the throttle (39) and slide it out of the spindle from the carburettor body.

8. Reassembly is a straight reversal of the dismantling sequence.

---

6. Carburettor - examination and repair

The S.U. Carburettor generally speaking is most reliable, but even so it may develop one of several faults which may not be readily apparent unless a careful inspection is carried out. The common faults the carburettor is prone to are:

1. Piston sticking;
2. Float needle sticking;
3. Float chamber flooding;
4. Water and dirt in the carburettor.

In addition the following parts are susceptible to wear after long mileage and as they vitally affect the economy of the engine they should be checked and renewed where necessary, every 24,000 miles:

a) The carburettor needle. If this has been incorrectly fitted at some time so that it is not centrally located in the jet orifice, then the metering needle will have a tiny ridge worn on it. If a ridge can be seen then the needle must be renewed. S.U. carburettor needles are made to very fine tolerances and should a ridge be apparent no attempt should be made to rub the needle down with fine emery paper. If it is wished to clean the needle it can be polished lightly with metal polish.

b) The carburettor jet. If the needle is worn it is likely that the rim of the jet will be damaged where the needle has been striking it. It should be renewed as otherwise fuel consumption will suffer. The jet can also be badly worn or ridged on the outside from where it has been sliding up and down between the jet bearing every time the choke has been pulled out. Removal and renewal is the only answer as well.

c) Check the edges of the throttle and the choke tube for wear. Renew if worn.

d) The washers fitted to the base of the jet and under the float chamber lid may leak after a time and can cause a great deal of fuel wastage. It is wisest to renew them automatically when the carburettor is stripped down.

e) After high mileages the float chamber needle and seat are bound to be ridged. They are not an expensive item to replace and must be renewed as a set. They should never be renewed separately.

PISTON STICKING

1. The hardened piston rod which slides in the centre guide tube in the middle of the dashpot is the only part of the piston assembly (which comprises the jet needle, suction disc, and piston choke) which should make contact with the dashpot. The piston rim and the choke periphery are machined to very fine tolerances so that they will not touch the dashpot or the choke tube walls.

2. After high mileages wear in the centre guide tube may allow the piston to touch the dashpot wall. This condition is known as sticking.

3. If piston sticking is suspected or it is wished to test for this condition, rotate the piston about the centre guide tube at the same time as sliding it up and down inside the dashpot. If any portion of the piston makes contact with the dashpot wall then that portion of the wall must be polished with a metal polish until clearance exists. In extreme cases fine emery cloth can be used.

The greatest care should be taken to remove only the minimum amount of metal to provide the clearance as too large a gap will cause air leakage and will upset the functioning of the carburettor. Clean down the walls of the dashpot and the piston rim and ensure that there is no oil on them. A trace of oil may be judiciously applied to the piston rod.

4. If the piston is sticking, under no circumstances try to clean it by trying to alter the tension of the light return spring.

FLOAT NEEDLE STICKING

1. If the float needle sticks, the carburettor will soon run dry and the engine will stop despite there being fuel in the tank.

The easiest way to check a suspected sticking float needle is to remove the inlet pipe at the carburettor and, where an mechanical fuel pump is fitted, turn the engine over on the starter motor by pressing the solenoid rubber button. Where an electrical fuel pump is fitted turn on the ignition but do not start the engine. If fuel spurts from the end of the pipe (direct it towards the ground or into a wad of cloth or jar) then the fault is almost certain to be a sticking float needle.

2. Remove the float chamber, dismantle the valve and clean the housing and float chamber out thoroughly.

FLOAT CHAMBER FLOODING

1. If fuel emerges from the small breather hole in the cover of the float chamber this is known as flooding. It is caused by the float chamber needle not seating properly in its housing; normally this is because a piece of dirt or foreign matter is jammed between the needle and needle housing. Alternatively the float may have developed a leak or be maladjusted so that it is holding open the float chamber needle valve even though the chamber is full of petrol. Remove the float chamber cover, clean the needle assembly, check the setting of the float as detailed on page 61 and shake the float to verify if any has leaked into it.

WATER OR DIRT IN THE CARBURETTOR

1. Because of the size of the jet orifice, water or dirt in the carburettor is normally easily cleaned. If dirt in the carburettor is suspected, lift the piston assembly and flood the float chamber. The normal level of the fuel should be about 1/16 inch below the top of the jet, so that on flooding the carburettor the fuel should flow out of the jet hole.

2. If little or no petrol appears, start the engine (the jet is never completely blocked) and with the throttle

fully open, blank off the air intake. This will cause a partial vacuum in the choke tube and help suck out any foreign matter from the jet tube. Release the throttle as soon as the engine speed alters considerably. Repeat this procedure several times, stop the engine and then check the carburettor as detailed in the first paragraph of this section.

3. If this failed to do the trick then there is no alternative but to remove and blow out the jet.

JET CENTERING

1. This operation is always necessary if the carburettor has been dismantled; but to check this is necessary on a carburettor in service, first screw up the jet adjusting nut as far as it will go without forcing it, and lift the piston and then let it fall under its own weight. It should fall onto the bridge making a soft metallic click. Now repeat the above procedure but this time with the adjusting nut screwed right down. If the soft metallic click is not audible in either of the two tests proceed as follows.

2. Disconnect the jet link (49), see Fig. 3:3, from the bottom of the jet, and the nylon flexible tube from the underside of the float chamber (25). Gently slide the jet and the nylon tube from the underside of the carburettor body. Next unscrew the jet adjusting nut (23) and lift away the nut and the locking spring. Refit the adjusting nut without the locking spring and screw it up as far as possible without forcing. Replace the jet and tube but there is no need to reconnect the tube.

3. Slacken the jet locking nut (21) so that it may be rotated with the fingers only. Unscrew the piston damper (10) and lift away the damper. Gently press the piston down onto the bridge and tighten the locknut (21). Lift the piston using the lifting pin (3) and check that it is able to fall freely under its own weight. Now lower the adjusting nut (23) and check once again and if this time there is a difference in the two metallic clicks repeat the centering procedure until the sound is the same for both tests.

4. Gently remove the jet and unscrew the adjusting nut. Refit the locking spring and jet adjusting nut. Top up the damper with oil if necessary and replace the damper. Connect the nylon flexible tube to the underside of the float chamber and finally reconnect the jet link.

FLOAT CHAMBER FUEL LEVEL ADJUSTMENT

1. It is essential that the fuel level in the float chamber is always correct as otherwise excessive fuel consumption may occur. On reassembly of the float chamber check the fuel level before replacing the float chamber cover in the following manner.

2. Invert the float chamber cover so that the needle valve is closed. It should be just possible to place a 3/16 inch bar (A) Fig. 3:4, parallel to the float chamber cover without fouling the float, or if the float stands proud of the bar then it is necessary to bend the float lever slightly until the clearance is correct.

NEEDLE REPLACEMENT

1. Should it be found necessary to fit a new needle, first remove the piston and suction chamber assembly, marking the chamber for correct reassembly in its original position.

2. Slacken the needle clamping screw and withdraw the needle from the piston.

3. Upon refitting a new needle it is important that the

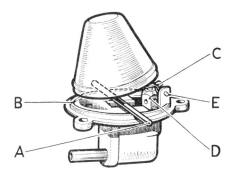

Fig. 3.4. FLOAT LEVER ADJUSTMENT CHECK
A 3/16 in. (5mm) bar   D Float needle and seat
B Machined lip   assembly
C Angle of float lever   E Lever hinge pin

shoulder on the shank is flush with the underside of the piston. Use a straight edge such as a metal rule for the adjustment. Refit the piston and suction chamber and check for freedom of piston movement.

7. Carburettor - adjustment and tuning

1. To adjust and tune the S.U. carburettor proceed in the following manner: Check the colour of the exhaust at idling speed with the choke fully in. If the exhaust tends to be black and the tailpipe interior is also black it is a fair indication that the mixture is too rich. If the exhaust is colourless and the deposit in the exhaust pipe is very light grey it is likely that the mixture is too weak. This condition may also be accompanied by intermittent misfiring, while too rich a mixture will be associated with 'hunting'. Ideally the exhaust should be colourless with a medium grey pipe deposit.

2. The exhaust pipe deposit should only be checked after a good run of at least 20 miles. Idling in city traffic and stop/start motoring is bound to produce excessively dark exhaust pipe deposit.

3. Once the engine has reached its normal operating temperature, detach the carburettor air intake cleaner.

4. Only two adjustments are provided on the S.U. carburettor. Idling speed is governed by the throttle adjusting screw (2) Fig. 3:5, and the mixture strength by the jet adjusting nut (1). The S.U. carburettor is correctly adjusted for the whole of its engine revolution range when the idling mixture strength is correct.

5. Idling speed adjustment is effected by the idling adjusting screw (3). To adjust the mixture set the engine to run at about 1000 r.p.m. by screwing in the idling screw.

6. Check the mixture strength by lifting the piston of the carburettor approximately 1/32 inch with the piston lifting pin so to disturb the air flow as little as possible. If:

   a) the speed of the engine increases appreciably the mixture is too rich;

   b) the engine speed immediately decreases the mixture is too weak;

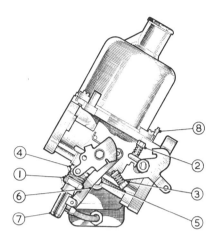

Fig. 3.5. S. U. CARBURETTOR MAIN EXTERNAL
PARTS

1 Jet adjusting nut   bolt
2 Throttle adjusting screw   6 Jet link
3 Fast-idle or choke screw   7 Jet head
4 Jet locking nut   8 Vacuum ignition take-
5 Float-chamber securing   off

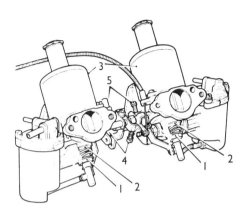

Fig. 3.6. A TWIN-CARBURETTOR INSTALLATION
1 Jet adjusting nuts   bers
2 Jet locking nuts   4 Fast-idle adjusting screws
3 Piston/suction cham-   5 Throttle adjusting screws

c) the engine speed increases very slightly the mixture is correct.

To enrich the mixture rotate the adjusting nut, which is at the bottom of the underside of the carburettor, in an anti-clockwise direction, i.e. upwards. Only turn the adjusting nut a flat at a time and check the mixture strength between each turn. It is likely that there will be a slight increase or decrease in r.p.m. after the mixture adjustment has been made so that the throttle idling adjusting screw should now be turned so that the engine idles at between 600 and 700 r.p.m.

8.   Carburettors (Twin) - removal and replacement

1.   Remove the air cleaner installation from the carburettor. Release the control linkage return spring.
2.   Disconnect the fuel feed pipe from the float chambers. Slacken the clip holding the breather hose to the 'V' piece and remove the hose.
3.   Unlock the nipple from the throttle linkage and disconnect the throttle cable stop. Also disconnect the throttle cable stop bracket from the inlet manifold.
4.   Disconnect the choke control cables and also the distributor vacuum advance pipe from the carburettor. Unscrew the four nuts and lift away together with the plain washers for each carburettor. Carefully withdraw the carburettor from the inlet manifold studs.
5.   Refitting is the reverse procedure to removal. Fit new gaskets between the carburettor flange and manifold.

9.   Carburettor (Twin) - installation - synchronization

1.   First ensure that the mixture is correct in each carburettor by disconnecting the linkage and adjusting each carburettor as described previously in this chapter. With a twin S. U. carburettor installation, not only

have the carburettors to be individually set to ensure correct mixture, but also the idling suction must be equal on both. It is best to use a vacuum synchronizing device such as that produced by Crypton. If this is not available it is possible to obtain fairly accurate synchronization by listening to the hiss made by the air flow into the intake throat of each carburettor. A rubber tube held to the ear is useful for this adjustment.
2.   The aim is to adjust the throttle butterfly disc so that an equal amount of air enters each carburettor. Slacken the throttle shaft levers on the throttle shaft which connects the two throttle discs together. Listen to the hiss from each carburettor intake and if a difference in intensity is noticed between them, then unscrew the throttle adjusting screw on the other carburettor until the hiss from both the carburettors is the same.
3.   With the vacuum synchronizing device all that it is necessary to do is to place the instrument over the intake of each carburettor in turn and adjust the adjusting screws until the reading on the gauge is identical for both carburettors.
4.   Tighten the levers on the interconnecting linkage to connect the two throttle discs of the two carburettors together, at the same time holding down the throttle adjusting screws against their idling stops. Synchronization of the two carburettors is now complete.

10.   Carburettors (Twin) - installation linkage adjustment

1.   On cars fitted with twin carburettors there must be a gap between the fork and lever so that when there is no pressure on the accelerator pedal the throttle butterfly valves will be in the fully closed position without any load from the accelerator linkage to the butterfly and spindle.
2.   Insert a spacer 3/8 inch thick between the intermediate throttle lever and the throttle spindle collar. Depress each actuating lever downwards until it just contacts its fork and tighten in this position. Extract

the spacer and check that there is a 0.013 inch gap between the ends of the actuating levers and the forks. These are illustrated in the inserts in Fig. 3:7.

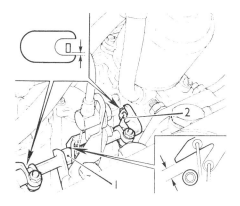

Fig. 3.7. THROTTLE LINKAGE ADJUSTMENT - TWIN CARBURETTOR INSTALLATION
1 Throttle spindle collar   2 Actuating lever

long outer body casing housing the diaphragm, armature and solenoid assembly with, at one end the contact breaker assembly protected by a bakelite cover, and at the other end a short casting containing the inlet and outlet ports, filter valve and pumping chamber. The joint between the bakelite cover and body casing is protected with a rubber sealing band.

2. The pump operates in the following manner: When the ignition is switched on, current travels from the terminal on the outside of the bakelite cover through the coil located around the solenoid core which becomes energized and, acting like a magnet, draws the armature towards it. The current then passes through the points to earth.

3. When the armature is drawn forward it brings the diaphragm with it against the pressure of the diaphragm spring. This creates sufficient vacuum in the pump chambers to draw in fuel from the tank through the fuel filter and non-return inlet valve.

4. As the armature nears the end of its travel a special 'throw over' mechanism operates which separates the points, so breaking the circuit.

5. The diaphragm return spring then pushes the diaphragm and armature forwards into the pumping chamber so forcing the fuel in the chamber out to the carburettor through the return outlet valve. When the armature is nearly fully forward the throw over mechanism again functions, this time closing the points and re-energizing the solenoid, so repeating the cycle.

11. Electric fuel pump - description

1. The S.U. pump type AUF 200 as shown in Fig. 3:8 operates from the 12 volt car battery and comprises a

12. Electric fuel pump - removal and refitting

1. Disconnect the positive terminal from the battery.
2. Disconnect the earth and supply wires from their

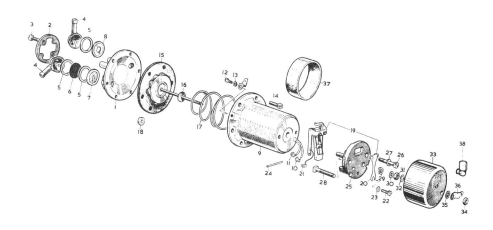

Fig. 3.8. EXPLODED VIEW OF S.U. ELECTRIC FUEL PUMP

No.	Description	No.	Description	No.	Description	No.	Description
1	Body	11	2 B.A. terminal tag	21	2 B.A. terminal tag	30	Lead washer for screw
2	Spring clamp plate	12	Earth screw	22	Screw for blade	31	Nut for screw
3	Screw	13	Spring washer	23	Dished washer	32	Spacer - nut to cover
4	Inlet/outlet nozzle	14	Screw housing to body	24	Spindle for contact breaker	33	End cover
5	Sealing washer	15	Diaphragm assembly	25	Pedestal	34	Nut for cover
6	Filter	16	Impact washer	26	Pedestal to housing screw	35	Shakeproof washer
7	Inlet valve	17	Spring	27	Spring washer	36	Lucar connector
8	Outlet valve	18	Roller	28	Screw for terminal	37	Sealing band
9	Coil housing	19	Rocker and blade	29	Spring washer	38	Non-return valve
10	5 B.A. terminal tag	20	Blade				

terminals on the pump body.

3. Disconnect the inlet, outlet and vent pipe connections from the pump body. It may be found that on pumps fitted to later cars there are in fact two vent pipes in which both should be disconnected.

4. Plug the inlet pipe with a bolt and tighten the clip around the hose so stopping fuel leaking from the tank.

5. Unscrew the two bolts and spring washers which hold the pump bracket to the rear panel and left away the pump.

6. Replacement of the pump is a reversal of the above process. Two particular points to watch are that:

　　a) The fuel inlet and outlet pipes are connected the right way round and that the outlet port is vertically above the inlet port.

　　b) A good electrical earth connection is made.

13. Electric fuel pump - dismantling

1. Refer to Fig. 3:8 and release the inlet and outlet nozzles (4), valves, sealing washers (5), and filter (6) by unscrewing the two screws (3) from the spring clamp plate (2) which holds them all in place.

2. Mark the flanges adjacent to the coil housing (9) and the body (1) and separate the coil housing holding the armature and solenoid assembly from the pumping chamber casting, by unscrewing the six screws (14) holding both halves of the pump together. Take great care not to tear or damage the diaphragm as it may stick to either of the flanges as they are separated.

3. The armature spindle which is attached to the armature head and diaphragm is unscrewed anti-clockwise from the trunnion (19) at the contact breaker end of the pump body. Lift out the armature, spindle, spring (17) and diaphragm and remove the eleven brass rollers (18) or armature guide plate shown in Fig. 3:9 retained behind the diaphragm. Slide off the impact washer (16) which is used to quieten the noise of the armature head hitting the solenoid core.

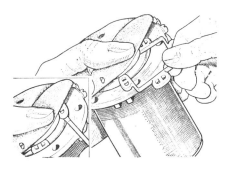

Fig. 3.9. ARMATURE GUIDE PLATE INSTALLATION Inserting the end lobes of the armature guide plate into the recess between the armature and coil housing. Inset. Probe the end lobes free from the coil recess.

4. Slide off the protective rubber sealing band (37) and unscrew the terminal nut (34), connector (36) and washer (35) from the terminal screw (28). Remove the bakelite contact braker cover (33).

5. Unscrew the 5B.A. screw (22) which holds the contact spring blade in position and remove it with the blade

(20) and screw washer (23).

6. Remove the cover retaining nut (31) on the terminal screw (28) and cut through the head washer under the nut on the terminal screw with a pocket knife.

7. Remove the 2B.A. screw (26) holding the bakelite pedestal to the coil housing and lift away the two spring washers (27). Also remove the braided copper earth lead (10) and (11) from the terminal screws.

8. Remove the pin (24) on which the rockers (19) pivot by pushing it out sideways and remove the rocker assembly. The pump is now fully dismantled. It is not possible to remove the solenoid core and coil and the rocker assembly must not be broken down as it is only supplied as a complete assembly if renewal is necessary.

14. Electric fuel pump - inspection and servicing

1. Although it is not in the official manufacturers servicing scheme it is considered good policy to service the S.U. fuel pump every 12,000 miles to minimise the possibility of failure.

2. Remove the filter as has already been detailed and thoroughly clean it in petrol. At the same time clean the points by gently drawing a piece of thin card between them. Do this very carefully so as not to disturb the tension of the spring blade. If the points are burnt or pitted they must be renewed and a new blade and rocker assembly fitted.

3. If, with the pump fitted to the car, fuel starvation occurred and was combined with rapid operation of the diaphragm there is an air leak on the suction side of the pump or the fuel level is too low. Check the level of the fuel in the tank and if satisfactory undo the fuel line at the top of the carburettor float chamber, and immerse the end of the pipe in a jam jar half full of petrol. With the ignition switched on and the pump operating, should a regular stream of air bubbles emerge from the end of the pipe, air is leaking in on the suction side.

4. If the filter is coated with a gum like substance very much like varnish, serious trouble can develop in the future unless all traces of this gum (formed by deposits from the fuel) are removed.

5. To do this boil all steel and brass parts in a 20% solution of caustic soda, then dip them in nitric acid and clean them in boiling water. Alloy parts can be cleaned with a clean rag after they have been left to soak for a few hours in methylated spirits.

6. With the pump stripped right down, wash and clean all parts thoroughly in paraffin and renew any that are worn, damaged, fractured or cracked. Examine the plastic valve assemblies for signs of kinking or the valve plates for damage. The easiest method of testing is to alternatively blow and suck with the mouth. Also inspect the narrow tongue on the valve cage for distortion and allow the valve to lift approximately 1/16 inch. Examine the valve recesses in the body for damage and corrosion, remove any corrosion as previously described or if the recesses are pitted a new body must be fitted.

7. Inspect the coil housing vent tube for signs of blockage, and the coil lead for correct fitting to the wire and the insulation of the wire is sound. Check that the bakelite pedestal is not cracked especially at the narrow ridge on the edge of the rectangular hole on which the contact blade rests.

8. Examine the non-return vent valve fitted in the end cover for damage. Check that the small bearing is free to move. Finally examine the diaphragm for signs of cracking, perishing or bad distortion and fit a new one if suspect.

---

15. Electric fuel pump - reassembly

---

1. Fit the rocker assembly (19) to the bakelite pedestal (25) and insert the rocker pivot pin (24). The pin is case hardened and wire or any other substitute must not be used if the pin is lost.

2. Place the spring washer, wiring tag from the short lead of the coil (10), new lead washer (30), and the nut (31) on the terminal screw (28), and tighten the nut down. Also refer to Fig. 3:10 for further illustrations of assembly sequence.

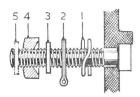

Fig. 3.10. TERMINAL SCREW ASSEMBLY SEQUENCE
1 Spring washer   4 Recessed nut
2 Wiring tag   5 End cover seal washer
3 Lead washer

3. Attach the copper earth wire (21) from the outer rocker immediately under the head of the nearest pedestal securing screw, and fit the pedestal to the solenoid housing (9) with the two pedestal securing screws (26) and lock washer (27). It is unusual to fit an earth wire immediately under the head of the screw but in this case it has been found not to be a particularly good electrical conductor.

4. Fit the lock washer (23) under the head of the spring blade contact securing screw (22) then the last lead from the coil and then the spring blade so that there is nothing between it and the bakelite pedestal. It is important that this order of assembly is strictly adhered to. Tighten the screw lightly.

5. The static position of the pump when it is not in use is with the contact points making firm contact as shown in Fig. 3:11 and this forces the spring blade to be bent slightly back. Move the outer rocker arm up and down, and position the spring blade so that the contacts on the rocker or blade wip over the centre of the other points. When open, the blade should rest against the small ledge on the bakelite pedestal just below the points. The points should come into contact with each other when the rocker is halfway forward. To check that this is correct, press the middle of the blade gently so that it rests against the ridge with the points just having come into contact. It should now be possible to slide a 0.070 inch feeler gauge between the rocker rollers and the solenoid housing. If the clearance is not correct, bend the top of the blade very carefully until it is.

With the outer rocker resting against the coil housing and the spring blade contact resting on the pedestal it should just be possible to insert a 0.030 inch feeler gauge between the points.

6. Tighten down the blade retaining screw, and check that there is a considerable gap existing between the underside of the spring blade and the pedestal ledge, with the rocker contact bearing against the blade contact and the rocker fully forward in the normal static position. With the rocker arm down, ensure that the

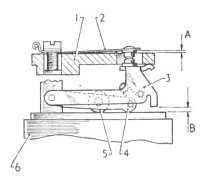

Fig. 3.11. ROCKER FINGER SETTING
A .035 in. $\pm$ .005 in.   B .070 in. $\pm$ .005 in.

1 Pedestal   4 Inner rocker
2 Contact blade   5 Trunnion
3 Outer rocker   6 Coil housing

underside of the blade rests on the ledge of the pedestal. Again if necessary remove the blade and very slightly bend it until it does.

7. Place the impact washer (16) (Fig. 3:8) on the underside of the armature head, fit the diaphragm return spring (17) with the wider portion of the coil against the solenoid body, place the brass rollers (18) in position under the diaphragm and insert the armature spindle through the centre of the solenoid core, and screw the spindle into the rocker trunnion.

8. It will be appreciated that the amount the spindle is screwed into the rocker trunnion will vitally affect the functioning of the pump. To set the diaphragm correctly, turn the steel blade to one side, and screw the armature spindle into the trunnion until, if the spindle was screwed in a further one sixth of a turn, the throw-over rocker would not operate the points closed to points open position. Now screw out the armature spindle four holes (2/3 of a turn) as shown in Fig. 3:12 to ensure that wear in the points will not cause the pump to stop operating. Return the steel blade back to its normal position. Refit the eleven brass rollers, or guide plate as shown in Fig. 3:9.

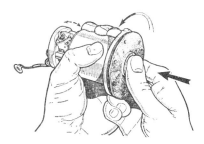

Fig. 3.12. Correct way to rotate diaphragm during rocker setting.

9.   Reassembly of the valves, filters and nozzles onto the pumping chamber is a reversal of the dismantling process. Always use new washers and gaskets throughout.
10.   With the pumping chamber reassembled, replace it carefully on the solenoid housing ensuring that the previously made mating marks on the flanges line up with each other. Screw in the six screws firmly.
11.   Fit the bakelite end cover, connector, lock washer and secure with the brass nut. Refit the rubber sealing band.

16. Mechanical fuel pump – description

The mechanically operated fuel pump is located on the rear left hand side of the crankcase and is operated by a separate lobe on the camshaft via a short pushrod. As the pushrod moves horizontally to and fro it actuates a rocker lever one end of which is connected to the diaphragm operating rod. The operation is shown in Fig. 3:13. When the pushrod is moved outwards by the cam lobe the diaphragm via the rocker arm moves downwards causing fuel to be drawn in through the filter, past the inlet valve flap and into the diaphragm chamber. As the cam lobe moves round, the diaphragm moves upwards under the action of spring, and fuel flows via the large outlet valve to the carburettor float chamber.

When the float chamber has the requisite amount of fuel in it, the needle valve in the top of the float chamber shuts off the fuel supply, causing pressure in the fuel delivery line to hold the diaphragm down against the action of the diaphragm spring until the needle valve in the float chamber opens to admit more fuel.

17. S.U. Mechanical fuel pump – removal and replacement

1.   Disconnect the positive terminal from the battery and remove the air cleaner assembly from the carburettor installation to give better access to the fuel pump.
2.   Remove the fuel inlet and outlet connections from the fuel pump.
3.   Unscrew the two pump mounting flange nuts and remove together with the two spring washers.
4.   Carefully slide the pump off the two studs followed by the insulating block assembly and gaskets. Withdraw the pushrod from its location in the side of the cylinder block.
5.   Replacement of the pump is a reversal of the above procedure. Remember to use new gaskets but on no account alter the original total thickness of the insulating block and gaskets. Do not forget to insert the pushrod into the cylinder block.

18. Mechanical fuel pump – dismantling, inspection and reassembly

1.   Thoroughly clean the outside of the pump in paraffin and dry. To ensure correct reassembly mark the upper and lower body flanges.
2.   Remove the cover retaining screws, (2) (Fig. 3:14) lift away the cover followed by the sealing ring (3) and fuel filter (4).
3.   Remove the six screws holding the upper body to the lower body making special note of the position of the three shorter screws. Separate the two halves (6 and 12).
4.   As the combined inlet and outlet valve is a press

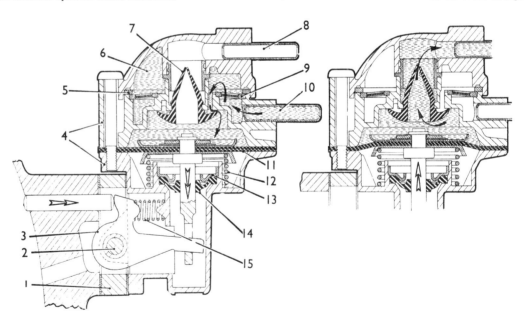

Fig. 3.13. S.U. MECHANICAL FUEL PUMP OPERATION

No.	Description	No.	Description	No.	Description	No.	Description
1	Insulating and joint washer assembly	4	Upper and lower bodies	8	Outlet nozzle	12	Crankcase seal
2	Pivot pin	5	Sealing washer	9	Filter	13	Retaining cup
3	Rocker lever	6	Outlet cover	10	Inlet nozzle	14	Crankcase seal
		7	Valve (inlet and outlet)	11	Diaphragm assembly	15	Rocker lever tension spring

fit into the body very carefully remove the valve (7) taking care not to damage the very fine edge of the inlet valve.

5. With the diaphragm (8) and rocker (14) held down against the action of the diaphragm spring (9) tap out the rocker lever pivot pin (15) using a parallel punch. Lift out the rocker lever (14) and spring (13).

6. Lift out the diaphragm (8) and spring (9) having first well lubricated the lower seal (11) to avoid damage as the spindle stirrup is drawn through.

7. It is recommended that unless the seal (11) is damaged it be left in position, as a special extractor is required for removal.

8. Carefully wash the filter gauge (4) in petrol and clean all traces of sediment from the upper body (6). Inspect the diaphragm (8) for signs of distortion, cracking, perishing and fit a new one if suspect.

9. Inspect the fine edge and lips of the combined inlet

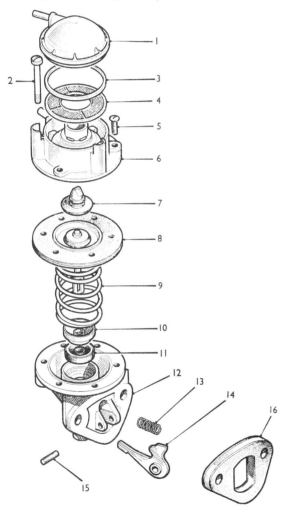

Fig. 3.14. EXPLODED VIEW OF S.U. MECHANICAL FUEL PUMP

No.	Description	No.	Description
1	Outlet cover	9	Diaphragm spring
2	Cover retaining screws	10	Crankcase seal cup
3	Sealing ring	11	Crankcase seal
4	Filter	12	Lower body
5	Body securing screws	13	Rocker lever tension
6	Upper body		spring
7	Combined inlet/outlet	14	Rocker lever
	valve	15	Rocker lever pivot pin
8	Diaphragm/stirrup as-	16	Insulating block as-
	sembly		sembly

and outlet valve (7) and also check that it is a firm fit in the upper body. Finally inspect the outlet cover (1) for signs of corrosion, pitting or distortion and fit a new component if necessary.

10. To reassemble first check that there are no sharp edges on the diaphragm spindle and stirrup and well lubricate the oil seal. Insert the stirrup and spindle into the spring (9) then through the oil seal (11) and position the stirrup ready for rocker lever engagement.

11. Fit the combined inlet/outlet valve (7) ensuring that the groove registers in the housing correctly. Check that the fine edge of the inlet valve contacts its seating correctly and evenly.

12. Match up the screw holes in the lower body and holes in the diaphragm and depress the rocker lever until the diaphragm lies flat, fit the upper body (6) and hold in place by the three short screws (5), but do not tighten fully. Refit the filter (4), new sealing washer (3) and the outlet cover (1) suitably positioned to connect to the outlet hose to the carburettor. Replace the three long screws (2) and then tighten all screws firmly in a diagonal pattern.

13. Insert the rocker lever (14) and spring (13) into the crankcase and hold in position using the rocker lever pivot pin (15).

19. S.U. Mechanical fuel pump - testing

If the pump is suspect or has been overhauled it may be quickly dry tested holding a finger over the inlet nozzle and operating the rocker lever through three complete strokes. When the finger is released a suction noise should be heard. Next hold a finger over the outler nozzle and press the rocker arm fully. The pressure generated should hold for a minimum of fifteen seconds.

20. Fuel tank - removal and replacement

1. Note how much fuel is in the tank, remove the hexagon drain plug and drain the fuel from the tank into a container of suitable size.

2. Remove the complete rear bumper assembly details of which are given in Chapter 14.

3. Disconnect the earth lead from the battery (positive terminal).

4. Remove the fuel filler tube from its neck on the tank. Also disconnect the electrical wire from the fuel tank gauge sender unit by pulling it off its connector.

5. Support the weight of the tank on a jack and remove the six nuts together with the plain and spring washers from the set screws and studs. Carefully lower and withdraw the tank. It should be noted that on later cars there are three setscrews used on the wheel side.

6. Refitting the fuel tank is the reverse procedure to removal.

21. Fuel tank gauge unit - removal and replacement

1. Disconnect the earth lead from the battery (positive terminal).

2. Remove the cover from the hole in the luggage compartment floor and disconnect the electrical connection from the gauge unit.

3. Undo the lock ring which holds the gauge unit to the tank with the aid of a hammer and thin metal drift (BLMC have a special gauge locking ring, part number 18G 1001

for this operation).

Carefully lift the complete unit away, ensuring the float lever is not bent or damaged in the process. Also lift away and discard the rubber sealing ring.

4. Replacement of the unit is the reverse procedure to removal. To ensure a fuel tight joint, scrape both the tank and sender gauge mating flanges clean, and always use a new rubber joint washer.

22. Fuel tank - cleaning

With time it is likely that sediment will collect in the bottom of the fuel tank. Condensation, resulting in rust and other impurities, will usually be found in the fuel tank of any car more than three or four years old.

When the tank is removed it should be vigorously flushed out and turned upside down, and if facilities are available, steam cleaned.

FUEL SYSTEM AND CARBURATION

FAULT FINDING CHART

Cause	Trouble	Remedy
SYMPTOM:	FUEL CONSUMPTION EXCESSIVE	
Carburation and ignition faults	Air cleaner choked and dirty giving rich mixture Fuel leaking from carburettor(s), fuel pumps, or fuel lines Float chamber flooding Generally worn carburettor(s) Distributor condenser faulty Balance weights or vacuum advance mechanism in distributor faulty	Remove, clean and replace air cleaner. Check for and eliminate all fuel leaks. Tighten fuel line union nuts. Check and adjust float level. Remove, overhaul and replace. Remove, and fit new unit. Remove, and overhaul distributor.
Incorrect adjustment	Carburettor(s) incorrectly adjusted mixture too rich Idling speed too high Contact breaker gap incorrect Valve clearances incorrect Incorrectly set sparking plugs Tyres under-inflated Wrong sparking plugs fitted Brakes dragging	Tune and adjust carburettor(s). Adjust idling speed. Check and reset gap. Check rocker arm to valve stem clearances and adjust as necessary. Remove, clean, and regap. Check tyre pressures and inflate if necessary. Remove and replace with correct units. Check and adjust brakes.
SYMPTOM:	INSUFFICIENT FUEL DELIVERY OR WEAK MIXTURE DUE TO AIR LEAKS	
Dirt in system	Petrol tank air vent restricted Partially clogged filters in pump and carburettor(s) Dirt lodged in float chamber needle housing Incorrectly seating valves in fuel pump	Remove petrol cap and clean out air vent. Remove and clean filters. Remove and clean out float chamber and needle valve assembly. Remove, dismantle, and clean out fuel pump.
Fuel pump faults	Fuel pump diaphragm leaking or damaged Gasket in fuel pump damaged Fuel pump valves sticking due to petrol gumming	Remove, and overhaul fuel pump. Remove, and overhaul fuel pump. Remove, and thoroughly clean fuel pump.
Air leaks	Too little fuel in fuel tank (Prevalent when climbing steep hills) Union joints on pipe connections loose Split in fuel pipe on suction side of fuel pump Inlet manifold to block or inlet manifold to carburettor(s) gasket leaking	Refill fuel tank. Tighten joints and check for air leaks. Examine, locate, and repair. Test by pouring oil along joints - bubbles indicate leak. Renew gasket as appropriate.

Chapter 4/Exhaust Emission Control System

Contents

Specifications

Special Tuning Data for 1800 Mk II models fitted with Exhaust Emission Control System

Engine

Type	18H359B, 18H360B, 18H361B, 18H362B, 18H363B, 18H364B
Compression Ratio	9:1
Compression Pressure.	160 lb/sq. inch
Idle Speed	800 r.p.m.
Fast Idle Speed	1,100 to 1,200 r.p.m.
Valve Rocker Clearance	.0.5 inch set cold
Stroboscopic Ignition Timing	14° B.T.D.C. at 1,000 r.p.m. (vacuum pipe disconnected)
Timing Mark Location	Pointer on timing case, notch on crankshaft pulley

Distributor

Make	Lucas
Type	25D4
Serial Number	41234
Contract Breaker Gap..	.014 to .016 inch
Rotation of rotor	Anti-clockwise
Dwell Angle	57° to 63°
Condenser Capacity	.18 to .24 mF
Crankshaft Degrees (Vacuum Pipe disconnected)	14° at 800 to 1,000 r.p.m.
	19° at 1,400 to 1,600 r.p.m.
	42° ± 1° at 6,000 r.p.m.

Vacuum Advance

Starts	4 in. Hg
Finishes	12 in. Hg
Total Crankshaft Degrees...	16° ± 2°

Carburettor(s)

Make	S.U.
Type/Specification	HS6/AUD314 (manual); AUD315 (automatic)
Choke Diameter...	$1\frac{3}{4}$ in.
Jet Size..	.100 inch
Needle...	BAJ
Piston Spring	Yellow
Initial Jet Adjustment	12 flats from bridge

Exhaust Emission

Exhaust gas analyser reading:
   At engine idle speed ... ...   3% CO (maximum)

Air pump test speed ... ...   1.000 r.p.m. (engine)

1.   General description

Due to the increasing concern of atmospheric pollution in various countries and the appearance of new regulations apertaining to motor cars, certain modifications have to be made to either the engines, the exhaust system or the fuel tank breathing system. In some cases a combination of two or three modifications has to be incorporated, depending entirely on the local regulations relative to the country in which the car is being operated.

These modifications are not at present enforced - in countries where the regulations exist - for visitors cars.

The three systems are:
1. Crankcase emission control.
2. Exhaust emission control.
3. Fuel evaporative loss control.

It is important for the reader to appreciate that electronic engine tune equipment is very necessary when finally setting the various engine adjustments i.e. carburettor settings or ignition timing, otherwise the engine and exhaust emission control modifications will not operate efficiently and could affect the overall engine performance.

At the end of this section are full details for diagnosing faults and these should be used as a guide to tracing the fault, but the rectification may have to be left to the local agents who will have the necessary servicing equipment.

2.   Crankcase emission control

1.   The valve control portion of the crankcase emission control comprises a diaphragm control valve which is connected by rubber hoses to the inlet manifold and the crankcase as shown in Fig 4:1. The outlet connection from the crankcase incorporates an oil separator which prevents oil being drawn up to the emission control valve with the oil vapour. A restricted orifice 9/64 inch diameter in the oil filler cap on the rocker cover acts as a source of fresh air into the crankcase, as the oil vapour or piston blow-by gas is drawn up into the inlet manifold by normal manifold depression.

2.   The emission control valve diaphragm is spring loaded to vary the opening to the inlet manifold depending on the depression within the manifold. When the inlet manifold depression decreases, or alternatively the crankcase pressure increases, the diaphragm opens and allows the oil vapour or piston blow-by gases to be drawn into the inlet manifold.

3.   When the engine speed is low or labouring under

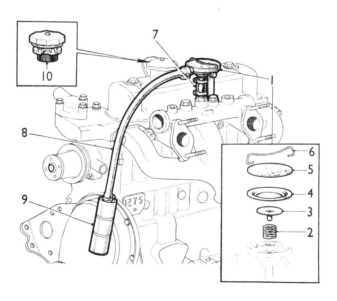

Fig. 4.1. CRANKCASE EMISSION VALVE CONTROL SYSTEM

No.	Description	No.	Description
1	Emission control valve	6	Spring clip
2	Valve spring	7	Manifold connection
3	Metering valve	8	Breather hose
4	Diaphragm	9	Oil separator
5	Cover plate	10	Filtered filler cap

load the diaphragm automatically closes the valve and therefore restricts the flow of oil vapour or piston blow-by gases into the inlet manifold which will therefore prevent the weakening of the petrol/air charge to the cylinders.

4. The carburettor control portion of the system comprises the engine breather outlet which is connected by rubber hoses to the controlled depression chamber (as shown in Fig 4:2), the part between the piston and the throttle disc butterfly valve of the carburettor installation.

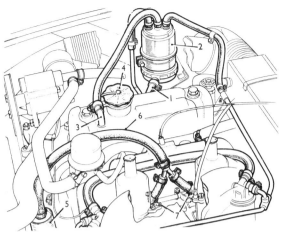

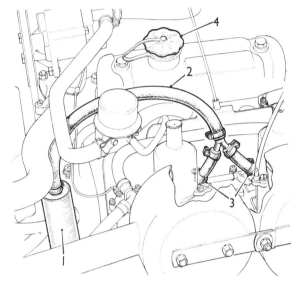

Fig. 4.2. CARBURETTOR CONTROL SYSTEM

No.	Description	No.	Description
1	Oil separator		nection
2	Breather hose	4	Filtered filler cap
3	Carburettor chamber con-		

5. The oil vapour or piston blow-by gas is drawn from the crankcase by the depression in the controlled depression chamber, through a special oil separator fitted into the engine crankcase connection and thereafter to the inlet manifold. Fresh air is supplied to the crankcase through a special oil filler cap with a small filter incorporated in it.

6. The carburettor control system - incorporating evaporative loss control equipment uses all the parts from the carburettor control system, with the exception of the special oil filler cap. The system is shown in Fig 4:3. The fresh air requirement for the crankcase is drawn through a filtered absorption canister of the evaporative loss control system fitted to the rocker cover. A special restrictor valve in the rocker cover connection acts to reduce the air flow to ensure that there is a depression in the crankcase at all times.

3. Servicing - testing the valve control

1. With the engine at normal operating temperature and running at an even idle speed, remove the oil filler cap. If the engine speed rises slightly this indicates that the valve is functioning correctly. On the other hand if the speed does not rise it is an indication that the control valve requires servicing.

Fig. 4.3. CARBURETTOR CONTROL SYSTEM - INCORPORATING EVAPORATIVE LOSS CONTROL

No.	Description	No.	Description
1	Ventilation air intake	5	Oil separator
2	Absorption canister	6	Breather hose
3	Restricted connection to rocker cover	7	Carburettor chamber connections
4	Sealed oil filler cap		

4. Service attention

1. The oil filler cap must be renewed every 12,000 miles or 12 months whichever is sooner.
2. The control valve may be removed for servicing or renewal by disconnecting the two rubber hoses. To dismantle, ease off the spring clip and lift away the cover plate, diaphragm, metering valve and spring.
3. The parts may be cleaned in petrol or paraffin and if deposits are difficult to remove allow to soak overnight. The diaphragm should be cleaned in methylated spirits.
4. All parts should be examined for signs of wear and new parts fitted as necessary.
5. During reassembly ensure that the metering valve fits correctly into its guide and also that the diaphragm is correctly seated. Finally test the valve as previously described.
6. If operation of the system is suspect check the rubber hoses and connections for leaks or blockage.
7. No servicing of the evaporative loss system is necessary other than the intake filter pad located in the absorption canister which should be renewed when blocked.

5. Exhaust port air injection - description

Air under pressure from a pump driven by a 'V' belt is passed to each exhaust valve port via a special air injection manifold. The system is shown in Fig 4:4. Blow back from high pressure exhaust gases into the air injection system is prevented by a check valve in the air delivery pipe.

The air pump also supplies air through a valve called a 'Gulp valve' to the inlet manifold to provide air during deceleration and overrun conditions, thus overriding the carburettor.

The air pump of the rotary vane type is mounted on the front of the cylinder head and is driven from the water pump double pulley. An adjustable lower mounting is fitted to provide adequate belt tension adjustment. Clean air via a dry type renewable element filter is drawn into the pump and is discharged through the pump discharge

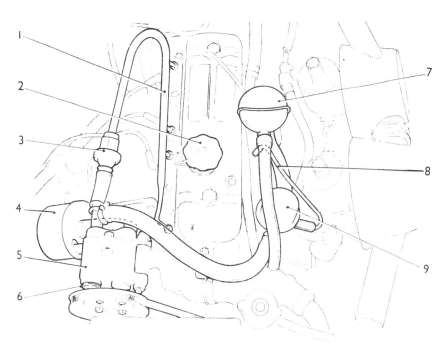

Fig. 4. 4. EXHAUST PORT AIR INJECTION EXHAUST EMISSION CONTROL SYSTEM

No. Description	No. Description	No. Description	No. Description
1 Air manifold	4 Emission air cleaner	6 Relief valve	8 Vacuum sensing tube
2 Filtered oil filler cap	5 Air pump	7 Crankcase emission valve	9 Gulp valve
3 Check valve			

port. A relief valve is fitted to the discharge port to prevent excessive pressure build up. A check valve is fitted between the air pump and injection manifold which is designed to prevent any exhaust gases passing to the air pump, causing it to be damaged. It closes if the air pressure drops whilst the engine is running, as for instance if the drive belt breaks.

As previously mentioned there is a gulp valve fitted to the inlet manifold and this is connected to the pump discharge line and controls the flow of air for weakening the air/petrol charge present in the inlet manifold immediately after the throttle is closed after full throttle operation. There is a little pipe called a 'Sensing pipe' which connects the inlet manifold depression direct to the underside of the diaphragm and through a small bleed hole to the upper side. Any sudden increases in inlet manifold depression occurring immediately after complete throttle closure acts on the underside of the diaphragm and the valve is opened and air is admitted to the inlet manifold. The little bleed hole will allow for any differences in inlet manifold depression acting on the diaphragm to equalise, causing the valve to close. It may be found that on some engines there is a restrictor fitted between the air pump discharge connection and the gulp valve to check any engine surging whilst the gulp valve is in operation.

The carburettors are specially modified incorporating a limit valve in the carburettor throttle disc which will control the inlet manifold depression, so that under conditions of a high inlet manifold depression the petrol/ air charge entering the combustion chambers is in the correct proportions for complete burning. It is important that the carburettors are set exactly right and for this electronic engine tune equipment is necessary.

6. Air pump

1. The air pump is pivot mounted so allowing adjustment to the drive belt to be made. A total deflection of $\frac{1}{2}$ inch should be evident under normal hand pressure at the mid-way point of the longest run of the belt between the two pulleys.

2. To adjust the tension of the belt first slacken the air pump mounting bolt (1) Fig 4:5, and also the two adjusting link bolts (2). Lift up the air pump, using the hand only, until the correct tension is achieved and tighten the adjusting bolts and mounting bolt using a torque wrench set at 10 lb ft.

3. As special equipment is necessary to test and service the air pump it is recommended that this item be left to the local agents.

7. Check valve

1. To remove the check valve, first disconnect the air supply hose at the check valve union and holding the

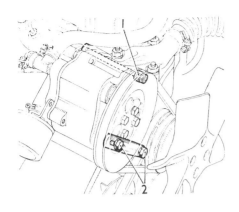

Fig. 4.5. AIR PUMP ADJUSTMENT

No.	Description	No.	Description
1	Pump mounting bolt	2	Adjusting link bolts

air manifold connection firmly in the hand to prevent it twisting, unscrew the check valve. Refitting is the reverse sequence to removal. A cross section view of the check valve is shown in Fig 4:6.

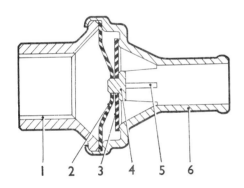

Fig. 4.6. CROSS SECTION VIEW THROUGH CHECK VALVE

No.	Description	No.	Description
1	Air manifold connection	4	Valve pilot
2	Diaphragm	5	Guides
3	Valve	6	Air supply connection

2. To test the check valve, using the mouth only, blow through each end of the valve in turn where it should be found that air will only pass through the valve when blown from the air supply hose end. If any air passes through when blown from the air manifold connection it is an indication that there is an internal fault and the valve must be renewed. It is important that a compressed air jet is NOT used for this test.

8. Air manifold and injectors

1. To test the air manifold and injectors first disconnect the air manifold from the cylinder head connections. Then slacken the air supply hose clip located at the check valve connection. Very carefully rotate the air manifold about its connection axis until the injector connections are easily accessible. Tighten the air supply hose clip again. Start the engine and allow to run at normal idle speed. It should be observed that there is a steady flow of air from each of the air manifold connection tubes. If however the flow is either non-existant or equal from any of the air manifold connection tubes, the manifold should be completely removed and the obstruction cleared using a compressed air jet. With the engine running again at normal idle speed check that there is exhaust gas passing from each cylinder head injector. It is important however that the injectors are free in their cylinder head locations and that they are not displaced during testing.

2. Should an injector be blocked with carbon it may be cleaned by using a 1/8 inch drill in a hand drill and carefully drilling down the injector bore ensuring that the tip of the drill does not touch the valve stem when passing through the end of the injector. Any dust remaining may be cleared using a compressed air jet.

9. Gulp valve and limit valve (inlet manifold depression)

If the operation of the gulp valve or limit valve is suspect the car should be taken to the local agents as accurate gauges are required for testing. For reference a cross section of the gulp valve is shown in Fig 4:7.

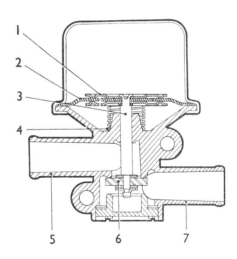

Fig. 4.7. CROSS SECTION VIEW THROUGH GULP VALVE

No.	Description	No.	Description
1	Metering balance orifice	5	Inlet manifold hose connection
2	Diaphragm	6	Valve
3	Valve spindle	7	Air pump hose connection
4	Return spring		

10. Engine modification system - description

This system as shown in Fig 4:8 is used with a high compression ratio engine fitted with a specially modified

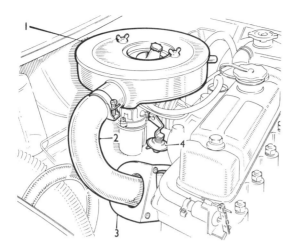

Fig. 4.8. ENGINE MODIFICATION EXHAUST EMISSION CONTROL SYSTEM. NOTE POSITION OF AIR INTAKE FOR LOW TEMPERATURE CONDITIONS

No.	Description	No.	Description
1	Air cleaner	3	Manifold shroud
2	Air intake tube	4	Throttle damper

carburettor installation.

The carburettor must be specially and accurately tuned to give maximum and most efficient engine performance and this can be done only by using electronic engine tune equipment. A limit valve is built into the carburettor throttle disc so that the inlet manifold depression is limited when under high inlet manifold depression conditions and the petrol/air charge into the combustion chamber is at the correct proportion for complete burning. Also a throttle damper is fitted to act on the throttle lever as it returns to the closed position when the accelerator pedal is released. This ensures a gradual closing of the throttle valve which will give a smooth and progressive deceleration of the car. This is adjustable but should be left to the local agent if the operation of the damper is suspect.

With cars operating in very low temperature conditions the air cleaner intake is positioned in a metal shroud formed over part of the exhaust manifold so that air drawn through by the air cleaner to the carburettor installation is warmed. The air intake may be repositioned away from the exhaust manifold for cars operating in warmer conditions by first slackening the intake tube retaining clip followed by removing the two air cleaner wing nuts. The intake tube can now be extracted from the exhaust manifold shroud and from the air cleaner. Refit the intake tube with its entry positioned adjacent to the rocker cover. Finally replace the wing nuts and tighten the securing clip.

The carburettors that are fitted to cars which have had the engines modified for exhaust emission control regulation purposes are accurately set and it is very important that they are not interchanged or substitute parts fitted. Furthermore resetting and tuning can only be done when the engine is connected up to electronic engine tune equipment, so that any work to be done in the way of testing or adjusting or overhauling the carburettors must be left to the local agents.

11. Evaporative loss control - description

The objective of this system is to collect any petrol vapour that could have evaporated from the petrol in the tank. Also as an ultimate, on the twin carburettor installations even the petrol in the carburettor float chambers is vented to the absorption unit (8) Fig 4:10. The idea is that the petrol vapour is stored in an absorption canister (7) Fig 4:9, whilst the engine is stationary but when the engine is restarted the vapour is passed through the crankcase emission control system to the combustion chambers. With the car in motion any vapours are automatically drawn to the crankcase emission control system. A special ventilation system comprises tubes on the fuel tank and ensures that petrol vapour is vented through the control system when the car is parked on a slope. An expansion tank (4) Fig 4:9 is of suitable capacity to prevent any spillage of fuel caused by a full tank of petrol becoming heated due to rises in ambient temperatures. The expansion tank connections are so positioned that it is not possible for liquid petrol to find its way to the storage canister (8). Both the petrol filler cap and the oil filler cap seal the complete system and to ensure correct and reliable operation they must always be correctly fitted.

The absorption canister, Fig 4:9, is located in the engine compartment and contains a special carbon grain

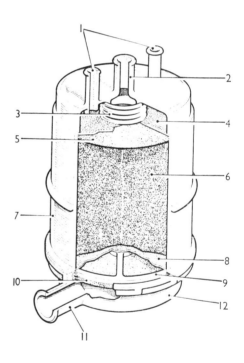

Fig. 4.9. COMPONENT PARTS OF ABSORPTION CANISTER

No.	Description	No.	Description
1	Vapour pipe connections	7	Canister
2	Purge pipe connection	8	Gauze
3	Spring	9	Retainer
4	Gauze	10	Filter pad
5	Filter pad	11	Air vent connection
6	Charcoal granules	12	End cap

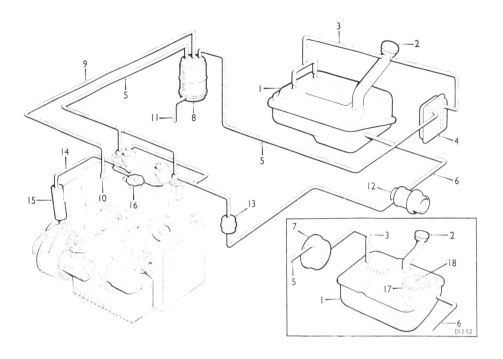

Fig. 4.10. EVAPORATIVE LOSS CONTROL SYSTEM
NOTE: Inset shows arrangement of a separation tank and capacity limiting fuel tank

No.	Description	No.	Description	No.	Description	No.	Description
1	Fuel tank	6	Fuel pipe	11	Air vent	15	Oil separator
2	Sealed fuel filler cap	7	Separation tank	12	Fuel pump	16	Sealed oil filler cap
3	Expansion/vapour line	8	Absorption canister	13	Fuel line filter	17	Capacity limiting tank
4	Expansion tank	9	Purge line	14	Breather pipe	18	Air lock bleed
5	Vapour pipe	10	Restricted connection				

with filter pad at each end so that ventilating air is filtered and the carbon grain keeps in position. The ventilation air filter pad (10) is renewable by unscrewing the end cap (12). The vapour tubes from the petrol tank, the carburettor float chambers and also the surge line from the engine crankcase breather system are connected to the three unions located at the top of the canister. The single union at the bottom of the canister is the connection for the ventilating air tube.

Any petrol vapour enters the canister through the vapour tubes and is absorbed and held by the charcoal. Once the engine is started air is drawn by the crankcase emission control system through the ventilation tube and into the canister. With the air passing between the carbon granules the petrol vapours are given up and are carried with the air through the crankcase emission system to the combustion chambers.

Two methods are used to ensure adequate capacity to accommodate petrol displaced by expansion due to high ambient temperature. Either a separate expansion tank of suitable capacity is fitted, and it is into this that any excess petrol flows, or as an alternate system an air lock chamber is designed into the petrol tank which will stop the tank being filled to maximum fluid capacity so providing additional space for expansion as it occurs. See inset Fig 4:10.

To act as a safeguard to stop dirt finding its way into the carburettor float chamber and unseating the little needle valve, a small fuel line filter is fitted into the system, this being shown in Fig 4:11.

A small temperature sensitive valve is sometimes fitted next to the carburettor and the valve is connected between the air cleaner and the controlled depression chamber of the carburettor. If the under bonnet temperatures are abnormally high, causing the petrol to be

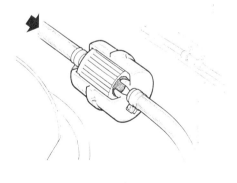

Fig. 4.11. Fuel line filter. Arrow shows flow of fuel.

excessively warm, the valve opens and allows a small quantity of air to pass into the carburettor by passing the jet assembly in the carburettor bridge. This air jet will weaken the charge which would otherwise gradually richen by the vapours from the evaporative loss control system and also by the increase in petrol flow through the carburettor due to the high fuel temperature.

12. Servicing

1. Leak testing. Should the correct operation of either one part of the system or the system as a whole, other than the absorption canister or fuel line filter, be suspect the car should be taken to the local agents as specialist equipment is necessary to trace the fault.

2. Fuel line filter. It is recommended that the filter be renewed every 12,000 miles. It is easily removed by releasing the two clips and easing the flexible pipes from either end. Do not forget to check that the ignition switch is off otherwise the electric fuel pump (if fitted as an alternative to the mechanical pump) will operate. With the new filter fitted run the engine for a few minutes and check the two hose connections for leaks.

3. Absorption canister. It is recommended that the air filter located in the bottom section of the canister is renewed every 12,000 miles for average motoring conditions or more often if the conditions are dusty. The complete absorption canister must be renewed every 50,000 miles or at any time should the carbon grains be saturated in liquid petrol.

4. To remove the canister first disconnect the air vent tube (1), see Fig 4:12, from the base of the canister. Then disconnect the vapour (2) and surge pipe (3) from the top of the canister and finally unscrew the mounting clip tightening nut and bolt (4) and lift away the canister.

5. The air filter may be removed by unscrewing

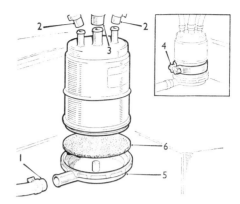

Fig. 4.12. ABSORPTION CANISTER AIR FILTER PAD
Note the correct hose connections

No.	Description	No.	Description
1	Air vent tube	4	Canister securing clip
2	Vapour pipes	5	End cap
3	Surge pipe	6	Air filter pad

the bottom end cap (5) of the canister which will then expose the filter (6). Lift it out and discard, wipe the inside of the cap with a non fluffy rag and fit a new filter pad followed by the cap.

6. Refit the canister to the mounting clip and reconnect the pipes. The surge pipe from the engine valve rocker cover must be fitted to the centre connection on the top of the canister.

Chapter 5/Ignition System

Contents

Specifications	1800 (1964 – 1967)	
Sparking plugs	Champion	
Size...	N5. 14mm.	
Plug gap	0.024 – 0.026 inch	
Firing order	1342	
Coil	Lucas HA12	
Resistance at 20°C (68°F) in Primary winding ...	3.1 to 3.5 ohms	
Consumption – ignition switched on	3.9 amp	
Distributor	Lucas 25D4	
Contact points gap setting	0.014 – 0.016 inch	
Rotation of rotor	Anti-clockwise	
Dwell angle	60° ± 3°	
Automatic advance...	Vacuum and centrifugal	
Condenser capacity	0.18 – 0.24 mF.	
Serial No. High compression distributor	40969	
Serial No. Low compression distributor	40970	
	High compression	Low compression
Automatic advance commences	700r.p.m.	700r.p.m.
Maximum advance (crankshaft degrees)	20°	32°
Vacuum advance (crankshaft degrees)	20°	16°
Decelerating check (crankshaft degrees)	20° @ 3,800r.p.m.	32° @ 4,600r.p.m.
	16° @ 2,600r.p.m.	18° @ 2,400r.p.m.
	11° @ 2,000r.p.m.	15° @ 2,000r.p.m.
	4° @ 1,200r.p.m.	3° @ 1,000r.p.m.
No advance below	700r.p.m.	700r.p.m.
Ignition timing		
Static timing – High compression...	14° B.T.D.C.	
Low compression	14° B.T.D.C.	
Stroboscopic timing – High compression	16° B.T.D.C. @ 600r.p.m.	
Low compression	16° B.T.D.C. @ 600r.p.m.	
Suppressors	Spark plug leads	

Ignition System – Specifications & Data – 1800 and 18/85 (1967 – 1968)
  The ignition system specifications are identical to the 1800 (1964 – 67) except for the differences listed below:

Distributor
  Serial No. High compression distributor   41034

Ignition System Specifications & Data - 1800 MkII & 18/85 MkII (1968 on)
The ignition system specifications are identical to the 1800 (1964 - 67) except for the difference listed below:

Sparking plugs
    Size... ... ...   N9Y
Distributor
    Serial No. High compression distributor 41234A
    Serial No. Low compression distributor   41035

	High compression	Low compression
Automatic advance commences	500r.p.m.	700r.p.m.
Maximum advance (crankshaft degrees)	26°	32°
Vacuum advance (crankshaft degrees)	12°	16°
Decelerating check (crankshaft degrees)	26° @ 4,400r.p.m.	32° @ 4,600r.p.m.
	20° @ 3,200r.p.m.	18° @ 2,400r.p.m.
	12° @ 2,200r.p.m.	15° @ 2,000r.p.m.
	4° @ 1,200r.p.m.	3° @ 1,000r.p.m.
No advance below	500r.p.m.	700r.p.m.

Ignition timing
    Stroboscopic timing - High compression   ... ...   12° B.T.D.C. @ 600r.p.m.
                        Low compression   ... ...   12° B.T.D.C. @ 600r.p.m.

Ignition System Specifications & Data - 1800 MkII 'S' and 18/85 MkII 'S' (1968 on)
The ignition system specifications are identical to the 1800 (1964 - 67) except for the differences listed below:

Sparking plugs
    Size... ... ...   N9Y
Distributor
    Serial No. High compression distributor   41238

	High compression
Automatic advance commences	600r.p.m.
Maximum advance (crankshaft degrees)	20°
Vacuum advance (crankshaft degrees)	16°
Decelerating check (crankshaft degrees)	20° to 24° @ 4,800r.p.m.
	14° to 18° @ 2,800r.p.m.
	11° to 15° @ 2,000r.p.m.
	10° to 14° @ 1,500r.p.m.
	4° to 8° @ 1,100r.p.m.
No advance below	600r.p.m.

Ignition timing
    Stroboscopic timing - High compression   ... ...   12° B.T.D.C. @ 600r.p.m.

1. General description

In order that the engine may run correctly it is necessary for an electrical spark to ignite the fuel/air charge in the combustion chamber at exactly the right moment in relation to engine speed and load. The ignition system is based on supplying low tension voltage from the battery to the ignition coil where it is converted to high tension voltage. The high tension voltage is powerful enough to jump the sparking plug gap in the cylinders many times a second under high compression pressure, providing that the ignition system is in good working order and that all adjustments are correct.

The ignition system comprises two individual circuits known as the low tension circuit and the high tension circuit.

The low tension circuit (sometimes known as the primary circuit) comprises the battery, lead to control box, lead to the ignition switch to the low tension or primary coil windings (terminal SW) and the lead from the low tension coil windings (coil terminal CB) to the contact breaker points and condenser in the distributor.

The high tension circuit (sometimes known as the secondary circuit) comprises the high tension or secondary coil winding, the heavily insulated ignition lead from the centre of the coil to the centre of the distributor cap, the rotor arm, the sparking plug leads and the sparking plugs.

The complete ignition system operation is as follows: Low tension voltage from the car battery is changed within the ignition coil to high tension voltage by the opening and closing of the contact breaker points in the low tension circuit. High tension voltage is then fed via the carbon brush in the centre of the distributor cap to the rotor arm of the distributor. The rotor arm revolves inside the distributor cap, and each time it comes in line with one of the four metal segments in the cap, these being connected to the sparking plug leads, the opening and closing of the contact breaker points causes the high tension voltage to build up, jump the gap from the rotor arm to the appropriate metal segment and so via the sparking plug lead to the sparking plug where it finally jumps the gap between the two spark plug electrodes, one being connected to the earth system.

The ignition time is advanced and retarded automatically to ensure the spark occurs at just the right instant for the particular load at the prevailing engine speed.

The ignition advance is controlled both mechanically and by a vacuum operated system. The mechanical governor mechanism comprises two lead weights, which move out under centrifugal force from the central distributor shaft as the engine speed rises. As they move outwards they rotate the cams relative to the distributor shaft, and so advance the spark. The weights are held in position by two light springs and it is the tension of the springs which is largely responsible for correct spark advancement.

The vacuum control comprises a diaphragm, one side of which is connected via a small bore tube to the carburettor, and the other side to the contact breaker plate. Depression in the induction manifold and carburettor, which varies with engine speed and throttle opening, causes the diaphragm to move, so moving the contact breaker plate and advancing or retarding the spark. A fine degree of control is achieved by a spring in the vacuum assembly.

2. Contact breaker - adjustment

1. To adjust the contact breaker points so that the correct gap is obtained, first release the two clips securing the distributor cap to the distributor body, and lift away the cap. Clean the inside and outside of the cap with a dry cloth. It is unlikely that the four segments will be badly burned or scored, but if they are the cap must be renewed. If only a small deposit is on the segments it may be scraped away using a small screwdriver.
2. Push in the carbon brush located in the top of the cap several times to ensure that it moves freely. The brush should protrude by at least a quarter of an inch.
3. Gently prise the contact breaker points (6) Fig. 5:1, open to examine the condition of their faces. If they are rough, pitted or dirty, it will be necessary to remove them for resurfacing, or for replacement points to be fitted.

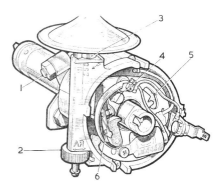

Fig. 5.1. ADJUSTMENT POINTS FOR THE DISTRIBUTOR

No.	Description	No.	Description
1	Clamp-plate pinch bolt	4	Fixed plate securing screw
2	Vernier adjusting nut	5	Screwdriver notches
3	Vernier scale	6	Points

4. Presuming the points are satisfactory, or that they have been cleaned or replaced, measure the gap between the points by turning the engine over until the contact breaker arm is on the peak of one of the four cam lobes. A 0.015 inch feeler gauge should now just fit between the points.
5. If the gap varies from this amount, slacken the contact plate securing screw (4) and adjust the contact gap by inserting a screwdriver in the notched hole (5) at the end of the plate, turning clockwise to decrease and anti-clockwise to increase the gap. Tighten the securing

screw and check the gap again.
6. Replace the rotor arm and distributor cap and clip the spring blade retainers into position.

3. Contact breaker points - removal and replacement

1. If the contact breaker points are burned, pitted or badly worn, they must be removed and either replaced, or their faces must be filed smooth.
2. To remove the points, unscrew the terminal nut and remove it together with the washer under its head. Remove the flanged nylon bush and then the condenser lead and the low tension lead from the terminal pin. Lift off the contact breaker arm and then remove the large fibre washer from the terminal pin.
3. The adjustable contact breaker plate is removed by unscrewing the one holding down screw and removing it, complete with spring and flat washer.
4. To reface the points, rub the faces on a fine carborundum stone, or on fine emery paper. It is important that the faces are rubbed flat and parallel to each other so that there will be complete face to face contact when the points are closed. One of the points will be pitted and the other will have deposits on it.
5. It is necessary to remove completely the built-up deposits, but not necessary to rub the pitted point right to the stage where all the pitting has disappeared, though obviously if this is done it will prolong the time before the operation of refacing the points has to be repeated.
6. To replace the points, first position the adjustable contact breaker plate, and secure it with its screw spring and flat washer. Fit the fibre washer to the terminal pin, and fit the contact breaker arm over it. Insert the flanged nylon bush with the condenser lead immediately under its head, and the low tension lead under that, over the terminal pin. Fit the steel washer and screw on the securing nut.
7. The points are now reassembled and the gap should be set as detailed in the previous section.

4. Condenser - removal, testing and replacement

1. The purpose of the condenser, (sometimes known as a capacitor), is to ensure that when the contact breaker points open there is no sparking across them which would wast voltage and cause wear.
2. The condenser is fitted in parallel with the contact breaker points. If it develops a short circuit, it will cause ignition failure as the points will be prevented from interrupting the low tension circuit.
3. If the engine becomes very difficult to start or begins to miss after several miles running and the breaker points show signs of excessive burning, then the condition of the condenser must be suspect. A further test can be made by separating the points by hand with the ignition switched on. If this is accompanied by a flash it is indicative that the condenser has failed.
4. Without special test equipment the only sure way to diagnose condenser trouble is to replace a suspected unit with a new one and note if there is any improvement.
5. To remove the condenser from the distributor, remove the distributor cap and the rotor arm. Unscrew the contact breaker arm terminal nut, and remove the nut, washer, and flanged nylon bush and release the condenser. Replacement of the condenser is simply a reversal of the removal process. Take particular care that the condenser lead does not short circuit against any portion of the breaker plate.

5.   Distributor - lubrication

1.   It is important that the distributor cam is lubricated with petroleum jelly at the specified mileages, and that the breaker arm, governor weights, and cam spindle, are lubricated with engine oil once every 6,000 miles. In practice it will be found that lubrication every 3,000 miles is preferable although this is not recommended by the makers.

2.   Great care should be taken not to use too much lubricant, as any excess that might find its way onto the contact breaker points could cause burning and misfiring.

3.   To gain access to the cam spindle, lift away the rotor arm. Drop no more than two drops of engine oil onto the screw head. This will run down the spindle when the engine is hot and lubricate the bearings. No more than ONE drop of oil should be applied to the pivot post.

6.   Distributor - removal and replacement

1.   To remove the distributor from the engine, start by pulling the terminals off each of the sparking plugs. Release the nut securing the low tension lead to the terminal on the side of the distributor and unscrew the high tension lead retaining cap from the coil and remove the lead.

2.   Unscrew the union holding the vacuum tube to the distributor vacuum housing.

3.   Remove the distributor body clamp bolts (two) which hold the distributor clamp plate (1) Fig. 5:2, to the engine and remove the distributor. NOTE: If it is not wished to disturb the timing, then under no circumstances should the clamp pinch bolt, which secures the distributor in its relative position in the clamp, be loosened. Providing the distributor is removed without the clamp being loosened from the distributor body and the engine is not turned, the timing will not be lost.

4.   Replacement is a reversal of the above process. If the engine has been turned it will be best to retime the ignition. This will also be necessary if the clamp pinch bolt has been loosened.

7.   Distributor - dismantling

1.   With the distributor removed from the car and on the bench, remove the distributor cap (2) Fig. 5:2 and lift off the rotor arm (4). If very tight, lever it off gently with a screwdriver.

2.   Remove the points from the distributor as detailed in Section 3.

3.   Remove the condenser (6) from the contact breaker plate (8) by releasing its securing screw.

4.   Unlock the vacuum unit spring from its mounting pin on the moving contact breaker plate.

5.   Remove the contact breaker plate.

6.   Unscrew the two screws and lockwashers which hold the contact breaker base plate (9) in position and remove the earth lead (10) from the relevant screw. Remember to replace this lead on reassembly.

7.   Lift out the contact breaker base plate.

8.   NOTE: the position of the slot in the rotor arm drive in relation to the offset drive dog at the opposite end of the distributor. It is essential that this is reassembled correctly as otherwise the timing may be 180° out.

9.   Unscrew the cam spindle retaining screw (21), which is located in the centre of the rotor arm drive shaft (14),

and remove the cam spindle.

10.   Lift out the centrifugal weights (13) together with their springs.

11.   To remove the vacuum unit (16), spring off the small circlip securing the advance adjustment knurled nut which should then be unscrewed. With the micrometer adjusting nut removed, release the spring and the micrometer adjusting nut lock spring clip. This is the clip that is responsible for the 'clicks' when the micrometer adjuster is turned, and it is small and easily lost, as is the circlip, so put them in a safe place. Do not forget to replace the lock spring clip on reassembly.

12.   It is necessary to remove the distributor drive shaft or spindle only if it is thought to be excessively worn. With a thin punch drive out the retaining pin (20) from the driving tongue collar (19) on the bottom end of the distributor drive shaft. The shaft can then be removed. The distributor is now completely dismantled.

8.   Distributor - inspection and repair

1.   Check the points that have already been described previously. Check the distributor cap for signs of tracking, indicated by a thin black line between the segments. Replace the cap if any signs of tracking are found.

2.   If the metal portion of the rotor arm is badly burned or loose, renew the arm. If slightly burnt clean the arm with a fine file. Check that the carbon brush moves freely in the centre of the distributor cover.

3.   Examine the fit of the breaker plate on the bearing plate and also check the breaker arm pivot for looseness or wear and renew as necessary.

4.   Examine the balance weights and pivot pins for wear, and renew the weights or cam assembly if a degree of wear is found.

5.   Examine the shaft and the fit of the cam assembly on the shaft. If the clearance is excessive compare the items with new units, and renew either, or both, if they show excessive wear.

6.   If the shaft is a loose fit in the distributor bushes and can be seen to be worn, it will be necessary to fit a new shaft and bushes. The old bushes in the early distributor, or the single bush in the later ones, are simply pressed out. NOTE: Before inserting new bushes they should be stood in engine oil for 24 hours.

7.   Examine the length of the balance weight springs and compare them with new springs. If they have stretched they should be renewed.

9.   Distributor - reassembly

1.   Reassembly is a straight reversal of the dismantling process, but there are several points which should be noted in addition to those already given in the section on dismantling.

2.   Lubricate the balance weights and other parts of the mechanical advance mechanism, the distributor shaft, and the portion of the shaft on which the cam bears, with S.A.E. 20 engine oil, during assembly. Do not oil excessively but ensure these parts are adequately lubricated.

3.   On reassembling the cam driving pins with the centrifugal weights, check that they are in correct position so that when viewed from above, the rotor arm should be at the six o'clock position, and the small offset on the driving dog must be on the right.

4.   Check the action of the weights in the fully advanced

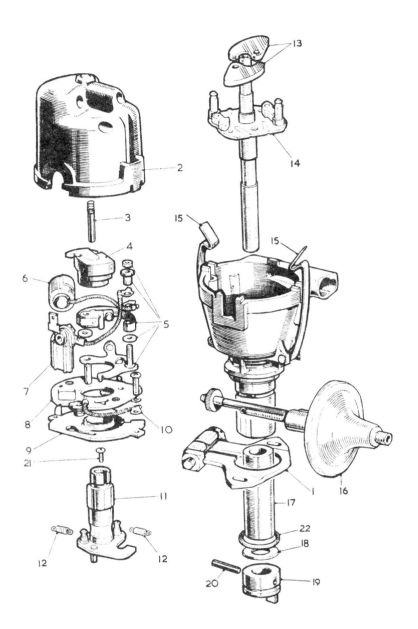

Fig. 5.2. EXPLODED VIEW OF THE DISTRIBUTOR

No.	Description	No.	Description	No.	Description
1	Clamping plate	7	Terminal and lead (low tension)	12	Automatic-advance springs	18	Thrust washer
2	Moulded cap			13	Weight assembly	19	Driving dog
3	Brush and spring	8	Moving contact-breaker plate	14	Shaft and action plate	20	Parallel pin
4	Rotor arm	9	Contact-breaker base plate	15	Cap-retaining clips	21	Cam screw
5	Contacts (set)	10	Earth lead	16	Vacuum unit	22	'O' ring oil seal
6	Capacitor	11	Cam	17	Bush		

and fully retarded positions a n d ensure they are not binding.

5.   Tighten the micrometer adjusting nut to the middle position on the timing scale.

6.   Finally, set the contact breaker gap to the correct clearance of 0. 015 inch.

10. Ignition - timing

1.   If the clamp plate pinch bolt has been loosened on the distributor and the static timing lost, or if for any other reason it is wished to set the ignition timing, proceed as follows:

2.   The static advance is checked at the exact moment of opening of the contact breaker points relative to the position of the notch in the crankshaft pulley periphery in relation to the points on the bottom of the timing gear cover case.   The longest pointer (as shown in Fig. 5:3) indicates T.D.C. and each of the three shorter points indicates 5° B.T.D.C., 10° B.T.D.C , and 15° B.T.D.C., respectively.

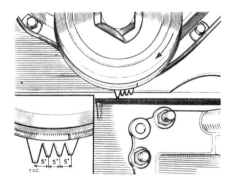

Fig. 5. 3. Ignition timing marks on pulley and cover.

3.   Check the 'Ignition specification' for correct position of the crankshaft pulley wheel when the points should just begin to open.   This is known as 'Static Setting'.

4.   Rotate the crankshaft so the No. 1 piston is coming to T. D. C. on t h e compression stroke.   This can b e checked by removing No. 1 sparking plug and feeling the pressure being developed in t h e cylinder, or by removing the rocker cover and noting when the valves in No. 4 cylinder are rocking, i. e. the inlet valve just opening and exhaust valve just closing.   If this check is not made it is all too easy to set the timing 180° out, as both No. 1 and 4 cylinders come up to T. D. C. at the same time, but only one on the firing stroke.

5.   Continue turning the engine until the notch on the crankshaft pulley is in line with the correct timing mark on the timing cover, or is in the correct position with regards to the pointers.

6.   Remove the distributor cover, slacken off the distributor body clamp bolt, and with the rotor arm towards the No. 1 terminal (check this position with the distributor cap and lead to No. 1 sparking plug), insert the distributor into the distributor housing.   The dog on the drive shaft should match up with the slot in the distributor driving spindle.

7.   Insert the two bolts holding the distributor in position.

8.   With the engine set in the correct position and the rotor arm opposite the correct segment for No. 1 cylinder turn the advance/retard knob on the distributor until the contact points are just beginning to open.   Eleven clicks of the knurled micrometer adjuster nut represent 1° of timing movement.

9.   If the range of adjustment provided by this adjuster is not sufficient, then, if the clamp bolt is not already slackened, it will be necessary to slacken it, and turn the distributor body half a graduation as marked on the adjusting spindle barrel.   (Each graduation represents 5° timing movement of 55 clicks of the micrometer adjuster).   Sufficient adjustment will normally be found available u s i n g the distributor micrometer adjuster.   When this has been achieved, the engine is statically timed.

10.   Difficulty is sometimes experienced in determining exactly when the contact breaker points open.   This can be ascertained most accurately by connecting a 12-volt bulb in parallel with the contact breaker points (one lead to earth and the other from the distributor low tension terminal).   Switch on the ignition, and turn the advance and retard adjuster until the bulb lights up, indicating that the points have just opened.

11.   If a stroboscopic timing light is being used, attach one lead to No. 1 sparking plug, and attach the other lead into the free end of No. 1 plug ignition cable leading from the distributor.   Start the engine and shine t h e light on the crankshaft pulley and timing indicators.   If the engine idles at more than 600 r. p. m. then the correct static timing will not be obtained as the centrifugal weights will have started to advance.

12.   If the light shows the notch in the pulley wheel to be to the right of the timing marks, then the ignition is too far advanced.   If t h e notch appears to the left of the timing marks, t h e n the ignition is too far retarded.   Turn the distributor body or micrometer adjuster until the timing notch appears in just the right position in relation to the timing marks.

13.   Tighten the clamp bolt and recheck that the timing is still correct, making any small correction necessary with the micrometer adjuster.

14.   A better result can sometimes be obtained by making slight readjustments under running conditions.

15.   First start the engine and allow to warm up to normal temperature, and then accelerate in top gear from 30 to 50 m. p. h., listening for heavy pinking of the e n gine.   If this occurs, the ignition needs to be retarded slightly until just the faintest trace of pinking can be heard under these operating conditions.

16.   Since the ignition advance adjustment enables the firing point to be related correctly in relation to the grade of fuel used, the fullest advantage of any change of fuel will only be attained by re-adjustment of the ignition settings.

17.   This is done by varying the setting of the index scale on the vacuum advance mechanism one or two divisions, checking to make sure that the best all-round result is attained.

11. Sparking plugs and leads

1.   The correct functioning of t h e sparking plugs is vital for the correct running and efficiency of the engine.

2.   At intervals of 6, 000 miles the plugs should be removed, examined, cleaned, and if worn excessively, replaced.   The condition of the sparking plug will also tell much about the overall condition of the engine.

3.   If the insulator nose of the sparking plug is clean

and white, with no deposits, this is indicative of a weak mixture, or too hot a plug. (A hot plug transfers heat away from the electrode slowly - a cold plug transfers heat away quickly).

4. The plugs fitted as standard are the Champion N5 15mm type on early models, and N9Y type on post 1968 models. If the top and insulator nose is covered with hard black-looking deposits, then this is indicative that the mixture is too rich. Should the plug be black and oily, then it is likely that the engine is fairly worn, as well as the mixture being too rich.

5. If the insulator nose is covered with light tan to greyish brown deposits, then the mixture is correct and it is likely that the engine is in good condition.

6. If there are any traces of long brown tapering stains on the outside of the white portion of the plug, then the plug will have to be renewed, as this shows that there is a faulty joint between the plug body and the insulator, and compression is being allowed to leak away.

7. Plugs should be cleaned by a sand blasting machine, which will free them from carbon more than cleaning by hand. The machine will also test the condition of the plugs under compression. Any plug that fails to spark at the recommended pressure should be renewed.

8. The sparking plug gap is of considerable importance, as, if it is too large or too small, the size of the spark and its efficiency will be seriously impaired. The sparking plug gap should be set to 0.025 inch for the best results.

9. To set it, measure the gap with a feeler gauge, and then bend open, or close, the outer plug electrode until the correct gap is achieved. The centre electrode should never be bent as this may crack the insulation and cause plug failure if nothing worse.

10. When replacing the plugs, remember to use new washers, and replace the leads from the distributor in the correct firing order, which is 1, 3, 4, 2, No. 1 cylinder being the one nearest the radiator.

11. The plug leads require no routine attention other than being kept clean and wiped over regularly. At intervals of 5,000 miles, however, pull each lead off the plug in turn and remove them from the distributor by slackening the screws located as shown in Fig. 5:4. Water can seep down into these joints giving rise to a white corrosive deposit which must be carefully removed from the end of each cable.

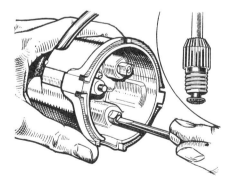

Fig. 5.4. H.T. cable clamping screw in distributor cap.

12. Ignition system - fault finding

By far the majority of breakdown and running troubles are caused by faults in the ignition system either in the low tension or high tension circuits as shown in Fig. 5:5.

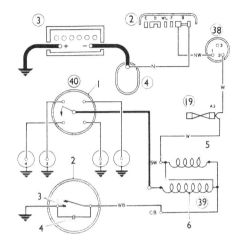

Fig. 5.5. DIAGRAM OF IGNITION SYSTEM

No.	Description	No.	Description
(2)	Control box - RB340	1	Distributor cap
(3)	Battery	2	Contact-breaker moving plate
(4)	Starter solenoid	3	Contact-breaker points
(19)	Fuse unit	4	Capacitor
(38)	Ignition and starter switch	5	Primary winding
(39)	Ignition coil	6	Secondary winding
(40)	Distributor		

13. Ignition system - fault symptoms

There are two main symptoms indicating ignition faults. Either the engine will not start or fire, or the engine is difficult to start and misfires. If it is a regular misfire i.e. the engine is only running on two or three cylinders, the fault is almost sure to be in the secondary, or high tension, circuit. If the misfiring is intermittent, the fault could be in either the high or low tension circuits. If the engine stops suddenly, or will not start at all it is likely that the fault is in the low tension circuit. Loss of power and overheating, apart from faulty carburation settings, are normally due to faults in the distributor or incorrect ignition timing.

14. Fault diagnosis - engine fails to start

1. If the engine fails to start and it was running normally when it was last used, first check there is fuel in the petrol tank. If the engine turns over normally on the starter motor and the battery is evidently well charged, then the fault may be in either the high or low tension circuits. First check the H.T. circuit. NOTE: If

the battery is known to be fully charged, the ignition comes on, and the starter motor fails to turn the engine, CHECK THE TIGHTNESS OF THE LEADS ON THE BATTERY TERMINALS and also the secureness of the earth lead to its CONNECTION TO THE BODY. It is quite common for the leads to have worked loose, even if they look and feel secure. If one of the battery terminal posts gets very hot when trying to work the starter motor this is a sure indication of a faulty connection to that terminal.

2. One of the commonest reasons for bad starting is wet or damp sparking plug leads and distributor. Remove the distributor cap. If condensation is visible internally dry the cap with a rag and also wipe over the leads. Replace the cap.

3. If the engine still fails to start, check that current is reaching the plugs, by disconnecting each plug lead in turn at the sparking plug end, and holding the end of the cable about 3/16 inch away from the cylinder block. Spin the engine on the starter motor by pressing the rubber button on the starter motor solenoid switch (under the bonnet).

4. Sparking between the end of the cable and the block should be fairly strong with a regular blue spark. (Hold the lead with rubber to avoid electric shocks). If current is reaching the plugs, then remove them and clean and regap them to 0.025 inch. The engine should now start.

5. Spin the engine as before, when a rapid succession of blue sparks between the end of the lead and the block indicate that the coil is in order, and that either the distributor cap is cracked; the carbon brush is stuck or worn; the rotor arm is faulty; or the contact points are burnt, pitted or dirty. If the points are in bad shape, clean and reset them as described in section 11.

7. If there are no sparks from the end of the lead from the coil, then check the connections of the lead to the coil and distributor head, and if they are in order, check out the low tension circuit starting with the battery.

8. Switch on the ignition and turn the crankshaft so the contact breaker points have fully opened. Then with either a 20-volt voltmeter or bulb and length of wire check that current from the battery is reaching the starter solenoid switch. No reading indicates that there is a fault in the cable to the switch, or in the connections at the switch or at the battery terminals. Alternatively, the battery earth lead may not be properly earthed to the body.

9. If in order, check that current is reaching terminal 'A' (the one with the brown lead) in the control box, by connecting the voltmeter between 'A' and an earth. If there is no reading this indicates a faulty cable or loose connections between the solenoid switch and the 'A' terminal. Remedy and the car will start.

10. Check with the voltmeter between the control box terminal 'A1' and earth. No reading means a fault in the control box. Fit a new control box and start the car.

11. If in order, then check that current is reaching the ignition switch by connecting the voltmeter to the ignition switch input terminal (the one connected to the brown/blue lead) and earth. No reading indicates a break in the wire or a faulty connection at the switch or 'A1' terminals.

12. If the correct reading (approx. 12 volts) is obtained check the output terminal on the ignition switch (the terminal connected to the white lead). No reading means that the ignition switch is broken. Replace with a new

unit and start the car.

13. If current is reaching the ignition switch output terminal, then check the 'A3' terminal on the fuse unit with the voltmeter. No reading indicates a break in the wire or loose connections between the ignition and the 'A3' terminal. Even if the A3-A4 fuse is broken current should still be reaching the coil as it does not pass through the fuse. Remedy and the car should now start.

14. Check the switch terminal on the coil (it is marked 'SW' and the lead from the switch connects to it). No reading indicates loose connections or a broken wire from the 'A3' terminal on the fuse unit. If this proves to be the fault, remedy and start the car.

15. Check the contact breaker terminal on the coil (it is marked 'CB') and if no reading is recorded on the voltmeter then the coil is broken and must be replaced. The car should start when a new coil has been fitted.

16. If a reading is obtained at the 'CB' terminal then check the wire from the coil for loose connections etc. If a reading is obtained then the final check on the low tension is across the breaker points. No reading means a broken condenser which when replaced will enable the car to finally start.

---

15. Fault diagnosis - engine misfires

---

1. If the engine misfires regularly, run it at a fast idling speed, and short out each of the plugs in turn by placing a short screwdriver across from the plug terminal to the cylinder. Ensure that the screwdriver has a WOODEN or PLASTIC INSULATED HANDLE.

2. No difference in engine running will be noticed when the plug in the defective cylinder is short circuited. Short circuiting the working plugs will accentuate the misfire.

3. Remove the plug lead from the end of the defective plug and hold it about 3/16 inch away from the block. Restart the engine. If the sparking is fairly strong and regular the fault must lie in the sparking plug.

4. The plug may be loose, the insulation may be cracked, or the points may have burnt away giving too wide a gap for the spark to jump. Worse still, one of the points may have broken off. Either renew the plug, or clean it, reset the gap, and then test it.

5. If there is no spark at the end of the plug lead, or if it is weak and intermittent, check the ignition lead from the distributor to the plug. If the insulation is cracked or perished, renew the lead. Check the connections at the distributor cap.

6. If there is still no spark, examine the distributor cap carefully for tracking. This can be recognised by a very thin black line running between two or more electrodes, or between an electrode and some other part of the distributor. These lines are paths which now conduct electricity across the cap thus letting it run to earth. The only answer is a new distributor cap.

7. Apart from the ignition timing being incorrect, other causes of misfiring have already been dealt with under the section dealing with the failure of the engine to start.

8. If the ignition timing is too far retarded, it should be noted that the engine will tend to overheat, and there will be a quite noticeable drop in power. If the engine is overheating and the power is down, and the ignition timing is correct, then the carburettor should be checked, as it is likely that this is where the fault lies. See Chapter 3 for details on this.

Too hot–white deposits

Chipped electrode

Pre-ignition damage

Too cold–dry, block fuel deposits

Badly burnt electrode

A normal clean plug with light deposits

Chapter 6/Clutch & Actuating Mechanism

Contents

Specifications

Make	Borg and Beck
Type	8 inch diaphragm type (narrow)
Clutch plate diameter	8 inch (20.32cm)
Facing material	Mintex H22 (All except 1800 MkII fitted with 18H engine)
	Wound yarn RYZ or WR7 (1800 MkII fitted with 18H engine)
Numbers of damper springs...	6
Damper spring load	125 – 135 lb
Damper spring colour	white and light green
Clutch release bearing	Graphite (MY3D)
Clutch fluid	Castrol Girling Brake Fluid Amber

1. General description

The object of the clutch unit being fitted between the engine and gearbox is so that the engine may be run without being connected to the transmission. Also it enables the engine torque to be progressively applied to the gearbox so enabling the car to move off gradually from rest and then for the gear to be changed easily as the speed increases or decreases.

The main parts of the clutch assembly are the clutch driven plate assembly (2), see Fig. 6:1, the cover assembly (1) and the release bearing assembly (3). When the clutch is in use the driven plate assembly being splined to the gearbox primary drive shaft is sandwiched between the flywheel and pressure plate, by the diaphragm spring. Engine torque is therefore transferred from the flywheel to the clutch driven plate assembly and then to gearbox primary drive shaft.

By depressing the clutch pedal the piston in the master cylinder moves forward so forcing hydraulic fluid through the clutch hydraulic pipe to the slave cylinder. The piston in the slave cylinder moves forward on the entry of the fluid and actuates the clutch withdrawal lever by means of a short pushrod. The release bearing assembly is pushed against the diaphragm spring which releases its pressure on the driven plate assembly and so breaks the drive between the engine and gearbox.

When the clutch pedal is released the pressure plate diaphragm spring forces the pressure plate into contact with the high friction linings on the clutch driven plate, at the same time forcing the clutch driven plate assembly against the flywheel and so taking the drive up.

As the friction linings on the clutch driven plate wear, the pressure plate automatically moves closer to the driven plate to compensate. This makes the centre of the diaphragm spring move nearer to the release bearing, so decreasing the release bearing clearance but not the clutch free pedal travel, as unless the master

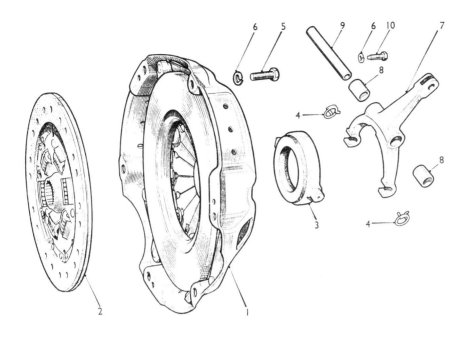

Fig. 6.1. EXPLODED VIEW OF CLUTCH

No.	Description	No.	Description
1	Cover assembly with straps, diaphragm spring, release plate, and pressure plate	5	Screw - clutch to flywheel
2	Driven plate assembly	6	Spring washers
3	Release bearing assembly	7	Clutch withdrawal lever
4	Bearing retainers	8	Bushes - withdrawal lever
		9	Fulcrum shaft
		10	Screw - fulcrum shaft

cylinder has been disturbed this is automatically compensated for.

2. Maintenance

1. Routine maintenance consists of checking the level of hydraulic fluid in the master cylinder every 1000 miles and topping up with Girling Amber Brake Fluid if the level has fallen.

2. If it is noted that the level of the liquid has fallen then an immediate check should be made to determine the source of the leak.

3. Before checking the level of the fluid in the master cylinder reservoir, carefully clean the cap and body of the reservoir unit with clean rag so as to ensure that no dirt enters the system when the cap is removed. On no account should paraffin or any other cleaning solvent be used in case the hydraulic fluid becomes contaminated.

4. Check that the level of the hydraulic fluid is up to within $\frac{1}{4}$ inch of the filler neck and that the vent hole in the cap is clear. Do not overfill.

3. Clutch system - bleeding

Whenever the clutch hydraulic system has been overhauled, a part renewed, or lever in the reservoir is too low, air will have entered the system necessitating the system to be bled. During this operation the level of hydraulic fluid in the reservoir should not be allowed to fall below half full otherwise air will be drawn in again.

1. Obtain a clean and dry glass jam jar, plastic tubing at least 12 inches long and able to fit tightly over the bleed nipple of the slave cylinder, a supply of Castrol Girling Brake Fluid Amber, and someone to help.

2. Check that the master cylinder reservoir is full and if not fill it, and cover the bottom inch of the jar with hydraulic fluid.

3. Remove the rubber dust cap from the bleed nipple on the slave cylinder and with a suitable spanner open the bleed nipple one turn.

4. Place one end of the tube securely over the nipple and insert the other end in the jam jar so that the tube orifice is below the level of the fluid.

5. The assistant should now pump the clutch pedal up and down quite quickly until the air bubbles cease to emerge from the end of the tubing. He should also check the reservoir frequently to ensure that the hydraulic fluid does not drop too far so letting air into the system.

6. When no more air bubbles appear, tighten the bleed nipple on the downstroke.

7. Replace the rubber dust cap over the bleed nipple.
NOTE: Never use the fluid bled from the hydraulic system immediately for topping up the master cylinder, but allow to stand for at least twenty four hours in a sealed air tight container so allowing the minute air bubbles held in suspension to escape.

4.   Clutch slave cylinder - removal and refitting

1.   It is not necessary to drain the clutch master cylinder when removing the slave cylinder. If fluid is to be left in the master cylinder however it is essential to seal the vent hole in the cylinder cap, by screwing the cap down hard over a piece of polythene sheeting, so preventing loss of fluid.
2.   Wipe the hydraulic pipe union at its connection on the slave cylinder with a clean non fluffy rag. Detach the union and wrap the end in a piece of clean non fluffy rag to prevent dirt ingress.
3.   Remove the two screws and spring washers securing the slave cylinder to the flywheel housing. Carefully withdraw the slave cylinder leaving the push rod attached to the clutch withdrawal fork.
4.   Refitting is the reverse procedure to removal. Bleed the hydraulic system and road test.

5.   Clutch slave cylinder - dismantling, examination and reassembly

1.   Clean the exterior of the slave cylinder using dry non fluffy rag.
2.   Carefully ease back the dust cover, (5) Fig. 6:2, from the cylinder body and lift away. Also remove the piston stop end cap (4) which is held in place by two crimped slots in the side of the cap.
3.   Remove the piston assembly (3) and spring (1) by carefully shaking out these components. Remove the piston seal (2) using a non metal pointed rod or fingers. Do not use a metal screwdriver as this could scratch the piston.
4.   Inspect the inside of the cylinder for score marks caused by impurities in the hydraulic fluid. If there are any found, the cylinder and piston will require renewal.
5.   If the cylinder is sound, thoroughly clean it out with fresh hydraulic fluid.
6.   The old rubber seal will probably be swollen and visibly worn. Smear the new rubber seal with hydraulic fluid and refit to the stem of the piston ensuring that the smaller periphery or back of the seal is against the piston.
7.   Place small end of the spring onto the piston stem. Thoroughly wet the seal and cylinder bore with clean hydraulic fluid and insert the piston assembly into the bore of the cylinder. Gently ease the edge of the seal into the bore so that it does not roll over. Refit the end cap into place and using a pair of engineer's pliers crimp the slots to retain it in position. Fit a new dust cover to the end of the cylinder.

6.   Clutch master cylinder - removal and refitting

1.   Drain the hydraulic fluid from the clutch hydraulic system by attaching a length of suitable size plastic tubing to the bleed screw on the slave cylinder. Place the other end in a clean jam jar. Open the bleed screw one turn and depress the clutch pedal. Tighten the bleed screw and allow the pedal to return. Repeat this procedure until the system has been drained.
2.   Wipe the master cylinder hydraulic pipe connection with a clean non fluffy rag and disconnect the union. Wrap the end in a piece of clean rag to stop dirt ingress or fluid dripping onto the paintwork. Plug the master cylinder union connection to stop accidental dirt entry into the master cylinder.
3.   Extract the split pin from the master cylinder to piston push rod clevis pin, remove the plain washer (12) Fig. 6:3, and withdraw the clevis pin (11). Separate the push rod (9) from the clutch pedal.
4.   Remove the fixing bolt (16) and spring washer (15) from the underside of the master cylinder, and the nut (17) and spring washer from the top of the master cylinder mounting flange to the bulkhead, and carefully ease the master cylinder away from the bulkhead.
5.   The master cylinder refitting procedure is the reverse to removal but care must be taken when offering up to the bulkhead that the pushrod is in line with the clutch pedal. Once connections have been made the hydraulic system must be bled and the car road tested.

7.   Clutch master cylinder - dismantling, examination and reassembly

1.   The numbers in the text refer to Fig. 6:3. Pull off the rubber dust cover (13) which exposes the circlip (10) which must be removed so the pushrod complete with metal retaining washer can be pulled out of the master cylinder.
2.   Pull the piston (8) and valve assembly as one unit from the master cylinder.
3.   The next step is to separate the piston and valve assemblies. With the aid of a small screwdriver prise up the inner leg of the piston return spring retainer (6) which engages under a shoulder in the front of the piston (8) and holds the retainer (6) in place.
4.   The retainer (6) spring (5) and valve assembly (1-4) can then be separated from the piston.
5.   To dismantle the valve assembly compress the spring (5) and move the retainer (6) which has an offset hole to one side in order to release the valve stem (3) from the retainer (6).

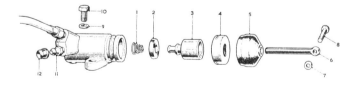

Fig. 6.2. COMPONENT PARTS OF CLUTCH SLAVE CYLINDER

No. Description	No. Description	No. Description	No. Description
1 Spring	4 End cap - piston stop	7 Plain washer	10 Screw - cylinder to housing
2 Piston seal	5 Dust cover	8 Clevis pin	11 Bleed screw
3 Piston	6 Push-rod	9 Spring washer	12 Bleed screw cover

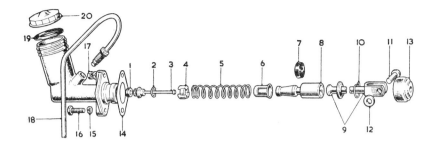

Fig. 6.3. COMPONENT PARTS OF CLUTCH MASTER CYLINDER

No.	Description	No.	Description	No.	Description	No.	Description
1	Valve seal	7	Piston seal	12	Plain washer	17	Nut - stud
2	Curved washer - valve stem	8	Piston	13	Dust cover	18	Master to slave cylinder pipe
3	Valve stem	9	Push-rod	14	Packing	19	Filler cap gasket
4	Valve spacer	10	Circlip - push-rod	15	Spring washer	20	Filler cap
5	Spring	11	Clevis pin - pedal to master cylinder	16	Screw		
6	Spring retainer						

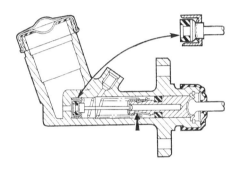

Fig. 6.4. The assembled clutch master cylinder. Inset shows the thimble leaf valve correctly assembled.

6. With the seat spacer (4) and curved valve seal washer (2) removed, the rubber seals can be removed.

7. Clean and carefully examine all parts, especially the piston cup and rubber washers, for signs of distortion, swelling, splitting, or other wear and check the piston and cylinder for wear and scoring. Renew any parts that are suspect. It is recommended that whenever a master cylinder is dismantled new rubber seals are always fitted.

8. Rebuild the piston and valve assembly in the following sequence ensuring that all parts are thoroughly wetted with clean brake fluid:

(a) Fit the piston seal (7) to the piston (8) so that the larger circumference of the lip will enter the cylinder bore first.

(b) Fit the valve seal (1) to the valve (3) in the same way as in (a).

(c) Place the valve spring seal washer (2) so that its convex face abuts against the valve stem flange (3) and then fit the seat spacer (4) and spring (5).

(d) Fit the spring retainer (6) to the spring (5) which must then be compressed so the valve stem (3) can be re-inserted in the retainer (6).

(e) Replace the front of the piston (8) in the retainer (6) and then press down the retaining leg so it locates under the shoulder at the front of the piston (8).

(f) With the valve assembly well lubricated with clean hydraulic fluid carefully insert it in the master cylinder

bore taking care that the rubber seal (7) is not damaged or the lip reversed as it is pushed into the bore.

(g) Fit the pushrod (9) and washer in place and secure with the circlip (10). Smear the sealing areas of the dust cover with Girling Grease and pack the cover with rubber grease to act as a dust trap, and fit to the master cylinder body. The master cylinder is now ready for refitting to the car.

8. Clutch - removal, inspection and replacement

1. Remove the combined engine and transmission assembly as described in Chapter 1, sections 5 and 6.

2. Remove the flywheel housing and primary drive gears as detailed in Chapter 1, (photo).

8.2

3. Before removing the pressure plate assembly it should be noted that it is located on the face of the flywheel by dowels. Look for marks on the pressure plate assembly coinciding with marks on the flywheel to ensure correct reassembly. If no marks are evident make identification lines on these two parts so that upon reassembly the pressure plate is reassembled in its original position. Slacken each of the six pressure plate to flywheel mounting bolts (5) Fig. 6:1, a turn at a time (photo) so releasing them evenly and progressively. As they are being released check that the pressure plate flange (1) is not binding on the dowels otherwise it could fly off causing an accident.

4. Lift away the six bolts (5) and spring washers (6)

8.3

followed by the pressure plate assembly (Fig. 6:5) and the driven plate assembly (2) (photo).

5. Using a stiff brush or clean rags dust the face of the flywheel, the pressure plate assembly and the driven plate assembly. Note that the dust is harmful to the lungs as it contains asbestos.

6. It is important that neither oil nor grease comes into contact with the clutch facings and that absolute cleanliness is observed at all times.

7. Inspect the friction surfaces of the driven plate and if worn, a complete new assembly must be fitted. The linings are completely worn out when the faces of the rivets are flush with the lining face. Check that the friction linings show no sign of heavy glazing or oil impregnation which, if evident, means that a new assembly must be fitted. If a small quantity of lubricant has found its way into the facing, due to heat generated by the resultant slipping, it will be burnt off. This will be indicated by darkening of the facings. This is not too serious provided that the grain of the facing material can be clearly identified. Fit a new assembly if there is any doubt at all. It is important that if oil impregnation is present, the cause of the oil leak is found and rectified to prevent recurrence.

8. Carefully inspect the driven plate contact faces of the flywheel for signs of overheating, distortion, cracking and scoring and if any are evident fit new parts as necessary.

9. Mount the driven plate onto the clutch shaft and check for looseness or wear on the hub splines. Also check the driven plate cushion springs for damage and looseness.

10. Inspect the clutch withdrawal lever assembly pivot shaft bushes (8) Fig. 6:1, for wear and fit a new lever assembly (7) or rebush if necessary.

11. Check that the graphite release bearing (3) is not badly worn or cracked. It is normally recommended that if a new pressure plate assembly and driven plate

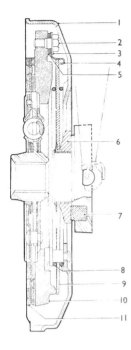

Fig. 6.5. CROSS SECTION OF COVER ASSEMBLY

No.	Description	No.	Description
1	Cover	7	Release bearing
2	Strap bolt	8	Annular rings
3	Washer	9	Diaphragm spring
4	Clip	10	Pressure plate
5	Pressure-plate strap	11	Driven plate
6	Release plate		

assembly are being fitted then a new graphite release bearing be fitted as well.

12. Refitting the clutch components is the reverse sequence to removal but the following points should be noted:

(a) Smear a light coating of high melting point grease to the bore of the shaft bush.

8.4

8.12b

8.12c

(b) Refit the pressure and driven plate assemblies making sure that the alignment marks previously noted or made are correctly matched and that the longer side of the clutch disc hub faces the flywheel (photo).

(c) The clutch disc must now be centralised by using either an old clutch shaft or a round wooden rod (photo) with one end shaped to the diameter of the crankshaft spigot and the other end to the diameter of the driven plate splined hub.

(d) Refit the flywheel housing and primary drive cover as described in Chapter 1.

NOTE: A modified clutch was incorporated into cars produced after engine Nos. 18AMW/U/H11020 and L2754 whereby the height of the clutch pressure plate assembly cover was increased. To enable the correct clearances at the release bearing, the release bearing withdrawal lever and flywheel housing were also modified.

If a new clutch pressure plate assembly is being fitted the latest release bearing clutch withdrawal lever, slave cylinder pushrod, and flywheel housing must be used on engines made prior to the engine numbers given below:

Engine No.	Item
H25030 and L20548 and also intermittently between engine Nos. H24647 and L25025 H29739 and L20568	Clutch withdrawal lever and release bearing Flywheel housing and slave cylinder pushrod.

9. Clutch withdrawal lever and release bearing - removal and replacement

1. Remove the combined engine and transmission assembly as described in Chapter 1, sections 5 and 6.
2. Remove the flywheel housing and primary drive gears as described in Chapter 1.
3. Ease the rubber sealing plug out from the flywheel housing. Unscrew the setscrew (10) Fig. 6:1, securing the withdrawal lever fulcrum shaft (9), and using a 5/16 inch UNF bolt screwed into the tapped end of the fulcrum shaft (9) withdraw the shaft. Lift away the withdrawal lever assembly.
4. To remove the release bearing (3) rotate the spring retainers (4) through 90° and lift away from the withdrawal lever.
5. Refitting is the reverse procedure to removal but refer to the note at the end of the previous section for details of a modification made by the manufacturers.

10. Clutch pedal - removal and refitting

The clutch and brake pedals are mounted on a common fulcrum point attached to a bracket on the toe board. To remove the clutch pedal is identical to that of the brake pedal, details of which are given in Chapter 11.

11. Clutch faults

There are four main faults to which the clutch and release mechanism are prone. They may occur by themselves or in conjunction with any of the other faults. They are clutch squeal, slip, spin and judder.

12. Clutch squeal - diagnosis and cure

1. If on taking up the drive or when changing gear, the clutch squeals, this is sure indication of a badly worn clutch release bearing. As well as regular wear due to normal use, wear of the clutch release bearing is much accentuated if the clutch is ridden, or held down for long periods in gear, with the engine running. To minimise wear of this component the car should always be taken out of gear at traffic lights and for similar hold-ups.
2. The clutch release bearing is not an expensive item.

13. Clutch slip - diagnosis and cure

1. Clutch slip is a self evident condition which occurs when the clutch friction plate is badly worn, the release arm free travel is insufficient, oil or grease have got onto the flywheel or pressure plate faces, or the pressure plate itself is faulty.
2. The reason for clutch slip is that, due to one of the faults listed above, there is either insufficient pressure from the pressure plate, or insufficient friction from the friction plate to ensure solid drive.
3. If small amounts of oil get onto the clutch, they will be burnt off under the heat of clutch engagement, in the process gradually darkening the linings. Excessive oil on the clutch will burn off leaving a carbon deposit which can cause quite bad slip, or fierceness, spin and judder.
4. If clutch slip is suspected, and confirmation of this condition is required, there are several tests which can be made:
(a) With the engine in second or third gear and pulling lightly up a moderate incline, sudden depression of the accelerator pedal may cause the engine to increase its speed without any increase in road speed. Easing off on the accelerator will then give a definite drop in engine speed without the car slowing.
(b) Drive the car at a steady speed in top gear and braking with the left leg, try and maintain the same speed by pressing down on the accelerator. Providing the same speed is maintained a change in the speed of the engine confirms that slip is taking place.
(c) In extreme cases of clutch slip the engine will race under normal acceleration conditions.

If slip is due to oil or grease on the linings a temporary cure can sometimes be effected by squirting carbon tetrochloride into the clutch. The permanent cure, of course, is to renew the clutch driven plate, and trace and rectify the oil leak.

14. Clutch spin - diagnosis and cure

1. Clutch spin is a condition which occurs when there is a leak in the clutch hydraulic actuating mechanism; the release arm free travel is excessive; there is an obstruction in the clutch either on the primary gear splines or in the operating lever itself; or oil may have partially burnt off the clutch linings and have left a resinous deposit which is causing the clutch disc to stick to the pressure plate or flywheel.
2. The reason for clutch spin is that due to any, or a combination of, the faults just listed, the clutch pressure plate is not completely freeing from the centre plate even with the clutch pedal fully depressed.
3. If clutch spin is suspected, the condition can be confirmed by extreme difficulty in engaging first gear from rest, difficulty in changing gear, and very sudden

take-up of the clutch drive at the fully depressed end of the clutch pedal travel as the clutch is released.

4.   Check the operating lever free travel.   If this is correct examine the clutch master and slave cylinders and the connecting hydraulic pipe for leaks.   Fluid in one of the rubber boots fitted over the end of either the master or slave cylinders, where fitted, is a sure sign of a leaking piston seal.

5.   If these points are checked and found to be in order then the fault lies internally in the clutch, and it will be necessary to remove the clutch for examination.

15. Clutch judder - diagnosis and cure

1.   Clutch judder is a self evident condition which occurs when the gearbox or engine mountings are loose or too flexible; when there is oil on the faces of the clutch friction plate; or when the clutch pressure plate has been incorrectly adjusted.

2.   The reason for clutch judder is that due to one of the faults just listed, the clutch pressure plate is not freeing smoothly from the friction disc, and is snatching.

3.   Clutch judder normally occurs when the clutch pedal is released in first or reverse gears, and the whole car shudders as it moves backwards or forwards.

Chapter 7/Manual Gearbox

Contents

Specifications	1800 Mk I	
Number of forward speeds..	4	
Synchromesh.	All forward speeds	
Ratio: Top	1.000:1	
Third	1.384:1	
Second	2.217:1	
First..	3.292:1	
Reverse	3.075:1	

	Standard	Alternative*
Overall ratio: Top	3.882:1	4.187:1
Third	5.371:1	5.795:1
Second	8.609:1	9.283:1
First	12.779:1	13.784:1
Reverse.	11.936:1	12.875:1

Road speed at 1,000 rpm in top gear..	17.69 mph	16.39 mph
Speedometer gear ratio	6/17	
Idler gear end float	0.008 to 0.010 inch	
1st and 3rd speed gear end floats	0.006 to 0.008 inch	
2nd speed gear end float	0.005 to 0.008 inch	
Lay gear end float	0.002 to 0.003 inch	
Synchromesh breakaway load	23 to 27 lb	

Spring...	Free length	Fitted length	Load at fitted length
Synchro hub	0.72 inch	0.385 inch	5.5 to 6 lb
Selector fork.	1.0625 inch	0.750 inch	18 to 20 lb
Lay gear thrust...	1.661 inch	**1.6161** inch	9 to 10 lb

*Standard ratio up to engine No. 18AMW/U/H27523, 18 AMW/U/L20548

Specifications and Data:	1800 Mk II, 18/85 Mk II and 18/85 with 18 H engine
	1800 Mk II 'S' and 18/85 Mk II 'S'
	1800 Mk II 'S' fitted with 18H engine

The specifications are identical to the 1800 Mk I except for the differences listed below:

Ratio: Second	2.06:1	

	Standard	Alternative
Overall ratio: Second	7.99:1	8.63:1
Road speed at 1,000 rpm in top gear..	18.2 mph	16.8 mph

Torque Wrench Settings (lb ft.)

Drain plug	40 to 50
Transmission case stud nuts 7/16 inch UNF ...	40 to 45
Transmission case stud nuts 3/8 inch UNF ...	25
Transmission case nuts 5/16 inch UNF	18 to 20
Adaptor plate to crankcase 5/16 inch UNF .	18 to 20
Clutch shaft bearing retainer 5/16 inch UNC ...	18 to 20
Adaptor plate crankcase 3/8 inch UNF.	33 to 35
Flywheel housing to adaptor plate 3/8 inch UNF.	33 to 35
Clutch operating cylinder 3/8 inch UNC	33 to 35
Flywheel housing to adaptor plate 5/16 inch UNF	23 to 25
Clutch lever fulcrum shaft $\frac{1}{4}$ inch UNF	12 to 14
Clutch shaft nut 1 1/8 inch UNS	60
First motion shaft nut – inner and outer	120
Third motion shaft nut 15/16 inch UNS	40
Third motion shaft nut 1 inch UNS	150 to 170
Retaining plate – change speed cables 5/16 inch UNC	13 to 15
Retaining plate – control box 5/16 inch UNC ...	10 to 12
Control box rubber mounting nut 5/16 inch UNF.	10 to 12
Locknut cable to jaws $\frac{1}{4}$ inch UNF	8 to 10
Top cover to control box $\frac{1}{4}$ inch UNF/UNC	8 to 10
Mounting bracket to control box $\frac{1}{4}$ inch UNC ...	8 to 10
Differential housing end cover bolts 5/16 inch UNC	8 to 13

1. General description

The four forward speed transmission unit has synchromesh action on all the forward speeds. The constant mesh gears are of helical cut profile. The third motion shaft and float is controlled by a double row ball bearing race placed at the final drive pinion end of the shaft and the spigot bearing at the other end of the shaft is a needle roller assembly in the end of the first motion shaft. Fig 7:2 and Fig 7:3 show cross sectional views of the transmission unit.

The laygear runs on two needle roller bearings and a spacer tube located between the inner spring clips to ensure correct positioning.

The final drive gear unit with its two drive shafts is attached parallel to the third motion shaft on the rear of the transmission unit and the whole transmission unit is positioned beneath the crankcase running parallel with the engine crankshaft.

Drive is taken to the transmission unit via the clutch shaft gear to a helical idler gear positioned on the end of the transmission unit first motion shaft.

The remote control gear change system consists of a floor mounted gear change lever and control box assembly connected to the transmission casing by three cable assemblies which operate the change speed levers positioned in the cable housing.

As with usual BLMC transverse power units the transmission unit, final drive and engine share a common lubrication system.

It is a characteristic of the transmission unit to give a whine in all gears including top and also an idler gear rattle at tick over speed which is more pronounced at normal operating temperatures. The gear change system, although positive in action, tends to be a little spongy due to whip in the long gear change lever.

2. Transmission - removal from the engine

The transmission unit must be removed together with the engine before any major work can be carried

out on it. Full details of the removal and replacement procedure are given in Chapter 1.

Before commencing work it is recommended that the exterior of the engine and transmission unit be thoroughly cleaned using a grease solvent such as paraffin or 'Gunk'. After the solvent has been applied and allowed to stand for a time, a vigorous jet of water will wash off the solvent together with all the grease and dirt. If the dirt is thick and deeply embedded, work the solvent into it with a wire brush. Finally wipe down the exterior of the unit with a dry non fluffy rag. The transmission unit may be separated from the engine as follows:

1. With the engine and transmission unit on a firm work bench or placed on a very clean floor surface, first remove the end cover by undoing the thirteen cover bolts and lifting away together with the spring washers (photo).

2.1

2. Carefully lift away the cover from the clutch housing (photo).
3. Using a screwdriver placed behind the idler gear, gently lever the gear out of mesh from the other two gears (photo). Make a note of the location of the thrust washers on either face of the idler gear.
4. Lift away the idler gear (photo).
5. Using a socket wrench undo the bolt located in the recess next to the first motion shaft (photo).

2.2

6. With a screwdriver or chisel knock back the bolt locking tab washer (photo), and remove the bolt together with spring washer.

7. Using a screwdriver or chisel knock back the first motion shaft drive gear retaining nut lock washer (photo).

8. With a box spanner or large socket wrench undo the first motion shaft drive gear retaining nut (photo A). Should this nut be very tight it may be necessary to replace the idler gear and lock it with a screwdriver (photo B).

9. Withdraw the first motion shaft drive gear from the first motion shaft (photo). If this is tight on the shaft use a screwdriver between the inner face of the gear teeth and the outer track of the first motion shaft roller bearing and lever forward.

10. If the starter motor is still in position undo the two retaining bolts and lift away the starter motor.

11. Undo the bolts and nuts holding the clutch housing to adaptor plate taking special note of the location of the bolts as they are of different lengths. Withdraw the clutch housing (photo).

12. Mark the position of the clutch cover assembly relative to the flywheel to ensure correct refitting and undo the six cover retaining bolts in a diagonal pattern half a turn at a time to avoid distortion. Note that the cover assembly is located on dowels and it may be necessary to insert a screwdriver between the cover and flywheel face as the bolts are being undone to ease the cover from the dowels, and so stop it flying off when the bolts are completely undone. Lift away the cover and drive plate assembly.

13. With a screwdriver or chisel knock back the six flywheel retaining bolt lock tabs (photo).

14. Using a socket wrench undo the six flywheel retaining bolts half a turn at a time in a diagonal manner. Lock the flywheel with a screwdriver placed through the starter motor aperture in the engine adaptor plate with the blade inserted in between two ring gear teeth (photo).

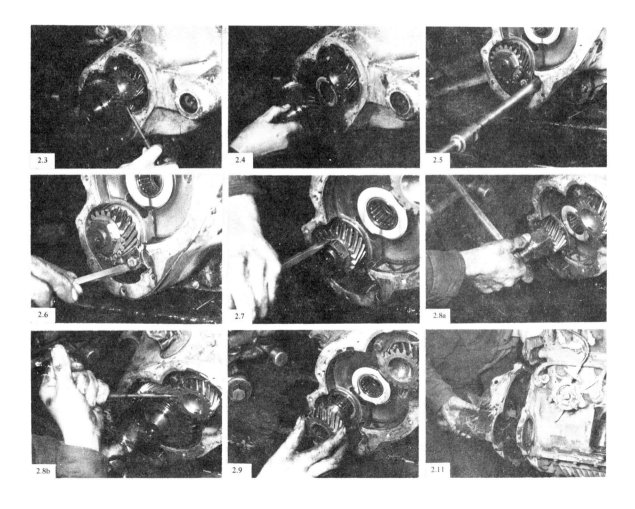

2.3   2.4   2.5

2.6   2.7   2.8a

2.8b   2.9   2.11

15. With all the bolts and locking tabs washers removed lift away the flywheel. Watch for sharp edges on the starter ring gear teeth and also remember that the flywheel is heavy (photo).

16. Refer to Fig. 7:1 and remove the fourteen retaining bolts together with spring washers making a special note of the bolt locations as they are of different threads and lengths. The photo shows two bolts of different lengths being removed.

17. Before it is possible to remove the adaptor plate it is necessary to knock off the horse shoe from the first motion shaft using a metal drift (photo).

18. With all bolts removed lift away the adaptor plate taking care not to damage the gasket placed between the adaptor plate and engine crankcase (photo).

19. Carefully lift away the adaptor plate gasket (photo). Make a note that there are four small springs (arrowed) under the gasket adjacent to the drive shaft. Lift these out and place in a jam jar for safety.

20. Turn to the front of the engine and remove the two short bolts that secure the transmission casing to the base of the cylinder block and crankcase (photo).

21. Remove the remaining bolts and nuts together with spring washers that hold the transmission case flange to the engine crankcase flange. Note that one of these bolts retains a metal tab with a grommet inserted through which goes the fuel overflow pipes from the carburettor installation (photo A). There are two bolts at

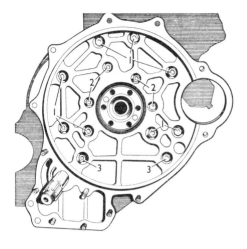

Fig. 7.1. ADAPTOR PLATE RETAINING BOLTS
1. 3/8in. UNF
2. 5/16 in. UNF
3. 5/16 in. UNC

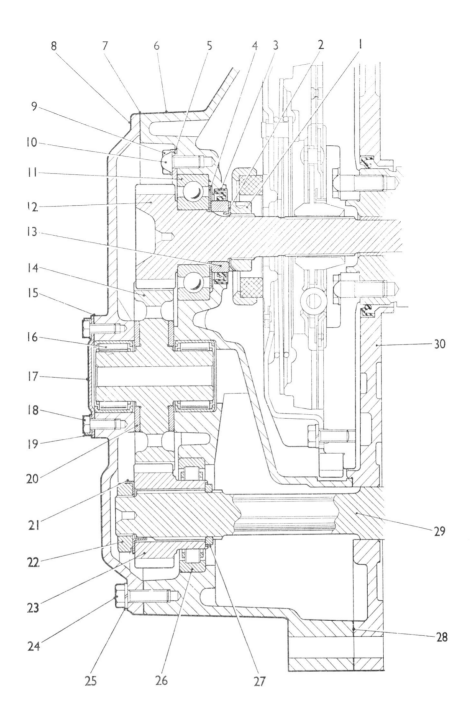

Fig. 7.2. FLYWHEEL HOUSING AND PRIMARY DRIVE GEARS

No.	Description	No.	Description	No.	Description	No.	Description
1	Clutch shaft nut		sembly	16	Needle roller bearings	23	Drive gear
2	Tab washer	9	Set screws	17	Bearing cap	24	Set screws
3	Oil seal	10	Lock washer tabs	18	Set screws	25	Spring washers
4	Oil flinger	11	Bearing	19	Lock washer tabs	26	Roller bearing
5	Bearing retainer	12	Clutch shaft	20	Thrust washers	27	Washer
6	Flywheel housing	13	Distance piece	21	Tab washer	28	Joint washer
7	Joint washer	14	Idler gear	22	Shaft nut	29	First motion shaft
8	Primary drive, cover as-	15	Joint washer			30	Adaptor plate

the rear of the engine which are easily overlooked. They are covered by the engine end plate. The one nearer the drive shaft is shorter than the other one (photo B).

2.21b

22. In order that the engine can be turned on its side without damaging anything, remove the union at the base of the dipstick tube and also the bolt holding the dipstick tube bracket to the side of the cylinder block (photo).

2.22

23. Place some pieces of wood on the floor, and with the assistance of a second person very carefully roll the engine and transmission assembly onto its side. Carefully part the transmission unit from the engine (photo). If the engine and transmission are on a bench with an overhead hoist available the two units may be separated by lifting up the engine.

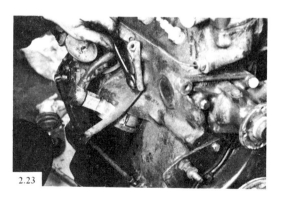

2.23

24. Do not damage the joint washer between the two

units. Lift away the oil suction 'O' ring and put in a safe place.

3. Transmission - dismantling

With the transmission unit separate from the engine and placed on a clean work bench dismantle the transmission unit in the following manner:
1. Mark the drive shafts and casing with blobs of paint (arrowed in photo) so that they may be refitted in their original positions.
2. Remove the two drive shafts by simply pulling outwards as shown in the photo taking care not to damage the oilseals with the splines on the ends of the drive shafts.
3. Remove the two brackets retaining bolts from the side of the differential assembly casing and lift away the bracket (photo).
4. Mark the drive shaft oil seal housings to ensure correct refitting and remove the six bolts that hold each housing to the differential assembly casing. Lift away the two covers together with their gaskets and any shims used. Note carefully the position of the oil return holes.
5. Undo the four 7/16 inch diameter, and the six 5/16 inch diameter, nuts and remove them together with the spring washers (photo).
6. Place a block of wood under the differential housing half as shown in the photo and carefully lift away the differential assembly casing half. If it is tight on the studs lightly tap using a soft faced hammer. Lift away the gasket.
7. Lift away the differential unit from the transmission casing (photo).
8. Undo the ten $\frac{1}{2}$ inch AF nuts which hold the end cover in place. Lift away the nuts and spring washers and withdraw the cover from the studs (photo).
9. Using a screwdriver select two gears as shown in the photo by moving the selector sleeves to the left.
10. With a screwdriver or chisel knock back the lockwasher which holds the large nut onto the end of the third motion shaft (photo).
11. Using an adjustable wrench, if a large spanner is not available, undo the large nut in a clockwise direction as it has a left hand thread (photo).
12. Withdraw the pinion gear from the end of the third motion shaft as shown in the photo.
13. Using a screwdriver or chisel knock back the tabs locking the mainshaft bearing locating plate retaining one nut and six bolts. Undo the nut and bolts and lift away together with the shaped tab washers (photo).
14. Withdraw the mainshaft bearing locating plate (photo).
15. With a screwdriver or tapered drift carefully drive out the bearing housing complete with bearing until it is possible to insert the blade of the screwdriver between the transmission casing web and the bearing housing flange (photo).
16. Complete removal is by judicious use of a screwdriver as shown in the photo. Be very careful when the housing comes out as the inner thrust ball bearings will immediately jump out.
17. The photo shows two of the ball bearings and the retainer that holds them in place. Gather all these together and place in a glass jar for safe keeping. There should be twelve ball bearings.
18. At this stage it is recommended that the lay gear end float at the small thrust washer, i.e. front end, be checked using either feeler gauges or a dial indicator gauge and a note made of any adjustment that may be

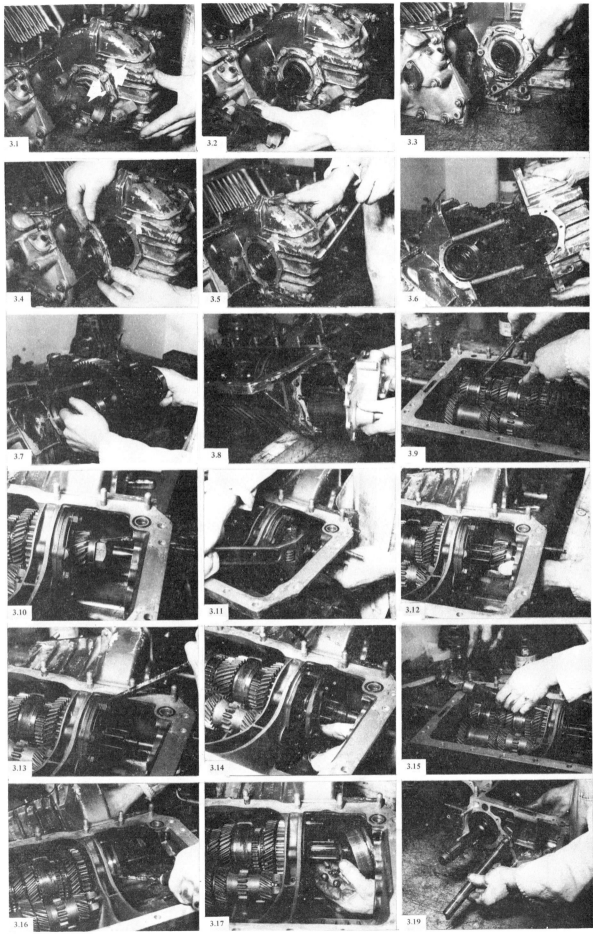

necessary upon reassembly. The correct end float should be 0.008 – 0.010 inch.

19. Using a soft metal drift carefully tap out the lay gear shaft from the front of the transmission casing until sufficient is exposed to pull out completely (photo).

20. Lift out the lay gear. The needle roller bearings are held in cages (photo).

21. There are two thrust washers fitted one each end of the lay gear. The small thrust washer is adjacent to the bridge piece or web in the middle of the transmission casing. The larger thrust washer is opposite at the other end (photo).

22. Using a pair of circlip pliers fitted with suitable size points release the circlip that secures the first motion shaft bearing in position (photo).

23. With the circlip removed lift away the distance piece located behind the circlip (photo).

24. From inside the transmission case drift the first motion shaft bearing outwards using a soft metal drift (photo).

25. Once the bearing has been released from the transmission casing the first motion shaft may now be lifted away (photo). Observe a caged needle roller bearing in the end of the first motion shaft which locates in a spigot on the end of the third motion shaft.

26. Slide out the reverse idler shaft as shown in the photo. This is a sliding fit normally held in place by one of the small bolts that also hold the third motion

shaft bearing retainer in place. If a little tight use a soft metal drift.

27. Now that the input shaft has been removed the main bearing and housing can be removed from the transmission casing completely (photo).

28. Locate the reverse selector fork rod and using a soft metal drift remove it from the casing (photo).

29. Lift out the reverse idle gear making a note of which way round it is fitted (photo). It may be necessary to move the third motion shaft.

3.29

3.20 3.21 3.22
3.23 3.24 3.25
3.26 3.27 3.28

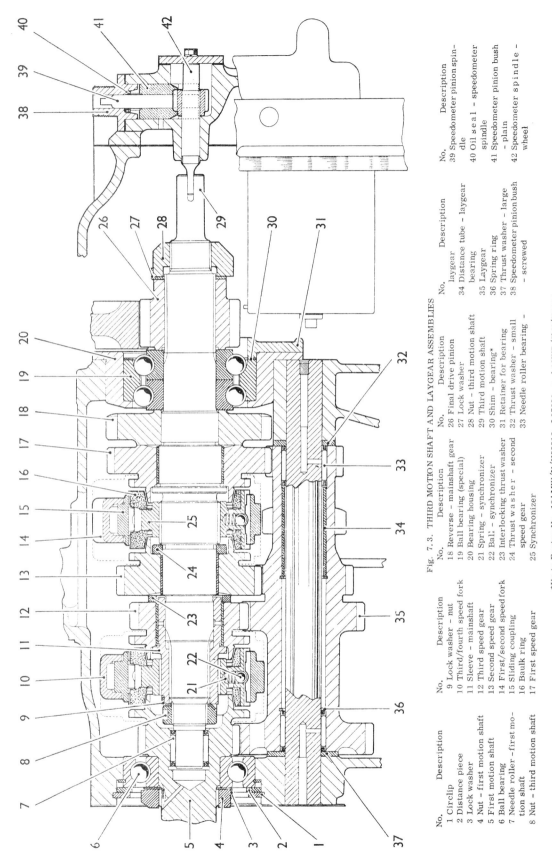

Fig. 7.3. THIRD MOTION SHAFT AND LAYGEAR ASSEMBLIES

No.	Description	No.	Description	No.	Description	No.	Description
1	Circlip	9	Lock washer – nut	18	Reverse – mainshaft gear	26	Final drive pinion
2	Distance piece	10	Third/fourth speed fork	19	Ball bearing (special)	27	Lock washer
3	Lock washer	11	Sleeve – mainshaft	20	Bearing housing	28	Nut – third motion shaft
4	Nut – first motion shaft	12	Third speed gear	21	Spring – synchronizer	29	Third motion shaft
5	First motion shaft	13	Second speed gear	22	Ball – synchronizer	30	Shim – bearing*
6	Ball bearing	14	First/second speed fork	23	Interlocking thrust washer	31	Retainer for bearing
7	Needle roller – first motion shaft	15	Sliding coupling	24	Thrust washer – second speed gear	32	Thrust washer – small
8	Nut – third motion shaft	16	Baulk ring	25	Synchronizer	33	Needle roller bearing –
		17	First speed gear				

No.	Description	No.	Description
	laygear	39	Speedometer pinion spindle
34	Distance tube – laygear bearing	40	Oil seal – speedometer spindle
35	Laygear	41	Speedometer pinion bush – plain
36	Spring ring	42	Speedometer spindle – wheel
37	Thrust washer – large		
38	Speedometer pinion bush – screwed		

*Up to Engine No. 18AMW/U/H99312, L97831, and 18WB/SbU/H1114.

101

30. Drift out the two remaining selector fork rods in the same manner as with the reverse selector fork rod.

31. Carefully lift away the third motion shaft from the transmission unit (photo). Take care about this step as it will be found that the selector forks can easily catch in the gears making withdrawal of the third motion shaft difficult. A second pair of hands is of great assistance in keeping the selector forks out of the way.

32. The photo shows the two forward speed selector forks. The one on the left is the 3rd and 4th speed selector fork whilst the one on the right is the 1st and 2nd speed selector fork. Retrieve the selector fork locating ball bearing and springs from the bottom of the transmission casing.

33. Place the mainshaft in a vice with soft faces placed between the jaws to prevent damage. The photo shows old bearing shells being used for this purpose.

34. Pull the 3rd and 4th speed synchronizer hub from the end of the third motion shaft (photo).

35. Very carefully tap back the locking tab in the two small indentations in the round nut on the end of the third motion shaft using a parallel punch or small chisel (photo).

36. Using a mole wrench as shown in the photo undo the circular nut.

37. Remove the tab washer. As the half of the splined boss acts as the bearing surface for the 3rd gear the

whole assembly including synchronizer may be slid from the third motion shaft (photo).

38. Remove the thrust distance washer followed by the second gear wheel and the synchronizer ring (photo).

39. Remove the thrust distance washer followed by

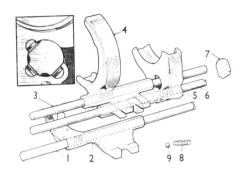

Fig. 7.4. GEAR SELECTOR FORKS AND RODS. INSET SHOWS END VIEW OF RODS WITH LOCKING PLATE FITTED

No.	Description	No.	Description
1	Reverse fork rod	6	3rd/4th fork rod
2	Reverse fork	7	Locating plate
3	1st/2nd fork rod	8	Spring
4	1st/2nd fork	9	Locating ball
5	3rd/4th fork		

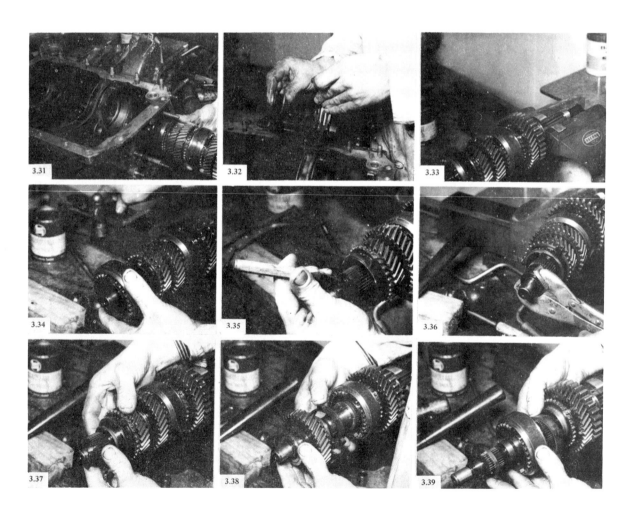

the 1st and 2nd gear synchronizer hub assembly and the synchronizer ring (photo).

40. The third motion shaft is now moved in the vice and placed in the vertical position as shown in the photo. Do not forget to use the soft faces to prevent damage to the gears. The remaining gear wheels and the inner portion of the ball bearing race are now drifted off the shaft.

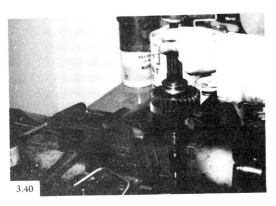
3.40

41. The photo shows the third motion shaft completely dismantled.

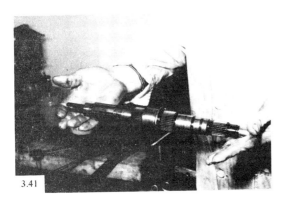
3.41

42. The first motion shaft may now be dismantled by holding between soft faces in a vice as shown in the photo and using a chisel or screwdriver to knock back the lock tab.

3.42

43. Undo the nut in the usual manner with a correct width spanner. If this is not available and as a last resort

use a drift as shown in the photo.

3.43

44. With the nut removed it is now possible to remove the first motion shaft bearing by placing in a vice and tapping the end of the shaft using a hammer and a block of soft wood. If the bearing is to be renewed remove the circlip from the outer track and transfer it to the new race if a new circlip is not available.

4. Transmission - components - examination and renovation

1. Carefully clean and then examine all the component parts starting with the baulk ring synchronizers, for general wear, distortion, and damage to machined faces and threads.

2. Examine the gear wheels for excessive wear and chipping of the teeth and renew them as necessary. It is advisable to renew the mating gear as well. If lay gear end float is above the permitted tolerance of 0.008 - 0.010 inch the thrust washers must be renewed. The small thrust washer is available in four thicknesses as follows: 0.123 - 0.125 inch, 0.1265 - 0.1285 inch, 0.130 - 0.132 inch, 0.133 - 0.135 inch.

3. Needle roller bearings are fitted at each end of the lay gear. Unless the car has done only a very small mileage they invariably need renewing. To examine them, carefully pull out the spring rings and with a finger pull out the rollers and distance tube. Renew the needle rollers if worn. To reassemble the roller bearings inside the lay gear, start by greasing the layshaft well and inserting it into the lay gear. Slide in the distance tube followed by a spring ring at each end of the distance tube. Insert some more grease in the gap between the layshaft and lay gear and insert the needle rollers. When one set is complete insert the outer spring ring. Invert the assembly taking care the layshaft does not drop out and insert the second set of needle rollers. Refit the outer spring ring and ensure that the two faces are flush with the ends of the lay gear. Place to one side until needed for refitting. Leave the layshaft in position to ensure the needle rollers do not move.

4. Examine the condition of the ball races used, the single one at the end of the first motion shaft and the double one on the third motion shaft. If there is looseness between the inner and outer races the bearings must be renewed.

5. Ensure that the ball races are a good fit in their housings.

6. Inspect the baulk rings and test them with their mating tapers on the gears. If they slip before they contact the edge of the dog teeth on the gear, the hub and

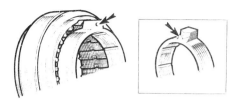

Fig. 7.5. The first and second speed sliding coupling showing the groove on the first speed side and the first speed baulk ring identified by the dimple or fillets (inset).

baulk ring must be renewed. Check the ball bearings are not pitted or worn and that the free length of the spring is 0.72 inch.

7. Check the locking detent ball bearings are not pitted or worn and that the springs when compared with a new one (if available) are all of equal length. The free length should be 1.0625 inch.

8. If there have been signs of oil leaks new seals must be fitted.

9. Examine all bushes for wear and if suspect fit new ones.

10. If the lay gear has a thrust spring fitted check that its free length is 1.661 inch.

11. Inspect the transmission case very carefully for signs of cracking or damage especially on the underside as well as at all mating surfaces, bearing housings and stud or bolt holes.

5. Transmission - reassembly

1. Always use new washers, gaskets and joint washers throughout reassembly. Generously lubricate all the gears, bushes and bearings with oil as they are being assembled except where indicated to the contrary.

2. Check that all oil ways are clear in the various parts of the transmission unit. Also ensure that the interior of the casing is clean and that there are no burrs on studs or bolt holes or the bearing housings.

3. Reassemble the third motion shaft bearing by placing the ball separator in place (photo).

5.3

4. Carefully drop the ball bearings into place leaving one out as it will not be possible to position the inner track with all the ball bearings in place (photo).

5. Place the inner track into the assembled bearings at an angle and then slip in the last ball bearing (photo).

6. Put the bearing assembly into a vice as shown in

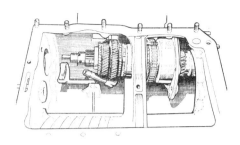

Fig. 7.6. Third motion shaft replacement

the photo and gently tighten so pressing the inner track into position.

7. Reassembly of the mainshaft commences by fitting the first gear in place followed by the reverse gear as shown in the photo.

8. Refit the third motion shaft bearing in place complete with its housing by using a piece of suitable diameter tubing placed over the inner track of the bearing and tapping the end of the tube with a hammer. The correct bearing fitting is shown in the photo.

9. As an alternative means of fitting the bearing, use a drift on alternate sides of the inner race with the third motion shaft held in a vice as shown in the photo.

10. Should refitting this bearing really prove obstinate place it in the vice as shown in the photo and tap the longer end of the third motion shaft with a soft faced hammer to drive the bearing fully home.

11. Reference to the photo shows the cut out at the centre portion of the synchronizer hub that must fit over the spline with no marking on the end at all. The 1st and 2nd gear synchronizer assembly can be fitted either way round but do make sure that the cut out in the centre does mate with the blind spline.

12. Put the large thrust washer on next making sure that the raised lip in this lies on the periphery of the thrust washer which engages with the groove cut in the third motion shaft (photo).

13. Having replaced 2nd gear, next refit 3rd gear ensuring that the cut out in the thrust washer is adjacent to the second gear, mating with the raised lip portion of the inner diameter of the sleeve fitted under 3rd gear (photo).

14. Fit a new tab locking washer and the circular lock nut. Tighten the circular nut securely using either a molewrench or a 'C' spanner as shown in the photo.

15. Using a suitable sized punch or chisel tap back the tag in the locking ring to lock the nut securely in place (photo).

16. The third motion shaft is now assembled as far as possible for the moment.

17. Place the first motion shaft on a block of soft wood and position the bearing with the circlip groove uppermost. Using a soft metal drift tap the bearing into place (photo). Use the drift only against the inner race.

18. Refit the tab washer and nut to the first motion shaft (photo).

19. If a suitable size spanner is not available tighten the nut securely using a soft metal drift and knock over the tab washer.

20. From a piece of 7/16 inch mild steel rod cut three pieces, approximately $\frac{1}{2}$ inch in length as shown in the photo.

21. Assemble the spring and ball to each of the selector forks in turn as shown in photo A, preferably by placing

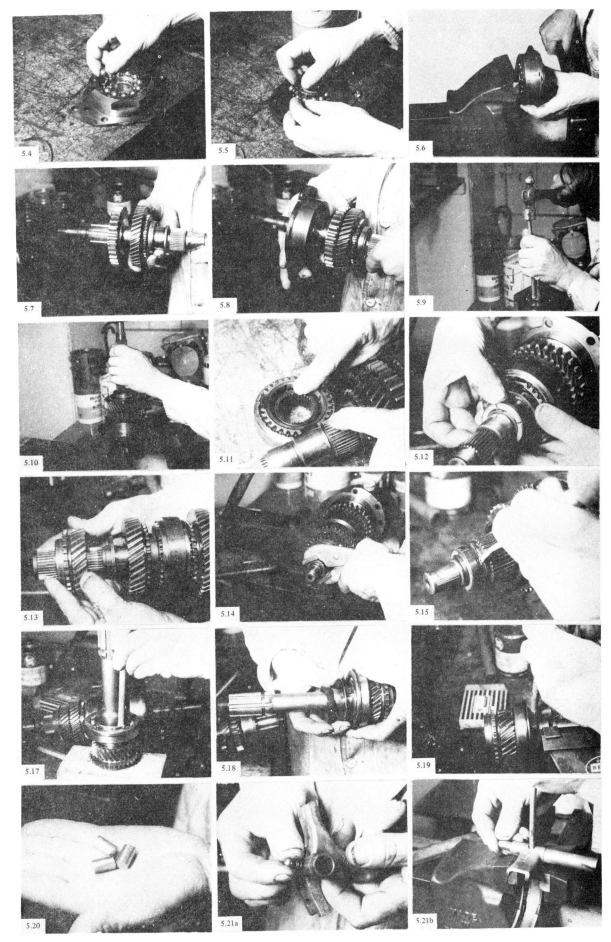

in a vice and pushing the ball and spring down with a metal rod whilst inserting one of the 7/16 inch diameter rods into the selector fork (photo B).

22. Refer to the photo and insert the two selector forks into the transmission casing. On the right is the 1st and 2nd selector fork whilst on the left is the 3rd and 4th selector fork approximately in their correct positions.

5.22

23. Carefully enter the third motion shaft into the transmission casing. Hold the selector forks out of the way of the third motion shaft (photo).

24. Slip the 3rd and 4th synchronizing sleeve over the end of the third motion shaft before it is finally positioned (photo).

25. Position the third motion shaft, at the same time aligning the synchronizer ring with the selector forks (photo).

26. Replace the reverse speed selector fork into the transmission casing. It may be necessary to put a hand through the differential unit aperture and move the other selector forks upwards to allow for this to be done (photo).

27. With the aid of a soft metal drift, tap the third motion shaft bearing housing fully home taking care that the centre portion of the bearing does not stick to the shaft otherwise all the ball bearings will be dislodged (photo).

28. Replace the shims previously removed and fit the housing retainer in position as shown in the photo.

29. Replace the bolts and one **nut that hold the** retainer in place not forgetting to fit the tab washers. DO NOT attempt to enter the bolt into the bottom left hand hole (arrowed in photo), as the bolt that enters this hole merely serves to hold the reverse idler shaft firmly in place.

30. Bend over the tab washers. The one at the bottom is not the easiest to get at and a mole wrench is ideal for this (see photo 5:29).

31. Refer to the photo and fit the 1st and 2nd selector rod into the top hole. Press the selector rod in until it meets resistance from the ½ inch piece of rod already

5.23 5.24 5.25

5.26 5.27 5.28

5.29 5.31 5.32

in position in the selector fork. The next part requires caution. To clear the fork of the rod a sharp tap with a soft faced hammer is necessary to stop the ball bearing flying out.

32. Repeat the previous operation for the 3rd and 4th selector rod (photo).

33. Using a wide blade screwdriver turn the two selector fork rods until the slots are positioned as shown in the photo. With the selector rods in this position push them in fully and the selector ball bearings will be heard

5.33

and felt to engage in the cut outs in each of the rods.

34. Replace the caged needle roller bearing onto the end of the third motion shaft (photo).

35. Ensure the synchronizer ring is in place and then carefully insert the gear end of the first motion shaft into the transmission casing as shown in the photo. Ensure that the synchromesh ring engages correctly on the first set of teeth on the first motion shaft.

36. Using a soft metal drift carefully tap the outer edge of the first motion shaft bearing into the casing as shown in the photo.

37. If a new bearing has been fitted a new distance piece must be selected and fitted. To do this refit the circlip and using feeler gauges determine the thickness of a distance piece which will be just too thick to allow the circlip to seat. Remove the circlip and original distance piece and select the next thinnest one and refit. The clearance between distance piece and circlip must not exceed 0.004 inch. Five distance pieces are available for this setting as follows: 0.117 – 0.118 inch, 0.121 – 0.122 inch, 0.125 – 0.126 inch, 0.129 – 0.130 inch and 0.133 – 0.134 inch (photos A and B).

38. Lubricate the gears and synchronizer rings (photo).

39. Place the reverse idler gear in position ensuring that the groove in the gear fits towards the front of the gearbox and lies in the fork of the reverse selector fork (photo).

40. Refit the reverse idler shaft with the machined

5.34

5.35

5.36

5.37a

5.37b

5.38

5.39

5.40

5.41

groove towards the outer end of the transmission casing. It will be necessary to manipulate the gear slightly to allow the shaft to pass through (photo).

41. Rotate the end of the reverse idler shaft until the milled end slots into place using a screwdriver as shown in the photo.

42. Refit the remaining screw and tab washer for the third motion shaft bearing retainer (photo). This screw also holds the reverse idler shaft in place.

5.42

43. Insert the reverse selector rod the procedure for which is covered in para. 31. Remove all three ½ inch metal rods from the transmission case.

5.43

44. Position the larger of the two lay gear thrust washers in the transmission casing ensuring that the tab is correctly positioned in the locating slot (photo).

5.44

45. It should be noted that when replacing the layshaft

it is essential that the large hole in the shaft is in direct line with the hole in the transmission case bridge piece (see holes arrowed in photo). This is an oil hole with oil entering the shaft and coming out of drillings to lubricate the caged needle roller bearings.

46. Fit the lay gear in position and slide the layshaft through from the outside end of the transmission case (photo).

47. Then slide the smaller thrust washer into position. The reason for this is that there is a slight recess for the larger end of the lay gear and it is not possible to fit both thrust washers first then following with the lay gear (photo).

48. Fit the final drive pinion in place with the boss facing towards the slim end of the shaft shown in the photo.

49. Fit the lock tab washer followed by the recessed nut. This nut has to be tightened to a torque wrench setting of 120 lb ft which is very very tight. If a torque wrench is not available tighten it as tight as possible. Do not forget it has a left hand thread. It will be necessary to lock the synchronizer sleeves by moving them both to the left before tightening the nut (photo).

50. Tap over the tab washer using a chisel or punch.

51. Fit a new end cover gasket and slide on the end cover as shown in the photo.

52. Carefully engage the speedometer drive gear in its slot in the end of the third motion shaft (photo) and tighten the end cover retaining nuts and spring washers.

53. Replace the differential unit into the transmission case so that it is offset towards the flywheel end of the casing as shown in the photo.

54. Refit the final drive cover with new gaskets and tighten the retaining nuts just sufficiently to hold the bearings and yet allow the assembly to be moved cross-wise by fitting the right hand end cover (photo).

55. Refer to Chapter 10/3 for full details of setting the differential unit. Fit a new crankcase to transmission casing flange joint washer taking care that the gasket is not torn when placing over the studs (photo).

56. Fit the oil suction 'O' ring correctly in position as shown in the photo and also ensure that the crankshaft front and rear main bearing sealing corks are still in position.

57. Carefully lower the engine onto the transmission case preferably using an overhead hoist (photo).

58. Refit the crankcase to transmission casing retaining nuts, bolts and spring washers finger tight and then one turn at a time in a diagonal manner to eliminate the possibility of distortion. Finally tighten using a torque wrench set to the recommendation at the beginning of this chapter.

59. Using a pair of pliers rotate the layshaft so as to align the recessed end of the shaft with the location in the backplate to prevent it rotating.

60. Refit the four springs to the layshaft thrust washer, these being arrowed in photo 5:62A.

61. Refit the locking plate shown in photo 5:62A to the ends of the selector rods.

62. Reference to photo B shows the correct positioning of the plate when fitted.

63. Fit a new adaptor plate gasket to cylinder block gasket and carefully replace the adaptor plate and secure the bolts located as shown in Fig 7:3. Tighten the bolts to a torque wrench setting given at the beginning of this chapter (photo).

64. Replace the flywheel onto the end of the crankshaft carefully pushing it over the dowels (photo).

65. Fit new locking tab washers, followed by the six bolts and tighten the bolts using a torque wrench set to read 40 lb ft (photo).

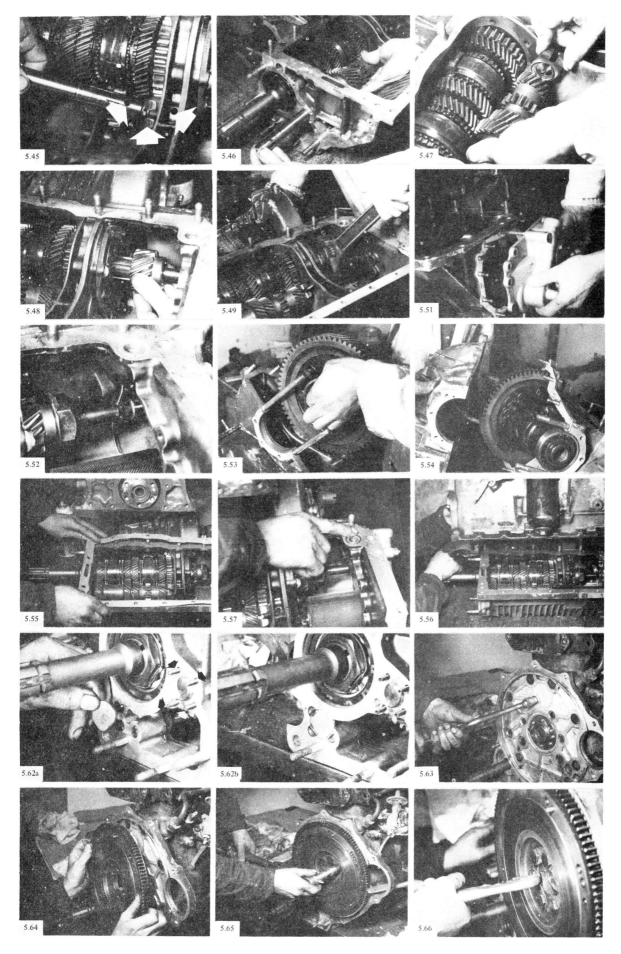

5.45

5.46

5.47

5.48

5.49

5.51

5.52

5.53

5.54

5.55

5.57

5.56

5.62a

5.62b

5.63

5.64

5.65

5.66

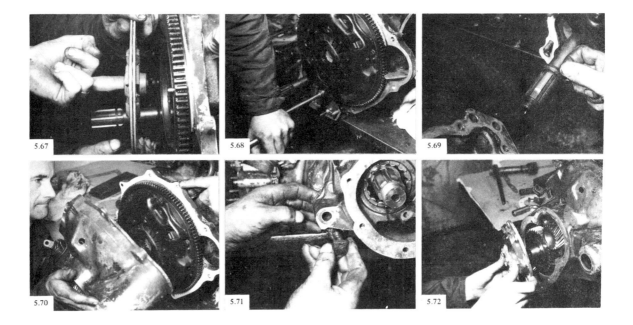

5.67   5.68   5.69

5.70   5.71   5.72

66. Using a mole wrench, bend over the flywheel bolt lock tabs as shown in the photo.

67. Place the clutch driven plate assembly against the flywheel face as shown in the photo.

68. Replace the clutch cover assembly on the flywheel dowels and tighten all the retaining bolts finger tight. Use a metal rod to line the clutch driven plate hub with the spigot bearing in the rear of the crankshaft and tighten the retaining bolts in a diagonal manner half a turn at a time. Lock the flywheel as shown in the photo.

69. Refit the horse shoe clip onto the end of the first motion shaft as shown in the photo.

70. Carefully fit the clutch housing to the engine adaptor plate as shown in the photo and tighten all the retaining nuts and bolts.

71. When refitting the clutch cover do not forget the specially shaped head bolt (photo).

72. Finally refit the idler gear and thrust washers followed by the end cover.

73. The power unit is now ready for refitting to the car.

---

6. Gear change mechanism

Gear selection is by a remote control gear lever linked to the selectors at the rear of the transmission unit by three special flexible cables. The remote control gear lever is attached to a change speed control box located on the underside of the floor.

---

7. Gear change mechanism - removal

1. Drain the oil from the complete transmission system into a clean container of suitable size (refill capacity of system $11\frac{1}{2}$ pints).

2. Carefully slide the gaiter up the gear change lever so that it is well clear of the bottom. Push down the spring loaded dust cover and rotate so that its bayonet fixing will be released. Lift up the gear change lever and it will be released from the control box. Move the floor carpeting clear of the control box area taking care

not to drop any dust or grit into the gear change lever location in the control box top cover and unscrew the floor cover plate retaining screws. Lift away the cover plate and joint washer.

3. Unscrew the three nuts and lift away together with the spring washers that hold the heat shield to the floor panel.

4. Extract the split pin from the clevis pin that holds the handbrake control cable to the handbrake pull rod. Remove the plain washer and withdraw the clevis pin.

5. Unscrew the nuts that hold the gear change remote control cable housing to the differential housing, lift away the nuts and spring washers and carefully ease the housing up the studs ready for removal. Place a piece of non fluffy rag into the aperture left in the differential housing to stop dirt ingress.

6. With the heat shield resting on the exhaust pipe remove the four bolts that secure the control box to the floor panel, and lift away the complete cable assembly.

---

8. Gear change mechanism - dismantling and inspection

1. The first part to dismantle is the cable housing. Unscrew the set screws and remove together with the cable retainers from the cable housing. Carefully withdraw the cables. Next release the circlip which retains the change speed lever pivot to the housing and remove the pivot by either pressing or using a soft metal drift. The levers and spacers will now be released and should be carefully lifted away, and the position of each component noted for correct refitting.

2. Turning to the control box remove the nuts and spring washers which hold the top cover to the remainder of the body. Lift away the top cover followed by the change speed guide and the interlock arm. Unscrew the two bolts, lift away the spring washers followed by the cable retaining plate and its two spacers. Remove the two adjustment nuts from each cable and carefully withdraw the cables. Finally release the operating shaft retainer and either drift or press the shafts from the control box. This will release the change speed jaws which may

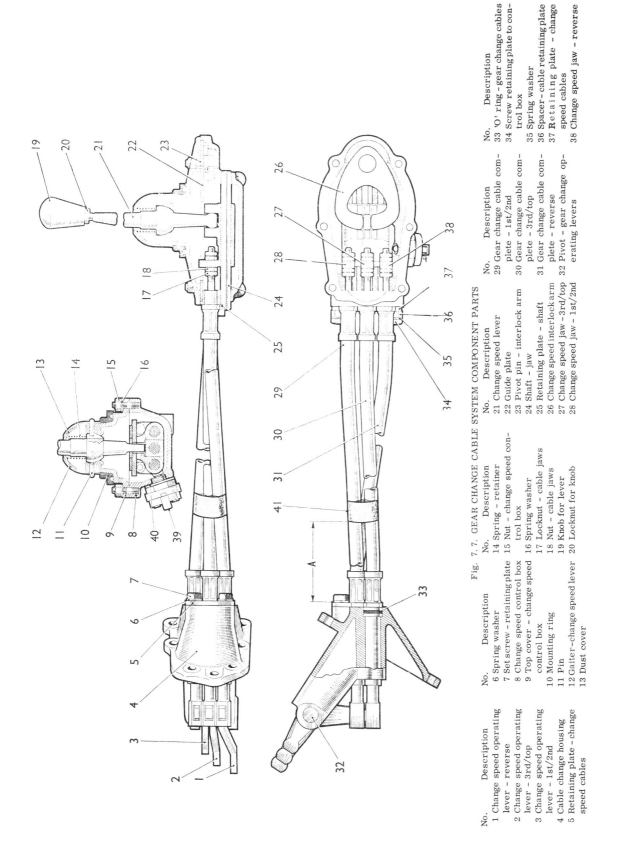

Fig. 7.7. GEAR CHANGE CABLE SYSTEM COMPONENT PARTS

No.	Description	No.	Description	No.	Description	No.	Description
1	Change speed operating lever – reverse	6	Spring washer	21	Change speed lever	33	'O' ring – gear change cables
2	Change speed operating lever – 3rd/top	7	Set screw – retaining plate	22	Guide plate	34	Screw retaining plate to control box
3	Change speed operating lever – 1st/2nd	8	Change speed control box	23	Pivot pin – interlock arm	35	Spring washer
4	Cable change housing	9	Top cover – change speed control box	24	Shaft – jaw	36	Spacer – cable retaining plate
5	Retaining plate – change speed cables	10	Mounting ring	25	Retaining plate – shaft	37	**Retaining plate – change speed cables**
		11	Pin	26	Change speed interlock arm	38	Change speed jaw – reverse
		12	Gaiter–change speed lever	27	Change speed jaw – 3rd/top		
		13	Dust cover	28	Change speed jaw – 1st/2nd		
		14	Spring – retainer	29	Gear change cable complete – 1st/2nd		
		15	Nut – change speed control box	30	Gear change cable complete – 3rd/top		
		16	Spring washer	31	Gear change cable complete – reverse		
		17	Locknut – cable jaws	32	Pivot – gear change operating levers		
		18	Nut – cable jaws				
		19	Knob for lever				
		20	Locknut for knob				

now be lifted out.

3. Thoroughly clean all parts and check for wear of the moving parts. Inspect the bodies for signs of cracking especially around stud or bolt holes. Any part that is suspect must be renewed.

---

9. Gear change mechanism – reassembly and installation

It is recommended that during reassembly all gaskets and 'O' ring seals should be renewed. To reassemble the mechanism proceed as follows:

1. Refer to Fig 7:7 and position the three change speed levers and spacers in their correct position in the cable housing and refit the pivot pin. The pivot pin should be locked in position with a new circlip.

2. Position the cable assemblies into the cable housing taking care to engage them correctly with the change speed levers. Refit the cable retainer followed by the mounting bolts and spring washers. Next place the change speed selector slides into the control box and press in the operating shafts. Replace the shaft retainer. To ensure adequate lubrication pour a little engine oil over the selector slides and operate so ensuring that each slides freely in the control box.

3. Replace the cables into the control box carefully ensuring that the threaded ends of each cable correctly enters its respective selector slide hole. The reverse gear cable may be easily identified as being longer than the other two and also having a yellow band on it. Do not forget the two nuts on the cable side of the threaded rod. Replace the second pair of nuts and temporarily tighten the nut and lock nut on each cable. Refit the cable retainer and spacers and secure in place with the two bolts and spring washers.

4. Fit a new gasket coated with a suitable jointing compound onto the cable housing. Move the change speed levers to the neutral position and carefully enter the change speed levers so correctly positioning the cable housing on the differential housing. Do not forget to remove the previously placed rag in the aperture of the differential housing. Secure with the nuts and spring washers.

5. Refit the control box to the heat shield and mount the assembly to the floor panel. Refit the handbrake cable to the handbrake pull rod not forgetting to use a new split pin. Adjust the three gear change cables as detailed in the following section.

6. Replace the change guide and interlock arm onto the pivot pin followed by the control box cover and a new gasket. Refit the securing nuts and spring washers.

7. Grease the gearchange lever pivot and insert into the top of the control box cover. Press down on the lever dust cover and rotate so engaging the bayonet coupling. Finally replace the floor cover plate and the carpeting. Position the gaiter correctly at the base of the gearchange lever and road test the car for correct gear change operation.

---

10. Gear change mechanism – adjustment

The system may be adjusted from within the car and must always be checked if noise or difficult gear changing is being experienced. This operation is very simple and should be carried out as follows:

1. Carefully slide the gaiter up the gear change lever so that it is well clear of the bottom. Push down the spring loaded dust cover and rotate it so that its bayonet fixing will be released. Lift up the gear change lever

and it will be released from the control box. Move the floor carpeting clear of the control box area taking care not to drop any dust or grit into the gear change location in the control box top cover and unscrew the floor cover plate retaining screws. Lift away the cover plate and joint washer.

2. Remove the nuts and spring washers and lift away the control box top cover followed by the change speed guide. Ensure that the three control cables are in the neutral position and check that the interlock arm swings freely through the change speed jaws and that there is a clearance of 0.030 inch each side.

3. Should the jaws not line up correctly the cables must be adjusted. Slacken the lock nuts and nuts on the cables that require adjustment. Position the jaw relative to the interlock arm and move the cable forwards and backwards so as to determine the mid point of the end play in the cable and relay levers. Carefully tighten the adjustment nuts followed by the locknuts.

4. Using feeler gauges as before check that the clearance between both sides of the interlock arm and jaw is equal at the required setting of 0.030 inch.

5. Refit the coverplate, gear change lever and carpeting as a reverse of the procedure detailed in para. 1 of this section.

---

11. Speedometer drive – removal and refitting

It is not usual for the speedometer drive gear to give any trouble but if after a process of elimination the gear is suspect the gear may be removed as follows:

1. Disconnect the speedometer drive cable from the special screws bush bolted to the drive cover on the transmission case. This is shown in Fig 7:8.

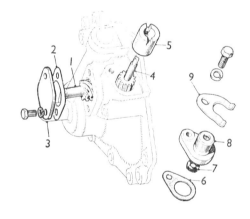

Fig. 7.8. SPEEDOMETER DRIVE ASSEMBLY

No.	Description	No.	Description
1	Drive wheel	6	Joint washer
2	Joint washer	7	Oil seal
3	End plate	8	Screwed bush
4	Pinion	9	Spring plate
5	Pinion bush		

2. Unscrew the two bolts from the coverplate and lift away together with the spring washers followed by the plate and gasket. Remove the screwed bush retaining bolt and lift away together with the spring washer followed by the spring plate, the screwed bush, its gasket and oil seal.

3. Carefully withdraw the speedometer pinion gear, rotating slightly to disengage meshing with the drive wheel. The pinion bush should be automatically unseated and able to be lifted out with the pinion gear.

4. Refitting the various parts is the reverse procedure to removal. Should excessive movement of the pinion shaft in the pinion bush be evident, the pinion bush must be renewed.

5. The spring plate now fitted to the drive assembly must replace the flat retaining washer as, with the latter, distortion can be caused. Always fit new gaskets and an oil seal.

12. Modified first motion shaft

Cars fitted with transmission after unit No. 937 had a modified first motion shaft whereby besides a new shaft being fitted this also meant a new retaining washer, drive gear, lock washer, retaining nut and the flywheel housing. The various parts are shown in Fig 7:9.

For replacement of items of the earlier type, the modified parts are not individually interchangeable and must be used only as a complete set.

Also a differential roller bearing may be found with a lip on the outer track as shown in the insert in Fig 7:9. The lip should be positioned towards the clutch housing.

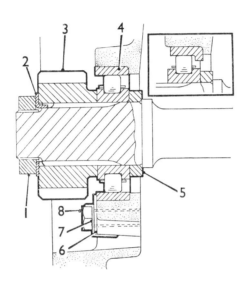

Fig. 7.9. MODIFIED FIRST MOTION SHAFT BEARING ASSEMBLY

No.	Description	No.	Description
1	Nut - 1 5/8 in. A. F.	5	Retaining ring
2	Lock washer	6	Location plate
3	Drive gear	7	Lock washer
4	Roller bearing	8	Setscrew

Inset: Alternative bearing

GEARBOX

FAULT FINDING CHART

Cause	Trouble	Remedy
SYMPTOM:	WEAK OR INEFFECTIVE SYNCHROMESH	
General wear	Synchronising cones worn, split or damaged.	Dismantle and overhaul gearbox. Fit new gear wheels and synchronising cones.
	Baulk ring synchromesh dogs worn, or damaged	Dismantle and overhaul gearbox. Fit new baulk ring synchromesh.
SYMPTOM:	JUMPS OUT OF GEAR	
General wear or damage	Broken gearchange fork rod spring	Dismantle and replace spring.
	Gearbox coupling dogs badly worn	Dismantle gearbox. Fit new coupling dogs.
	Selector fork rod groove badly worn	Fit new selector fork rod.
	Selector fork rod securing screw and locknut loose	Remove side cover, tighten securing screw and locknut.
SYMPTOM:	EXCESSIVE NOISE	
Lack of maintenance	Incorrect grade of oil in gearbox or oil level too low	Drain, refill, or top up gearbox with correct grade of oil.
General wear	Bush or needle roller bearings worn or damaged	Dismantle and overhaul gearbox. Renew bearings.
	Gearteeth excessively worn or damaged	Dismantle, overhaul gearbox. Renew gearwheels.
	Laygear thrust washers worn allowing excessive end play	Dismantle and overhaul gearbox. Renew thrust washers.
SYMPTOM:	EXCESSIVE DIFFICULTY IN ENGAGING GEAR	
Clutch not fully disengaging	Clutch pedal adjustment incorrect	Adjust clutch pedal correctly.
	Remote Control cables require attention	Adjust cables

Chapter 8/Automatic Gearbox

Contents

Specifications

Automatic transmission type	AS1 - 35TA
Torque converter ratio range	1:1 to 1:1
Primary drive:	
Type	Sprockets and chain
Ratio	1.03:1
Gearbox	
Ratio - First	2.39:1
Second	1.45:1
Top	1.00:1
Reverse	2.09:1

1. General description

Borg-Warner automatic transmissions have been fitted to medium and large sized cars for many years and the popular model 35 was modified allowing it to be fitted to front wheel drive cars. In the original design it takes the place of the clutch and gearbox and is mounted in the usual position behind the engine. However, as with front wheel drive models where the manual gearbox is fitted underneath the engine, so is this automatic transmission, and the layout can be seen in Fig. 8:1.

From the illustration it will be noted that the torque converter is not mounted in line with the gear train but fitted above it. The torque developed by the engine is transmitted to the gear train by a special type of chain as shown in Fig. 8:2. With this layout there is a division between the engine and the automatic transmission unit so that the engine oil is retained in the engine and normal automatic transmission fluid in the automatic transmission and differential unit. This is of course a deviation from normal BLMC transverse unit design.

The drivers control, called the selector, is mounted on the fascia panel and connected to the unit by flexible control cables which are also made by Borg-Warner.

The internal parts comprising the gear train and clutches are identical to those used in the popular model 35. The main difference is in the direction of rotation of the planet carrier which turns in the opposite direction to normal.

The hydraulic valve body also uses a considerable number of model 35 parts, the hydraulic oil being supplied by only one front pump and not two pumps. Access to the servos and valve body is via cover plates on the underside of the casing. There is an electric switch which controls the starter motor inhibitor and this switch, together with the reverse light switch, is not mounted as is usual on the side of the transmission unit. Instead there are separate micro-switches mounted on the drivers selector quadrant.

As was previously mentioned a special drive chain called a 'Hy-Vo' chain is fitted between the torque converter and the planetary drive gear train. It is of endless, pre-stressed design and operates without the need of a tensioner. If it is ever wished to renew the chain because of excessive wear it should be noted that both the sprockets and chain are obtainable from agents as

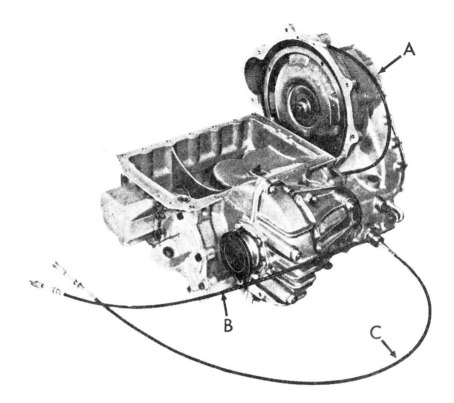

Fig. 8.1. The Automatic Transmission Unit

individual components. They are, however, designed to outlive the life of the automatic transmission unit.

Due to the complexity of the automatic transmission unit, if performance is not up to standard or overhaul is necessary, it is imperative that this be left to your local main agents who will have all the special equipment and knowledge for fault diagnosis and rectification. The successful overhaul of an automatic transmission

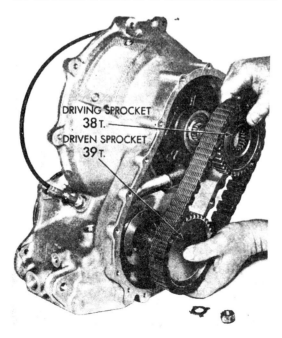

Fig. 8.2. Morse Hy-Vo Chain drive

unit requires the use of many very special tools and the content of this chapter is therefore confined to supplying general information and any service information that will be of practical use to the owner.

2. Driving technique

The selector lever is mounted on the fascia panel and controls the operation of the automatic transmission. There are five lever positions marked on the quadrant and these are 'P', 'R', 'N', 'D' and 'L'. As a safety factor to prevent direct selection from 'N' the lever must be moved to the left against the action of a spring before 'L' or 'R' can be selected. To select 'P' the lever must be moved as far as it will go to the left. Each selector lever position controls the system as follows:

'P' This is the park position whereby no engine power is transmitted to the driving wheels and the transmission is locked by mechanical means. For safety reasons it is recommended that this position be used whenever the car is parked or when the engine is to be run for tuning or adjustment. Serious damage will result if this position is selected whilst the car is moving.

'R' Reverse position whereby the car can be driven in reverse and, to assist control, full engine braking is available. As with the 'P' position it is important not to select 'R' whilst the car is moving forwards.

'N' This is the neutral or normal position whereby no engine torque is transmitted to the driving wheels. Always apply the handbrake when the selector is in the 'N' position and the car is stationary.

'D' For normal driving conditions; this is the usual

position for the selector lever and gives a full automatic range of the three forward ratios, all of which are progressively engaged up and down depending on the position of the accelerator pedal and the speed of the car.

'L' In this position the automatic ratio change is overridden for first and second ratios together with the engine braking.

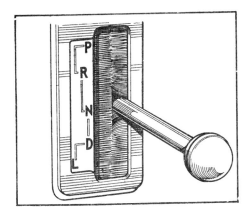

Fig. 8.3. Selector lever positions

3. Starting the engine

1. The starter motor may be operated only when the selector lever is in the 'P' or 'N' positions, this being controlled by a micro switch behind the selector fascia, For safety reasons always apply either the handbrake or foot brake before starting the engine.

2. Care should be taken when starting the engine from cold using the choke control. Stalling should be avoided if this control is left out just sufficiently to increase engine speed until the engine has reached normal operating temperature. At the faster idling speed when the selector lever is moved to 'D' or 'L' a firm engagement will be obtained but has no ill effects on the automatic transmission unit.

4. Normal driving conditions

1. Once the engine has been started and is running evenly, with the brake firmly applied move the selector lever to the 'D' position; to drive away just release the brake and gently depress the accelerator pedal. In the 'D' position all forward ratios will be progressively and automatically engaged as the speed increases or decreases. This means that the ratio automatically selected will be suitable for both the speed of the car as well as road conditions determining engine power required.

2. If a minimum accelerator pedal pressure is utilised the automatic transmission is changed up at low road speeds and conversely if the accelerator pedal is depressed to the full throttle position the changes will be at higher road speeds. Further pressure on the accelerator pedal will produce a 'kick-down' condition and will give change up speeds at maximum road speeds.

3. A smooth start from rest is always obtained and is not dependant on the accelerator pedal position. Care **must** be taken when driving over slippery surfaces and

for maximum fuel economy.

5. Selector in 'L' position

1. With the selector lever in this position from rest, the transmission will be in first speed ratio and will remain in this ratio irrespective of road speed or accelerator pedal position. This first ratio gives maximum engine braking.

2. If the transmission is in the third ratio of the 'D' range with a road speed of below 55 m.p.h. selection of 'L' will immediately down change the system to the second ratio with moderate engine braking. Should the road speed drop to below 5 m.p.h. first ratio will automatically be selected.

3. The 'L' position is best used in the following conditions:

(a) To give the driver engine braking assistance, whilst the car is descending a steep hill. Depress the foot brake until the road speed decreases to below 55 m.p.h. and then select the 'L' position. To obtain maximum engine braking assistance first ratio may be obtained below 25 m.p.h. by depressing the accelerator to the 'kick-down' position.

(b) To prevent considerable ratio changing when the car is being driven up a long hill of unequal gradients.

(c) To give immediate extra engine torque as would be necessary when it is desired to overtake another vehicle.

6. Increased acceleration

1. If a lower ratio is required, as when it is necessary to overtake another vehicle, depress the accelerator pedal down as far as it will go into the 'kick-down' position.

2. The use of the 'kick-down' position is under direct control from the driver except that the maximum down change speeds have been previously set to give the best car performance, yet without excessive engine speed.

3. If correctly set, the 'kick-down' changes will not operate above the following tabulated speeds:

Ratio Change	Road Speed
3rd to 2nd	53 - 56 m.p.h.
2nd to 1st	23 - 30 m.p.h.

7. Special driving or recovery considerations

1. Stopping. To slow down or stop, remove the foot from the accelerator pedal and depress the foot brake in the usual way. The engine will not stall.

2. Parking. With the car stationary move the selector to the 'P' position and apply the handbrake. If the car has been parked on a steep gradient move the selector to the 'D' position and increase the engine speed slightly if facing uphill, or if facing downhill, move the selector to the 'R' position and increase the engine speed slightly, then release the handbrake.

3. Soft surfaces. When the front wheels will not grip the road surface due to snow, ice or mud conditions, rock the car forwards and backwards by moving the selector alternatively to the 'R' and 'D' positions and raising the engine speed slightly.

4. Towing caravan. If a caravan or trailer is being towed always select the 'L' position before ascending or descending steep hills to stop overheating of the special transmission fluid and also to receive benefit from engine braking assistance.

5.   Recovery towing. Should it be necessary to have the car towed to a garage, do not tow in the usual way using a tow rope unless an additional 3 pints ($3\frac{1}{2}$ U.S. pints, 1.7 litres) of transmission oil has been added to the unit; and then do not tow at speeds higher than 30 m.p.h. for a distance not exceeding 40 miles. If there are noises coming from the transmission do not tow with the front wheels on the road but suspend the front end and tow the car in this position.

6.   Tow-starting. Due to the design characteristics of the automatic transmission it is not possible to tow start the car.

---

8.   Automatic transmission - hydraulic fluid

It is important that only transmission fluid manufactured to specification Type A, Suffix A fluid is used. The capacity of the unit is approximately 15 pints (18.014 U.S. pints; 8.524 litres).

---

9.   Maintenance

---

1.   Ensure that the converter housing stoveguard is always kept clean of dust or mud otherwise overheating will occur.

2.   Regularly check the automatic transmission fluid level. With the engine at its normal operating temperature, move the selector to the 'P' position and allow to idle for two minutes. Remove the dipstick, wipe it clean, and with the engine idling, insert the dipstick and quickly withdraw again. If necessary add enough of the clean correct grade fluid to bring the level to the

Fig. 8.4. Dipstick location

'High' mark. The difference between the two dipstick graduations is 1 pint (1.2 U.S. pints; 0.568 litres).

3.   If the unit has been drained always use new fluid. Fill up to the correct 'high' level gradually refilling the unit. The exact amount will depend on how much was left in the converter after draining but the usual average required is 5 pints (6.005 U.S. pints; 2.841 litres). Check the level as detailed in paragraph 2 of this section.

---

10.   Automatic transmission - removal & replacement

Full details are given in Chapter 1/6. Once again it is important to note that any suspected faults must be referred to the main agent before unit removal as with this type of unit the fault must be confirmed using special equipment before it has been removed from the car.

---

11.   Automatic transmission unit - separating from and replacing to the engine

---

1.   With the engine and transmission unit away from the car and the exterior thoroughly cleaned using paraffin or a good quality degreasing solvent, remove the two starter motor retaining bolts and lift away the motor.

2.   Remove the screws which hold the drive plate to the torque converter through the starter motor aperture, rotating the drive plate by the starter ring gear.

3.   Turning to the converter housing, remove the four uppermost nuts that hold the housing to the engine end plate. It will be observed that two of the nuts each hold a wiring clip, one holds the engine earthing strap and the other one secures the engine damper.

4.   A thin socket will now be required to remove the ten screws that hold the automatic transmission casing to the front and side of the engine crankcase flange. Also remove the screw that is located at the centre between the automatic transmission casing and the crankcase. This one can be easily missed.

5.   Using the same socket, remove the six screws that hold the automatic transmission casing to the rear of the engine crankcase flange.

6.   With an engine hoist or four strong men, lift the engine upwards from the automatic transmission casing taking care that it is lifted away squarely.

7.   Replacing the engine to the automatic transmission casing is the reverse sequence to removal. It is, however, recommended that the engine is held about 1/8 inch away from the case whilst the converter spigot is correctly engaged in the crankshaft. Then lower until engine is on the casing. Replace all the screws that were removed holding the two units together but do not tighten until the adaptor plate to converter housing screws have been fully tightened. Then fully tighten the unit mounting screws in a diagonal pattern.

Chapter 9/Drive Shafts & Universal Joints

Contents

1. General description

Drive is transmitted from the differential to the front wheels by means of two drive shafts. Fitted at either end of each shaft are universal joints which allow for vertical movement of the front wheels.

The outer universal joints are of the Hardy Spicer Birfield constant velocity joint type. The drive shaft fits inside the circular outer constant velocity joint which is also on the driven shaft. Drive is transmitted from the drive shaft to the driven shaft by six steel balls which are located in curved grooves machined in line with the axis of the shaft on the inside of the driven shaft and outside of the drive shaft. This allows the driven shaft to hinge freely on the drive shaft, but at the same time keeps them together. The constant velocity joint is packed with a special grease and enclosed in a rubber boot.

Two types of connections were used at the coupling end of the drive shaft, the earlier type being fixed to the shaft and the later type being a sliding joint as shown in Fig. 9:1. The sliding joint like the constant velocity joint is packed with a special grease and sealed by a rubber boot.

2. Routine maintenance

1.   At intervals of 3,000 miles inspect the rubber boots which protect the outer universal joints. If they are torn, split, or damaged they should be renewed as soon as possible as they are open to road dust, grit and water which would lead to rapid deterioration of the ball bearings in the joint. Should a new rubber boot be necessary it requires the removal of the drive shaft and release of the drive shaft from the inner race or sliding joint. Full details are given in subsequent sections of this chapter.
2.   Wear in the constant velocity joint is detected by a regular knocking when the front wheels are turned on full lock. In severe cases it will be necessary to turn the wheels only slightly for the noise to begin.

3. Drive shaft removal and refitting (early type)

The removal and refitting of drive shafts calls for the use of special tools and these are listed in this section - no way to avoid their use is known. Before you commence work ensure these tools can be borrowed or hired from your local BLMC agent.
1.   Insert a $\frac{1}{2}$ inch metal or hard wood block between the upper suspension arm and the lower rebound rubber. Carefully jack up the front of the car and place a firmly based stand under the front side member. Remove the wheel from the shaft which is to be renewed.
2.   Remove the steering rod ball joint from the steering arm using tool 18G1063 or a suitable universal ball joint separator.
3.   Remove the two bolts holding the disc brake caliper unit to the front swivel hub. Lift the caliper away from the disc and using strong string or wire hang the caliper on the sub-frame so that the flexible hydraulic hose is not strained. Do not depress the brake pedal.
4.   Extract the split pin and remove the drive shaft nut. Using a soft faced hammer gently tap the end of the shaft, and lift away the outer cone.

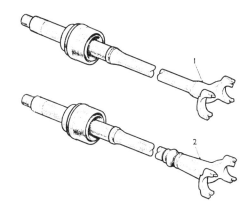

Fig. 9.1. THE TWO TYPES OF DRIVE SHAFTS WHICH CAN BE FITTED
1 First type with fixed flange
2 Second type with sliding joint flange

5. Suitably mark the drive shaft flange and the flexible coupling and also the differential shaft flange positions relative to the flexible coupling, so that upon reassembly they may be fitted in their original positions.

6. Remove the eight lock nuts from the four U bolts securing the flexible coupling to both the drive and differential shafts.

7. Select wood blocks of suitable size, and support the disc brake and drive flange assembly. Ease back the lock plate, remove the nut and separate the swivel hub ball joint at the outer end of the upper suspension arm. Carefully allow the swivel hub to pivot outwards and disengage the drive shaft coupling. Pull the drive shaft from the hub assembly if necessary raising the shaft so that it clears the hub.

8. Although refitting is the reverse procedure to removal certain important points must be adhered to otherwise difficulties may be experienced. Repack the hub with grease ensuring complete penetration without over packing which would cause early bearing failure. Should the hub bearings be a tight fit onto the drive shaft hold the drive shaft between soft faces in a vice, borrow and use the BLMC tool 18G1104 as shown in Fig 9:2. Screw the guide onto the end of the drive shaft, place the hub in its correct position ensuring that it is the correct way round and finally place the tool in position. Screw the centre bolt of the tool into the guide as far as it will go and using an open ended spanner tighten the nut on the centre bolt so drawing the drive shaft through the hub.

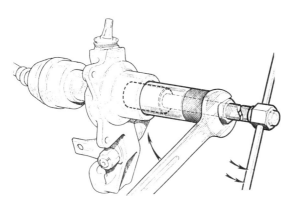

Fig. 9. 2. Drawing the drive shaft through the hub.

9. With the flexible type coupling, new self lock nuts must always be used. Tighten the nuts on each U bolt evenly until the coupling metal faces are brought together with at least 1/16 inch of the threaded part of the U bolt showing. Drive shafts having couplings of the flange type should have the nuts tightened in a diagonal pattern one turn at a time and finally tightened using a torque wrench set to 28 lb ft. NOTE: Drive shafts are not interchangeable unless a modification to the differential shaft assembly has been completed, so do not attempt to fit a drive shaft with a sliding joint in place of the fixed flange type. Details of the modification are given in Chapter 10.

10. Tighten the drive shaft hub nut using a torque wrench set to 150 lb ft, and using a dial indicator gauge check the run out of the disc at its maximum circumference. If it is in excess of 0.008 inch the hub must be removed from the drive shaft and repositioned. Also check the hub bearing end float which should be between 0 and 0.004 inch. For further details refer to Chapter 13.

4. Drive shaft - removal and refitting (later type)

1. Insert a $\frac{1}{2}$ inch thick x $\frac{1}{2}$ inch wide metal or hard wood block between the upper suspension arm and the lower rebound rubber. Carefully jack up and place a firmly based stand under the front side member and remove the road wheel.

2. Remove the steering rod ball joint from the steering arm using a suitable universal ball joint separator or a soft faced hammer.

3. Slacken the bleed screw on the disc brake caliper and drain the hydraulic system. Disconnect the flexible hose from the metal hydraulic pipe at the connection, refer to chapter 11/5 for full details.

4. Remove the two bolts holding the caliper unit to the front swivel hub. Lift away the caliper from the hub.

5. Extract the split pin and remove the drive shaft nuts. Using a soft faced hammer gently tap the end of the shaft and lift away the outer cone. Carefully pull the driving flange and disc assembly away from the shaft and disconnect the dust shield.

6. Mark the coupling to ensure correct reassembly and disconnect the drive shaft at the couplings.

7. Release the locknuts securing the upper and lower ball joints and separate, using a suitable ball joint separator. Carefully withdraw the combined hub and drive shaft assemblies.

8. A special BLMC tool No. 18G.1063 plus adaptors 18G.47. AT are required to remove the drive shaft from hub. This operation is shown in Fig 9:3. Lower the drive shaft through the base of the tool and position the two halves of the adaptors round the rubber boot so that the hub rests on the support legs (arrowed in Fig 9:3). Manipulate the shaft so that it is in line with the centre bolt of the tool and press the shaft out from the hub.

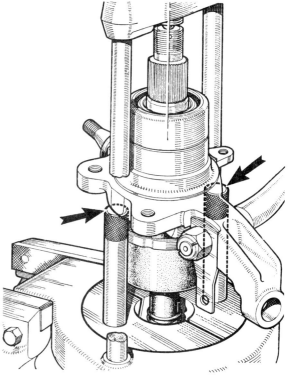

Fig. 9.3. Removing the drive shaft from the hub.

Ensure that whilst the tool is being operated the underside of the drive shaft is held so that when released from the hub it does not fall on the floor. It is possible to perform this operation using a good quality three leg puller.

9. The inner hub bearing must now be removed from drive shaft using BLMC tool 18G.47.C together with adaptor 18G.47.AT as shown in Fig 9:4. If this tool is not available a large three leg puller may be used provided care is taken.

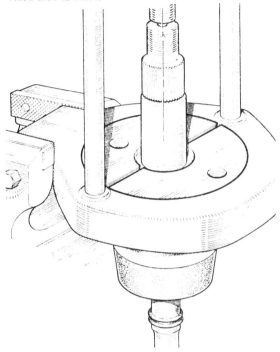

Fig. 9.4. Removing the inner hub bearing.

10. Although refitting is the reverse procedure to removal certain important points must be adhered to otherwise difficulties could be experienced. Repack the hub with grease ensuring complete penetration, without over packing which could cause early bearing failure. Hold the drive shaft between soft faces in a vice and use the BLMC tool No. 18G.1104 as shown in Fig 9:2. Screw the guide onto the end of the drive shaft. Carefully refit the inner hub bearing into the hub ensuring that it is the correct way round. Then place the tool in position. Screw the centre bolt of the tool into the guide as far as it will go and using an open ended spanner tighten the nut on the centre bolt so drawing the drive shaft through the hub.

11. Refit the driving flange and brake disc assembly onto the shaft, replace the outer cone and tighten the nut using a torque wrench set to read 150 lb ft.

12. Replace the dust shield and the disc brake caliper. Remake the hydraulic pipe connection. Refit the ball end joint to the steering lever and completely bleed the hydraulic brake system as detailed in Chapter 11.

13. Replace the road wheel and remove the stand. Road test the car.

5. Constant velocity joint - removal, inspection and reassembly

There is little point in dismantling the outer constant velocity joints if they are known to be badly worn.

In this case it is better to remove the old joint from the shaft and fit a new unit. To remove and then dismantle the constant velocity joint proceed as follows:

1. Remove the drive shaft from the car as detailed in the Section 3 or 4 depending on which type of shaft is fitted.

2. Thoroughly clean the exterior of the drive shaft and rubber, preferably not using a liquid cleaner.

3. Mount the drive shaft vertically in a vice with the constant velocity joint facing downwards.

4. Before the joint can be dismantled it must be removed from the drive shaft. This is easily done by firmly tapping the outer edge of the constant velocity joint with a hide or plastic headed hammer as shown in Fig 9:5. The constant velocity joint is held to the shaft by an internal circular section circlip, and tapping the joint in the manner described forces the circlip to contract into a groove so allowing the joint to slide off the shaft.

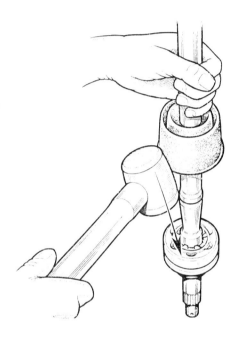

Fig. 9.5. Removing the shaft from the joint inner race.

5. Mark the position of the inner and outer races with a dab of paint so that upon reassembly the mated parts can be correctly replaced.

6. Refer to Fig 9:6 and tilt the inner race until one ball bearing is released. Repeat this operation easing out each ball bearing in turn, using a small screwdriver.

7. Manipulate the cage until the special elongated slot coincides with the lands of the bell housing. Drop one of the lands into the slot and lift out the cage and race assembly (see Fig 9:7).

8. Turn the inner race at right angles to the cage and in line with the elongated slot. Drop one land into the slot and withdraw the inner race as shown in Fig 9:8.

9. Thoroughly clean all component parts of the joint by washing in paraffin.

10. Examine each ball bearing in turn for cracks, flat

Fig. 9.8. Inner race to be positioned as shown by arrow to enable it to be removed from cage

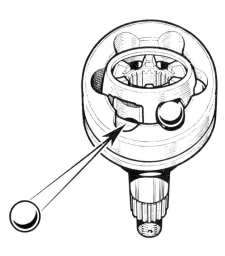

Fig. 9.6. Tilt the inner race so that the ball bearings may be removed.

Fig. 9.7. Removal of cage and inner race assembly from bell housing

spots or signs of the surface pitting. Check the inner and outer race tracks for widening which will cause the ball bearings to be a loose fit. This, together with excessive wear in the ball cage, will lead to the characteristic 'knocking' on full lock. The cage which fits between the inner and outer races must be examined for wear in the ball cage windows and for cracks which are likely to develop across the narrower portions between the outer rims and the holes for the ball bearings. If wear is excessive then all the parts must be renewed as a matched set.

11. The majority of cages used in the original fitment to the car are of a standard size but it is possible for some drive shafts to have a 0.010 inch oversize cage and bell housing fitted. A joint will only accept a replacement cage of the same size as the original. As it is very important that a new cage is not fitted until its size has been determined use a BLMC tool 18G.1064. A standard cage will pass through the gauge whereas an oversize cage will not. In the service kits supplied for constant velocity joint overhaul the standard cage has a part number 18G8069 plus a white paint identification mark. The oversize cage has part number 18G8070 and has a red paint identification mark.

12. To reassemble first ensure that all parts are very clean and then lubricate with Duckham's M-B grease which is supplied under BLMC part number AKF1540. Do not under any circumstances use any other grease. Provided all parts have been correctly selected and are clean and well lubricated they should fit together easily without force.

13. Refit the inner race into the cage by manipulating one of the lands into the elongated slot in the cage. Insert the cage and inner race assembly into the ball joint by fitting one of the elongated slots over one of the lands in the outer race. Rotate the inner race to line up with the bell housing in its original previously marked position.

14. Taking care not to lose this position, tilt the cage until one ball bearing can be inserted into a slot. Repeat this procedure until all six ball bearings are in their correct positions. Ensure that the inner race moves freely in the bell housing throughout its movement range taking care that the ball bearings do not fall out.

15. Using the remainder of the special grease, pack the joint evenly. Smear the inside of a new rubber boot with Duckham's M-B grease and fit the rubber boot and a new circlip to the end of the shaft.

16. Hold the shaft in a vice and locate the inner race on the splines. By pressing the constant velocity joint against the circlip, position the ring centrally and contract it in the chamber in the inner race leading edge with two screwdrivers as shown in Fig 9:9. Using a soft faced hammer, sharply tap the end of the stub shaft to compress the ring and then tap the complete assembly onto the drive shaft. Double check that the shaft if fully engaged and the circlip fully locked against the inner race.

17. Ease the rubber boot over the constant velocity joint and ensure the moulded edges of the boot are seating correctly in the retaining grooves of the shaft and bell

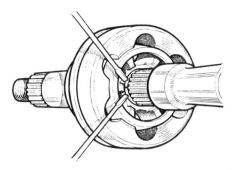

Fig. 9.9. It is important that the circlip is centralised before the shaft is pushed onto the splines.

housing. Secure in position with the large and small clips. Check that the tab of the large clip is pulled away from the direction of normal forward rotation as shown in Fig 9:10. Do not use wire as this cuts into the rubber boot.

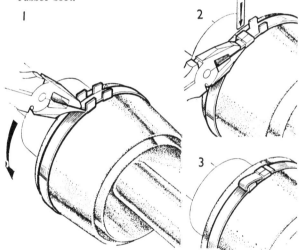

Fig. 9.10. THE CORRECT FITTING OF CLIPS TO THE RUBBER BOOT

1 Pull clip as tight as possible. Pull the free end, hold and take a further grip, and pull downwards again.

2 Hold in position, fold over and secure front tabs.

3 Bend free end over and secure clip end with rear tabs.

---

6. Sliding joint - removal, inspection and replacement

---

1. Remove the drive shaft as described previously in this chapter.

2. Thoroughly clean all dirt and grease from the drive shaft flange area.

3. Remove the rubber housing sealing clips and carefully pull the rubber housing from the flange. Mark the drive shaft and flange so that they may be correctly reassembled in their original position.

4. Using two small screwdrivers close the end of the circlip and release it from the groove. Withdraw the shaft from the flange.

5. Thoroughly clean all parts and inspect the rubber housing for signs of damage, the splines for wear and, if

a new shaft or housing is to be fitted, the spline clearance.

6. It is important that only Duckham's Laminoid Grease is used, this being obtained under BLMC part number 97H2465 for a 1 lb tin.

7. Well lubricate the splined end of the drive shaft and also the inside of the rubber housing seal. Slide the rubber housing onto the shaft followed by the circlip. Now fill the flange sleeve with approximately 1 ounce of grease.

8. Position the shaft spring and push the shaft onto the flange. Insert the circlip into its seating as shown by the arrow in Fig 9:8.

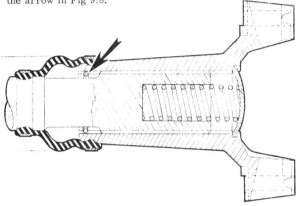

Fig. 9.11. THE SLIDING JOINT ASSEMBLY

1 Ensure that the diameter of rubber housing does not exceed 2 in. (A).

2 The arrow shows the securing clip.

9. Fit the rubber housing into the shaft and sleeve grooves. Slip the blade of a screwdriver under one rubber housing outer clip and allow air and any excess grease to seep out. The external diameter of the rubber housing should not exceed 2 inch. If greater, squeeze the housing by hand until it is of the required diameter.

10. Withdraw the drive shaft slightly and fit new retaining clips as described in this chapter.

---

7. Universal joints - dismantling, inspection and reassembly

Before servicing the universal joint it is as well to determine the source of wear. This is best done by holding the shaft and testing for circumferential movement at the flange by attempting to rotate it with the shaft firmly held. Any movement will indicate that either the bearings or the splines have worn. Next lift the joint with the drive shaft held firm and any movement will indicate worn bearing thrust faces.

To overhaul the universal joint proceed as follows:

1. Remove the complete drive shaft assembly as previously described in this chapter. Clean the shaft and universal joint preferably not using a liquid cleaner but a stiff brush.

2. Using a pair of circlip or pointed pliers remove the four circlips from the journals. If difficulty is experienced in contracting a circlip, lightly tap the end of the bearing so relieving pressure on the circlip and then remove.

3. Hold the universal joint firmly in the hand and lightly tap the yoke whereupon the bearing opposite should start to emerge. If it does not do so hold the universal joint in a vice and referring to Fig 9:12 using a small diameter rod and light hammer, tap the sticking bearing out from

Fig. 9.12. Universal joint bearing removal using a small diameter rod.

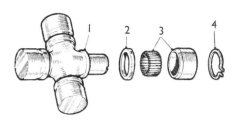

Fig. 9.13. UNIVERSAL JOINT COMPONENT PARTS

No.	Description	No.	Description
1	Journal spider	3	Needle rollers and bearing
2	Rubber seal	4	Circlip

inside the joint.   Repeat this operation for the opposite bearing.

4.   To remove the two remaining bearings, rest the exposed journals on the journal spider on a soft wood surface, and tap the lug of the yoke to remove the two remaining races.

5.   Wash all dismantled parts in paraffin and dry. Inspect the bearing needle rollers for signs of pitting, ovality or damage. Also inspect the bearing for cracking and internal wear. The rubber seals should be a snug fit on the journal spider. If any part is suspect it should be renewed.   The new bearing should be a good push fit in the yoke.

6.   To reassemble, first pad the hole in the journal spider with a high melting point grease. Ensure that all air is expelled from the drilling inside the spider otherwise it will not be adequately lubricated. Pack each

bearing with grease to a depth of 1/8 inch.

7.   Fit new seals to the four spider journals and carefully insert the spider into the flanges by tilting to engage into the bores.

8.   Insert one bearing into the bore from the bottom position so that no needles fall out. Use a copper drift to tap it down the yoke bore until the circlip groove is just completely visible. Fit the circlip ensuring it is seating correctly.

9.   Fit the opposite bearing in the manner just described, always from the bottom and inserting upwards. Repeat for the other two bearings, fitting the circlips once each bearing is in place.

10. If the joint appears to be tight lightly tap the flanges to relieve pressure on the bearings, using a soft face hammer. Wipe away excess grease and the drive shaft is ready for refitting.

Chapter 10/Differential Unit

Contents

Specification

Type ... ...   Helical gears and differential
Ratio: Standard 3.882:1
     *Alternative 4.187:1
     Automatic transmission.. ... ...   3.830:1

    * Standard ratio up to engine numbers:
       18AMW/U/H27523
       18AMW/U/L20548
      Preload, differential bearing.. ... ...   0.003 - 0.005 inch
      Speed at 1,000 rpm in top gear manual gear-
      box... ... ...   17.69 mph
      Alternative ratio manual gearbox .. ..   16.39 mph
      No speed quoted on automatic due to percentages slippage.

1. General description

The differential unit is located on the bulkhead side of the combined engine and transmission unit. It is held in place by nuts and studs. The crownwheel or drive gear together with the differential gears are mounted in the differential unit. The drive pinion is mounted on the third motion shaft.

All repairs can be carried out to the component parts of the differential unit only after the engine/transmission unit has been removed from the car. If it is wished to attend to the pinion, it will be necessary to separate the transmission casing from the engine.

The differential housing and gearbox are machined when assembled so that they are a matched pair and are not interchangeable. Also the final drive gear and pinion are mated and must be changed as a pair and not as individual gears.

2. Differential unit - removal and dismantling

1. Remove the engine and transmission assembly as detailed in Chapter 1.

2. Mark each differential drive shaft (6) and (22) see Fig. 10:3, so that they may be refitted in their original positions. Very carefully withdraw each shaft taking care not to damage the oil seals with the splines on the end of the shaft.

3. Remove the bolts (4) and spring washers (3) holding the final drive end covers (2) to the differential casing and lift away the end covers and joint washers (1). Note carefully the position of the oil return holes and the

number of shims (9) fitted between the differential bearing (10) and end cover on each side of the unit. Mark the end covers to ensure that they are replaced in their original positions.

4. Remove the four 7/16 inch diameter and six 5/16 inch nuts and spring washers holding the differential cover, followed by the final drive gear and differential assembly.

5. Use a good quality three leg puller to remove the bearing outer ring and bearing on each side of the differential carrier. It should be noted that the thrust sides of the bearings are marked for correct reassembly.

6. Release the lock washer tabs (12) and remove the eight bolts (11) holding the drive gear (13) to the differential case (20). Again mark the drive gear and differential case to ensure correct reassembly in their original positions.

7. Using a small diameter pin punch tap out the roll pins (16) retaining the centre pinion pin (17). Carefully drive out the centre pinion pin (17) using a suitable sized copper drift. Push the differential pinions (19) and concave thrust washers (18) around and remove from the case. Ease the two side gears (15) and thrust washers (14) towards the centre of the differential case and lift away through the openings in the case.

8. Clean all the removed parts in paraffin and dry. Examine the gears for wear, and chipped or damaged teeth; the thrust washers for wear or cracking; and the centre pinion for wear or loose fit in the differential housing.

9. If there was excessive noise in the drive or over run conditions this may be caused by excessive back lash between the differential pinions and differential

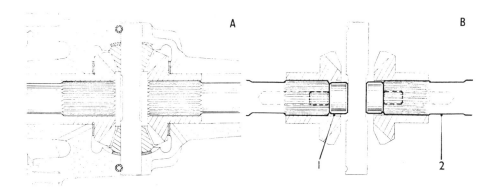

Fig. 10.1. DIFFERENTIAL ASSEMBLY - FIRST TYPE

A Plunging differential shafts   Up to 18AMW/U/H54626,   B Modified for plunging drive   1 Distance piece
  and fixed-length drive shafts   L42211   shafts   2 Second-type differential shaft

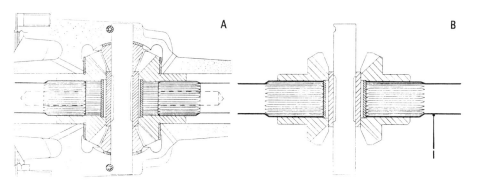

Fig. 10.2. DIFFERENTIAL ASSEMBLY - SECOND TYPE

A Plunging differential shafts   fixed-length drive shafts   to 89667, L42212 to 42273   shafts
  with foam-filled drilling,   Between 18AMW/U/H54627   B Modified for plunging drive   1 First-type differential shaft
  Welch-plugged gear, and

gears. Fit new pinion and/or differential gear thrust washers.

10. Check the bearings for side play and the races for general wear. Inspect the inner tracks for signs of movement on their mounting or the outer tracks rotating in their housing and if either of the conditions exists fit new parts.

11. Reassembly is the reverse procedure to dismantling. It is important that the differential gear thrust washers are fitted correctly. The slightly chamfered bores should be positioned against the machined face of the differential gears.

12. If new ball races are to be fitted to the differential case and new seals to the end covers a suitable press and assorted supporting blocks may be used provided care is taken to ensure that upon initial insertion they are fitting squarely.

13. Two types of differential assemblies have been used: these are shown in Fig. 10:1 and 10:2. When reassembling the first type of drive shafts, i.e. the sliding splines in the yoke type, the differential shafts should be modified to give a fixed condition. This is achieved by fitting a distance piece between the pinion centre pin and the differential shaft. Drive shafts of the later type as shown in Fig. 10:2 should be fitted.

If drive shafts with sliding splines are to be fitted to the second type unit it should be modified by fitting differential shafts of the first type as shown in Fig. 10:2.

3. Differential unit - reassembly and refitting

1. Replace the differential unit into the transmission case so that it is offset towards the flywheel end of the casing. Refit the final drive cover and just sufficiently tighten the retaining nuts so as to hold the bearings and yet allow the assembly to be moved crosswise by fitting the right hand end cover.

2. Replace the right hand end cover and a new gasket, taking care to ensure that the slots in the gasket line up with the oil holes in the end cover and the final drive cover. Refit the set screws and very carefully tighten in an even manner so ensuring maximum contact between the register on the inner face of the cover and the

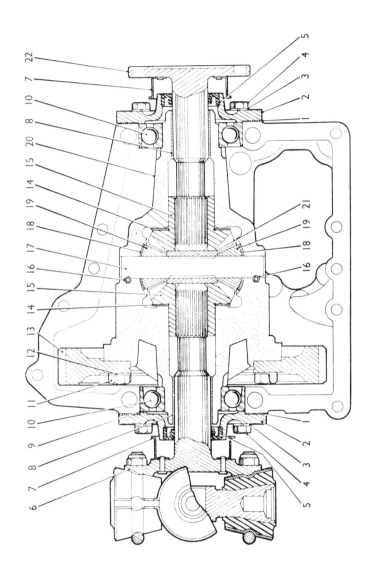

Fig. 10.3. THE DIFFERENTIAL UNIT

No.	Description	No.	Description	No.	Description
1	Joint washer	9	Shim – ball bearing to end cover	15	Differential gear
2	End cover	10	Ball bearing (double-purpose)	16	Roll pin – pinion centre
3	Spring washer	11	Bolt – final drive wheel	17	Pinion centre
4	Set screw – end cover to transmission case	12	Lock washer	18	Washer for differential pinion
5	Oil seal	13	Final drive wheel	19	Differential pinion
6	Differential shaft – flexible coupling type	14	Washer for differential gear	20	Differential case
7	Dust cover			21	Distance piece
8	Bush			22	Differential shaft – flange type

differential bearing outer track. It should be observed that as the setscrews are being tightened so the final drive assembly will move slightly away from the flywheel side of the engine.

3.   NOTE: Upon initial dismantling it may be found that there were shims on the flywheel side of the differential. If this were so the differential should be assembled in the transmission casing so that it is offset away from the flywheel end of the casing.

4.   The differential bearings must be preloaded and there are two methods of performing this adjustment Either is equally effective.

5.   Assemble the left hand final drive cover less its gasket and gently tighten the setscrews until the cover register just abuts to the bearing outer track. If the setscrews are over tightened the cover flange will be distorted necessitating fitting a new cover.

6.   With the aid of feeler gauges measure the slight clearance between the cover flange and the differential housing and transmission casing. Take this measurement in several places and the clearance should be identical in all cases. If differences are found the reason will be due to the setscrews being unevenly tightened causing the differential assembly to be drawn out of alignment. Slacken the setscrews and retighten again, taking care not to overtighten and so cause excessive tension on the cover. Re-measure the clearance.

7.   When a new gasket is fitted, its compressed thickness is 0.008 inch and the installed bearing must be pre-loaded by between 0.003 - 0.005 inch. The gap must therefore be 0.011 - 0.013 inch. Any excess gap, as determined with the feeler gauges and a small calculation, must be shimmed using special shims available in 0.0015 and 0.0025 inch thicknesses.

8.   Remove the end cover and fit a new gasket plus the required shims. Tighten the cover set screws in a diagonal pattern using a torque wrench set between 8 and 13 lb. ft.

9.   The second method requires an accurate depth gauge. First tighten the transmission casing nuts fully and eliminate all end clearance in the bearings by using a soft drift and hammer, and moving the bearing and differential towards the right hand end cover. Use the depth gauge and measure the depth from the casing to the bearing. The thickness of shim required, taking into account the pre-load, may be determined from the table below:

Depth of bearing (inch)	Shim thickness (inch)
0.113 - 0.114	none
0.115 - 0.116	0.0025
0.117 - 0.118	0.004
0.119 - 0.120	0.006
0.121 - 0.122	0.008
0.123 - 0.124	0.010

10.   Fit the end cover together with a new gasket and shims the thickness of which was determined from the above table. Tighten the end cover nuts in a diagonal pattern using a torque wrench set to between 8 and 13 lb ft.

11.   The differential shafts may now be refitted, the method being dependant on the type fitted.

12.   First type

Smear the splines of the differential shafts with Duckham's Lammol grease and refit the shaft.

13.   Second type

Carefully clean out all traces of oil and grease from the differential shaft cavities and refit each cavity with 3/8 ounce of Duckham's Lammol grease. Also smear the splines with the same grade grease and refit the shafts. Once the complete differential unit has been reassembled test the differential shafts by rotating together and ensuring that they both have equal resistance to turning. If unequal resistance is felt in one shaft compared with the other, this will cause the steering to pull in one direction.

Chapter 11/Braking System

Contents

Specifications

1800 1964-1967
1800 Mk II and 18/85 with 18H engine

Make	Girling hydraulic
Footbrake	Hydraulic on all four wheels
Handbrake (on rear wheel only)..	Mechanical
Type of brakes:	
Front	Disc - self adjusting
Rear	Drum - single leading screw
Disc diameter	9 $\frac{9}{32}$ inch (236 mm)
Drum diameter	9 inch (229 mm)
Total disc pad area	21 sq. in. (135.5 cm^2)
Total disc swept area..	183 sq. in. (1,180.6 cm^2)
Disc brake pad material	M78 (red/green/red/green/red)
Minimum pad wear thickness	1/16 inch (1.6 mm)
Drum brake lining dimensions	1.75 x 8.687 in. (44.5 x 220.65 mm)
Total swept area (drum brakes)..	99 sq. in. (639 cm^2)

Drum brake lining material   ... ...   DON 242
Minimum lining thickness... ... ...   Replace when worn to rivets
Wheel cylinder ... ...   .700 in. (17.8 mm) dia.
Early cars... ... ...   .75 in. (19.0 cm) dia.
Brake servo unit type.. ... ...   Girling Powerstop Mk II
Later cars... ... ...   Girling Powerstop Mk IIB
Master cylinder:

       Single type ... ...   C.V. with integral reservoir
                                               Diameter   .75 inch (19 mm)

       Tandem type . ...   C.V./I.V. with integral reservoir
                                               Diameter   .812 inch

Pressure regulating valve:

       Mounting angle - early cars ... ... 13°
                      later cars . ... 17°

Limiting valve ... ... 25°
Brake fluid... ... ...   Castrol Girling Amber

---

Brake Specifications and Data: 1800 Mk II 'S' and 18/85 Mk II 'S' with 18 H engine

The brake specification is identical to the 1800 Mk I except for the differences listed below:

Disc diameter ... ...   9.7 in. (246 mm)
Total disc pad area ... ...   27.6 sq in. ($178 cm^2$)
Total disc swept area.. ... ...   195 sq. in. (1,258 cm^2)
Disc brake pad material ... ...   DC1 (yellow/blue/blue/blue/yellow)

1. Drum brakes - general description

The two rear wheel drum brakes fitted are of the internal expanding type and are operated by either the hand brake, or by the brake pedal which is coupled to the brake master cylinder and hydraulic fluid reservoir mounted on the front bulkhead. The same hydraulic system also operates the front disc brakes.

The rear brakes are of the single leading shoe type, with one brake cylinder per wheel operating two shoes. Attached to each of the rear wheel operating cylinders is a mechanical expander operated by the handbrake lever through a cable which runs from the brake lever to the back-plate brake levers. This provides an independent means of rear brake application.

Drum brakes have to be adjusted periodically to compensate for wear in the linings. It is unusual to have to adjust the handbrake system as the efficiency of this system is largely dependant on the condition of the brake linings and the adjustment of the brake shoes. The handbrake can, however, be adjusted separately to the footbrake operated hydraulic system.

The hydraulic brake functions in the following manner: On application of the brake pedal, hydraulic fluid under pressure is pushed from the master cylinder to the brake operating cylinders at each wheel, by means of a four way union, steel pipe lines and flexible hoses.

A pressure regulating valve fitted into the pipe line leading to the rear brakes is mounted at an angle on the right hand wing valance. Under normal light brake action the valve does not operate and brake fluid passes freely to the rear brake wheel cylinders. If the brake pedal is suddenly depressed the ball in the valve assembly rolls up an incline and closes the valve. Pressure is built up in the hydraulic pipe lines and in the valve which will be sufficient to displace a spring loaded plunger. This will limit the pressure applied to the rear brakes. The pressure in the brake lines leading to the front disc brakes will rise as the brake pedal is further depressed. The action of this valve limiting the hydraulic pressure to the rear brake wheel cylinders will practically eliminate the tendency for the rear brakes to lock under emergency stopping conditions. The stop light switch is attached to the underside of the valve body.

2. Preventative maintenance - general

It is important that the complete braking system is at the peak of condition at all times. To safeguard against any premature wear or deterioration it is suggested that the following points be adhered to:

1. The front disc brake pads, rear drum linings, hoses, metal pipes and unions be examined at intervals of 3,000 miles.

2. The brake hydraulic fluid should be completely changed every 18 months or 24,000 miles whichever is sooner.

3. All seals in the brake master cylinder and wheel cylinders, and the flexible hoses should be examined and preferably renewed every 3 years or 40,000 miles whichever is sooner. The working surfaces of the master cylinder and wheel cylinders should be inspected for signs of wear or scoring and new parts fitted as considered necessary.

4. Only Castrol Girling Brake Fluid Amber should be used in the hydraulic system. Never leave brake hydraulic fluid in open unsealed containers as it absorbs moisture from the atmosphere which lowers the safe operating temperature of the fluid. Also any fluid drained or used for bleeding the system should not be re-used immediately.

5. Any work performed on the hydraulic system must be done under conditions of extreme care and cleanliness.

---

3. Drum brakes - maintenance

---

1. Every 3,000 miles, carefully clean the top of the brake master cylinder reservoir, (see Fig 11:1), remove the cap, and inspect the level of fluid which should be $\frac{1}{4}$ inch below the bottom of the filler neck. Ensure that the breather valve in the cap is free from dirt.

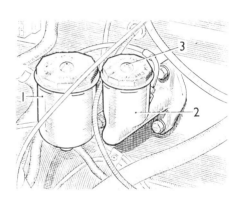

Fig. 11.1. MASTER CYLINDER LOCATION

No.	Description	No.	Description
1	Brake	3	Vent hole in cap
2	Clutch		

2. If the hydraulic fluid is below this level top up the reservoir with Castrol Girling Brake Fluid Amber. It is important that no other type of fluid is used. Use of a non-standard fluid will result in brake failure caused by the perishing of the special seals in the master and brake cylinders. If topping up becomes frequent then check the metal piping and flexible hoses for leaks, and check for worn brake or master cylinders which will also cause loss of fluid.

3. At intervals of 3,000 miles, or more frequently if pedal travel becomes excessive, adjust the brake shoes to compensate for wear of the brake linings.

4. At the same time lubricate all joints in the handbrake mechanism with an oil can filled with Castrolite or similar grade oil.

4. Brake system - bleeding

Whenever the brake hydraulic system has been overhauled, a part renewed or the level in the reservoir becomes too low, air will have entered the system necessitating its bleeding. During the operation the level of hydraulic fluid in the reservoir should not be allowed to fall below half full, otherwise air will be drawn in again.

1. Obtain a clean and dry glass jam jar, plastic tubing at least 12 inches long and able to fit tightly over the bleed nipples, and a supply of Castrol Girling Brake Fluid Amber.

2. Check that on each rear brake backplate the wheel cylinder is free to slide. Ensure that all connections are tight and all bleed screws are closed. Firmly apply the handbrake.

3. Fill the master cylinder and the bottom inch of the jam jar with hydraulic fluid. Take extreme care that no fluid is allowed to come into contact with the paintwork as it acts as a solvent and will damage the finish.

4. NOTE: The front disc brakes should be bled first EXCEPT where a tandem master cylinder is fitted when the rear brakes must be bled first. Remove the rubber dust cap from the bleed nipple and attach the bleed tube to the bleed screw on the front caliper which is furthest away from the master cylinder. Insert the other end of the bleed tube in the jar containing one inch hydraulic fluid. Use a suitable size open ended spanner and unscrew the bleed screw $\frac{1}{2}$ a turn.

5. A second person should now pump the brake pedal up and down commencing with one fast full stroke of the pedal followed by three short but rapid strokes and allow the pedal to fly back. Check the fluid level in the reservoir. Carefully watch the flow of fluid into the glass jar and when the air bubbles cease to emerge with the fluid during the next down stroke tighten the bleed screw. Remove the plastic tubing and replace the rubber dust cap. Using a torque wrench set to between 4 - 6 lb ft finally tighten the bleed screw. Top up the fluid in the reservoir.

6. Repeat operations in paragraphs 4 and 5 for the second front brake caliper as applicable.

7. The rear brakes should be bled in the same manner as the front except that each brake pedal stroke should be slow with a pause of three or four seconds between each stroke. This is to ensure that the ball in the 'G' valve does not seat on the valve insert. If the ball does move it can usually be heard to make contact with the valve insert and the brake pedal will be unable to continue its downward stroke. Should this occur, tighten the bleed screw and whilst depressing the brake pedal release the handbrake. This will unseat the ball from the valve insert. Re-apply the handbrake and continue the bleed sequence taking care that the fluid level in the reservoir does not drop below half full.

8. In several cases it has been found that the bleed operation for one or more cylinders is taking a considerable time and the cause is probably due to air being drawn past the bleed screw threads when the screw is loose. To counteract this condition it is recommended that at the end of each downward stroke the bleed screw be tightened to stop air being drawn past the threads.

10. If after the bleed operation has been completed the brake pedal operation still feels spongy this is an indication that there is still air in the system, or that the master cylinder is faulty.

NOTE: Never use the fluid bled from the hydraulic system immediately for topping up the master cylinder but allow to stand for at least twenty four hours in a sealed air tight container so allowing the minute air bubbles held in suspension to escape.

5. Flexible hose - inspection, removal and replacement

Inspect the condition of the flexible hydraulic hoses leading from the body mounted metal pipe to the brake backplate. If any are swollen, damaged, cut or chaffed, they must be renewed.

1. Unscrew the metal pipe union nut from its connection to the hose, and then holding the hexagon on the hose with a spanner, unscrew the attachment nut and washer.

2. The body end of the flexible hose can now be withdrawn from the chassis mounting bracket and will be quite free.

3. Disconnect the flexible hydraulic hose at the backplate by unscrewing it from the brake cylinder. NOTE: When releasing the hose from the backplate the chassis end must always be freed first.

4. Replacement is a straight reversal of the above procedure.

5. If a rear hose bracket is being renewed on early cars a bracket without a spigot will have been used. The new bracket will probably have a spigot requiring a hole 3/16 inch clearance and 1/8 inch deep along the centre line of the bracket.

6. Drum brakes - adjustment

1. Jack up the rear of the car and place on firm stands to avoid any accidents. Also check the front wheels to ensure that the car does not roll forwards or backwards.

2. The brakes on all models covered by this manual are taken up by turning the square headed adjuster located toward the top of each backplate, the position being shown in Fig 11:2. The edges of the adjuster are easily burred if an adjustable wrench or open ended spanner is used. Use a square headed brake adjusting spanner if possible. NOTE: When adjusting the rear brakes make sure that the handbrake is fully off.

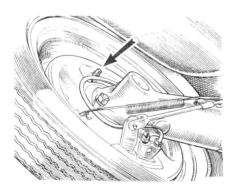

Fig. 11. 2. Rear brake shoe adjuster

3. Turn the adjuster a quarter of a turn at a time until the wheel is locked, do not force the adjuster. Then turn back the adjuster one notch so that the wheel will rotate without binding.

4. Spin the wheel and apply the brakes hard to centralise the shoes. Re-check that it is not possible to turn the adjusting screw further without locking the wheel.

NOTE: A rubbing noise when the wheel is spun is usually due to dust on the brake drum and shoe lining. If there is no obvious slowing of the wheel due to brake bonding there is no need to slacken off the adjusters until the noise disappears. It is better to remove the drum and de-dust taking care not to inhale any dust.

5. Repeat this process for the other brake drum. A good tip is to paint the head of the adjusting screws white which will facilitate future adjusting by making the adjuster heads easier to see. Also a little graphite penetrating oil on the adjuster threads will check any possible future seizure caused by rusting.

7. Drum brake shoe - inspection, removal and replacement

After high mileages it will be necessary to fit replacement brake shoes with new linings. Refitting new brake linings to shoes is not considered either economic or possible without the use of special equipment. However, if the services of a local garage or workshop having brake relining equipment are available then there is no reason why the original shoes should not be successfully relined. Ensure that correct specification linings are fitted to the shoes.

1. Check the front wheels, remove the rear wheel hub caps and loosen the wheel nuts. Jack up the rear of the car and place on firm supports to avoid any accidents. Remove the road wheel nuts and put in a safe place. Lift away the road wheel.

2. Using a wide blade screwdriver remove the two countersunk head screws holding the brake drum to the hub (photo A). Remove the brake drum (photo B). If

7.2a

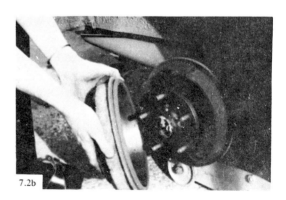

7.2b

the brake drum is tight slacken off the brake adjuster. If it will still not move away from the hub use a soft faced hammer and tap outwards on the circumference rotating the drum whilst completing this operation.

3. The brake linings should be renewed if they are so worn that the rivet heads are flush with the surface of the lining. If bonded linings are fitted they must be renewed when the lining material has worn down to 1/16 inch at its thinnest point.

4. Release the brake shoe web anti-rattle springs (photo) and slacken off the brake shoe adjustment if not previously done.

7.4

5. Make a note that the lining on the leading brake shoe is fitted towards the trailing end. Observe the position of the brake shoe return springs; the interrupted springs being at the wheel cylinder end. Also note into which holes the springs located in the brake shoe webs.

6. To remove the brake shoes lift the trailing end of the shoe from the abutment on the adjuster and the leading end from the wheel cylinder. Unhook the springs from the shoe webs and lift away (photo). It is recommended that strong elastic bands be used to keep the pistons in the wheel cylinders. If the shoes are to be left off for a while put a warning notice on the steering wheel not to depress the brake pedal otherwise the pistons will be ejected from the cylinder causing unnecessary work.

7.6

7. Thoroughly clean all traces of dust from the shoes, backplates and brake drums using a stiff brush. It is not recommended to use compressed air as it causes dust and it is important that it is not inhaled. Brake dust can cause judder or squeal and therefore it is important to clean out the brakes thoroughly.

8. Check that the piston is free in its cylinder and that

the rubber dust covers are undamaged and in position, and that there are no hydraulic fluid leaks. Ensure that the handbrake lever assembly is free and also that the brake adjuster operates correctly. Lubricate the threads on the adjusting wedge with a graphite based penetrating oil.

9. Prior to reassembly, smear a trace of Girling brake grease to all sliding surfaces and steady posts. Do not allow any grease to come into contact with the linings or rubber parts. Refit the shoes in the reverse sequence to removal taking care that the two pull off springs are located in the correct web holes, correctly positioned between web and backplate, and also that the shoes register correctly into the slotted ends of the wheel cylinder and adjuster.

10. Back off the adjuster and replace the brake drum, retaining counter sunk screws and road wheel. Adjust the brake as detailed in the previous section. Check correct adjustment of the handbrake and finally road test.

8. Rear brake wheel cylinder - removal, inspection and overhaul

If hydraulic fluid is leaking from the brake cylinder it will be necessary to dismantle the cylinder and replace the seal. If brake fluid is found running down the side of the wheel, or it is noticed that a pool of liquid forms alongside one wheel and the level in the master cylinder has dropped, proceed as follows:

1. Remove the brake drum and brake shoes as detailed in section 7. Clean down the rear of the backplate using a stiff brush. Place a quantity of rag under the backplate or a tray to catch any hydraulic fluid that may issue from the open pipe or wheel cylinder.

2. Carefully detach the hydraulic pipe from the rear of the wheel cylinder. Also disconnect the handbrake cable from the handbrake lever assembly at the rear of the backplate by removing the split pin and extracting the clevis pin noting that the head is uppermost. Remove the rubber boots.

3. Using a wide blade screwdriver separate the locking plate and wheel cylinder retaining spring plate, and carefully tap the retaining plate upwards so enabling it to be removed from its location in the neck of the wheel cylinder.

4. Withdraw the handbrake lever assembly from the wheel cylinder followed by the spring plate and shaped distance washer. Carefully pull the wheel cylinder assembly from the hub side of the brake backplate.

5. Ease away the retainer (20) Fig 11:3, followed by the piston dust cover (19) and withdraw the piston (17) from the cylinder. Remove the piston seal (18) using a non metal pointed rod or fingers. Do not use a metal screwdriver as this could scratch the piston.

6. Inspect the inside of the cylinder for score marks caused by impurities in the hydraulic fluid. If any are found the cylinder and piston will require renewal. NOTE: If the wheel cylinder requires renewal ensure that it is of the same diameter as originally fitted. The bodies are marked .7 for vehicles after commission number A17S12614A. Previously bodies marked $\frac{3}{4}$ were used.

7. If the cylinder is sound thoroughly clean it out with fresh hydraulic fluid.

8. The old rubber seal will probably be swollen and visibly worn. Smear the new rubber with hydraulic fluid and reassemble in the cylinder. Fit a new dust seal (19) and cylinder retaining clip (20).

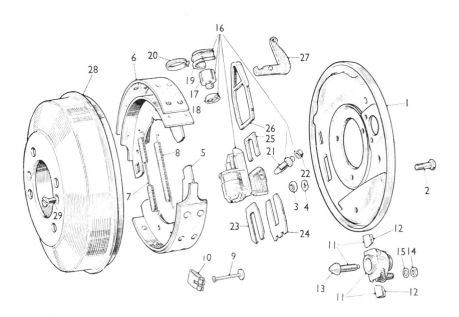

Fig. 11.3. REAR DRUM BRAKE COMPONENT PARTS

No.	Description
1	Backplate - with water ex-cluder
2	Bolt - backplate to radius arm
3	Nut for bolt
4	Spring washer
5	Brake-shoe assembly
6	Liner
7	Spring - shoe return - cy-linder end.

No.	Description
8	Spring - shoe return - adjuster end
9	Pin - brake-shoe steady
10	Spring - brake-shoe steady
11	Adjuster assembly
12	Tappet
13	Wedge
14	Nut - adjuster to backplate
15	Washer for nut (shakeproof)
16	Cylinder assembly - wheel

No.	Description
17	Piston
18	Seal for piston
19	Cover for piston - dust
20	Retainer for dust cover
21	Screw - bleeder
22	Cover for bleed screw - dust
23	Spring - retaining - wheel cylinder
24	Plate - locking

No.	Description
25	Washer - distance
26	Cover - dust - wheel cylinder to backplate
27	Lever assembly - hand brake
28	Drum - brake
29	Screw - drum to hub
30	Set screw - backplate to radius arm
31	Spring washer

9. Using Girling white brake grease smear the back-plate where the wheel cylinder slides and refit the brake wheel cylinder ensuring it is the correct way round. Refit the distance washer (25) between the wheel cylinder neck and the backplate ensuring that the cranked end of the distance washer is away from the handbrake lever assembly movement area. Also the two cranked lips must face away from the backplate. Replace the hand-brake lever assembly, followed by the locking plate (24) to be placed between the spring plate (23) and the distance washer (25). Carefully tap the locking plate into position until the two cranked lips of the spring plate locate in the locking plate (24).

10. Refit the rubber cover, connect the hydraulic pipe to the wheel cylinder and the handbrake cable to the handbrake lever. Replace the clevis with the head uppermost and lock using a new split pin.

11. Replace the brake shoes, drum and road wheel and finally bleed the hydraulic system and adjust the brakes.

9. **Brake shoes adjuster - removal and replacement**

1. Should it be found necessary to remove the brake

adjuster, first remove the road wheel, brake drum and brake shoes. Release the adjuster retaining nuts (14), Fig 11:3, and lift away the star washers (15). The adjuster can now be lifted away from the backplate.

2. Check that the screw (13) can be screwed both in and out to its fullest extent without showing signs of tightness.

3. Lift away the two tappets and thoroughly clean the adjuster assembly. Inspect the adjuster body and tappets for signs of excessive wear and fit new parts as necessary.

4. Lightly smear the tappets with Girling white brake grease and reassemble. Double check correct operation by holding the two tappets between the fingers and rotate the wedge whereupon the two tappets should move out together.

5. Refitting is the reverse procedure to dismantling. The two adjuster retaining nuts should be tightened to a torque wrench set to between 4 and 5 lb ft.

10. **Drum brake backplate - removal and replacement**

1. To remove the brake backplate first withdraw the hub, details of this operation being given in Chapter 13.

Next the flexible brake pipe must be disconnected from the rear of the wheel cylinder. Finally remove the handbrake attachment and the two screws and nuts, also one set screw that holds the brake backplate to the radius arm. The backplate may now be lifted away with the brake shoes, adjuster and wheel cylinder still in position.

2. Upon refitting it is important that a sealant is coated onto the face of the backplate which is in contact with the mounting face of the radius arm. Reassembly is the reverse procedure to removal.

---

11. Handbrake - adjustment

It is usual that when the rear brakes are adjusted any excessive free movement of the handbrake will automatically be taken up. However, in time the handbrake cables will stretch and it will be necessary to take up the free play by shortening the cable at the point where it is attached to the intermediate lever.

Never try to adjust the handbrake to compensate for wear on the rear brake linings. It is usually badly worn brake linings that lead to the excessive handbrake travel. If upon inspection the rear brake linings are in good condition or recently renewed and the handbrake tends to reach the end of its ratchet travel before the brakes operate, adjust the handbrake as follows:

1. Lock the rear brake shoes by rotating the adjustment screw as far as it will turn without forcing it.
2. Apply the handbrake on the fourth notch of its ratchet.
3. Adjust the nuts at the brake intermediate lever until the cable slackness has been removed. DO NOT OVERTIGHTEN the cables or the rear brakes will bind.
4. Release the handbrake and check that neither of the rear wheels are binding. It is very important that the wheels give equal resistance so that full braking benefit will be obtained. If it is found that both wheels do not offer the same resistance, remove the brake drum of the wheel which tends to bind and check that the brake shoe push off springs are fitted correctly and also that the wheel cylinder has not seized. Clean the brake backplate, shoes and drum and replace the drum. Adjust the brakes and finally road test.

---

12. Handbrake cable - removal and replacement

If the handbrake cables have stretched to the extent that adjustment is no longer possible, or if they are badly corroded or worn, they can be replaced as follows:

1. Chock the front wheels and release the handbrake.
2. Remove the two bolts and plain washers securing the handbrake control to the parcel shelf. Also remove the two bolts and spring washers retaining the handbrake control body to the toe-board.
3. Refer to Fig 11:5 and from underneath the car remove the split pin and plain washer from the clevis pin (13) holding the control cable fork (3) onto the uppermost part of the intermediate lever (11).
4. Remove the split pin and plain washer from the second clevis pin (13) securing the fork (20) to the lower part of the intermediate lever.
5. Remove the split pin locking the adjusting nut (18) to the fork (20) and unscrew both nuts (17 and 18).
6. Unscrew the two self tapping screws holding the cable bracket (52) to the under floor and lift away the screws and bracket.
7. Release the outer cable locknut from the heat shield

bracket. Withdraw the clevis pins placed between the cable rod forks and compensation lever (48). Extract the complete compensator unit once the locknut and flat washer have been removed. Carefully withdraw the cable through the heat shield to clear the guides.

8. The return spring (38) should now be unhooked if the brake rod (37) is to be removed, followed by extracting the split pins and plain washers from the clevis pins (13) on either end of the brake rod (37). Lift out the brake rod.

9. Replacement is the direct reversal of the above procedure but the following points should be noted:
(a) If there are no grease nipples fitted to the outer casing coat the inner cable with a graphite grease before refitting.
(b) Lubricate the compensation linkage.
(c) Adjust the intermediate cable as described in the previous section.

---

13. Reducing valve - removal, overhaul and reassembly

The objective of the reducing valve shown in Fig 11:4 is to provide maximum braking efficiency by controlling the brake line pressure to the front and rear brakes due to weight transference in conjunction with deceleration of the car. It is mounted at a pre-determined angle on the right hand wing valance. On early cars the valve was mounted on a bracket set at 17° with no identification mark, but on later cars a 13° mounting bracket with the figures 13 stamped on it was used. The brackets are not interchangeable. To remove the valve assembly proceed as follows:

1. Using a stiff brush clean the exterior of the valve body. Slacken a wheel cylinder bleed screw and using a piece of plastic tubing partially drain the hydraulic system.
2. Disconnect the four hydraulic fluid pipes from the

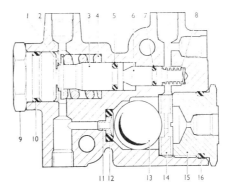

Fig. 11.4. REDUCING VALVE COMPONENT PARTS

No.	Description	No.	Description
1	Circlip - retainer	9	End plug
2	Abutment washer	10	Seal - end plug
3	Primary piston	11	Valve insert
4	Main spring	12	Valve seal
5	Seal 'O' ring - large	13	Ball
6	Secondary piston	14	Spacer - ball
7	Seal 'O' ring - small	15	Inlet plug
8	Spring - secondary	16	Seal - inlet plug

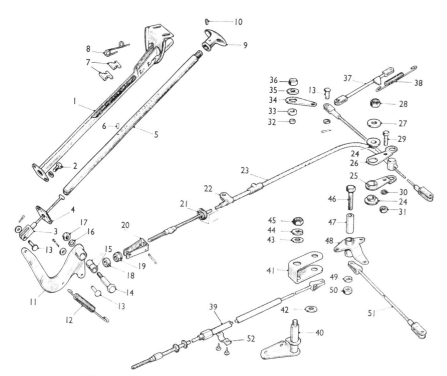

NOTE: Items 39-52 Hand brake cable and compensator assembly
From A17S-042816A, M17S-000671A.

Fig. 11.5. HANDBRAKE SYSTEM COMPONENT PARTS

No.	Description	No.	Description	No.	Description	No.	Description
1	Control body	15	Bushes	27	Plain washer	40	Pivot assembly - handle brake compensator
2	Screw - control to dash	16	Plain washer	28	Locknut		
3	Control cable	17	Locknut	29	Bolt)	41	Bracket
4	Joint washer	18	Locknut	30	Spring washer) Lever	42	Anti-rattle washer
5	Pull rod	19	Adjusting nut (use with split	31	Nut)	43	Plain
6	Pin - pull rod		pin)	32	Distance piece	44	Spring washer
7	Pawls	20	Fork	33	Bush	45	Nut
8	Spring - pawl pressure	21	Grommet - cable guide	34	Relay lever	46	Bolt
9	Tee handle	22	Clip - cable to floor	35	Plain washer	47	Distance tube
10	Pin - handle	23	Cable - intermediate to relay	36	Locknut	48	Compensating lever
11	Intermediate lever assembly		lever	37	Brake rod	49	Spring washer
12	Tension spring	24	Bush	38	Return spring	50	Nut
13	Clevis pin assemblies	25	Compensator lever - bottom	39	Cable - intermediate to re-	51	Cable right- or left-hand
14	Pivot pin	26	Compensator lever - top		lay lever	52	Clip - cable to floor

reducing valve and also the two wires from the stop light switch.

3. Unscrew the two securing bolts and lift away the reducing valve having first put an absorbant rag around the valve to absorb any hydraulic fluid which could drip onto the paintwork. Also wrap a clean non-fluffy rag around the ends of the four disconnected hydraulic pipes.

4. It is very important that if the valve is to be dismantled absolute cleanliness is observed at all times. Ensure that no mineral oil or grease is allowed to be anywhere near the valve assembly. Unscrew the inlet plug and invert the valve so that the spacer and ball can fall out.

5. Using a Whitworth tap of suitable size firmly screwed into the valve bore extract the valve and seal.

6. Remove the end plug and, by inverting and shaking the valve body, the primary and secondary piston assemblies should drop out.

7. Before inspecting the component parts, discard all old seals and thoroughly wash all parts using either Girling Cleaning Fluid or Industrial grade methylated spirits. Inspect the piston bores for score marks or ridges which if evident, mean that the unit must be renewed.

8. When reassembling utmost cleanliness must be observed and new seals fitted to ensure reliable operation.

9. Using Girling Red Rubber grease on the 'O' ring seals first fit the larger one to the primary piston after the circlip washer and main spring. The smaller 'O' ring should then be fitted to the secondary piston.

10. Carefully insert the secondary piston together with spring into the bore ensuring that the spring is not tilting but seating correctly at the bottom of the bore. Insert the primary piston with the circlip facing outwards into the bore taking care that no hydraulic fluid is trapped under the piston.

11. Screw the end plug with a new seal correctly fitted and lubricated into the body and tighten using a torque wrench set to 25 to 35 lb ft.

12. Using a mild steel drift with a 0.1 inch spigot and a 120° included angle shoulder machined at one end, very carefully fit a new valve seal and insert, correctly positioning them with the valve upright and lightly tapping the drift until they are in position.

13. Insert the ball followed by the spacer ensuring that it is correctly seating on the machined shoulder of the valve body. Fit a new seal to the inlet plug, lubricate with a smear of Girling Red Rubber grease, screw the plug into position and finally tighten using a torque wrench set at 25 to 35 lb ft. Refit the stop light switch.

14. The unit is now ready for refitting to the front right wing valance using the two securing bolts. It should be mounted at an angle of 13° (There will be a figure 13 stamped on the bracket) to the horizontal this being measured from across the top of the outlet faces, or 17° if of the earlier unmarked type. Remember that the brackets are not interchangeable and the angles cannot be altered under any circumstances.

15. Reconnect the stop light switch wires followed by the four hydraulic pipes. Take care that the unions are correctly seated and that the threads are not crossed before tightening. Finally fill the master cylinder reservoir and completely bleed the hydraulic system, full details of this operation being given in Section 4 of this Chapter.

14. Disc brakes - general description

Disc brakes are fitted to the front wheels of all models covered by this manual. They are of the rotating disc and rigid caliper design having two friction pads in each caliper.

Application of the foot brake creates hydraulic pressure in the master cylinder and this travels from the cylinder along the steel pipes and flexible hoses to two cylinders, one in each half of the caliper body. The hydraulic fluid pushes on the back of the pistons, which are in contact with the friction pads, and so by this action the rotating disc is squeezed on either side creating friction, thus giving the desired braking action.

Two rubber seals are fitted to the mouth of the operating cylinders. The outer seal prevents moisture and road dirt from entering the cylinder. The inner seal, which is retained in a groove just inside the cylinder, prevents hydraulic fluid leakage, and provides a running clearance for the pad irrespective of how worn it is, by moving it back a fraction when the brake pedal is released.

As the friction pad thickness decreases due to wear, so the pistons move further out of the cylinders and the level of the hydraulic fluid in the master cylinders reservoir drops. Disc pad wear is thus taken up automatically and eliminates the need for periodic adjustments by the owner.

15. Disc brakes - maintenance

1. Every 3,000 miles, check the level of the hydraulic fluid in the master cylinder reservoir, as detailed in Section 3.

2. At the same time examine the wear in the brake disc pads and change them round if one is very much more worn on one side of the rotating disc than on the other.

16. Disc brake friction pad (two piston design) - inspection, removal and replacement

1. Apply the hand brake. Chock the rear wheels, jack up the front of the car and place on firmly based supports. Remove the road wheels.

2. Inspect the thickness of the pad friction lining material and if it is less than 1/8 inch the pads must be renewed.

3. Remove the brake master cylinder reservoir cap and, using a plastic tube, syphon off hydraulic fluid to a new level of approximately half the available capacity. This operation is important as, when the pistons are moved into the caliper body to accommodate the new and thicker pads, fluid will be displaced from the caliper hydraulic cylinders to the master cylinder reservoir. This preparatory work will stop any accidental damage to paintwork due to hydraulic fluid overflowing.

4. Extract the split pins (1), see Fig 11:6 (photo A), from the pad retaining pins (2), and withdraw the two retaining pins (photo B).

5. Using a pair of pliers (photo) or hook lift away the pads (3) and anti-squeal shims if fitted. Note the correct location of the anti-squeal shims for correct reassembly.

6. Wipe down the piston faces using a dry non-fluffy rag and carefully push the two pistons back into the caliper body.

7. Replace the anti-squeal shims in their previously noted correct position followed by the new pads, ensuring that the pad friction material is facing towards the disc.

8. Insert the retaining pins with their heads on the same side as the four caliper body half clamping bolts and insert the split pins.

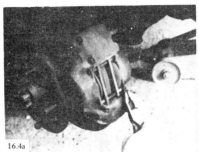
16.4a

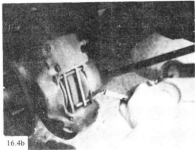
16.4b

16.5

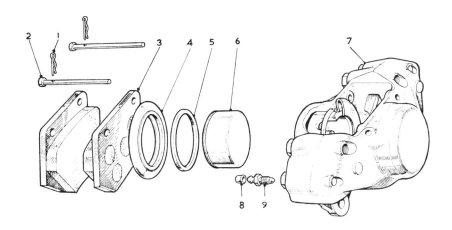

Fig. 11.6. EXPLODED VIEW OF FRONT BRAKE CALIPER UNIT

No.	Description	No.	Description
1	Split pin	6	Piston
2	Retaining pin	7	Caliper body
3	Pad assembly	8	Bleed nipple dust cover
4	Dust cover	9	Bleed nipple
5	Sealing ring		

9. Depress the brake pedal firmly several times to re-set the pistons and top up the hydraulic fluid in the master cylinder reservoir. Replace the road wheels, remove the supports and finally road test the car.

---

17. Disc and brake caliper (two piston design) - removal and dismantling

---

1. Apply the handbrake. Chock the rear wheels, jack up the front of the car and place on firmly based supports. Remove the road wheels.
2. Slacken the bleed screw and drain the hydraulic fluid from the brake pipe. Disconnect the flexible hose from the metal hydraulic pipe at the connection, referring to Section 5 for full details.
3. Remove the two bolts holding the caliper unit to the front hub. Lift away the caliper from the hub.
4. Extract the split pins (1) Fig 11:6, from the pad retaining pins (2) and withdraw the two retaining pins. Using a pair of pointed pliers or hook lift away the pads (3) and any anti-squeal shims for correct reassembly.
5. Thoroughly clean the exterior of the caliper taking care to remove all traces of any cleaning fluid before progressing further.
6. Using a small 'G' clamp hold the piston in the mounting half of the caliper. Temporarily re-connect the caliper to the flexible brake pipe. Do not allow the caliper to hang on the flexible hose but support it. Carefully depress the footbrake pedal and this will push the piston, in the rim half of the caliper, outwards. Release the dust cover (4) and then depress the footbrake pedal again until the piston (6) has been ejected enough to continue removal by hand. It is advisable to have a container or non-fluffy rag available to catch any hydraulic brake fluid once the piston is removed.
7. Using a tapered wooden rod or an old plastic knitting needle carefully extract the fluid seal (5) from its bore in the caliper half.

8. Remove the 'G' clamp from the mounting half piston. Temporarily refit the rim half piston and repeat the operations in paragraphs 6 and 7 above.
9. Thoroughly clean the internal parts of the caliper using only Girling Cleaning Fluid or Industrial Methylated spirits. Any other fluid cleanser will damage the internal seals between the two halves of the caliper. DO NOT SEPARATE THE TWO HALVES OF THE CALIPER.
10. To reassemble the caliper first wet a new fluid seal with Castrol Girling Brake Fluid Amber and carefully insert it into its groove in the rim half of the caliper seating, ensuring that it is correctly fitted. Refit the dust cover into its special groove in the cylinder.
11. Release the bleed screw in the caliper one complete turn. Coat the side of the piston with hydraulic fluid and with it positioned squarely in the top of the cylinder bore ease the piston in until approximately 5/16 inch is left protruding. Engage the outer lip of the dust cover in the piston groove and push the piston into the cylinder as far as it will go.
12. Repeat the operations in paragraphs 10 and 11 above for the mounting half of the caliper.
13. Refit the caliper to the hub and tighten the two mounting bolts using a torque wrench set at 45 to 50 lb ft.
14. Replace or renew the pads as necessary together with the anti-squeal shims. Insert the retaining pins and lock with the split pins. Reconnect the flexible hydraulic brake pipe and bleed the system as described in Section 4. Replace the road wheels, remove the supports and finally road test the car.

It is usually unnecessary for the disc to be removed from the front hub except when the run out at the outer periphery of the braking surface is in excess of 0.008 inch or there is deep scoring.

If the maximum runout is exceeded the disc should be removed, details of which are given in Chapter 13, and repositioned on the drive shaft splines. Score marks are not serious provided that they are concentric but not excessively deep. It is far better to fit a new disc rather than to re-grind the original one.

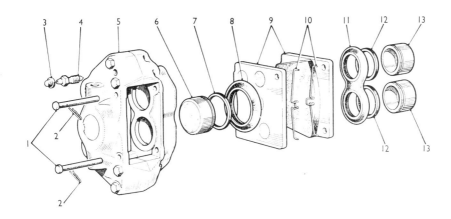

Fig. 11.7. EXPLODED VIEW OF FRONT BRAKE CALIPER UNIT AS FITTED TO 1800 MK II 'S' MODELS

No.	Description	No.	Description	No.	Description	No.	Description
1	Retaining pin	5	Caliper body	8	Boot	11	Boot
2	Split pin	6	Piston (inner)	9	Pad assembly	12	Sealing ring
3	Bleed nipple dust cover	7	Sealing ring	10	Anti-rattle spring	13	Piston (outer)
4	Bleed nipple						

18. Disc brake friction pad (three piston design) - inspection, removal and replacement

The 1800 Mk II, 1800 Mk II 'S' and later 18/85 models were fitted with a larger disc brake caliper unit having three pistons instead of two, see Fig 11:7. To check and fit new pads, if necessary, proceed as follows:

1. Apply the handbrake, chock the rear wheels, jack up the front of the car and place on firmly based supports. Remove the road wheels.
2. Inspect the thickness of the pad friction lining material and if it is less than 1/8 inch the pads must be renewed.
3. Remove the brake master cylinder reservoir cap and, using a plastic tube, syphon off hydraulic fluid to a new level approximately half the capacity of the reservoir when full. This operation is important as, when the pistons are moved into the caliper body to accommodate the new and thicker pads, fluid will be displaced from the caliper hydraulic cylinders to the master cylinder reservoir. This preparatory work will stop any accidental damage to paintwork due to the hydraulic fluid overflowing.
4. Extract the split pins (2) see Fig 11:7, from the pad retaining pins (1) and withdraw the two retaining pins. Take great care that the anti-rattle springs (10) do not fly out as the retaining pins are withdrawn. A hand suitably placed over the caliper will stop this happening.
5. Using a pair of pointed pliers or hook lift away the pads (9) and any anti-squeal shims. Note the correct location of the anti-squeal shims for correct reassembly.
6. Wipe down the piston faces using a non-fluffy rag and carefully push the three pistons back into the caliper body.
7. Replace the anti-squeal shims in their previously noted correct position followed by the new pads ensuring that the pad friction material is facing towards the disc. Replace the retaining pins (1) and anti-rattle springs (10) and lock in place using the split pins.

8. Depress the brake pedal firmly several times to re-set the three pistons and top up the hydraulic fluid in the master cylinder reservoir. Replace the road wheels, remove the supports and finally road test the car.

19. Disc and brake caliper (three piston design) - removal and dismantling.

The procedure for removing the disc and also the caliper is identical to that for the two piston design. Also identical is the overhaul procedure for the caliper except that there are two pistons on one side and one on the other. Remove the rim half pistons first, followed by the mounting half piston.

20. Brake pedal - removal and replacement

1. The brake pedal is removed by first withdrawing the split pin from the brake master cylinder push rod clevis pin and extracting the cotter pin. Unhook the brake pedal return spring and undo the nut from the end of the brake pedal fulcrum bolt. Lift away the washer. Carefully withdraw the fulcrum bolt together with the brake pedal, an internal distance sleeve and a spacing washer.
2. Refitting is the reverse procedure to removal. Ensure that the head of the fulcrum bolt is facing towards the outside of the pedal assembly. The brake pedal mounting fitted to a car with automatic transmission is identical to that fitted to a manual transmission except that care must be taken to note the location of an additional spacer between the pedal and bracket and a flat washer to the pedal fulcrum bolt.

21. Brake master cylinder (Girling type C.U. - single) - removal and replacement

1. Apply the handbrake and chock the front wheels.

Drain the fluid from the master cylinder reservoir by attaching a rubber tube to one of the brake bleed screws, undoing the screw one turn, and then pumping the fluid out into a suitable container by means of the brake pedal. Hold the pedal against the floor at the end of each stroke and tighten the bleed nipple. When the pedal has returned to its normal position, loosen the bleed nipple and repeat the process until the master cylinder reservoir is empty.

2. Wipe the master cylinder hydraulic pipe connection with a clean non-fluffy rag and disconnect the union. Wrap the end in a piece of clean rag to stop dirt ingress or fluid dripping onto the paintwork. Plug the master cylinder union connection to stop accidental dirt entering into the master cylinder.

3. Extract the split pin from the yoke on the end of the push rod (9), Fig 11:8, lift away the plain washer (12) and withdraw the clevis pin (11).

4. Remove the fixing bolt (16) and spring washer (15) from the underside of the master cylinder and the nut (17) and spring washer from the top of the master cylinder mounting flanges to the bulkhead and carefully ease the master cylinder away from the bulkhead.

5. The master cylinder refitting procedure is the reverse to removal but care must be taken when offering up to the bulkhead that the pushrod is in line with the brake pedal. Once connections have been made the complete hydraulic system must be bled and the car road tested.

Fig. 11.8. MASTER CYLINDER COMPONENT PARTS (NON SERVO

No.	Description	No.	Description
1	Valve seal		cylinder
2	Spring washer - curved	12	Plain washer
3	Valve stem	13	Dust cover
4	Valve spacer	14	Packing
5	Spring	15	Spring washer
6	Spring retainer	16	Screw
7	Plunger seal	17	Nut - stud
8	Plunger	18	Master cylinder to servo uni
9	Push-rod and retaining washer		pipe
		19	Filler cap gasket
10	Circlip - push-rod	20	Filler cap
11	Clevis pin - pedal to master		

NOTE: Inset shows correct assembly of spring washer in centre valve

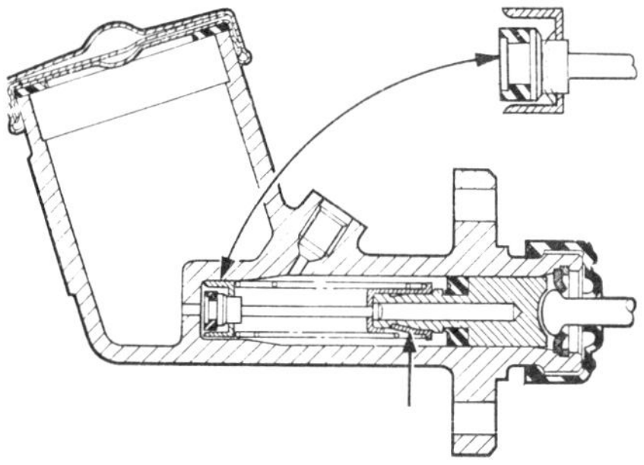

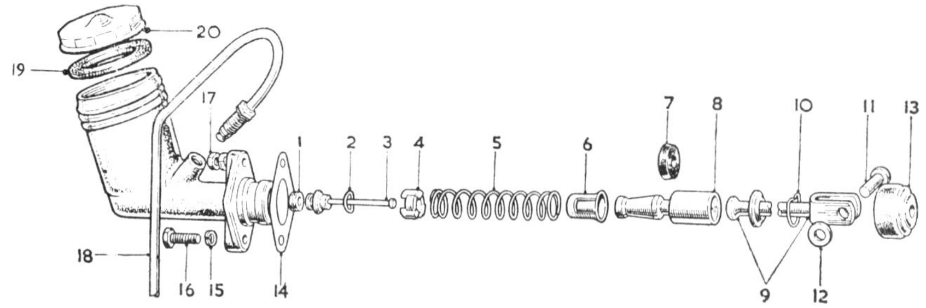

22. Brake master cylinder (Girling type C.U. - single) - dismantling and reassembly

If a replacement master cylinder is to be fitted it will be necessary to lubricate the seals before fitting to the car as they have a protective coating when originally assembled. Remove the blanking plug from the hydraulic pipe union seating. Ease back and remove the pushrod dust cover so that clean brake fluid can be injected at these points. Operate the piston several times so that the fluid will spread over all internal working surfaces.

If the master cylinder is to be dismantled after removal proceed as follows:

1. Ease back the pushrod cover (13), Fig 11:8, and remove the circlip (10) so that the pushrod and dished washer (9) can be withdrawn. This exposes the plunger (8) with a seal (7) attached, and this must be removed as a unit. The assembly is separated by lifting the thimble leaf over the shouldered end of the plunger. The seal should then be eased off using the fingers only.

2. Depress the plunger return spring (5) allowing the valve stem (3) to slide through the keyhole in the thimble (6), thus releasing the tension in the spring.

3. Detach the valve spacer (4) taking care of the spacer spring washer (2) which will be found located under the valve head.

4. Examine the bore of the cylinder carefully for any signs of scores or ridges, and if this is found to be smooth all over, new seals can be fitted. If there is

any doubt of the condition of the bore then a new cylinder must be fitted.

5. If examination of the seals shows them to be apparently oversize or swollen, or very loose on the plunger, suspect oil contamination in the system. Ordinary lubricating oil will swell these rubber seals, and if one is found to be swollen it is reasonable to assume that all seals in the braking system will need attention.

6. Thoroughly clean all parts in either Girling Cleaning Fluid or Industrial methylated spirits. Ensure that the bypass ports are clean.

7. All components should be assembled wet by dipping in clean brake fluid. Fit a new valve seal (1), Fig 11:8, the correct way round so that the flat side is correctly seating on the valve head. Place the dished washer (2) with the dome against the underside of the valve head as shown in Fig 11:8. Hold it in position with the valve spacer (4) ensuring that the legs face towards the valve seal.

8. Replace the plunger return spring (5) centrally on the spacer, insert the thimble (6) into the spring and depress until the valve stem (3) engages in the keyhole of the thimble.

9. Ensure that the spring is central on the spacer before fitting a new plunger seal (7) onto the plunger with the flat face against the face of the plunger (8), and also fit a new back seal (13).

10. Insert the reduced end of the plunger (8) into the thimble (6) until the thimble engages under the shoulder of the plunger and press home the thimble leaf.

11. Check that the master cylinder bore is clean and smear with clean brake fluid. With the plunger suitably wetted with brake fluid carefully insert the assembly into the bore with the valve end first. Ease the lips of the plunger seal carefully into the bore.

12. Replace the pushrod (9) and refit the circlip (10) into the groove in the cylinder body. Smear the sealing areas of the dust cover with Girling Rubber Grease and pack the cover with the rubber grease to act as a dust trap and fit the master cylinder body. The master cylinder is now ready for refitting to the car.

---

23. Brake master cylinder (single-servo mounted) – dismantling and reassembly

---

The master cylinder although of a slightly different construction in having a detachable reservoir instead of being integral with the body, is serviced in an identical manner to the master cylinder previously described. Fig 11:9 shows all the components. The bolt adaptor (5) must be tightened using a torque wrench set to 20 - 25 lb ft upon reassembly and there is no joint washer between the master cylinder mounting flange and the servo unit.

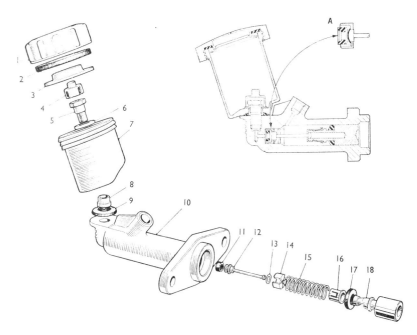

Fig. 11.9. MASTER CYLINDER COMPONENT PARTS (DIRECT ACTING SERVO)

No.	Description	No.	Description	No.	Description	No.	Description
1	Filler cap)	6	Washer	11	Valve seal	15	Spring
2	Gasket) assembly	7	Reservoir	12	Valve stem	16	Spring retainer
3	Baffle)	8	Spacer	13	Spring washer - curved	17	Seal
4	Baffle	9	Washer-seal	14	Valve spacer	18	Plunger
5	Adaptor	10	Cylinder body				

NOTE: Inset A shows correct assembly of spring washer in centre valve.

24. Brake master cylinder (tandem-servo mounted) – removal and replacement

The tandem master cylinder shown in Fig 11:10 comprises two independent cylinders, one known as the primary is connected to the front disc brakes, and the other known as secondary is connected to the rear drum brakes. By having this arrangement, should one system fail the second system will usually be operative.

The combined operation comes into effect when the brake pedal is depressed and the servo pushrod moves the primary plunger up its bore and the tipping valve closes the primary supply port. Once closed any further movement of the servo pushrod applies pressure to the front brakes. Simultaneously this pressure, together with the increasing pressure of the intermediate spring, overcomes the secondary spring and the secondary plunger moves down the bore. As with the primary plunger, first movement closes the secondary supply port and hydraulic pressure is transmitted to the rear drum brakes via the hydraulic pipes.

To remove the master cylinder proceed as follows:

1. Apply the handbrake and chock the front wheels. Slacken the bleed screw on one of the rear wheel cylinder bleed screws and drain the hydraulic master cylinder secondary bore and reservoir fluid. Slacken the front wheel caliper bleed screw and drain hydraulic fluid from

the master cylinder primary bore.

2. Wipe the master cylinder hydraulic pipe connections with a clean non-fluffy rag and disconnect the unions. Wrap the end in a piece of clean rag around the unions to stop dirt ingress or fluid dripping onto the paintwork. Plug the master cylinder union connections to stop accidental dirt entering into the master cylinders.

3. Remove the two master cylinder to servo unit mounting nuts, lift away the spring washers and withdraw the master cylinder.

4. The master cylinder refitting procedure is the reverse to removal. Bleed the complete hydraulic system and road test the car to check for satisfactory operation.

25. Brake master cylinder (tandem-servo mounted) – dismantling and reassembly

1. Refer to Fig 11:10 and remove the two screws holding the reservoir (4) to the cylinder body (10). Lift away the reservoir. Using a suitable size Allen key or wrench unscrew tipping valve nut (7) and lift away the seal (9). Using a suitable diameter rod push the primary plunger (20) down the bore, this operation enabling the tipping valve (8) to be withdrawn.

2. Using a compressed air jet very carefully applied to the rear outlet pipe connection blow out all the master

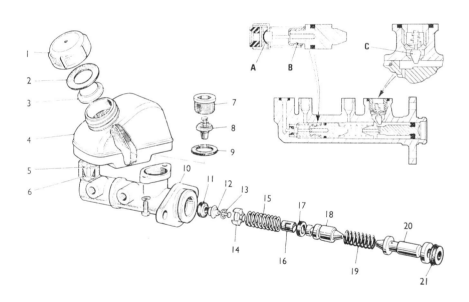

Fig. 11.10. MASTER CYLINDER COMPONENT PARTS (TANDEM, DIRECT ACTING SERVO)

No. Description	No. Description	No. Description	No. Description
1 Filler cap)	7 Securing nut	12 Valve stem	17 Seal
2 Gasket)Assembly	8 Tipping valve	13 Spring washer – curved	18 Secondary plunger
3 Baffle)	9 Face seal	14 Valve spacer	19 Intermediate spring (black)
4 Reservoir – dual	10 Cylinder body	15 Secondary spring	20 Primary plunger
5 Circlip – internal	11 Valve seal	16 Spring retainer	21 Gland seal
6 Seal			

A Correct assembly of spring washer in centre valve
B Leaf of spring retainer

C As the brakes are applied the primary plunger moves down the cylinder and al-

lows the tipping valve (C) to close the primary supply port. The assembly

shows the unit in the off position.

cylinder internal components. Alternatively shake out all the parts. Take care that adequate precautions are taken to ensure all parts are caught as they emerge.

3. Separate the primary and secondary plungers from the intermediate spring. Use the fingers to remove the gland seal (21) from the primary plunger.

4. The secondary plunger assembly should be separated by lifting the thimble leaf (16) over the shouldered end of the plunger (18). Using the fingers remove the seal (17) from the secondary plunger.

5. Depress the secondary spring (15) allowing the valve stem (12) to slide through the keyhole in the thimble (16) thus releasing the tension on the spring.

6. Detach the valve spacer (14) taking care of the springwasher (13) which will be found located under the valve head.

7. Examine the bore of the cylinder carefully for any signs of scores or ridges, and if this is found to be smooth all over, new seals can be fitted. If there is any doubt of the condition of bore, then a new cylinder must be fitted.

8. If examination of the seals shows them to be apparently oversize or swollen, or very loose on the plungers, suspect oil contamination in the system. Oil will swell these rubber seals, and if one is found to be swollen, it is reasonable to assume that all seals in the braking system will need attention.

9. Thoroughly clean all parts in either Girling Cleansing Fluid or Industrial methylated spirits. Ensure that the by-pass ports are clear.

10. All components should be assembled wet by dipping in clean brake fluid. Using fingers only, fit new seals (17 and 21) to the primary and secondary plungers (8 and 20) ensuring that they are the correct way round. Place the dished washer (13) with the dome against the underside of the valve seat as shown in Fig 11:10. Hold it in position with the valve spacer (14) ensuring that the legs face towards the valve seal.

11. Replace the plunger return spring (15) centrally on the spacer, insert the thimble (16) into the spring (15) and depress until the valve stem (12) engages in the keyhole of the thimble.

12. Insert the reduced end of the plunger (18) into the thimble (16) until the thimble engages under the shoulder of the plunger and press home the thimble leaf. Replace the intermediate spring (19) between the primary (20) and secondary (18) plungers.

13. Check that the master cylinder bore is clean and smear with clean brake fluid. With the complete assembly suitably wetted with brake fluid carefully insert the assembly into the bore. Ease the lips of the plunger seals (17 and 21) carefully into the bore. Push the assembly fully home.

14. Refit the tipping valve assembly (8) and seal (9) to the cylinder bore and tighten the securing nut to a torque wrench setting of 35 - 45 lb ft. Replace the hydraulic fluid reservoir (4) and tighten the two retaining screws.

15. The master cylinder is now ready for refitting to the servo unit. Bleed the complete hydraulic system and road test the car.

26. Vacuum servo unit - general

A vacuum servo unit is fitted into the brake hydraulic circuit in series to provide assistance to the driver when the brake pedal is depressed. This reduces the effort required by the driver to operate the brakes under normal and emergency braking conditions.

The unit operates by vacuum obtained from the induction manifold and comprises basically a booster diaphragm, control valve, slave cylinder and a non-return valve.

Two different servo units can be found on the cars covered by this manual, the Girling 'Powerstop' Mk II and the Girling 'Super Vac'. Both of these are shown in illustration form together with details of servicing. It is recommended that a service exchange unit be fitted in preference to overhaul.

The servo unit and hydraulic master cylinder are connected together so that the servo unit piston rod acts as the master cylinder pushrod. The driver's braking effort is transmitted through another pushrod to the servo unit piston and its built-in control system. The servo unit piston does not fit tightly into the cylinder but has a strong diaphragm to keep its edges in constant contact with the cylinder walls so assuring an air tight seal between the two pads. The forward chamber is held under vacuum conditions created in the inlet manifold of the engine and during periods when the brake pedal is not in use, the controls open a passage to the rear chamber so placing it under vacuum conditions as well. When the brake pedal is depressed the vacuum passage to the rear chamber is cut off and the chamber opened to atmospheric pressure. The consequent rush of air pushes the servo piston forward in the vacuum chamber and operates the main push rod to the master cylinder.

The controls are designed so that assistance is given under all conditions and when the brakes are not required, vacuum in the rear chamber is established when the brake pedal is released. All air from the atmosphere entering the rear chamber is passed through a small air filter.

Three types of brake servo unit are to be found on models covered by this manual and service instructions for each of the three units are given under their respective model headings. It must be emphasised that if a servo unit requires overhaul it is far better to obtain a service exchange unit rather than repair the original unit.

27. Girling 'Powerstop' Mk II - removal and refitting

1. Wipe the area around the two hydraulic pipe connections on the servo unit with a clean rag, and unscrew the two connections. Plug the two pipes to stop dirt entry.

2. Remove the connection of the vacuum hose from the non-return valve on the servo unit. Finally unscrew the three bolts holding the servo unit to the mounting brackets and carefully lift away the unit.

3. Refitting is the reverse procedure to removal but it will be necessary to bleed the brake hydraulic system, instructions for which are given in Section 4 of this Chapter.

28. Girling 'Powerstop' Mk II - dismantling, inspection and reassembly

Thoroughly clean the outside of the unit using a stiff brush and wipe with a non-fluffy rag. It cannot be too strongly emphasised that cleanliness is vitally important when working on the unit. To dismantle proceed as follows:

1. Mount the unit in a firm vice holding it by the mounting lugs on the body. For figures in brackets refer to Fig 11:12.

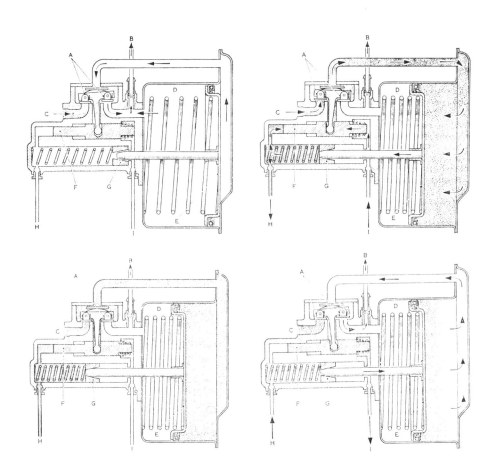

Fig. 11.11. DIAGRAMMATIC OPERATION OF VACUUM SERVO UNIT

No.	Description	No.	Description
A	Air valves	F	Control piston assembly
B	To inlet manifold	G	Output piston
C	Air inlet	H	From wheel cylinders
D	Vacuum cylinder	I	To master cylinder
E	Vacuum piston		

2. Unscrew the seven nuts (35) and bolts (36) holding the cylinder cover (45) to the vacuum cylinder (37). Take care about this operation as the cover will be under pressure from the piston return spring (41). It will be observed that two of the nuts retain the vacuum pipe cover. Lift away the end cover (45), joint washer (44), piston and seal assembly (42) and the return spring (41).

3. Carefully inspect the piston rod for signs of score marks. If these are evident it is not worthwhile continuing to dismantle and overhaul, so reassemble the unit and obtain a service exchange unit.

4. Remove the three screws (40) together with their copper washers (39) and lift away the clamp plate (38) from inside the vacuum cylinder. Carefully separate the body from the cylinder at the same time easing the

vacuum pipe (25) from its rubber grommet (34) in the cylinder flange. If tight, lubricate lightly.

5. Unscrew the screw (30) and lift away the air filter cover and air filter element (29). Also unscrew the four screws (27) holding the valve chest cover (25) to the body (1). Lift away the cover with the vacuum pipe attached and the gasket (24).

6. Locate and remove the two screws (23) from inside the valve and chest and withdraw the valve retaining plate and the valves with their rocking lever (20). It will be observed that the two valve plates are attached to the rocking lever by two separate clips.

7. Carefully separate the gasket (19) from the face of the body (1) and tap the face of the body on a soft wood block so as to remove the plug (10) which seals the upper

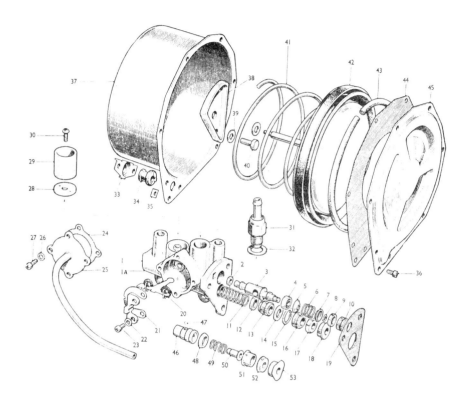

Fig. 11.12. GIRLING "POWERSTOP" MK II SERVO UNIT COMPONENT PARTS

No.	Description	No.	Description	No.	Description	No.	Description
1	Body - with circlip groove*	14	Flat washer*	28	Seal - air filter to body	41	Vacuum piston spring
1a	Body ⨍	15	Circlip*	29	Air filter element	42	Vacuum piston
2	Control piston seal - small	16	Spacer*	30	Screw	43	Seal - backing ring
3	Control piston	17	Gland seal*	31	Non-return valve	44	Joint washer - 2 off
4	Control piston seal - large	18	Guide bush*	32	Gasket	45	End cover
5	Spring abutment	19	Gasket - cylinder to body	33	Retaining plate	46	Output piston ⨍
6	Piston return spring	20	Valve assembly	34	Rubber grommet	47	Ball - fluid return ⨍
7	Spring retainer	21	Valve return spring	35	Nut	48	Taper seal ⨍
8	Circlip - retainer	22	Flat washer	36	Set screw	49	Spring - sleeve return ⨍
9	Taper seal - plug	23	Set screw	37	Vacuum cylinder	50	Sleeve ⨍
10	Plug	24	Gasket - vacuum pipe to body	38	Clamping plate	51	Spacer ⨍
11	Piston return spring	25	Vacuum pipe	39	Washer - copper	52	Gland seal ⨍
12	Taper seal*	26	Shakeproof washer	40	Set screw	53	Guide bush ⨍
13	Output piston*	27	Set screw				

*First-type output piston

⨍ Second-type output piston

valve control piston bore. Assisted by the piston return spring (6) withdraw the control piston assembly. If it is necessary to dismantle the control piston assembly compress the spring (6) and using a pair of circlip pliers or suitable equivalent extract the circlip (8) from the larger diameter end. This will release the spring retainer (7) and spring (6). Note the way the seals (4 and 5) are fitted and remove these with the fingers.

8. The next item to remove is the output piston but one of two types may be fitted, these being shown in Fig 11: 12. With the first type extract the valve guide bush (18) and using a small electrician's screwdriver lift out the

nylon spacer (16). Remove the circlip (15) from its groove using a pair of circlip pliers. The piston return spring (11) will then push the output piston assembly from the bore.

With the second type assembly withdraw the valve guide bush (53) and placing the thumb over the side of the bore carefully ease up the gland seal (52) using an electrician's screwdriver. The piston return spring will then push the piston assembly (46) forward. Lift the ball bearing (47) from the piston and put in a safe place to prevent loss.

9. A tapered seal (52) is situated in a groove on the

outside of the piston whilst a second seal is retained in place by a washer (second type) or cup (first type) in the end of the piston. The latter acts as a seal so that when the brakes are applied the end of the piston rod is sealed. This item cannot be serviced on its own so if at all suspect a new output piston assembly must be fitted.

10. The component parts are now ready for inspection. Remove all the old seals and clean all parts, except the bore of the vacuum cylinder, with Girling Cleaning Fluid or Industrial methylated spirits. The vacuum cylinder bore must not be cleaned as it is pre-lubricated with a special lubricant during initial assembly. Carefully examine the piston bores for signs of pitting, scoring or ridging and, if satisfactory, new seals can be fitted. If the bores are suspect a new unit must be fitted. Inspect the piston return springs for signs of cracking or loss of tension and fit new as necessary.

11. When reassembling all parts relative to the hydraulic system they should be well lubricated and absolute cleanliness observed. Always fit new seals upon reassembly.

12. Fit a new taper seal (12 or 28) to the output piston so that the taper faces away from the seal in the end of the piston. As was noted upon dismantling, two types of output piston assemblies have been fitted so these will be dealt with individually.

With the first type refit the return spring (11), the piston (13) and the washer (14). Carefully press these components into the bore against the piston spring pressure and very gently insert the circlip (5) into the groove. Check that it seats correctly. Insert the large end of the seal spacer (16) so that the taper is towards the guide bush followed by the gland seal (17) and finally insert and push home the guide bush (18).

When reassembling the second type place the ball bearing (47) into the location and assemble the sleeve return spring (49), the sleeve (50), and return spring (11). Use the operating piston rod to hold the spacer (51), gland seal (52) and guide bush (53) against the sleeve (50) and carefully push the above assembled parts down the bore. This operation is shown in Fig 11:13.

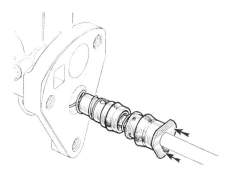

Fig. 11.13. Correct way of inserting the second type output piston assembly using the operating piston rod.

13. Lubricate and fit new seals to the valve control piston (3) ensuring that the large tapered seal is positioned so that the taper is facing away from the spring. Position the abutment washer (5) and spring retaining washer (7) on the piston and press the spring down and insert the circlip (8) into its groove. Check that it is seating correctly.

14. Insert the above piston assembly into its bore and carefully align the hole in the piston with the hole situated in the side of the bore.

15. Refit the valve plates to the valve rocking lever (20) and replace the assembly into the valve chest. Engage the ball end of the lever into the valve control piston (3). Place the valve spring (21) and retainer over the valve assembly and hold in position by tightening the two screws (23) and washers (22). Depress and release the valve operating piston and ensure that the valves operate freely. The valve nearest the body flange should be open and the other valve closed when in the normal position.

16. Fit a new seal into the groove in the valve control bore plug (10). Position the plug (10) into the bore until its face stands 1/16 inch proud of the body face. Refit the valve chest cover with pipe attached (25) with a new gasket (24) and secure using four screws (27) and washers (26).

17. Fit a new air filter element (29) followed by the cover and tighten the retaining screw (30). Position the retaining plate (33) onto the vacuum pipe (25). Fit a new gasket between the body and the cylinder and position the cylinder (37) carefully easing the vacuum pipe (25) into the centre of the grommet (34) in the flange of the cylinder. Offer the clamp plate (38) to the inside of the cylinder and tighten the three bolts (40) and washers (39) using a torque wrench set to between 10 and 12 lb ft.

18. Very lightly lubricate the piston seal (42) with 'Rocol Moly Cue' servo unit lubricant and fit a new sponge rubber joint ring (43). Replace the return spring (41) and insert the piston assembly into the cylinder taking care not to damage the piston seal or the rod and central bearing guide bush (18). Ease the piston down the bore, fit a new joint washer (44) between the cylinder and end cover (45) and secure the end cover with the seven screws and nuts. Do not forget to refit the retaining plate (33) whilst replacing the three screws at the lower corner of the cover.

19. The servo unit is now ready for refitting to the car.

---

29. Girling 'Super Vac' - removal and refitting

---

1. Slacken the bleed nipple on one of the brake caliper units, attach a piece of plastic pipe to the nipple and place the free end in a clean glass jar. Pump the brake pedal until the reservoir is empty. Tighten the bleed nipple.

2. Extract the split pin from the brake pedal to push-rod clevis pin, remove the washer and withdraw the clevis pin.

3. Wipe the area around the two hydraulic pipe connections on the master cylinder and the servo unit with a clean rag and unscrew the two connections. Plug the two pipes to stop the entry of dirt.

4. Disconnect the vacuum hose from the inlet manifold adaptor.

5. Remove the four nuts and spring washers holding the servo unit to the bulkhead panel bracket and carefully lift away the unit. Finally remove the master cylinder.

---

30. Girling 'Super Vac' - dismantling, inspection and reassembly

---

Thoroughly clean the outside of the unit using a stiff brush and wipe with a non-fluffy rag. It cannot be too strongly emphasised that cleanliness is important when working on the unit. Before any attempt be made to dismantle refer to Fig 11:15 where it will be seen two

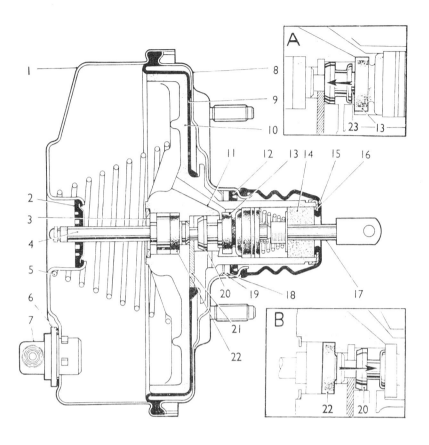

Fig. 11.14. GIRLING "SUPER VAC" SERVO UNIT COMPONENT PARTS

No. Description	No. Description	No. Description	No. Description
1 Front shell	7 Non-return valve	13 Control valve	19 Retainer
2 Seal and plate assembly	8 Rear shell	14 Filter	20 Control piston
3 Retainer (sprag washer)	9 Diaphragm	15 Dust cover	21 Valve retaining plate
4 Push-rod – hydraulic	10 Diaphragm plate	16 End cap	22 Reaction disc
5 Diaphragm return spring	11 Vacuum port	17 Valve operating rod assembly	23 Atmospheric port
6 'O' ring	12 Seal	18 Bearing	

NOTE: A. Control valve closed, control piston moved forward – atmospheric port open.

B. Pressure from diaphragm plate causes reaction disc to extrude, presses back control piston and closes atmospheric por

items of equipment are required. Firstly, a base plate (2) must be made to enable the unit to be safely held in a vice. Secondly, a lever (1) must be made similar to the form shown. Without these items it is impossible to dismantle satisfactorily.

To dismantle the unit proceed as follows:

1. Refer to Fig 11:14 and using a file or scriber mark a line across the two halves of the unit to act as a datum for alignment.

2. Fit the previously made base plate into a firm vice and attach the unit to the plate using the master cylinder studs as shown in Fig 11:15.

3. Fit the lever to the four studs on the rear shell as shown in Fig 11:15.

4. Use a piece of long rubber hose and connect one end to the adaptor on the engine inlet manifold and the other end to the non-return valve. Start the engine and this will create a vacuum in the unit so drawing the two halves together.

5. Rotate the lever in an anti-clockwise direction until the front shell indentations are in line with the recesses in the rim of the rear shell. Then press the lever assembly down firmly whilst an assistant stops the car engine and quickly removes the vacuum pipe from the

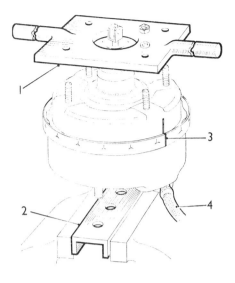

Fig. 11.15. SPECIAL TOOLS REQUIRED TO DISMANTLE GIRLING "SUPER VAC" SERVO UNIT

No.	Description	No.	Description
1	Lever	3	Scribe line
2	Base plate	4	Vacuum applied

inlet manifold connector. Depress the operating rod (17) so as to release the vacuum, whereupon the front (1) and rear (8) halves should part. If necessary use a soft faced hammer and lightly tap the front half to break the bond.

6.   Lift away the rear shell followed by the diaphragm return spring (5), the dust cover, end cap and the filter. Also withdraw the diaphragm (9). Press down the valve rod (17) and shake out the valve retaining plate (21) then separate the valve rod assembly from the diaphragm plate.

7.   Gently ease the spring washer from the diaphragm plate and withdraw the pushrod (4) and reaction disc (22).

8.   The seal and plate assembly in the end of the front shell are a press fit. It is recommended that unless the seal is to be renewed it be left in situ.

9.   Thoroughly clean all parts in Girling Cleaning Fluid and wipe dry using a non-fluffy rag. Inspect all parts for signs of damage, stripped threads etc. and fit new parts as necessary. All seals should be renewed and for this a 'major repair kit' should be purchased. This kit will also contain two separate greases which must be used as directed and not interchanged.

10. To reassemble first smear the seal (12) and bearing with grease numbered 64949008 and refit the rear shell (8) positioning it such that the flat face of the seal is towards the bearing. Press into position and refit the retainer (19).

11. Lightly smear the disc and hydraulic pushrod (4) with grease numbered 64949008. Refit the reaction disc (22) and pushrod (4) to the diaphragm plate (10) and press in the large sprag washer. The small sprag washer supplied in the 'major repair kit' is not required. It is important that the length of the pushrod (4) is not in any way altered and any attempt to move the adjustment bolt will strip the threads. If a new hydraulic

pushrod has been required the length will have to be set. Details of this operation are given at the end of this section.

12. Lightly smear the outer diameter of the diaphragm plate neck and the bearing surfaces of the valve plunger with grease numbered 64949008. Carefully fit the valve rod assembly into the neck of the diaphragm and fix with the retaining plate.

13. Fit the diaphragm into position and also the non-return valve (7) to the front shell (1). Next smear the seal and plate assembly with grease numbered 64949008 and press into the front shell (1) with the plate facing inwards.

14. Fit the front shell to the base plate and the lever to the rear shell. Reconnect the vacuum hose to the non-return valve and the adaptor on the engines induction manifold. Position the diaphragm return spring in the front shell. Lightly smear the outer bead of the diaphragm with grease numbered 64949009 and locate the diaphragm assembly into the rear shell. Position the rear shell assembly on the return spring and line up the previously made scribe marks.

15. The assistant should start the engine. Watching one's fingers very carefully press the two halves of the unit together and, using the lever tool, turn clockwise to lock the two halves together. Stop the engine and disconnect the hose.

16. Press a new filter into the neck of the diaphragm plate, refit the end cap and position the dust cover onto the special lugs of the rear shell.

17.   Hydraulic pushrod adjustment applies only if a new pushrod has been fitted. It will be seen by referring to Fig 11:16 that there is a bolt screwed into the end of the pushrod. The amount of protrusion has to be adjusted in the following manner: Remove the bolt and coat the threaded portion with Loctite Grade B. Reconnect the vacuum hose to the adaptor on the inlet valve and non-return valve. Start the engine and screw the prepared bolt into the end of the pushrod. Adjust the position of the bolt head so that it is 0.011 inch to 0.016 inch below the face of the front shell as shown by dimension A in Fig 11:16. Leave the unit for a minimum of 24 hours to allow the Loctite to set hard.

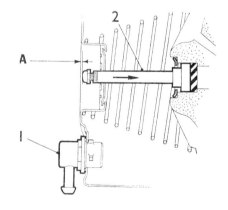

Fig. 11.16. THE CORRECT HYDRAULIC PUSH-ROD SETTING

No.	Description	No.	Description
A	Pushrod setting 0.011 to 0.016 in. below face	2	Push-rod against reaction disc
1	Vacuum applied		

18.   Refit the servo unit to the car as detailed in the previous section. To test the servo unit for correct operation after overhaul first start the engine and run

for a minimum period of two minutes and then switch off. Wait ten minutes and apply the footbrake very carefully listening to hear the rush of air into the servo unit. This will indicate that vacuum was retained and therefore operating correctly.

31. Girling 'Powerstop' Mk II B - description

The servo unit is shown in Fig 11:17 and although the vacuum cylinder and piston are different to the original Mark II, the air valve and filter are identical so that the service procedure is the same. Refer to section 28 for full information.

Due to its design, the vacuum cylinder sealing ring must not be removed which means that all the cylinder components are not able to be serviced. Therefore if proved to be in need of attention, an exchange service unit must be fitted.

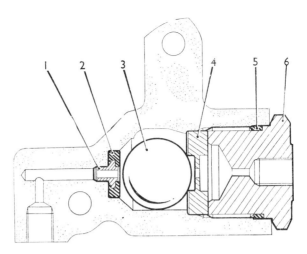

Fig. 11.18. LIMITING VALVE COMPONENT PARTS

No.	Description	No.	Description
1	Valve insert	4	Spacer - ball
2	Valve seal	5	Seal - end plug
3	Ball	6	End plug

internal puller is required to remove the insert and valve so it is recommended that unless specific trouble is being experienced with this part it be left alone. Remove the old seals using fingers only.

5. Thoroughly wash all parts using either Girling Cleaning Fluid or Industrial methylated spirits and examine the ball and ramp area for signs of corrosion wear and ridging.

6. Well lubricate the new seals with brake fluid and fit to the insert and end plug using fingers only.

7. If the valve and insert have been removed fit a new valve seal and insert by first positioning them in the bore at the bottom of the valve chamber. Check that the valve insert is upright and carefully tap the insert into its seating using a mild steel drift with a 0.1 inch spigot and 120° included angle shoulder machined on the end.

8. Replace the ball and spacer ensuring that the spacer

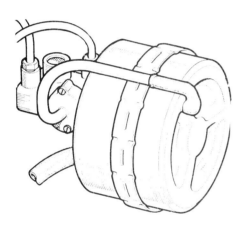

Fig. 11.17. Girling "Powerstop" Mk IIB Servo unit.

32. Pressure limiting valve - removal and replacement

When a servo unit is fitted into the braking system a limiting valve of the type shown in Fig 11:18 is fitted instead of the reducing valve previously described in this chapter. It is mounted and set at an angle of 25° so that at a certain rate of deceleration the steel ball rolls up the ramp and closes the valve. Any further increase in hydraulic pressure will be directed to the front brakes only.

To remove and check the unit proceed as follows:
1. The exterior of the unit should be cleaned with a stiff brush. Drain the brake hydraulic system from one of the rear drum brake bleed screws.
2. Disconnect the two pipe unions and wrap the ends in a non-fluffy rag to stop dirt ingress and hydraulic fluid dripping onto the paintwork.
3. Remove the two valve unit mounting bolts and lift away the unit taking care that no brake fluid drips onto the paintwork.
4. Unscrew the end plug and carefully tip the unit so that the spacer and ball may be removed. A special

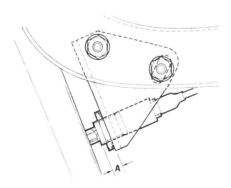

Fig. 11.19. MECHANICALLY OPERATED STOPLIGHT SWITCH SETTING
A 3/16 inch from bracket prior to adjustment

is correctly seating on its shoulder. Refit the end plug and tighten using a torque wrench set to 25 - 35 lb ft.

9. Refit the unit, bleed the complete hydraulic system and road test.

33. Stop light switch - adjustment

1. Cars covered by this manual having a servo unit fitted to the braking system do not have the reducing valve normally fitted on the front wing valance. A separate switch is fitted operated by the brake pedal.

2. Check that the switch operates correctly by holding the brake pedal down fully and depress the switch plunger. The lights should go out. Release the plunger and the lights should come on. If the operation is incorrect the switch probably requires adjustment. Refer to Fig 11:19 and slacken the locknut. Re-position the switch so that it protrudes 3/16 inch from the bracket (Dimension A).

3. Release the two nuts holding the switch bracket in position and re-position the bracket until the plunger is in contact with the pedal with no free play in the switch. Carefully tighten the switch bracket nuts so as not to move the bracket.

4. Screw the switch into the bracket until the contacts are open and then screw in one more turn. Tighten the switch locknut and re-check for correct operation. It is important that the switch does not act as a stop for the brake pedal.

Cause	Trouble	Remedy
SYMPTOM:	BRAKES TEND TO BIND, DRAG, OR LOCK-ON	
Incorrect adjustment	Brake shoes adjusted too tightly Handbrake cable over-tightened Master cylinder push rod out of adjustment giving too little brake pedal free movement	Slacken off brake shoe adjusters two clicks. Slacken off handbrake cable adjustment. Reset to manufacturer's specifications.
Wear or dirt in hydraulic system or incorrect fluid	Reservoir vent hole in cap blocked with dirt Master cylinder by-pass port restricted – brakes seize in 'on' position Wheel cylinder seizes in 'on' position	Clean and blow through hole. Dismantle, clean, and overhaul master cylinder. Bleed brakes. Dismantle, clean, and overhaul wheel cylinder. Bleed brakes.
Mechanical wear	Brake shoe pull off springs broken, stretched or loose	Examine springs and replace if worn or loose.
Incorrect brake assembly	Brake shoe pull off springs fitted wrong way round, omitted, or wrong type used	Examine, and rectify as appropriate.
Neglect	Handbrake system rusted or seized in the 'on' position	Apply 'Plus Gas' to free, clean and lubricate.

BRAKING SYSTEM
FAULT FINDING CHART

Cause	Trouble	Remedy
SYMPTOM:	PEDAL TRAVELS ALMOST TO FLOORBOARDS BEFORE BRAKES OPERATE	
Leaks and air bubbles in hydraulic system	Brake fluid level too low	Top up master cylinder reservoir. Check for leaks.
	Wheel cylinder leaking	Dismantle wheel cylinder, clean, fit new rubbers and bleed brakes.
	Master cylinder leaking (Bubbles in master cylinder fluid)	Dismantle master cylinder, clean, and fit new rubbers. Bleed brakes.
	Brake flexible hose leaking	Examine and fit new hose if old hose leaking. Bleed brakes.
	Brake line fractured	Replace with new brake pipe. Bleed brakes.
	Brake system unions loose	Check all unions in brake system and tighten as necessary. Bleed brakes.
Normal wear	Linings over 75% worn	Fit replacement shoes and brake linings.
Incorrect adjustment	Brakes badly out of adjustment	Jack up car and adjust brakes.
	Master cylinder push rod out or adjustment causing too much pedal free movement	Reset to manufacturer's specification.
SYMPTOM:	BRAKE PEDAL FEELS SPRINGY	
Brake lining renewal	New linings not yet bedded-in	Use brakes gently until springy pedal feeling leaves.
Excessive wear or damage	Brake drums badly worn and weak or cracked	Fit new brake drums.
Lack of maintenance	Master cylinder securing nuts loose	Tighten master cylinder securing nuts. Ensure spring washers are fitted.
SYMPTOM:	BRAKE PEDAL FEELS SPONGY & SOGGY	
Leaks or bubbles in hydraulic system	Wheel cylinder leaking	Dismantle wheel cylinder, clean, fit new rubbers, and bleed brakes.
	Master cylinder leaking (Bubbles in master cylinder reservoir)	Dismantle master cylinder, clean, and fit new rubbers and bleed brakes. Replace cylinder if internal walls scored.
	Brake pipe line or flexible hose leaking	Fit new pipeline or hose.
	Unions in brake system loose	Examine for leaks, tighten as necessary.
SYMPTOM:	EXCESSIVE EFFORT REQUIRED TO BRAKE CAR	
Lining type or condition	Linings badly worn	Fit replacement brake shoes and linings.
	New linings recently fitted - not yet bedded-in	Use brakes gently until braking effort normal.
	Harder linings fitted than standard causing increase in pedal pressure	Remove linings and replace with normal units.
Oil or grease leaks	Linings and brake drums contaminated with oil, grease, or hydraulic fluid	Rectify source of leak, clean brake drums, fit new linings.
SYMPTOM:	BRAKES UNEVEN & PULLING TO ONE SIDE	
Oil or grease leaks	Linings and brake drums contaminated with oil, grease, or hydraulic fluid	Ascertain and rectify source of leak, clean brake drums, fit new linings.
Lack of maintenance	Tyre pressures unequal	Check and inflate as necessary.
	Radial ply tyres fitted at one end of car only	Fit radial ply tyres of the same make to all four wheels.
	Brake backplate loose	Tighten backplate securing nuts and bolts.
	Brake shoes fitted incorrectly	Remove and fit shoes correct way round.
	Different type of linings fitted at each wheel	Fit the linings specified by the manufacturers all round.
	Anchorages for front suspension or rear axle loose	Tighten front and rear suspension pick-up points including spring anchorage.
	Brake drums badly worn, cracked or distorted	Fit new brake drums.

Chapter 12/Electrical System

Contents

Specifications

System	12 volt positive earth
Fuses...	17 amp (current rating)
Battery	Lucas D11/13 11 plate or Lucas D13 13 plate
Capacity at 20 hour rate	Lucas D11/13 - 50 amp hour
	Lucas D13 - 57 amp hour
Charging system..	Current voltage control

Regulator

Make/type	Lucas RB 340
Setting at 20°C at 3,000 r.p.m. dynamo – (1800 1964-67, 1800 and 18/85 1967-68)	14.5 - 15.5 volts
Setting at 20°C at 2,250 r.p.m. dynamo – (1800 Mk II, 18/85 and 18/85 Mk II and Mk II 'S' ...	14.5 - 15.5 volts
Cut in voltage	12.7 - 13.3 volts
Drop off voltage	9.5 - 11.0 volts

Dynamo

Type	Lucas C40/1 or C40/PS
Maximum output	22 ± 1 amps
Cut in speed..	1,585 r.p.m. at 13.5 volts
Field resistance	6.0 ohms at 20°C
Brush spring tension	20 to 30 oz
Brush min. length.	¼ inch

Alternator

Type	Lucas 11AC - 12 volts

Control unit

Type	Lucas 4TR

Field Isolating relay

Type	Lucas 6RA

Warning light control

Type	Lucas 3AW

Starter motor

Type	Lucas M418G four brush inertia type
Lock torque..	17 lb ft at 420 amps
Torque at 1,000 r.p.m.	8 lb ft at 320 amps and 8.6 volts
Light running current..	45 amps at 7,400 - 8,500 r.p.m.
Brush spring tension..	30 - 40 oz
Brush min. length	5/16 inch
Starter gear ratio.	13.3:1

Wiper motor

Type	Lucas 6WA single speed
or	Lucas 14W two speed
Drive to wheelboxes	Rack and cable
Armature end float	0.008 - 0.012 inch
Running current...	2.6 - 3.4 amps
Wiper speed (after 60 seconds)	44 - 48 cycles per minute
Resistance:	
Armature winding	0.29 - 0.35 ohm at 16°C
Field winding..	8.0 - 9.5 ohms at 16°C
Brush spring tension...	4.4 to 4.9 oz
Angle of wipe	110°

Horns

Type	Lucas 9H/9H modified
or	Clear hooters F725N
9H modified..	4 amps with connectors set wide apart

Bulbs	BMC part No.	Volts	Watts
Headlamps...	BFS410	12	45/50
Sidelamps - 1800	BFS510	12	5
Sidelamps - 1800 Mk II, Wolseley repeater flasher and grille badge - Wolseley.	BFS989	12	6
Side and indicator lamps (alternator)	BFS380	12	6/21
Repeater, and number plate lamps	BFS510	12	5
Direction indicator lamps...	BFS382	12	21
Tail and stop lamps	BFS380	12	6/21
Panel lights and warning lights	BFS987	12	2. 2
Clock, automatic, heated backlight and indicators	BFS281	12	2
Direction indicator, warning (Lilliput bulb) ...	BFS280	12	1. 5
Interior and luggage boot lamps..	BFS254	12	6
Reversing lamp - Wolseley	BFS273	12	21
Clock battery	13H3834	1. 35	-

1. General description

The electrical system is of the 12 volt type and the major components comprise a 12 volt 50 amp/hour battery of which the positive terminal is earthed; a voltage regulator and cut out; a Lucas dynamo or alternator which is fitted to the front right hand side of the engine and is driven by the fan belt from the crankshaft pulley wheel; and a starter motor which is fitted to the end plate and clutch housing on the right hand side of the engine.

The six plate 12 volt battery supplies a steady amount of current for the ignition, lighting, and other electrical circuits, and provides a reserve of electricity when the current consumed by the electrical equipment exceeds that being produced by the dynamo.

The dynamo is of the two brush type and works in conjunction with the voltage regulator and cut out. The dynamo is cooled by a multi-bladed fan mounted behind the dynamo pulley, and blows air through cooling holes in the dynamo end brackets. The output from the dynamo is controlled by the voltage regulator which ensures a high output if the battery is in a low state of charge or the demands from the electrical equipment high, and a low output if the battery is fully charged and there is little demand from the electrical equipment.

2. Battery - removal and replacement

1. The battery is in a special carrier fitted in the right hand wing valance of the engine compartment. It should be removed once every three months for cleaning and testing. Disconnect the positive and then the negative leads from the battery terminals by slackening the retaining nuts and bolts, or by unscrewing the retaining screws if these are fitted.
2. Remove the battery clamp and carefully lift the battery out of its compartment. Hold the battery vertical to ensure that none of the electrolyte is spilled.
3. Replacement is a direct reversal of this procedure. NOTE: Replace the negative lead before the earth (positive) lead and smear the terminals with petroleum jelly (vaseline) to prevent corrosion. NEVER use an ordinary grease as applied to other parts of the car.

3. Battery - maintenance and inspection

1. Normal weekly battery maintenance consists of checking the electrolyte level of each cell to ensure that the separators are covered by $\frac{1}{4}$ inch of electrolyte. If the level has fallen, top up the battery using distilled water only. Do not overfill. If a battery is overfilled or any electrolyte spilled, immediately wipe away the excess as electrolyte attacks and corrodes any metal it comes into contact with very rapidly.
2. As well as keeping the terminals clean and covered with petroleum jelly, the top of the battery, and especially the top of the cells, should be kept clean and dry. This helps prevent corrosion and ensures that the battery does not become partially discharged by leakage through dampness and dirt.
3. Once every three months remove the battery and inspect the battery securing bolts, the battery clamp plate, tray and battery leads for corrosion (white fluffy deposits on the metal which are brittle to touch). If any corrosion is found, clean off the deposit with ammonia and paint over the clean metal with an anti-rust anti-acid paint.
4. At the same time inspect the battery case for cracks. If a crack is found, clean and plug it with one of the proprietary compounds marketed by firms such as Holts for this purpose. If leakage through the crack has been excessive then it will be necessary to refill the appropriate cell with fresh electrolyte as detailed later. Cracks are frequently caused to the top of the battery cases by pouring in distilled water in the middle of winter AFTER instead of BEFORE a run. This gives the water no chance to mix with the electrolyte and so the former freezes and splits the battery case.
5. If topping up the battery becomes excessive and the case has been inspected for cracks that could cause leakage, but none are found, the battery is being overcharged and the voltage regulator will have to be checked and reset.
6. With the battery on the bench at the three monthly interval check, measure the specific gravity with a hydrometer to determine the state of charge and condition of the electrolyte. There should be very little variation between the different cells and if a variation in excess of 0. 025 is present it will be due to either:

(a) loss of electrolyte from the battery at some time caused by spillage or a leak, resulting in a drop in the specific gravity of the electrolyte when the deficiency was replaced with distilled water instead of fresh electrolyte.

(b) an internal short circuit caused by buckling of the plates or a similar malady pointing to the likelihood of total battery failure in the near future.

7. The specific gravity of the electrolyte for fully charged conditions at the electrolyte temperature indicated, is listed in Table A. The specific gravity of a fully discharged battery at different temperatures of the electrolyte is given in Table B.

TABLE A

Specific gravity - battery fully charged
1.268 at 100°F or 38°C electrolyte temperature
1.272 at 90°F or 32°C   "   "
1.276 at 80°F or 27°C   "   "
1.280 at 70°F or 21°C   "   "
1.284 at 60°F or 16°C   "   "
1.288 at 50°F or 10°C   "   "
1.292 at 40°F or 4°C   "   "
1.296 at 30°F or -1.5°C "   "

TABLE B

Specific gravity - battery fully discharged
1.098 at 100°F or 38°C electrolyte temperature
1.102 at 90°F or 32°C   "   ""
1.106 at 80°F or 27°C   "   "
1.110 at 70°F or 21°C   "   "
1.114 at 60°F or 16°C   "   "
1.118 at 50°F or 10°C   "   "
1.122 at 40°F or 4°C   "   "
1.126 at 30°F or -1.5°C "   "

4. Battery - electrolyte replenishment

1. If the battery is in a fully charged state and one of the cells maintains a specific gravity reading which is .025 or more lower than the others, and a check of each cell has been made with a voltage meter to check for short circuits (a four to seven second test should give a steady reading of between 1.2 and 1.8 volts), then it is likely that electrolyte has been lost from the cell with the low reading at some time.

2. Top the cell up with a solution of 1 part sulphuric acid to 2.5 parts of water. If the cell is already fully topped up draw some electrolyte out of it with a pipette. The total capacity of each cell is $\frac{3}{4}$ pint.

3. When mixing the sulphuric acid and water NEVER ADD WATER TO SULPHURIC ACID - always pour the acid slowly onto the water in a glass container. IF WATER IS ADDED TO SULPHURIC ACID IT WILL EXPLODE.

4. Continue to top up the cell with the freshly made electrolyte and then recharge the battery and check the hydrometer readings.

5. Battery - charging

1. In winter time when heavy demand is placed upon the battery such as when starting from cold, and much electrical equipment is continually in use, it is a good idea to occasionally have the battery fully charged from an external source at the rate of 3.5 to 4 amps.

2. Continue to charge the battery at this rate until no further rise in specific gravity is noted over a four hour period.

3. Alternatively, a trickle charger, charging at the rate of 1.5 amps can be safely used overnight.

4. Specially rapid 'boost' charges which are claimed to restore the power of the battery in 1 to 2 hours are most dangerous as they can cause serious damage to the battery plates through overheating.

5. While charging the battery note that the temperature of the electrolyte should never exceed 100°F.

6. Dynamo - maintenance

1. Routine maintenance consists of checking the tension of the fan belt, and lubricating the dynamo rear bearing once every 6,000 miles.

2. The fan belt should be tight enough to ensure no slip between the belt and the dynamo pulley. If a shrieking noise comes from the engine when the unit is accelerated rapidly, it is likely that it is the fan belt slipping. On the other hand, the belt must not be too taut or the bearings will wear rapidly and cause dynamo failure or bearing seizure. Ideally $\frac{1}{2}$ inch of total free movement should be available at the fan belt midway between the fan and the dynamo.

3. To adjust the fan belt tension, slightly slacken the three dynamo retaining bolts, and swing the dynamo on the upper two bolts outwards to increase the tension, and inwards to lower it.

4. It is best to leave the bolts fairly tight so that considerable effort has to be used to move the dynamo, otherwise it is difficult to get the correct setting. If the dynamo is being moved outwards to increase the tension and the bolts have only been slackened a little, a long spanner acting as a lever placed behind the dynamo with the lower end resting against the block works very well in moving the dynamo outwards. Re-tighten the dynamo bolts and check that the dynamo pulley is correctly aligned with the fan belt.

5. Lubrication on the dynamo consists of inserting three drops of S.A.E. 30 engine oil in the small oil hole in the centre of the commutator end bracket. This lubricates the rear bearing. The front bearing is pre-packed with grease and requires no attention.

7. Dynamo - testing in position

1. If, with the engine running, no charge comes from the dynamo, or the charge is very low, first check that the fan belt is in place and is not slipping. Then check that the leads from the control box to the dynamo are firmly attached and that one has not come loose from its terminal.

2. The lead from the 'D' terminal on the dynamo should be connected to the 'D' terminal on the control box, and similarly the 'F' terminals on the dynamo and control box should also be connected together. Check that this is so and that the leads have not been incorrectly fitted.

3. Make sure none of the electrical equipment such as the lights or radio, is on, and then pull the leads off the dynamo terminals marked 'D' and 'F'. Join the terminals together with a short length of wire.

4. Attach to the centre of this length of wire the negative clip of a 0-20 volts voltmeter and run the other clip to earth on the dynamo yoke. Start the engine and allow it to idle at approximately 750 rpm. At this speed the dynamo should give a reading of about 15 volts on the

voltmeter. There is no point in raising the engine speed above a fast idle as the reading will then be inaccurate.

5. If no reading is recorded then check the brushes and brush connections. If a very low reading of approximately 1 volt is observed then the field winding may be suspect.

6. If a reading of between 4 to 6 amps is recorded it is likely that the armature winding is at fault.

7. On early dynamos it was possible to remove the dynamo cover band and check the dynamo and brushes in position. With the Lucas C40-1 windowless yoke dynamo it must be removed and dismantled before the brushes and commutator can be attended to.

8. If the voltmeter shows a good reading, then with the temporary link still in position, connect both leads from the control box to 'D' and 'F' on the dynamo ('D' to 'D' and 'F' to 'F'). Release the lead from the 'D' terminal at the control box end and clip one lead from the voltmeter to the end of the cable, and the other lead to a good earth. With the engine running at the same speed as previously, an identical voltage to that recorded at the dynamo should be noted on the voltmeter. If no voltage is recorded there is a break in the wire. If the voltage is the same as recorded at the dynamo then check the 'F' lead in similar fashion. If both readings are the same as at the dynamo then it will be necessary to test the control box.

---

8. Dynamo - removal and replacement

---

1. Slacken the two dynamo retaining bolts, and the nut on the sliding link, and move the dynamo in towards the engine so that the fan belt can be removed.

2. Disconnect the two leads from the dynamo terminals.

3. Remove the nut from the sliding link bolt, and remove the two upper bolts. The dynamo is then free to be lifted away from the engine.

4. Replacement is a reversal of the above procedure. Do not finally tighten the retaining bolts and the nut on

the sliding link until the fan belt has been tensioned correctly.

---

9. Dynamo - dismantling and inspection

---

1. Mount the dynamo in a vice and unscrew and remove the two through bolts (17), Fig 12:1, from the commutator end bracket (1) (see photo).

9.1

2. Mark the commutator end bracket and the dynamo casing so the end bracket can be replaced in its original position. Pull the end bracket off the armature shaft. NOTE: Some versions of the dynamo may have a raised pip on the end bracket which locates in a recess on the edge of the casing. If so, marking the end bracket and casing is unnecessary. A pip may also be found on the drive end bracket at the opposite end of the casing (photo).

3. Lift the two brush springs and draw the brushes out of the brush holders (arrowed in photo).

4. Measure the brushes and if worn down to 9/32 inch or less unscrew the screws holding the brush leads to the end bracket. Take off the brushes complete with

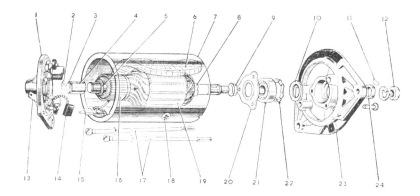

Fig. 12.1. EXPLODED VIEW OF LUCAS C40/1 DYNAMO

No. Description	No. Description	No. Description	No. Description
1 Commutator end bracket	7 Yoke	13 Output terminal 'D'	19 Armature
2 Felt ring	8 Shaft collar	14 Brushes	20 Bearing retaining plate
3 Felt ring retainer	9 Shaft collar retaining cup	15 Field terminal 'F'	21 Ball bearing
4 Bronze bush	10 Felt ring	16 Commutator	22 Corrugated washer
5 Thrust washer	11 Shaft key	17 Through-bolts	23 Driving end bracket
6 Field coils	12 Shaft nut	18 Pole-shoe securing screws	24 Pulley spacer

9.2

9.8

leads. Old and new brushes are compared in the photograph.

5. If no locating pip can be found, mark the drive end bracket and the dynamo casing so the drive end bracket can be replaced in its original position. Then pull the drive end bracket complete with armature out of the casing (photo).

6. Check the condition of the ball bearing (21) in the drive end plate by firmly holding the plate and noting if there is visible side movement of the armature shaft in relation to the end plate. If play is present, the armature assembly must be separated from the end plate. If the bearing is sound there is no need to carry out the work described in the following two paragraphs.

7. Hold the armature in one hand (mount it carefully in a vice if preferred) and undo the nut holding the pulley wheel and fan in place. Pull off the pulley wheel and fan.

8. Next remove the woodruff key (11) (arrowed in photo) from its slot in the armature shaft and also the

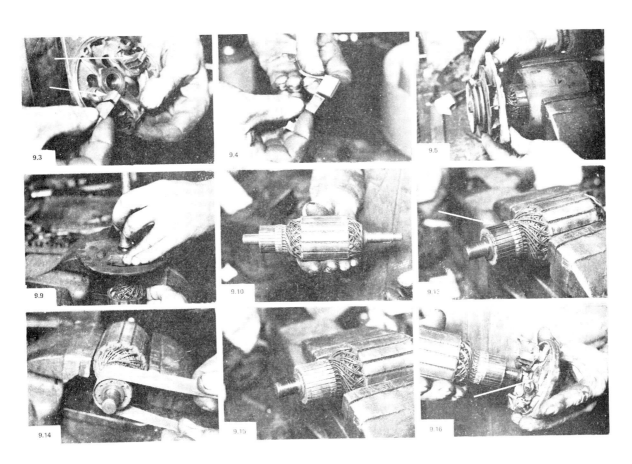

9.3

9.4

9.5

9.9

9.10

9.13

9.14

9.15

9.16

bearing locating ring (20).

9. Place the drive end bracket across the open jaws of a vice with the armature downwards and gently tap the armature shaft from the bearing (see photo) in the end plate with the aid of a suitable drift.

10. Carefully inspect the armature and check it for open or short circuited windings. It is a good indication of an open circuited armature when the commutator segments are burnt. If the armature has short circuited the commutator segments will be very badly burnt, and the overheated armature windings badly discoloured. If open or short circuits are suspected then test by substituting the suspect armature for a new one (see photo).

11. Check the resistance of the field coils. To do this, connect an ohmmeter between the field terminal and the yoke and note the reading on the ohmmeter which should be about 6 ohms. If the ohmmeter reading is infinity this indicates an open circuit in the field winding. If the ohmmeter reading is below 5 ohms this indicates that one of the field coils is faulty and must be replaced.

12. Field coil replacement involves the use of a wheel operated screwdriver, a soldering iron, caulking and riveting and this operation is considered to be beyond the scope of most owners. Therefore if the field coils are at fault either purchase a rebuilt dynamo, or take the casing to a BLMC dealer or electrical engineering works for new field coils to be fitted.

13. Next check the condition of the commutator. If it is dirty and blackened as shown in the photo clean it with a petrol damped rag. If the commutator is in good condition the surface will be smooth and quite free from pits or burnt areas, and the insulated segments clearly defined.

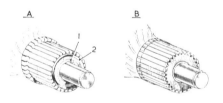

Fig. 12.2. THE DYNAMO COMMUTATOR

No.	Description	No.	Description
A	Fabricated type	1	Metal roll-over
B	Moulded type	2	Insulating cone

14. If, after the commutator has been cleaned, pits and burnt spots are still present, wrap a strip of glass paper round the commutator taking great care to move the commutator $\frac{1}{4}$ of a turn every ten rubs till it is thoroughly clean (photo).

15. In extreme cases of wear the commutator can be mounted in a lathe and with the lathe turning at high speed, a very fine cut may be taken off the commutator. Then polish the commutator with glass paper. If the commutator has worn so that the insulators between the segments are level with the top of the segments, then undercut the insulators to a depth of 1/32 inch (8mm), see Fig 12:3. The best tool to use for this purpose is half a hacksaw blade ground to a thickness of the insulator, and with the handle end of the blade covered in insulating tape to make it comfortable to hold. The photo shows the sort of finish the surface of the commutator should have when finished.

16. Check the brush bearing in the commutator end bracket for wear by noting if the armature spindle rocks when placed in it. If worn it must be renewed.

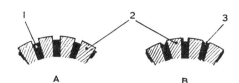

Fig. 12.3. CORRECT METHOD OF UNDERCUTTING THE COMMUTATOR

No.	Description	No.	Description
A	Correct way	2	Segments
B	Incorrect way	3	Insulator
1	Insulator		

17. The bush bearing can be removed by a suitable extractor or by screwing a 5/8 inch tap four or five times into the bush. The tap complete with bush is then pulled out of the end bracket.

18. NOTE: The bush bearing is of the porous bronze type and, before fitting a new one, it is essential that it is allowed to stand in S.A.E. 30 engine oil for at least 24 hours before fitment. In an emergency the bush can be immersed in hot oil (100°C) for 2 hours.

19. Carefully fit the new bush into the end plate, pressing it in until the end of the bearing is flush with the inner side of the end plate. If available press the bush in with a smooth shouldered mandrel the same diameter as the armature shaft.

10. Dynamo - repair and reassembly

1. To renew the ball bearing fitted to the drive end bracket drill out the rivets which hold the bearing retainer plate to the end bracket and lift off the plate.

2. Press out the bearing from the end bracket and remove the corrugated and felt washers from the bearing housing.

3. Thoroughly clean the bearing housing and the new bearing, and pack with high melting point grease.

4. Place the felt washer and corrugated washer in that order in the end bracket bearing housing (photo).

5. Then fit the new bearing as shown (photo).

6. Gently tap the bearing into place with the aid of a suitable drift (photo).

7. Replace the bearing plate and fit three new rivets (photo).

8. Open up the rivets with the aid of a suitable cold chisel (photo).

9. Finally peen over the open end of the rivets with the aid of a ball hammer as illustrated.

10. Refit the drive end bracket to the armature shaft. Do not try and force the bracket on but with the aid of a suitable socket abutting the bearing, tap the bearing on gently, so pulling the end bracket down with it (photo).

11. Slide the spacer up the shaft and refit the woodruff key (photo).

12. Replace the fan and pulley wheel and then fit the spring washer and nut and tighten the latter. The drive bracket end of the dynamo is now fully assembled as shown (photo).

13. If the brushes are little worn and are to be used again then ensure that they are placed in the same holders from which they were removed. When refitting brushes either new or old, check that they move freely in their holders. If either brush sticks, clean with a petrol moistened rag and if still stiff, lightly polish the sides of the brush with a very fine file until the brush moves quite freely in its holder.

14. Tighten the two retaining screws and washers which hold the wire leads to the brushes in place (photo).

10.14

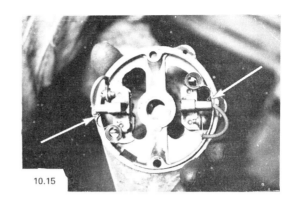

10.15

15. It is far easier to slip the end piece with brushes over the commutator, if the brushes are raised in their holders as shown in the photo and held in this position by the pressure of the springs resting against their flanks.
16. Refit the armature to the casing and then the commutator end plate, and screw up the two through bolts.
17. Finally, hook the ends of the two springs off the flanks of the brushes and onto their heads so the brushes are forced down into contact with the armature.

11. Dynamo - type C40/PS

On models with power assisted steering the above dynamo is fitted instead of the C40/1 type to accommodate the drive to the hydraulic pump which operates the power steering.

Servicing procedures as well as technical specification is identical except that the commutator end bracket has a ball race instead of the bush. Also the drive end

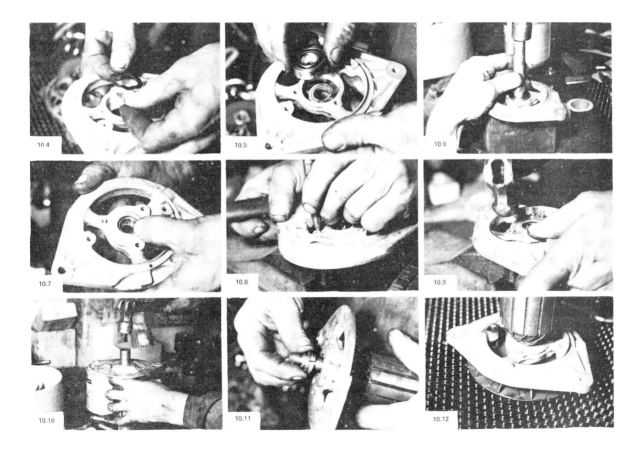

10.4
10.5
10.6
10.7
10.8
10.9
10.10
10.11
10.12

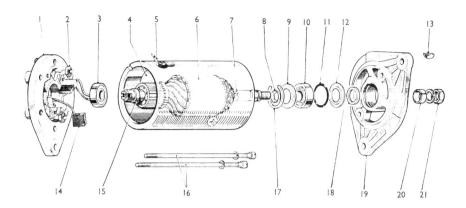

Fig. 12.4. EXPLODED VIEW OF LUCAS C40/PS DYNAMO

No.	Description	No.	Description	No.	Description	No.	Description
1	Commutator end bracket	7	Shaft collar	12	Felt retaining washer	17	Circlip
2	Brush tension spring	8	Bearing ring retainer	13	Shaft key	18	Felt washer
3	Bearing - commutator end	9	Bearing retaining plate	14	Brushes	19	Drive end bracket
4	Field coils	10	Bearing - drive end	15	Bearing collar	20	Drive end collar
5	Field terminal	11	'O' ring - oil seal	16	Through-bolts	21	Shaft nut
6	Armature						

bearing is retained by a circlip and an 'O' ring seal is used. The terminal connections are re-positioned. An exploded view of this dynamo is shown in Fig 12:4, and the following notes should be of additional assistance when removing or overhauling this later type:

1. Before the dynamo can be removed it will be necessary to disconnect the hoses from the power steering pump.

2. The power steering pump must be removed from the rear of the dynamo before dismantling. Once the through bolts have been removed it will be necessary to lever or press the commutator end bracket from the shaft. Note that a collar is fitted between the bearing and commutator.

3. A circlip (17) Fig 12:4 retains the drive end bearing (10) together with a retaining plate (9) and the 'O' ring oil seal (11) is fitted between the bearing (10) and the felt washer (18)

4. For testing the field coils the procedure is identical to that for the C40/1 except that the field coil connections are assembled to the yoke with the large eyelet earthed to the frame whilst the smaller one is to be insulated from the frame beneath the head of the rivet. Rivet the yoke in the normal fashion.

5. The commutator end bearing is of a fully shielded pre-packed design so that it does not require lubrication upon refitting. Fibre thrust washers are not fitted.

---

12. Alternator and control unit

If the car is fitted with an alternator certain precautions must be taken otherwise very expensive damage can result.

Special equipment is required for the servicing or testing of the alternator and control units together with specialist knowledge so it is not recommended that overhaul is undertaken by the Do-it-yourself motorist. Note

the following points which are very important:

1. If any electric arc welding is to be done on the car always disconnect the alternator and control unit.

2. Should a replacement alternator be fitted it must be of the same type and polarity as the original. The terminal polarity is very clearly marked.

3. The battery connections must never be reversed as this will damage the alternator rectifiers. Always connect the earth terminal of the battery first.

4. If a high rate battery charger is to be used to recharge a discharged battery on the car expensive damage will occur to the control unit if the ignition starter switch is moved to the auxiliary position. Always disconnect the control unit as a safety measure before boost charging. Remember to re-connect the control unit after charging.

5. If a high rate charger is being used to start the engine with a discharged battery, disconnect the control unit before using the charger. Do not re-connect the control unit until the charger has been disconnected and the engine is running at a normal idle speed.

6. Never disconnect the battery when the engine is running and never run the alternator with the main output cable disconnected at either the alternator or battery end.

7. The heavy duty cable connecting the battery to the alternator is always live. Take great care not to earth the alternator terminal or the cable end if removed from the terminal. Do not make or break any connections in the charging circuit with the engine running except as in paragraph 5 above.

8. Always keep the driving belt correctly tensioned so that a deflection of $\frac{1}{2}$ inch can be obtained under normal finger pressure at the mid point of its longest run.

9. Do not apply any leverage to the alternator except at the drive end bracket.

10. Keep the slip ring end cover ventilation holes clean at all times.

13. Starter motor - general description

The starter motor is mounted on the right hand lower side of the engine end plate, and is held in position by two bolts which also clamp the bellhousing flange. The motor is of the four field coil, four pole piece type, and utilises four spring loaded commutator brushes. Two of these brushes are earthed, and the other two are insulated and attached to the field coil ends.

14. Starter motor - testing in engine

1. If the starter motor fails to operate then check the condition of the battery by turning on the headlamps. If they glow brightly for several seconds and then gradually dim, the battery is in an uncharged condition.

2. If the headlamps glow brightly and it is obvious that the battery is in good condition then check the tightness of the battery wiring connections (and in particular the earth lead from the battery terminal to its connection on the bodyframe). Check the tightness of the connections at the relay switch and at the starter motor. Check the wiring with a voltmeter for breaks or shorts.

3. If the wiring is in order then check that the starter motor switch is operating. To do this press the rubber covered button in the centre of the relay switch under the bonnet. If it is working the starter motor will be heard to 'click' as it tries to rotate. Alternatively check it with a voltmeter.

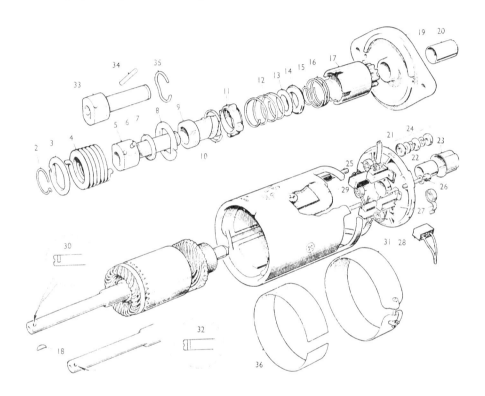

Fig. 12.5. EXPLODED VIEW OF LUCAS STARTER MOTOR

No.	Description	No.	Description	No.	Description	No.	Description
1	Drive assembly	10	Retaining ring*	19	Drive end bracket	28	Brush
2	Retaining ring	11	Control nut	20	Bush - driving end	29	Field coils
3	Anchor plate - front	12	Restraining spring	21	Commutator end bracket	30	Armature*
4	Main spring	13	Thrust washer - control nut	22	Bush - commutator end	31	Cover band ⁄
5	Centre sleeve*	14	Locating collar	23	Cap - shaft	32	Armature ⁄
6	Retaining pin*	15	Retaining ring	24	Terminal nuts and washers	33	Centre sleeve ⁄
7	Thrust washer (fibre)	16	Spring	25	Terminal post	34	Spiral pin ⁄
8	Anchor plate - rear	17	Pinion and barrel	26	Through-bolt	35	Waved circlip ⁄
9	Screwed sleeve	18	Woodruff - key*	27	Spring - brush tension	36	Seal - cover band ⁄

*For starter motors Serial No. 25555   ⁄ For starter motors Serial No. 25599

4.   If the battery is fully charged, the wiring in order, and the switch working and the starter motor fails to operate then it will have to be removed from the car for examination. Before this is done, however, ensure that the starter pinion has not jammed in mesh with the flywheel. Check by turning the square end of armature shaft with a spanner. This will free the pinion if it is stuck in engagement with the flywheel teeth.

15.   Starter motor - removal and replacement

1.   Disconnect the battery positive terminal and also the starter motor cable from the terminal on the starter motor end plate.

2.   Remove the two bolts which secure the starter motor to the flywheel housing and engine rear plate. Lift the starter motor away by manipulating downwards from the underside of the power unit compartment.

3.   Refitting is the reverse procedure to removal. Make sure that the starter motor cable when secured in position by its terminal does not touch any part of the body or power unit which could damage the insulation.

16.   Starter motor and drive gear - dismantling and re-assembly

1.   With the starter motor on the bench, loosen the screw on the cover band and slip the cover band off. An exploded view of the starter motor is shown in Fig 12:5.

2.   With a piece of wire bent into the shape of a hook, lift back each of the brush springs in turn and check the movement of the brushes in their holders by pulling on the flexible connectors.

3.   If the brushes (28) are so worn that their faces do not rest against the commutator, or if the ends of the brush leads are exposed on their working face, they must be renewed.

4.   If any of the brushes tend to stick in their holders then wash them with a petrol moistened cloth and, if necessary, lightly polish the sides of the brush with a very fine file, until the brushes move quite freely in their holders.

5.   If the surface of the commutator is dirty or blackened, clean it with a petrol dampened rag. Secure the starter motor in a vice and check it by connecting a heavy gauge cable between the starter motor terminal and a 12 volt battery.

6.   Connect the cable from the other battery terminal to earth in the starter motor body. If the motor turns at high speed it is in good order.

7.   If the starter motor still fails to function or if it is wished to renew the brushes, then it is necessary to further dismantle the motor.

8.   Start by lifting the brush spring (27) with the aid of a wire hook, off the brushes, and then take out the brushes from their holders one at a time.

9.   Working from the drive end of the starter motor, remove the circlip (2) from off the outer end of the drive head sleeve, and then remove the front spring anchor plate (3), the main spring (4), and then the rear spring anchor plate.

10.   Pull out the pin (6 or 34) which holds the drive head sleeve (5 or 33) to the armature shaft (30-32) and slide the sleeve assembly down the shaft. Then remove the woodruff key (18).

11.   The complete drive assembly (1) can now be pushed off the armature shaft (30 or 32).

12.   Extract the barrel retaining ring (10) from the in-

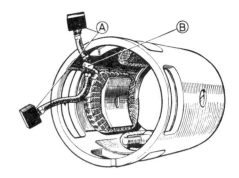

Fig. 12. 6. STARTER MOTOR BRUSH CONNECTIONS
No.	Description	No.	Description
A	Brushes	B	Tapping on field coils

side of the pinion and barrel assembly (17) and pull off the barrel and anti-drift spring (16) from the screwed sleeve (9).

13.   From the inner end of the drive head sleeve take off the circlip (15), locating collar (14), control nut thrust washer (13), cushioning spring (12), control nut (11), screwed sleeve (9) and the drive head thrust washer (7).

14.   Undo the terminal nuts and washers (24) from the terminal post (25) and unscrew and remove the two through bolts and spring washers (26).

15.   The commutator end bracket (21), the drive end bracket (19), and the armature (30) can now be removed.

16.   At this stage if the brushes are to be renewed their flexible connectors must be unsoldered and the connectors of new brushes soldered in their place. Check that the new brushes move freely in their holders. If cleaning the commutator with petrol fails to remove all the burnt areas and spots then wrap a piece of glass paper round the commutator and rotate the armature.

17.   If the commutator is very badly worn mount the armature in a lathe and with the lathe turning at high speed, take a very fine cut out of the commutator and finish the surface by polishing with glass paper. DO NOT UNDERCUT THE MICA INSULATORS BETWEEN THE COMMUTATOR SEGMENTS.

18.   With the starter motor dismantled, test the four field coils for an open circuit. Connect a 12 volt battery with a 12 volt bulb in one of the leads between the field terminal post and the tapping point of the field coils to which the brushes are connected. An open circuit is proved by the bulb not lighting.

19.   If the bulb lights, it does not necessarily mean that the field coils are in order, as there is a possibility that one of the coils will be earthing to the starter yoke or pole shoes. To check this, remove the lead from the brush connector and place it against a clean portion of the starter yoke. If the bulb lights the field coils are earthing.

20.   Replacement of the field coils calls for the use of a wheel operated screwdriver, a soldering iron, caulking and riveting operations and is beyond the scope of the majority of owners. The starter yoke should be taken to an automobile electrical engineering works for new field coils to be fitted. Alternatively, purchase an exchange Lucas starter motor.

21.   If the armature is damaged this will be evident after visual inspection. Look for signs of burning, discolouration, and for conductors that have lifted away from the

commutator. Ensure that if any parts of the drive gear are worn or damaged they are renewed.
22. Reassembly is a straight reversal of the dismantling procedure.

17. Starter motor bushes - inspection, removal and replacement

1. With the starter motor stripped down check the condition of the bushes. They should be renewed when they are sufficiently worn to allow visible side movement of the armature shaft.
2. The old bushes are simply driven out with a suitable drift and the new bushes inserted by the same method. As the bearings are of the phosphor bronze type it is essential that they are allowed to stand in S.A.E. 30 engine oil for at least 24 hours before fitment.

18. Control box - general description

1. The control box is positioned on the right hand wing valance and comprises three units: two separate vibrating armature - type single contact regulators and a cut out relay. One of the regulators is sensitive to change in current and the other to changes in voltage.
2. Adjustments can be made only with a special tool which resembles a screwdriver with a multi-toothed blade. This can be obtained through Lucas agents.
3. The regulators control the output from the dynamo depending on the state of the battery and the demands of the electrical equipment, and ensure that the battery is not overcharged. The cut out is really an automatic switch and connects the dynamo to the battery when the dynamo is turning fast enough to produce a charge. Similarly it disconnects the battery from the dynamo when the engine is idling or stationary so that the battery does not discharge through the dynamo.

19. Cut out and regulator contacts - maintenance

1. Every 12,000 miles check the cut out and regulator contacts. If they are dirty or rough or burnt place a piece of fine glass paper (DO NOT USE EMERY PAPER OR CARBORUNDUM PAPER) between the cut out contacts, close them manually and draw the glass paper through several times.
2. Clean the regulator contacts in exactly the same way, but use emery or carborundum paper and not glass paper. Carefully clean both sets of contacts from all traces of dust with a rag moistened in methylated spirits.

20. Voltage regulator - adjustment

1. The regulator requires very little attention during its service life, and if there should be any reason to suspect its correct functioning, tests of all circuits should be made to ensure that they are not the reason for the trouble.
2. These checks include the tension of the fan belt, to make sure that it is not slipping and so providing only a very low charge rate. The battery should be carefully checked for possible low charge rate due to a faulty cell, or corroded battery connections.
3. The leads from the generator may have been crossed during replacement, and if this is the case then the regulator points will have stuck together as soon as the generator starts to charge. Check for loose or broken leads from the generator to the regulator.
4. If after a thorough check it is considered advisable to test the regulator this should be carried out only by an electrician who is well acquainted with the correct method, using test bench equipment.
5. Pull off the Lucas connections from the two adjacent

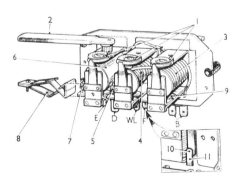

Fig. 12.7. CONTROL BOX (COVER REMOVED)

No.	Description	No.	Description
1	Adjustment cams	7	Voltage regulator contacts
2	Setting tool	8	Clip - contacts
3	Cut-out relay	9	Armature back stop
4	Current regulator	10	Cut-out contacts
5	Current relay contacts	11	Fixed contact bracket
6	Voltage regulator		

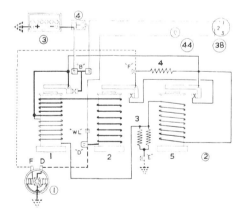

Fig. 12.8. CHARGING CIRCUIT WIRING DIAGRAM

No.	Description	No.	Description
(1)	Dynamo	1	Cut-out relay
(2)	Control box (RB340)	2	Current regulator
(3)	Battery	3	Swamp resistor
(4)	Starter solenoid	4	Contacts resistor
(38)	Starter/ignition switch	5	Voltage regulator
(44)	Ignition warning light		

control box terminals 'B'. To start the engine it will now be necessary to join together the ignition and battery leads with a suitable wire.

6.   Connect a 0-20 volt voltmeter between terminal 'D' on the control box and terminal 'WL'. Start the engine and run it at 3,000 rpm. The reading on the voltmeter should be steady and lie between the limits detailed in the specification.

7.   If the reading is unsteady this may be due to dirty contacts. If the reading is outside the specified limits stop the engine and adjust the voltage regulator in the following manner:

8.   Take off the control box cover and start and run the engine at 3,000 rpm. Using the correct tool turn the voltage adjustment cam anti-clockwise to raise the setting and clockwise to lower it. To check that the setting is correct, stop the engine, and then start it and run it at 3,000 rpm noting the reading. Refit the cover and the connections to the 'WL' and 'D' terminals.

21. Current regulator - adjustment

1.   The output from the current regulator should equal the maximum output from the dynamo which is 22 amps. To test this it is necessary to bypass the cut out by holding the contacts together.

2.   Remove the cover from the control box and with a bulldog clip hold the cut out contacts together.

3.   Pull off the wires from the adjacent terminals 'B' and connect a 0-40 moving-coil ammeter to one of the terminals and to the leads.

4.   All the other load connections including the ignition must be made to the battery.

5.   Turn on all the lights and other electrical accessories and run the engine at 3,000 rpm. The ammeter should give a steady reading between 19 and 22 amps. If the needle flickers it is likely that the points are dirty. If the reading is too low turn the special Lucas tool clockwise to raise the setting and anti-clockwise to lower it.

22. Cut out - adjustment

1.   Check the voltage required to operate the cut out by connecting a voltmeter between the control box terminals 'D' and 'WL'. Remove the control box cover, start the engine and gradually increase its speed until the cut out closes. This should occur when the reading is between 12.7 to 13.3 volts.

2.   If the reading is outside these limits turn the cut out adjusting cam by means of the adjusting tool, a fraction at a time clockwise to raise the voltage, and anti-clockwise to lower it.

3.   To adjust the drop off voltage bend the fixed contact blade carefully. The adjustment to the cut out should be completed within 30 seconds of starting the engine as otherwise heat build-up from the shunt-coil will affect the readings.

4.   If the cut out fails to work, clean the contacts, and if there is still no response, renew the cut out and regulator unit.

23. Fuses - general

The fuses are mounted in a holder located on the harness connector situated next to the control box on the engine bulkhead as shown in Fig 12:9.

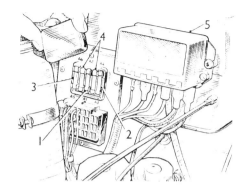

Fig. 12.9. THE REGULATOR AND FUSE BOX WITH THE FUSE BOX
COVER REMOVED

No.	Description	No.	Description
1 Fuse A1-A2		4 Spare fuses	
2 Fuse A3-A4		5 Control box	
3 Fuse A5-A6			

A 35 amp fuse is placed between the terminals A1 and A2 and gives protection to the accessories which operate whether the ignition is switched on or not. A second 35 amp fuse is placed between the terminals A3 and A4 and gives protection to the accessories which operate only when the ignition is switched on.

Fitted between terminals A5 and A6 is a 35 amp fuse which protects the front and tail side light circuits. Two spare fuses are provided on the fuse holder.

If any of the fuses blow due to a short circuit or similar trouble, trace the source of the trouble and rectify before fitting a new fuse.

24. Flasher unit

The actual flasher unit is enclosed in a small cylindrical metal container and is operated when the ignition is on by a composite switch mounted on the steering column.

If the flasher unit fails to operate, or works very slowly or very rapidly, check out the flasher indicator circuit as detailed below, before assuming there is a fault in the unit itself.

1.   Examine the direction indicator bulbs front and rear for broken filaments.

2.   If the external flashers are working but the internal flasher warning light has ceased to function check the filament of the warning bulb and replace as necessary.

3.   With the aid of the wiring diagram check all the flasher circuit connections if a flasher bulb is sound but does not work.

4.   In the event of total direction indicator failure, check the A3-A4 fuse.

5.   With the ignition turned on check that current is reaching the flasher unit by connecting a voltmeter between the 'plus' or 'B' terminal and earth. If this test is positive connect the 'plus' or 'B' terminal and the 'L' terminal and operate the flasher switch. If the flasher bulb lights up the flasher unit itself is defective and must be replaced as it is not possible to dismantle and repair it.

It is important that the flasher unit is mounted in the horizontal position with the terminal marked 'P' in the 3 or 9 o'clock position to ensure long and reliable operation.

25. Windscreen wiper mechanism - maintenance

Renew the windscreen wiper blades at intervals of 12,000 miles, or more frequently if necessary.

The cable which drives the wiper blades from the gearbox attached to the windscreen wiper motor is pre-packed with grease and requires no maintenance. The washer round the wheelbase spindle can be lubricated with several drops of glycerine every 6,000 miles.

26. Windscreen wiper mechanism - fault diagnosis and rectification

Should the windscreen wipers fail, or work very slowly, then check the terminals for loose connections, and make sure the insulation of the external wiring is not cracked or broken. If this is in order then check the current the motor is taking by connecting up a 1-20 volt voltmeter in the circuit and turning on the wiper switch. Consumption should be between 2.3 to 3.1 amps.

If no current is passing through check the A3-A4 fuse. If the fuse has blown replace it after having checked the wiring of the motor and other electrical circuits serviced by this fuse for short circuits. If the fuse is in good condition check the wiper switch.

If the wiper motor takes a very high current check the wiper blades for freedom of movement. If this is satisfactory check the gearbox cover and gear assembly for damage and measure the armature end float which should be between .009 to .012 inch (.20 to .30 mm). The end float is set by the adjusting screw. Check that excessive friction in the cable connecting tubes caused by too small a curvature is not the cause of the high current consumption.

If the motor takes a very low current ensure that the battery is fully charged. Check the brush gear after removing the commutator end bracket and ensure that the brushes have freedom of movement and if necessary, renew the tension spring. If the brushes are very worn they should be replaced with new ones. The brush levers should be quite free on their pivots. If stiff, loosen them by moving them backwards and forwards by hand and by applying a little thin machine oil. Check the armature by substitution if this unit is suspected.

27. Windscreen wiper blades - fail to park

If the windscreen wipers fail to park or only park intermittently, then the fault is almost certain to be that the limit switch is incorrectly set.

To reset the limit switch remove the four screws which hold the gearbox cover in position and turn the circular cover until the setting pip on top of the cover lines up, and is nearest to, the slightly offset groove in the gearbox cover.

28. Windscreen wiper blades - changing wiping arc

If it is wished to change the area through which the wiper blades move this is simply done by removing each blade in turn from each splined drive, and then replacing it on the drive in slightly different position.

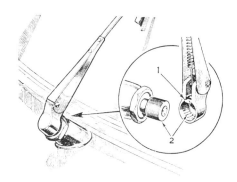

Fig. 12.10. WINDSCREEN WIPER ARM ATTACHMENT TO WHEEL-BOX SPINDLE

No.	Description	No.	Description
1	Retaining clip	2	Splined drive

29. Windscreen wiper motor (single speed) - gearbox and wheelbox - removal and replacement

1. Remove the windscreen wiper arms by lifting the blades, carefully raising the retaining clip and then pulling the arms off the splined drive shafts.
2. Disconnect the positive terminal of the battery and also the electrical cables from the motor housing.
3. Using an open ended spanner remove the Bundy pipe union nut from the end of the wiper motor gearbox. Remove the two bolts which hold the mounting bracket to the wing valance and carefully withdraw the motor and cable rack clear of the Bundy pipe.
4. From behind the fascia panel slacken the two cover screws in each wheelbox and remove the Bundy pipe in each case. Also remove the nut and front distance collar from outside the car. Push in the spindle and remove the wheelbox together with the rear bush from inside the car. NOTE: On Wolseley models covered by this manual the fascia panel must be removed. Full details of this operation are given in Chapter 14.
5. Replacement is a straight reversal of the above sequence but take care that the cable rack emerges properly and that the wheelboxes are correctly aligned.

30. Windscreen wiper motor (single speed) - dismantling, inspection and reassembly

If the motor is not functioning check first that current is reaching it. If this test is positive then the motor can be dismantled, inspected, and reassembled in the following sequence:
1. Undo the four bolts holding the motor gearbox cover in place and remove the cover (1) Fig 12:11.
2. Unscrew and remove the two through bolts (16) at the commutator bracket end and pull off the connectors.
3. Pull the commutator end bracket away from the yoke (23) so exposing the brushes (18).
4. Note which way round the brushes fit so that they can be replaced in their original positions. Remove the brushes in their assembly as one piece.
5. If it is wished to remove the field coil, first mark the two screws which hold the pole piece to the yoke so the screws can be replaced in their original positions. Undo them.
6. Press out the pole piece and field coil, mark the pole piece so it can be replaced in its original position

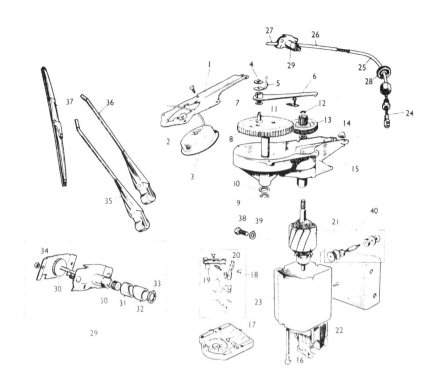

Fig. 12.11. EXPLODED VIEW OF LUCAS 6 W.A. SINGLE SPEED WIPER MOTOR

No. Description	No. Description	No. Description	No. Description
1 Gearbox cover	12 Circlip	23 Yoke	31 Rear bush
2 Gearbox cover locking plate	13 Intermediate gear	24 Cross-head and rack	32 Front bush
3 Parking switch	14 Plain washer	25 Motor to wheelbox - outer casing	33 Nut for wheelbox to dash
4 Circlip	15 Gearbox	26 Wheelbox to wheelbox - outer casing	34 Nut for wheelbox cover
5 Earth connector	16 Bolts	27 Wheelbox end - outer casing	35 Wiper arm - R.H.D.
6 Cross-head connecting link	17 Commutator end bracket	28 Grommet	36 Wiper arm - L.H.D.
7 Plain washer	18 Brush assembly	29 Wheelbox assembly	37 Wiper arm blade
8 Final gear	19 Brushes	30 Spindle and gear	38 Screw for motor to valance
9 Circlip	20 Brush spring		39 Shakeproof washer
10 Plain washer	21 Armature		40 Fixing stud assembly
11 Armature end-play stop	22 Field coil		

inside the yoke, and then press the pole piece out of the field coil.

Inspect the internal wiring in the motor for signs of burning indicating a short circuit. Insulate any chaffed or burnt wire. Examine the internal wiring for breaks and repair as necessary.

Small pieces of carbon can short circuit adjacent commutator segments. The pressure of carbon will also cause high current consumption. Clean both the commutator and the brushes and replace the latter if badly worn.

Check the resistance between adjacent segments of the commutator. The correct reading is between 0.34 and 0.41 ohms. Check the resistance of the field coil. It should be between 12.8 and 14 ohms. If it is lower than 12.8 ohms it is likely that there is a short circuit in the winding, which means that a new field coil must be fitted.

Reassembly is a straightforward reversal of the dismantling instructions. NOTE: The armature bearings, the commutator end of the armature shaft and the

felt lubricator in the gearbox must be lubricated with S.A.E. 20 engine oil during reassembly. The self aligning bearing should be immersed in the same grade of oil for 24 hours before it is refitted. The cable rack and wheelhoses, the worm wheel bearings, cross head, guide channel, connecting rod, crankpin, worm and final gear shaft should all be packed generously with a grease such as Castrolease LM or similar.

---

31. Windscreen wiper motor (single speed) - Limit switch resetting

---

If the wiper motor has been dismantled or the wiper arms moved it may be necessary to reset the self parking mechanism. This is achieved by loosening the gearbox cover (1), Fig 12:11, by slackening the retaining screws and rotating the parking switch (3) until by trial and error the correct setting is found. Re-tighten the cover retaining screws.

32. Windscreen wiper motor (two speed) - gearbox and wheelbox - removal and replacement

1. Remove the windscreen wiper arms by lifting the blades, carefully raising the retaining clip and then pulling the arms off the splined drive shafts, (see Fig 12:10).
2. Disconnect the positive terminal of the battery and also the electrical cable terminal connector from the motor housing.
3. Using an open ended spanner, remove the Bundy pipe union nut from the end of the wiper motor gearbox. Release the mounting bracket from the wing valance and carefully withdraw the motor and cable rack clear of the Bundy pipe.
4. Remove the parcel tray tops, the instruments and demister ducts. Slacken the cover of each wheel box.
5. Unscrew the nuts and lift away the distance collars from outside the car. Release the bulkhead grommet and finally push down on the spindles and remove from behind the fascia panel.
6. Replacement is a straightforward reversal of the above sequence but take care that the cable rack emerges properly and that the wheelboxes are correctly aligned.

33. Windscreen wiper motor (two speed) - dismantling, inspection and reassembly

1. Refer to Fig 12:12 and remove the four gearbox cover retaining screws (2) and lift away the cover (1). Release the circlip (4) and flat washer (5) securing the connecting rod (3) to the crankpin on the shaft and gear (7). Lift away the connecting rod (3) followed by the second flash washer (5).
2. Release the circlip (4) and washer (5) securing the shaft and gear (7) to the gearbox body (9).
3. De-burr the gear shaft and lift away the gear making a careful note of the location of the dished washer (8).
4. Scribe a mark on the yoke assembly (15) and gearbox body (9) to ensure correct reassembly and unscrew the two yoke bolts (16) from the motor yoke assembly (15). Part the yoke assembly including armature (14) from the gearbox body. As the yoke has residual magnetism ensure that the yoke is kept well away from metallic dust.
5. Unscrew the two screws (13) securing the brush gear and the terminal and switch assembly and remove both the assemblies.
6. Inspect the brushes for signs of excessive wear. If

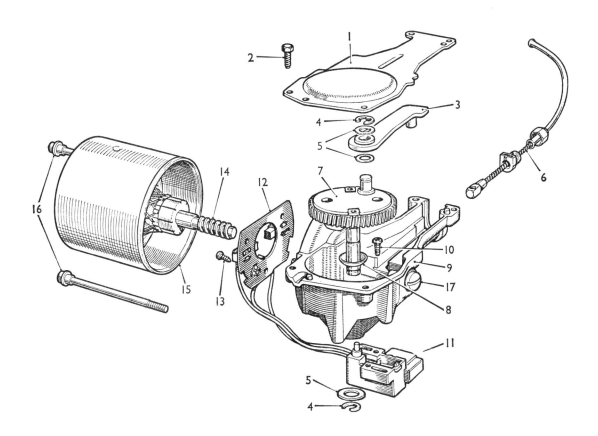

Fig. 12.12. EXPLODED VIEW OF LUCAS 14 W TWO SPEED WIPER MOTOR

No.	Description	No.	Description	No.	Description	No.	Description
1	Gearbox cover	6	Cross-head and rack	10	Screw for limit switch	14	Armature
2	Screw for cover	7	Shaft and gear	11	Limit switch assembly	15	Yoke assembly
3	Connecting rod	8	Dished washer	12	Brush gear	16	Yoke bolts
4	Circlip	9	Gearbox	13	Screw for brush gear	17	Armature thrust screw
5	Plain washers						

the main brushes are worn to a limit of 3/16 inches or the narrow section of the third brush is worn to the full width of the brush fit a new brush gear assembly. Ensure that the three brushes move freely in their boxes. If a push type spring gauge is available check the spring rate which should be between 5 to 7 ounces when the bottom of the brush is level with the bottom of the slot in the brush box. Again if the spring rate is incorrect fit a new brush gear assembly.

7.   If the armature is suspect take it to an automobile electrician to test for open or short circuiting.

8.   Inspect the gear wheel for signs of excessive wear or damage and fit a new one if necessary.

9.   Reassembly is the reverse procedure to dismantling but there are several points that require special attention:

10.   Use only Ragosine Listate grease to lubricate the gear wheel teeth and cam, the armature shaft worm gear, connecting rod and its connecting pin, the cross head slide and cable rack and wheelbox gear wheels.

11.   Use only Shell Turbo 41 oil to lubricate the bearing bushes, the armature shaft bearing journals (sparingly), the gear wheel shaft and crankpin, the felt washer in the yoke bearing (thoroughly soak) and the wheelbox spindles.

12.   The yoke assembly fixing bolts should be tightened using a torque wrench set to 14 lbs in.

13.   When a replacement armature is to be fitted, slacken the thrust screw (17) Fig 12:12 so as to provide end float for fitting the yoke.

14.   The thrust disc inside the yoke bearing should be fitted with the concave side towards the end face of the bearing.   The dished washer fitted beneath the gear wheel should have its concave side towards the gear wheel as shown in Fig 12:12.

15.   The larger of the two flat washers is fitted underneath the connecting rod and the smaller one on top under the retaining circlip.

16.   To adjust the armature end float, tighten the thrust screw, shown in Fig 12:13, and then turn back one quarter of a turn so giving an end float of between 0.002 and 0.008 inch.   The gap should be measured under the head of the thrust screw.   Fit a shim of suitable size beneath the head and tighten the screw.

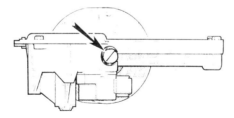

Fig. 12.13. Position of armature end-float adjusting screw

34.   Horn and horn push

It is important that if the horn works badly or completely fails, the wiring leading to it is checked for short circuiting or loose connections.   Ensure that the horn is firmly secured and that there is nothing lying on the horn body.

If the fault is not an external one remove the horn cover and check the leads inside the horn.   If these are sound, check the contact breaker contacts.   If these are burnt or dirty, clean them with a fine file and wipe all traces of dirt and dust away with a petrol moistened rag.

Test the current consumption of the horn which should be between 3 and 3½ amps.

To adjust the contact breaker to compensate for wear, unhook the locknut and turn the small serrated adjustment screw anti-clockwise, at the same time pushing the horn push to sound the horn.   As soon as the horn stops, turn the screw clockwise about a quarter of a turn.   This will start the horn again and represents the correct adjustment.

On models fitted with twin horns adjust each horn singly by disconnecting the other instrument.   Wrap a piece of insulating tape round the disconnected wires to prevent the live one touching an earth and blowing the '1' to '2' fuse.

If clear type horns are fitted turn the small serrated adjustment screw located on the top of the horn body in a clockwise direction and then turn back in an anti-clockwise direction as far as possible without losing volume.

The horn push in the centre of the steering wheel is removed by depressing the horn push centre and turning it in an anti-clockwise direction so releasing it from its bayonet fixing in the steering wheel hub.

35.   Headlamp - removal, replacement and adjustment

The headlamp units fitted to cars being used in the United Kingdom or North America are of the sealed beam type.   Due to their design they may be serviced only as a complete unit.

1.   Remove the screw which secures the outer rim (3) Fig 12:14 to the light assembly and lift away the outer rim.

2.   Remove the three screws which hold the inner rim (5) to the seating rim (7) and lift away the inner rim.

3.   Carefully draw the sealed beam unit (2) forwards until the connector (6) is exposed and disconnect the sealed beam unit from the connector.

4.   Refitting is the reverse sequence to the above.

36.   Headlamp - beam adjustment

The headlights may be adjusted for both vertical and horizontal beam position by the three screws (1) Fig 12:14 for vertical movement and (8), only one shown,

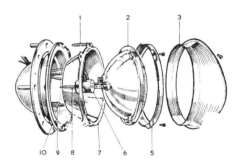

Fig. 12.14. HEADLAMP MOUNTINGS AND ADJUSTMENT SCREW POSITIONS

No.	Description	No.	Description
1	Vertical adjustment	6	Connector
2	Sealed-beam unit	7	Seating rim
3	Rim	8	Horizontal adjustment
4	Rim fixing screw	9	Spring - unit seating
5	Unit retaining plate	10	Seating washer

for horizontal movement.

They should be set so that on full or high beam the beams are set slightly below parallel with a level road surface. Do not forget that the beam position is affected by how the car is normally loaded for night driving and set the beams loaded to this condition.

37. Headlamp - relay unit

A relay unit is fitted onto the side and headlight circuits so that when the side lights are switched on and the direction indicator or stop lamps operated they are dimmed to stop glare for following drivers. The unit is sealed and cannot be adjusted so that if the unit is suspect it should be checked by substitution for a known good unit. It is located in the rear luggage compartment through the right hand rear light access panel.

38. Rear screen

To test the electrically heated rear screen, switch on the ignition and heater booster motor. The warning light operates when the switch is in the 'ON' position only. Should the rear screen not warm up as it should, check for current at the snap connector situated in the rear luggage compartment. Ensure that there is a good earth electrical connection on the body panel. If current is reaching the connector remake the connection and re-test and this time if the heater does not operate it is probable that the element has failed necessitating a new rear screen to be fitted.

39. Electrical system - fitting accessories

Provision has been made for the fitting of additional electrical accessories into the system at the bulkhead connection panel. First release the panel by undoing the retaining screws.

Next decide w h i c h electrical supply is required either controlled by ignition switch (A4 and green cables) or always live (A2 and purple cables).

For an accessory to be fitted at some location in front of the panel, carefully withdraw a purple or green cable and fit a 'pick-a-back' with cable attached in its place and then slide the existing cable socket onto the 'pick-a-back'. (These are obtainable from most garages or motor accessory shops). Then connect the connector to a switch.

Select one of the 'LM' positions and gently insert a terminal blade from t h e back making sure that its locking tongue engages correctly. Join the switch and the terminal blade cables with a snap connector. Finally

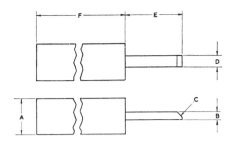

Fig. 12.15. TERMINAL EXTRACTOR TOOL, USEFUL WHEN FITTING ACCESSORIES TO TERMINAL BLOCK

No.	Description	No.	Description
A	.250 in. (6.4 mm)	D	.075 in. (1.9 mm)
B	.045 in. (1.1 mm)	E	.500 in. (13 mm)
C	.035 in. (0.9 mm) at 45°	F	1.5 in. (38 mm)

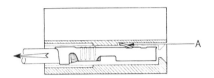

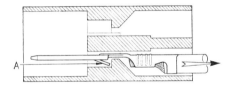

Fig. 12.16. METHOD OF REMOVING TERMINAL FROM TERMINAL BLOCK

No.   Description
1 Depress tab 'A'
2 Pull terminal from terminal block

remove the six way plug moulding and fit in a snap in socket with cable attached taking care that the socket and terminal positions match. Terminate the lead at t h e accessory and complete the electrical circuit by selecting a good earth return point on the body.

If the accessory is to be fitted back from the rear of the panel, carefully withdraw a purple or green cable and fit a 'pick-a-back' with cable attached in its place and slide the existing cable socket into the 'pick-a-back'. Then connect the accessory to a switch.

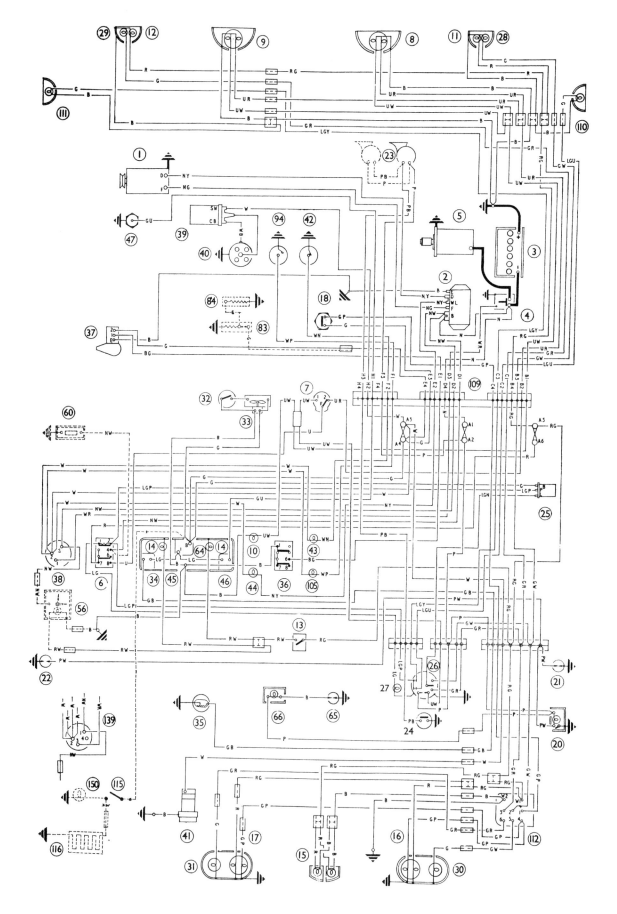

Fig. 12.17. WIRING DIAGRAM, AUSTIN & MORRIS 1800 MK I

Fig. 12.17. WIRING DIAGRAM, AUSTIN AND MORRIS
1800 MK I

1 Dynamo
2 Control box
3 Battery (12-volt)
4 Starter solenoid
5 Starter motor
6 Lighting switch
7 Headlight dip switch
8 R.H. headlamp
9 L.H. headlamp
10 Main-beam warning light
11 R.H. sidelamp
12 L.H. sidelamp
13 Panel light switch
14 Panel lights
15 Number-plate lamp
16 R.H. stop and tail lamp
17 L.H. stop and tail lamp
18 Stop light switch
20 Interior lamp
21 R.H. door switch
22 L.H. door switch
23 Horn (twin horns when fitted)
24 Horn-push
25 Flasher unit
26 Direction indicator switch with headlamp flasher
27 Direction indicator warning light
28 R.H. front flasher
29 L.H. front flasher
30 R.H. rear flasher
31 L.H. rear flasher
32 Heater or fresh-air motor switch
33 Heater or fresh-air motor
34 Fuel gauge
35 Fuel gauge tank unit
36 Windscreen wiper switch
37 Windscreen wiper
38 Starter and ignition switch
39 Ignition coil
40 Distributor
41 Fuel pump
42 Oil pressure switch
43 Oil pressure warning light
44 Ignition warning light
45 Speedometer
46 Coolant temperature gauge
47 Coolant temperature transmitter
56 Clock*
60 Radio*
64 Bi-metal instrument voltage stabilizer
65 Luggage compartment lamp switch
66 Luggage compartment lamp
83 Induction heater and thermostat ⚡
84 Suction chamber heater ⚡
94 Oil filter switch
105 Lubrication warning light
109 Multi-connector board with three 35-amp fuses
110 R.H. repeater flasher
111 L.H. repeater flasher
112 Day/night direction indicator and stop lamp relay
139 Starter and ignition switch - 4-position alternative

*Accessory   ⚡Special market fitment

CABLE COLOUR CODE

N. Brown P. Purple W. White U. Blue G. Green
Y. Yellow R. Red L.G. Light Green B. Black

When a cable has two colour code letters the first denotes the main colour and the second denotes the tracer
colour

Fig. 12.18. WIRING DIAGRAM, AUSTIN AND MORRIS
1800 MK II AND MK II 'S'

1 Dynamo
2 Regulator
3 Battery (12-volt)
4 Starter solenoid
5 Starter motor
6 Lighting switch
7 Headlight dip switch
8 R.H. headlamp
9 L.H. headlamp
10 Main-beam warning light
11 R.H. sidelamp
12 L.H. sidelamp
13 Panel lights switch
14 Panel lights
15 Number-plate lamp
16 R.H. stop and tail lamp
17 L.H. stop and tail lamp
18 Stop light switch
20 Interior lamp
21 R.H. door switch
22 L.H. door switch
23 Horn (twin horns when fitted)
24 Horn-push
25 Flasher unit
26 Combined direction indicator/headlamp flasher/
   headlamp high-low beam/horn-push switch
27 Direction indicator warning light
28 R.H. front flasher
29 L.H. front flasher
30 R.H. rear flasher
31 L.H. rear flasher
32 Heater or fresh-air motor switch
33 Heater or fresh-air motor
34 Fuel gauge
35 Fuel gauge tank unit
37 Windscreen wiper
38 Starter and ignition switch
39 Ignition coil
40 Distributor
43 Oil pressure warning light
44 Ignition warning light
45 Speedometer
46 Coolant temperature gauge
47 Coolant temperature transmitter
56 Clock*
60 Radio*
64 Bi-metal instrument voltage stabilizer
65 Luggage compartment lamp switch
66 Luggage compartment lamp
76 Indicator lamp - automatic transmission*
77 Electric windscreen washer
83 Induction heater and thermostat ⚡
84 Suction chamber heater ⚡
94 Oil filter switch
105 Oil filter warning light
109 Multi-connector board with three 17 amp fuses -
    current rated
110 R.H. repeater flasher
111 L.H. repeater flasher
112 Day/night direction indicator and stop lamp relay
115 Demist switch) Rear window*
116 Demist unit   )
131 Reverse and automatic transmission safety switches
150 Warning light - rear window demist*
*Accessory or optional extra ⚡Special market fitment
CABLE COLOUR CODE
N. Brown P. Purple W. White U. Blue G. Green
Y. Yellow R. Red L.G. Light Green B. Black
When a cable has two colour code letters the first denotes the main colour and the second denotes the tracer
colour

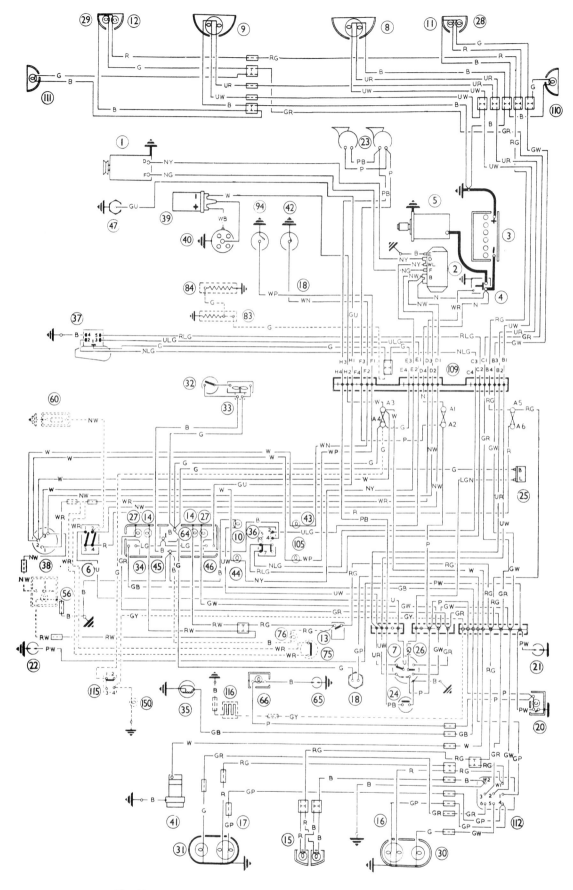

Fig. 12.18. WIRING DIAGRAM, AUSTIN & MORRIS 1800 MK II and MK II 'S'

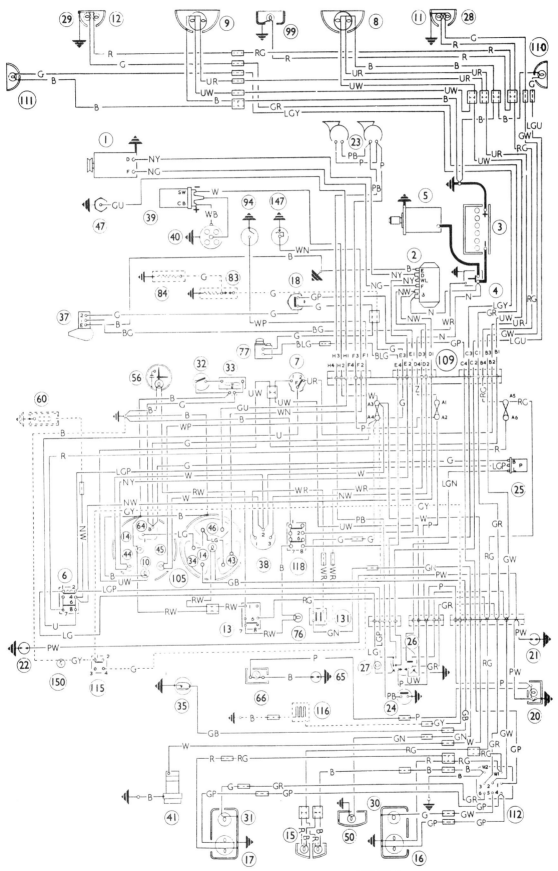

Fig. 12.19. WIRING DIAGRAM, WOLSELEY 18/85 MK I

Fig. 12. 19. WIRING DIAGRAM, WOLSELEY 18/85 MK I

1 Dynamo
2 Control box
3 Battery (12-volt)
4 Starter solenoid
5 Starter motor
6 Lighting switch
7 Headlight dip switch
8 R. H. headlamp
9 L. H. headlamp
10 Main-beam warning light
11 R. H. sidelamp
12 L. H. sidelamp
13 Panel lights switch
14 Panel lights
15 Number-plate lamp
16 R. H. stop and tail lamp
17 L. H. stop and tail lamp
18 Stop light switch
20 Interior lamp
21 R. H. door switch
22 L. H. door switch
23 Horns
24 Horn-push
25 Flasher unit
26 Direction indicator switch with headlamp flasher
27 Direction indicator warning light
28 R. H. front flasher
29 L. H. front flasher
30 R. H. rear flasher
31 L. H. rear flasher
32 Heater or fresh-air motor switch
33 Heater or fresh-air motor
34 Fuel gauge
35 Fuel gauge tank unit
37 Windscreen wiper
38 Starter and ignition switch
39 Ignition coil
40 Distributor
41 Fuel pump S. U. electric
43 Oil pressure gauge
44 Ignition warning light
45 Speedometer
46 Coolant temperature gauge
47 Coolant temperature transmitter
50 Reverse lamp
56 Clock*
60 Radio*
64 Bi-metal instrument voltage stabilizer
65 Luggage compartment lamp switch
66 Luggage compartment lamp
76 Indicator lamp – automatic transmission*
77 Electric windscreen washer
83 Induction heater and thermostat ⟋
84 Suction chamber heater ⟋
94 Oil filter switch
99 Radiator badge lamp
105 Oil filter warning light
109 Multi-connector board with three 35-amp fuses
110 R. H. repeater flasher
111 L. H. repeater flasher
112 Day/night direction indicator and stop lamp relay
115 Demist switch) Rear window*
116 Demist unit   )
118 Combined windscreen wiper and washer switch
131 Reverse and automatic transmission safety switches
147 Oil pressure transmitter
150 Warning light – rear window demist*
*Accessory or optional extra   ⟋Special market fitment
CABLE COLOUR CODE
N. Brown P. Purple W. White U. Blue G. Green
    Y. Yellow R. Red L. G. Light Green B. Black
When a cable has two colour code letters the first denotes
the main colour and the second denotes the tracer colour

Fig. 12. 20. WIRING DIAGRAM WOLSELEY 18/85 MK II
AND MK II 'S'

1 Dynamo
2 Regulator
3 Battery (12-volt)
4 Starter solenoid) Inertia-type starter
5 Starter motor   )
6 Lighting switch
7 Headlight dip switch
8 R. H. headlamp
9 L. H. headlamp
10 Main-beam warning light
11 R. H. sidelamp
12 L. H. sidelamp
13 Panel lights switch
14 Panel lights
15 Number-plate lamp
16 R. H. stop and tail lamp
17 L. H. stop and tail lamp
18 Stop light switch
20 Interior lamp
21 R. H. door switch
22 L. H. door switch
23 Horn (twin horns when fitted)
24 Horn-push
25 Flasher unit
26 Combined direction indicator/headlamp flasher/
   headlamp high-low beam/horn-push switch
27 Direction indicator warning light
28 R. H. front flasher
29 L. H. front flasher
30 R. H. rear flasher
31 L. H. rear flasher
32 Heater or fresh-air motor switch
33 Heater or fresh-air motor
34 Fuel gauge
35 Fuel gauge tank unit
36 Windscreen wiper
37 Windscreen wiper motor
38 Ignition/starter switch
39 Ignition coil
40 Distributor
43 Oil pressure gauge
44 Ignition warning light
45 Speedometer
46 Coolant temperature gauge
47 Coolant temperature transmitter
50 Reverse lamp
56 Clock
60 Radio*
64 Bi-metal instrument voltage stabilizer
65 Luggage compartment lamp switch
66 Luggage compartment lamp
76 Indicator lamp – automatic transmission*
77 Electric windscreen washer
78 Electric windscreen washer switch
83 Induction heater and thermostat ⟋
84 Suction chamber heater ⟋
99 Radiator badge lamp
109 Multi-connector board with three 17-amp fuses
110 R. H. repeater flasher
111 L. H. repeater flasher
112 Day/night direction indicator and stop lamp relay
115 Demist switch) Rear window*
116 Demist unit   )
131 Reverse and automatic transmission safety switches
147 Oil pressure transmitter
150 Warning light – rear window demist*
*Accessory or optional extra   ⟋Special market fitment
CABLE COLOUR CODE
N. Brown P. Purple W. White U. Blue G. Green
    Y. Yellow R. Red L. G. Light Green B. Black
When a cable has two colour code letters the first denotes
the main colour and the second denotes the tracer colour

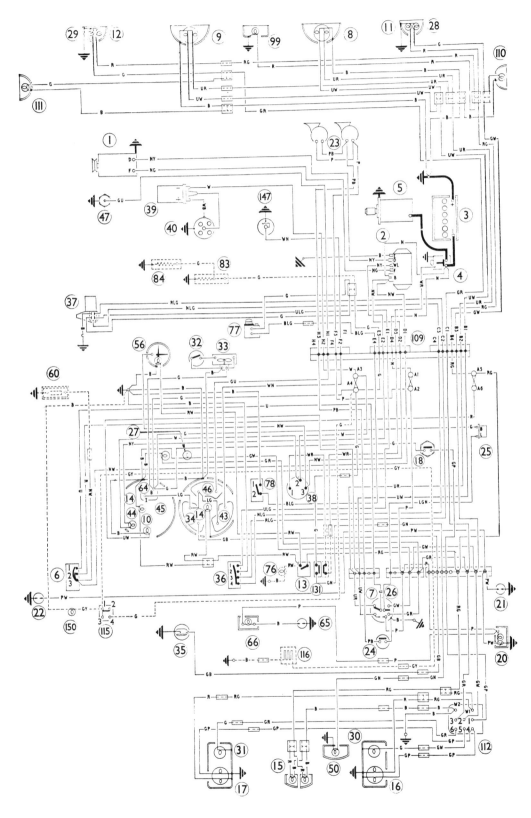

Fig. 12.20. WIRING DIAGRAM, WOLSELEY 18/85 MK II and MK II 'S'

FAULT FINDING CHART

Cause	Trouble	Remedy
SYMPTOM:	STARTER MOTOR FAILS TO TURN ENGINE	
No electricity at starter motor	Battery discharged Battery defective internally Battery terminal leads loose or earth lead not securely attached to body Loose or broken connections in starter motor circuit Starter motor switch or solenoid faulty	Charge battery. Fit new battery. Check and tighten leads. Check all connections and tighten any that are loose. Test and replace faulty components with new.
Electricity at starter motor: faulty motor	Starter motor pinion jammed in mesh with flywheel gear ring Starter brushes badly worn, sticking, or brush wires loose Commutator dirty, worn, or burnt Starter motor armature faulty Field coils earthed	Disengage pinion by turning squared end of armature shaft. Examine brushes, replace as necessary, tighten down brush wires. Clean commutator, recut if badly burnt. Overhaul starter motor, fit new armature. Overhaul starter motor.
SYMPTOM:	STARTER MOTOR TURNS ENGINE VERY SLOWLY	
Electrical defects	Battery in discharged condition Starter brushes badly worn, sticking, or brush wires loose Loose wires in starter motor circuit	Charge battery. Examine brushes, replace as necessary, tighten down brush wires. Check wiring and tighten as necessary.
SYMPTOM:	STARTER MOTOR OPERATES WITHOUT TURNING ENGINE	
Dirt or oil on drive gear	Starter motor pinion sticking on the screwed sleeve	Remove starter motor, clean starter motor drive.
Mechanical damage	Pinion or flywheel gear teeth broken or worn	Fit new gear ring to flywheel, and new pinion to starter motor drive.
SYMPTOMS:	STARTER MOTOR NOISY OR EXCESSIVELY ROUGH ENGAGEMENT	
Lack of attention or mechanical damage	Pinion or flywheel gear teeth broken or worn Starter drive main spring broken Starter motor retaining bolts loose	Fit new gear teeth to flywheel, or new pinion to starter motor drive. Dismantle and fit new main spring Tighten starter motor securing bolts. Fit new spring washer if necessary.
SYMPTOM:	BATTERY WILL NOT HOLD CHARGE FOR MORE THAN A FEW DAYS	
Wear or damage	Battery defective internally Electrolyte level too low or electrolyte too weak due to leakage Plate separators no longer fully effective Battery plates severely sulphated	Remove and fit new battery. Top up electrolyte level to just above plates Remove and fit new battery. Remove and fit new battery.
Insufficient current flow to keep battery charged	Fan/dynamo belt slipping Battery terminal connections loose or corroded Dynamo not charging properly Short in lighting circuit causing continual battery drain Regulator unit not working correctly	Check belt for wear, replace if necessary, and tighten. Check terminals for tightness, and remove all corrosion. Remove and overhaul dynamo. Trace and rectify. Check setting, clean, and replace if defective.
SYMPTOM:	IGNITION LIGHT FAILS TO GO OUT, BATTERY RUNS FLAT IN A FEW DAYS	
Dynamo not charging	Fan belt loose and slipping, or broken Brushes worn, sticking, broken, or dirty Brush springs weak or broken Commutator dirty, greasy, worn, or burnt	Check, replace, and tighten as necessary. Examine, clean, or replace brushes as necessary. Examine and test. Replace as necessary. Clean commutator and undercut segment separators.

	Armature badly worn or armature shaft bent	Fit new or reconditioned armature.
	Commutator bars shorting	Undercut segment separations.
	Dynamo bearings badly worn	Overhaul dynamo, fit new bearings.
	Dynamo field coils burnt, open, or shorted.	Remove and fit rebuilt dynamo.
	Commutator no longer circular	Recut commutator and undercut segment separators.
	Pole pieces very loose	Strip and overhaul dynamo. Tighten pole pieces.
Regulator or cut-out fails to work correctly	Regulator incorrectly set	Adjust regulator correctly.
	Cut-out incorrectly set	Adjust cut-out correctly.
	Open circuit in wiring of cut-out and regulator unit	Remove, examine, and renew as necessary.

Failure of individual electrical equipment to function correctly is dealt with alphabetically, item by item, under the headings listed below:

FUEL GAUGE

Fuel gauge gives no reading	Fuel tank empty!	Fill fuel tank.
	Electric cable between tank sender unit and gauge earthed or loose	Check cable for earthing and joints for tightness.
	Fuel gauge case not earthed	Ensure case is well earthed.
	Fuel gauge supply cable interrupted	Check and replace cable if necessary.
	Fuel gauge unit broken	Replace fuel gauge.
Fuel gauge registers full all the time	Electric cable between tank unit and gauge broken or disconnected	Check over cable and repair as necessary.

HORN

Horn operates all the time	Horn push either earthed or stuck down	Disconnect battery earth. Check and rectify source of trouble.
	Horn cable to horn push earthed	Disconnect battery earth. Check and rectify source of trouble.
Horn fails to operate	Blown fuse	Check and renew if broken. Ascertain cause.
	Cable or cable connection loose, broken or disconnected	Check all connections for tightness and cables for breaks.
	Horn has an internal fault	Remove and overhaul horn.
Horn emits intermittent or unsatisfactory noise	Cable connections loose	Check and tighten all connections.
	Horn incorrectly adjusted	Adjust horn until best note obtained.

LIGHTS

Lights do not come on	If engine not running, battery discharged	Push-start car, charge battery.
	Light bulb filament burnt out or bulbs broken	Test bulbs in live bulb holder.
	Wire connections loose, disconnected or broken	Check all connections for tightness and wire cable for breaks.
	Light switch shorting or otherwise faulty	By-pass light switch to ascertain if fault is in switch and fit new switch as appropriate.
Lights come on but fade out	If engine not running battery discharged	Push-start car, and charge battery.
Lights give very poor illumination	Lamp glasses dirty	Clean glasses.
	Reflector tarnished or dirty	Fit new reflectors.
	Lamps badly out of adjustment	Adjust lamps correctly.
	Incorrect bulb with too low wattage fitted	Remove bulb and replace with correct grade
	Existing bulbs old and badly discoloured	Renew bulb units.
	Electrical wiring too thin not allowing full current to pass	Rewire lighting system.

ELECTRICAL SYSTEM

Cause	Trouble	Remedy
Lights work erratically - flashing on and off, especially over bumps	Battery terminals or earth connection loose Lights not earthing properly Contacts in light switch faulty	Tighten battery terminals and earth connection. Examine and rectify. By-pass light switch to ascertain if fault is in switch and fit new switch as appropriate.
WIPERS		
Wiper motor fails to work	Blown fuse Wire connections loose, disconnected, or broken Brushes badly worn Armature worn or faulty Field coils faulty	Check and replace fuse if necessary. Check wiper wiring. Tighten loose connections. Remove and fit new brushes. If electricity at wiper motor remove and overhaul and fit replacement armature. Purchase reconditioned wiper motor.
Wiper motor works very slowly and takes excessive current	Commutator dirty, greasy, or burnt Drive to wheelboxes too bent or un-lubricated Wheelbox spindle binding or damaged Armature bearings dry or unaligned Armature badly worn or faulty	Clean commutator thoroughly. Examine drive and straighten out severe curvature. Lubricate. Remove, overhaul, or fit replacement. Replace with new bearings correctly aligned. Remove, overhaul, or fit replacement armature.
Wiper motor works slowly and takes little current	Brushes badly worn Commutator dirty, greasy, or burnt Armature badly worn or faulty	Remove and fit new brushes. Clean commutator thoroughly. Remove and overhaul armature or fit replacement.
Wiper motor works but wiper blades remain static	Driving cable rack disengaged or faulty Wheelbox gear and spindle damaged or worn Wiper motor gearbox parts badly worn	Examine and if faulty, replace. Examine and if faulty, replace. Overhaul or fit new gearbox.

Chapter 13/Suspension - Dampers - Steering

Contents

Specifications

1800 Mk I
Front Suspension

Type..	Independent with arms of unequal length, and tie-rod. Hydrolastic displacers interconnected front to rear.

	Normal Steering	Power Steering
Swivel hub inclination (unladen)	$12^o \pm \frac{3}{4}^o$	$11\frac{1}{2}^o \pm \frac{3}{4}^o$
Camber angle (unladen)...	$1\frac{1}{2}^o \pm \frac{3}{4}^o$ positive	$2^o \pm \frac{3}{4}^o$ positive
Castor angle (unladen)	$\frac{1}{4}^o \pm 1^o$ positive	$2^o \pm 1^o$ positive
Wheel bearing end float	Zero to 0.004 in	
Upper support arm bearing pre-load	Equal to between 5 to 10 lb in. torque	
Suspension arm bearings: Front and Rear ...	Roller race	

Rear Suspension

Type..	Independent with trailing arms. Hydrolastic displacers. Anti-roll bar fitted up to A-HS10-32802.
Wheel alignment (unladen)	Parallel
Camber (unladen)	$\frac{1}{2}^o$

Wheel bearing end-float	Zero to 0.002 in.
Radius arm bearing pre-load..	Equal to between 5 to 10 lb in. torque
Anti-roll bar fitment	Up to A-HS10-32802

Suspension
Trim and pressure:

	Adjust to trim height	Approximate fluid pressure
1st type drive shaft coupling (unladen)... ...	$14\frac{5}{8} + \frac{1}{4}$ in.	230 lb/sq in.
2nd type drive shaft coupling (unladen)	$14\frac{7}{8} \pm \frac{1}{4}$ in.	245 lb/sq in.
Automatic transmission (unladen)..	$14\frac{7}{8} \pm \frac{1}{4}$ in.	245 lb/sq in.

Wheels:

Type..	Ventilated disc $4\frac{1}{2}$ J x 13

Tyres:

Size and type	175 - 13. Dunlop SP41 tubeless
Pressures: (Normal) Front	28 lb/sq in.
Rear	22 lb/sq in.

Standard Steering:

Type..	Rack and pinion
Steering wheel turns - lock to lock	3.8
	4.4*
Steering wheel diameter..	$16\frac{1}{2}$ in.
Turning circle..	37 ft.
Front wheel alignment	$1/_8$ in. toe in - unladen

Power-assisted Steering

Type..	Rack and pinion with integral power assistance
Steering wheel turns - lock to lock	3.56
Steering wheel diameter..	$16\frac{1}{2}$ in.
Turning circle..	37 ft.
Front wheel alignment	$1/_8$ in. toe in - unladen

* Earlier models

Specifications and data:
1800 Mk II, 18/85 Mk II, 18/85 fitted with 18H Engine

The specifications are identical to the 1800 Mk I except for the differences listed below.

Front Suspension

Swivel hub inclination (unladen)	$12^o \pm \frac{3}{4}^o$
Camber angle (unladen)..	$1\frac{1}{2}^o \pm \frac{3}{4}^o$ positive
Castor angle (unladen)	See text for full details
Suspension arm bearings: Front and Rear ...	Metalastik Slipflex D.X. Bearings

Suspension
Trim and pressure:

	Adjust to trim height	Approximate fluid pressure
2nd type drive shaft coupling (unladen).. ...	$14\frac{7}{8} \pm \frac{1}{4}$ in.	245 lb/sq in.

Wheels:

Type:	Ventilated $4\frac{1}{2}$ J x 14

Tyres:

Size and type	165SR-14. Dunlop SP68 tubeless
Pressures: (Normal):	
Front..	30 lb/sq in.
Rear	24 lb/sq in.

Specifications and data
1800 Mk II and 18/85 Mk II 'S'

The specifications are identical to the 1800 Mk I except for the differences listed below.

Wheels:

    Type.. ... ...   Ventilated disc $4\frac{1}{2}$ J x 14

Tyres:

    Size and type ... ...   1655SR-14. Dunlop SP68 tubeless
    Pressures (Normal):
        Front.. ... ...   30 lb/sq in.
        Rear .. ..   24 lb/sq in.

Specifications and data
1800 Mk II 'S' fitted with 18H Engine

The specifications are identical to the 1800 Mk I except for the differences listed below:

Front Suspension	Normal Steering	Power-assisted Steering
Swivel hub inclination (unladen)	$12^{0} {}^{+}_{-} \frac{3}{4}^{0}$	
Camber angle (unladen)...	$1\frac{1}{2}^{0} {}^{+}_{-} \frac{3}{4}^{0}$	
Castor angle (unladen)	3^{0} negative	$2^{0} \pm 1^{0}$ positive
Suspension arm bearings: Front and rear	Metalastik Slipflex D.X. Bearings	

Suspension	Adjust to trim height	Approximate fluid pressure
Trim and pressure:		
2nd type drive shaft coupling (unladen)	$14^{7}/_{8} \pm \frac{1}{4}$ in.	245 lb/sq in.

---

1. Suspension - general description

The hydrolastic suspension system makes use of a special displacer unit at each wheel. The front and rear displacer units are connected together front to rear, side by side only, by strong metal tubes and flexible piping.

Made from sheet steel and rubber, as shown in Fig. 13:1, each displacer unit comprises a lower and upper chamber housing, a nylon reinforced diaphragm to - gether with a compressed rubber conical spring. Damper valves in the top of the fluid separating chamber perform the function done by separate telescopic dampers on other cars.

The displacer units are filled with a mixture of water, alcohol, and anti-corrosive additives. They work in the following manner:

When either of the front wheels hit a bump the piston moves up with the suspension and displaces the dia- phragm. This increases the pressure in the unit and so forces some of the fluid from the lower to the upper chamber.

This causes the rubber spring to deflect and to trans - fer some of the liquid, via the interconnecting pipe, to the rear displacer unit on the same side. As the fluid enters the rear top chamber, it pushes down on the piston which results in the rear of the car being raised. This all occurs far more quickly than it takes to describe, but is shown in diagrammatic form in Fig. 13:2.

The same process happens when a rear wheel meets a bump, but in reverse, as the fluid is now forced into one of the front displacer units. In this way it is pos - sible to obtain a very comfortable ride with the mini- mum of rolling and pitching.

The front suspension units each comprise a pair of unequal length swinging arms pivoting at the inner ends

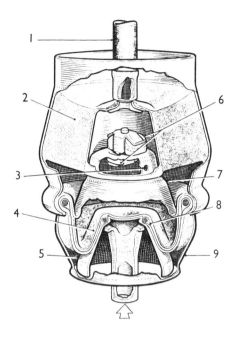

Fig. 13.1. HYDROLASTIC SUSPENSION DISPLACER UNIT (REAR)

No.	Description	No.	Description
1	Interconnecting pipe	6	Damper valves
2	Rubber spring	7	Fluid-separating member
3	Damper bleed	8	Rubber diaphragm (nylon-reinforced)
4	Butyl liner		
5	Tapered piston	9	Tapered cylinder

to the mounting bracket, and attached by ball joints at the outer ends to the swivel hub. The upper arm pivots on a pair of taper roller bearings and the lower suspension arm uses two flanged rubber bushes.

When the car is in forward motion, the rearward movement of the outer end of the lower suspension arm is controlled by a tie bar which connects with the front of the lower suspension arm using a nut and bolt placed just inwards of the outer end of the arm. The front end of the tie bar pivots in a pair of rubber bushes mounted in a bracket mounted to the front frame.

It is necessary to depressurize the hydrolastic system fitted to all cars if it is wished to overhaul the system. On reassembly it will be necessary to repressurize the system. This involves the use of special servicing tools which most BLMC agents now possess.

---

2.   Front hubs - removal and replacement

---

1.   Remove the hub cap from the appropriate front wheel. Slacken the wheel nuts and chock the rear wheels. Position a block of metal or hard wood approximately $\frac{1}{2}$ inch thick and $\frac{1}{2}$ inch wide between the upper suspension arm and the bump rubber. Jack up the front of the car and place on a firm stand. Undo the wheel nuts and remove the road wheel.

2.   Remove the two bolts holding the caliper unit to the front swivel hub and lift away the caliper from the hub. It should not be necessary to disconnect the hydraulic flexible hose but, to avoid unnecessary strain, tie a piece of string around the caliper and suspend so that it hangs away from the hub. Put a notice on the steering warning not to depress the brake pedal otherwise the pistons will be ejected.

3.   Extract the split pin (4) Fig. 13:3, and remove the drive shaft nut (3). Using a soft faced hammer gently tap the end of the shaft (11) and lift away the outer cone (5).

4.   Suitably mark the drive shaft flange (1) and the flexible coupling so that upon reassembly they may be fitted in their original positions. Carefully pull the driving flange (1) and disc brake assembly (8) from the shaft using a suitable two leg puller.

5.   Remove the dust shield (9) from the swivel hub (12). Mark the drive shaft coupling to ensure correct reassembly and by referring to Chapter 9/3 or 9/4 disconnect the drive shaft at the coupling. Use a universal ball joint extractor and separate the steering rod ball joint from the steering arm.

6.   Undo the locknuts which secure the upper and lower ball joints and remove the nuts and flat washers. It will be necessary to use a suitable two leg puller to release the upper and lower joint pins. Lift away the hub and drive shaft assembly.

7.   A special BLMC tool No. 18G47 plus adaptors 18G.47.AT., are required to remove the drive shaft from the hub. This operation is shown in Chapter 9, Fig. 9:3. Lower the drive shaft through the base of the tool and position the two halves of the adaptors round the rubber boot so that the hub rests on the support legs (arrowed in Fig. 9:3). Manipulate the shaft so that it is in line with the centre bolt of the tool and press the shaft out from the hub. Ensure that whilst the tool is being operated the underside of the drive shaft is held so that when released from the hub it does not fall on the floor. It is possible to perform this operation using a good quality three leg puller.

8.   Remove the outer oil seal (6) (Fig 13:3) followed by the outer bearing (13). It is recommended that the bearing cones are left in position inside the hub and the inner bearing race should be left in position on the drive shaft stub unless it is to be specifically renewed. The bearing cones may be removed by using a soft metal drift having first removed the inner seal (10). The inner bearing race may be removed by carefully using a good quality two leg puller.

9.   The bearings should be washed in paraffin and thoroughly dried using a non-fluffy rag. Carefully examine the rollers for signs of chipping, pitting, cracking or overheating. Inspect the rollers for security in their cages and cracking of the cages, especially at the thin sections. Finally examine the inner and outer cones for signs of chipping, pitting, and cracking and ensure that they do not spin on their mountings. Any bearing that is suspect should be renewed. Once inspection has been completed immerse in a good quality mineral oil.

10.   Examine the oil seals for signs of wear, hardening or deterioration, especially around the lip.

11.   To reassemble, first smear the drive shaft stub and the interior of the hub with grease to prevent rusting. Pack the bearings with the correct recommended grease and refit the inner bearing (13) followed by the spacer (7). Use a drift of suitable size and fit a new inner oil seal (10) and outer oil seal (6) well lubricating to ensure no damage. Pack the space between the bearing cones and seal with grease.

12.   If new bearings are to be fitted they will be supplied

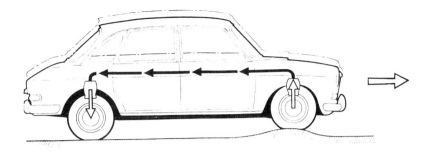

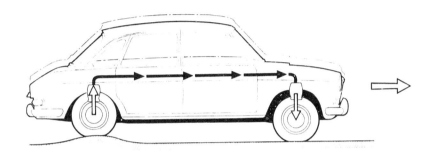

Fig. 13. 2. PRINCIPLE OF OPERATION OF HYDROLASTIC SUSPENSION

(a) Tail rises in response to upward motion of front wheels   (b) Nose rises in response to upward motion of rear wheels

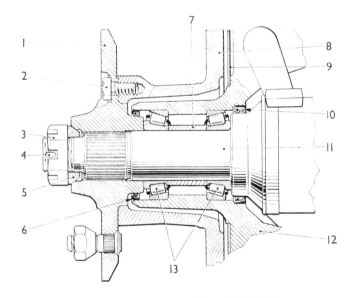

Fig. 13. 3. FRONT HUB COMPONENT PARTS

No.	Description	No.	Description	No.	Description	No.	Description
1	Driving flange assembly	5	Cone – outer	9	Dust shield	11	Drive shaft
2	Bolt – flange to disc	6	Oil seal – outer	10	Oil seal – inner (single lip – second type)	12	Swivel hub
3	Nut – hub	7	Distance tube			13	Taper bearings
4	Split pin	8	Disc				

by the agent in a matched pair plus a spacer. The old spacer should be discarded. Check that the hub bore and shoulders are not bruised or have burrs. Any should be removed using a hand scraper. Refit the bearing cones right up to the hub registers and pack the bearings with the correct recommended grease and fit to the hub together with the new spacer. Fit new inner and outer seals using a drift of suitable size, well lubricating to ensure no damage. Smear grease on the spacer and fill the space between the bearing cones and seals with grease.

13. Although refitting thereafter is the reverse procedure to removal certain important points must be adhered to otherwise difficulties could be experienced. Hold the drive shaft between soft faces in a vice and use BLMC tool No. 18G. 1104 as shown in Chapter 9 Fig. 9:2. Screw the guide onto the end of the drive shaft. Pass the hub assembly over the guide followed by the BLMC tool screwing it fully into the guide. Using an open ended spanner turn the nut until the hub is pressed fully home. Remove the service tool.

14. Place the driving flange (1) (Fig 13:3) and brake disc (8) along the shaft and screw the guide and BLMC service tool back onto the end of the shaft and turn the nut until the assembly is pressed fully home. Remove the tool once more.

15. Refit the outer cone followed by the drive shaft nut. By using a dial indicator gauge check the end float in the bearings which should be between 0 and 0.004 inch. However if after fitting a new set of bearings the end float is not to specification a new hub should be tried.

16. Tighten the drive shaft nut using a torque wrench set to read 150 lb. ft. Using the dial gauge again check the runout of the disc at its circumference. This must not exceed 0.008 inch. Fit a new split pin so locking the nut. If exceeded the disc and flange assembly should be repositioned on the drive shaft flange. Replace the assembly to the car upper and lower ball end pins followed by the dust shield, brake caliper and tie rod ball end joint to the steering lever and tighten the nuts. Replace the road wheel and lower the car.

The reason why such detail has been given is that unless these operations are performed correctly hub bearing life can be very limited.

---

3. Rear hubs - removal and replacement

---

1. Check the front wheels and remove the respective rear wheel hub cap. Slacken the wheel nuts.

2. Unscrew the two screws (1) Fig. 13:4, holding the brake drum (8) to the hub (7) and remove the brake drum.

3. Using a wide blade screwdriver carefully lever the grease retaining cap (6) from the centre of the hub. Withdraw the hub nut locking split pin (4) and undo the hub nut on the left hand side of the car which has a left hand thread so that to slacken the nut must be unscrewed clockwise. Conversely the hub nut on the right hand side of the car has a right hand thread so to slacken, the nut must be unscrewed anti-clockwise. Remove the nut (5) and the thick plain washer (3).

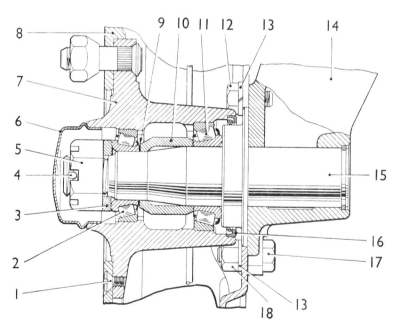

Fig. 13.4. REAR HUB COMPONENT PARTS

No. Description	No. Description	No. Description	No. Description
1 Screw - drum to hub	7 Hub assembly	11 Taper bearing - inner	15 Stub shaft
2 Taper bearing - outer	8 Brake drum	12 Set screw - back plate to	16 Oil seal
3 Washer	9 Shims (when fitted)	radius arm	17 Bolt - back plate to radius
4 Split pin	10 Distance piece or spacer-	13 Spring washer	arm
5 Nut - R. H. or L. H. thread	bearing	14 Radius arm	18 Nut
6 Grease retaining cap			

4. A hub puller will probably be needed to remove the hub from the stub shaft although a good quality three leg puller will do the job just as well. Take care not to damage the sub shaft thread whilst completing this operation.

5. It is recommended that the bearing cones are left in the hub unless they are to be renewed in which case they may be removed using a soft metal drift. Extract the distance piece or shim (9) and spacer (10) from the shaft.

6. The bearings should be washed in paraffin and thoroughly dried using a non-fluffy rag. Carefully examine the rollers for signs of chipping, pitting, cracking or overheating. Inspect the rollers for security in their cages and cracking of the cages especially at the thin sections. Finally examine the inner and outer cones for signs of chipping, pitting, cracking and ensure that they do not spin in their mountings. Any bearing that is suspect should be renewed. Once inspection has been completed immerse in a good quality mineral oil.

7. Examine the oil seal (16) for signs of wear, hardening or deterioration, especially around the lip.

8. To reassemble the hub if the original bearings are to be used again, first pack the bearings with grease making sure that there are no air pockets. If a new oil seal is to be fitted lubricate it well to ensure no damage and very gently tap into position referring to Fig. 13:4, to check the correct way round it should go. Carefully pack the space between the bearing cone and the oil seal with grease.

9. Offer up the hub assembly to the stub shaft reusing the distance piece or spacer and shims that were removed upon dismantling. Replace the washer and the hub retaining nut and tighten using a torque wrench set to read 40 lb. ft. Always use a new split pin to lock the nut in position.

10. If a new bearing is to be used there are certain points that should be noted:

(a) Hub assemblies fitted to the earlier models used a standard bearing spacer and shims whilst those fitted to later models had a variable distance piece.

(b) When new bearings are to be used a standard spacer with a BLMC part No. BTB593 together with shims must be used.

(c) When fitting new bearing cones always ensure that they are pressed fully home against their seatings in the hub using a soft metal drift.

(d) Any apparent excess end float should be eliminated by using shims and checked as described in paragraph 11, having first fitted the nut and washer and set to a torque wrench setting of 40 lb. ft.

11. Using a dial indicator gauge check the end float of the hub bearings. This should be between 0 and 0.002 inch. If it is not within the prescribed limits the hub assembly must be removed and shims inserted to give the desired end float. Three different thickness of shims are available, these being 0.003 inch, 0.005 inch and 0.010 inch.

12. Replace the grease retaining cap without packing it with grease as it is not necessary.

13. Replace the brake drum and the road wheel. If a brake overhaul has been completed at the same time, adjust the brake shoe to drum clearance. Lower the car to the floor.

---

4. Lower support arm - removal, inspection and replacement

---

1. Remove the hub cap from the appropriate front wheel. Slacken the wheel nuts and check the rear wheels.

Position a hard wood or metal packing piece approximately 1 inch thick, 1½ inch wide and 4 inches deep between the upper bump rubber and the upper suspension arm.

2. Carefully remove the nut (12) see Fig. 13:5, the bolt (11) and spring washer (13), from the tie rod (6) to the front suspension. Remove the split pin (1), Fig. 13:6

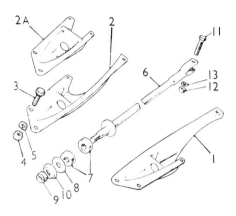

Fig. 13.5. TIE ROD AND BRACKETS

No.	Description	No.	Description
1	Tie-rod bracket - L. H.	7	Pad - tie-rod
2	Tie-rod bracket - R. H.	8	Cup washer - compression
2A	Second type and automatic	9	Locknut
3	Screw - bracket to body	10	Plain washer
4	Nut	11	Bolt - tie-rod to lower arm
5	Spring washer	12	Nut
6	Tie-rod	13	Spring washer

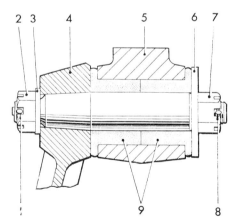

Fig. 13.6. LOWER SUPPORT ARM BEARING ASSEMBLY

No.	Description	No.	Description
1	Split pin	6	Plain washer
2	Nut - pivot pin to arm	7	Nut - pivot pin to bracket
3	Plain washer	8	Split pin
4	Lower arm	9	Bush - rubber
5	Mounting bracket		

nut (2) and washers (3) from the arm side of the pivot pin and release the lower support arm (4).

3. Remove the pivot pin and rubber bushes (9) from the mounting bracket (5), by drawing the pin towards the rear.

4. Clean and inspect the dismantled components for signs of cracking or excessive rusting. Check the rubber bushes for signs of cracking, perishing and splitting, and if they are worn or have been contaminated with oil fit new ones as necessary. Examine the pin for straightness.

5. To reassemble, first position the bushes in the mounting bracket and slide the pivot pin into position. Place the support arm onto the pin and hold it in position with the flat washer and nut.

6. Position the tie rod fork over the arm and fit the arm to the swivel hub. Tighten the nut using a torque wrench set to read 45 lb. ft. Then with no load on the bushes and the lower support arm in its normal position tighten the pivot pin nut and lock it using a new split pin.

7. Replace the bolt, spring washer and nut securing the tie rod to the arm. Refit the road wheel, extract the metal or wood block and remove the stand.

---

5. Suspension - removal and replacement

For this operation it will be necessary for the hydrolastic system to be de-pressurized for which special equipment is necessary. Most BLMC agents have this equipment so select the one nearest to where the car is to be worked upon and request that they de-pressurize the system. As the car will be very much lower it must be driven with extreme care avoiding rough road surfaces at a speed no greater than 30 miles per hour. The suspension is then removed as follows:

1. Remove the hub caps and slacken the road wheel nuts. Place wheel chocks behind the rear wheels and jack up the front of the car. Place on firm stands positioned under the front side member and under the rear suspension unit housing. Remove the road wheels.

2. Release the brake system flexible hose from its bracket and the caliper from the swivel hub as described in Chapter 11. Tie the caliper up out of the way, thus making it unnecessary to bleed the brake hydraulic system later. Put a notice on the steering wheel warning not to depress the brake pedal, otherwise the pistons will be ejected from the caliper. It may be found that on some early models the hose bracket is attached to the steering lever and in this case it will be necessary to release the hose at the bracket followed by the caliper.

3. Disconnect the tie-rod from the lower support arm by removing the nut, spring washer and bolt. Also disconnect the steering tie-rod from the steering lever using a universal ball joint separator, having first of course removed the split pin and retaining nut.

4. Mark the position of the drive shaft flange relative to the joint for guidance for correct reassembly, and disconnect the coupling.

5. From the underside, locate the five positions where the mounting brackets are retained to the valance. Undo the nuts and bolts and remove the complete suspension system forwards from the front of the car.

6. With the front suspension assembly away it is an ideal time to clean and check for rust on body panels not usually accessible and the required preventative action taken as necessary.

7. Refitting the suspension system is the reverse sequence to that of removal. Care must be taken at one point when refitting to ensure that the displacer unit is correctly engaged by its spring loaded strut.

8. If the brake caliper has been removed the brake hydraulic system must be bled before the car is returned to the agent for the hydrolastic suspension system to be pressurized once more.

---

6. Suspension tie-rod - removal and replacement

The suspension tie-rod connects the lower suspension arm to the body to control its position and, to a lesser extent, movement when the car is being driven. To remove the tie-rod proceed as follows:

1. Chock the rear wheels, jack up the front of the car and place on secure stands. Remove the nut (12) Fig. 13:5, spring washer (13) and bolt (11) holding the tie-rod (6) to the lower support arm. Do not allow the suspension to take the vehicle weight whilst the tie-rod is away from the car.

2. Remove the four nuts (4), spring washers (5) and bolts (3) holding the shaped bracket (1 or 2) to the body panel. Release the locknut (9) and extract the tie-rod (6) from the bracket.

3. Clean the tie-rod and carefully inspect the weld for signs of failure, the tie-rod threads for damage or the tie-rod itself for bending. Renew if at all suspect. Inspect the rubber pads for signs of cracking, splitting, perishing or oil contamination and fit new rubbers as necessary.

4. Reassembly is the reverse sequence to removal but there are several points to be noted:

(a) Fit a new polythene seal between the tie-rod bracket and the gusset plate.

(b) Tie-rods with a 'P' stamped at the fork end must be used only on cars fitted with power assisted steering.

(c) Two types of tie-rod assemblies have been fitted and parts are interchangeable only in sets so that the later type tie-rod bracket can be fitted only to the second type gusset plate. The differences can be seen in Fig. 13:5.

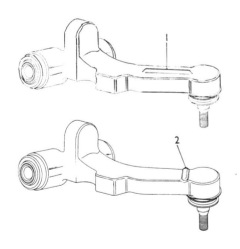

Fig. 13.7. UPPER SUPPORT ARM, (MODIFIED, SECOND TYPE)

No.	Description	No.	Description
1	Manual steering - bar along top face	2	Power steering - bar across top face

7.   Modified tie-rod

On MkII models of cars covered by this manual which
are fitted with manual steering, the correct suspension
system is identified by a longitudinal rib cast on the
upper support arm as shown in Fig. 13:7. A letter 'M'
is stamped on the steering lever and is designed to give
a negative castor angle of 3°.

If after using accurate steering geometry testing
equipment the castor angle is shown to be incorrect, a
new front suspension tie-rod assembly must be fitted to
each side. This carries a BLMC part No. 0.11H1942
and is easily identified by a band of red paint next to
the fork end.

The original nuts should not be refitted at the forward end of the tie-rod but new Nyloc nuts fitted. Once
the modified tie-rods have been fitted, the front wheel
alignment must be checked and reset if necessary.

8.   Front upper support arm - removal, inspection and
replacement

The upper support arm is of forged steel construction and houses a balljoint at its outer end. It rotates
about a roller bearing fulcrum point transmitting suspension movement to and from the Hydrolastic suspension displacer unit. Access to this component is gained
once the complete suspension assembly has been removed from the car as described earlier in this Chapter.
Once this has been done proceed as follows:
1.   Release the outer end of the upper support arm
from the swivel hub by removing the retaining nut (9)
Fig. 13:8, and special flat washer (8) and using a universal ball joint separator part the taper.
2.   Unscrew the nut (1) Fig. 13:9 from the bolt (8) and
remove the nut and washer (2). Withdraw the bolt (8)
from the assembly. Lift away the upper support arm and
the hydrolastic displacer strut noting the positioning of
the special distance collars (3) and (7). The mounting
tube may be removed from the bearings by using a press.

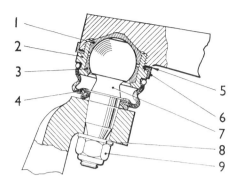

Fig. 13.8. BALLJOINT COMPONENT PARTS

No.	Description	No.	Description
1	Bottom socket	6	Lock washer
2	Housing	7	Ball pin
3	Top socket	8	Flat washer (special)
4	Dust cover	9	Locknut
5	Shim		

If renewal of the bearings outer cones is essential, a
universal internal puller should be used.
3.   Thoroughly wash the bearings and parts in paraffin
and dry using a non-fluffy rag. Carefully examine the
rollers for signs of chipping, pitting, c r a c k i n g or
rusting. Inspect the rollers for security in their cages,
and cracking of the cages especially at the thin sections.
Finally examine the inner and outer cones for signs of
chipping, pitting and cracking, and ensure that they do not
spin on their mountings. Any bearing that is suspect
should be renewed. Once inspection is complete immerse
in a good quality mineral oil.
4.   To reassemble if the original bearings are being
used again, the same spacing c o l l a r must be used.
Whilst refitting always rotate the bearings to ensure
that they are seating correctly. The torque which is required to rotate the shaft by using a pull scale or small
torque wrench should be between 5 and 10 lb. in. If a

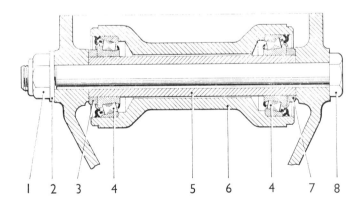

Fig. 13.9. COMPONENT PARTS OF UPPER SUPPORT ARM BEARING ASSEMBLY

No.	Description	No.	Description	No.	Description	No.	Description
1	Nut - nyloc	3	Spacer	5	Mounting tube	7	Distance collar
2	Plain washer	4	Taper bearing with seal	6	Upper support arm	8	Bolt

high reading is obtained, a thinner spacer will be necessary or, alternatively, a low reading will indicate a thicker spacer to be fitted. From experience it has been found that a thickness change of 0.003 inch will give a difference in torque of about 5 lb. inch. A range of nine spacers are available ranging from 0.200 inch to 0.224 inch in increments of 0.003 inch. It is important to note that the bearings must be rotated whilst the variable width type spacer is to be fitted. It is essential to ensure that the bearing inner race assembly is rotating with the shaft and NOT on it whilst the pre-load is being measured.

5. If a new bearing is to be fitted, first press or carefully drift the bearing cones into the upper support arm ensuring that they are well located against their shoulders. Pack both bearing assemblies with a Molybdenum disulphide base grease and fit them into the upper support arm. Take care not to damage the two oil seals, one placed at each end of the upper support arm.

6. Press the fixed length distance collar onto the pivot tube making sure that the flat face of the collar is flush and square with the end of the pivot tube. Push the pivot tube through the bearings from the rear face of the upper support arm and fit a spacer which gives a clearance at the end of the mounting bracket making sure that the fixed length collar is fitting flush with the end of the mounting tube. Replace the flat washer and tighten the nut until it just nips.

7. Using a feeler gauge measure the gap between the spacer and the distance collar and add 0.001 to 0.004 inch to this gap. This will give a figure to which the spacer thickness used during reassembly must be added, giving a final spacer thickness to be used. Unscrew the nut and remove together with the plain washer. Extract the spacer used for assembly and fit a spacer of required thickness. Check rotational torque as described in paragraph 4 of this section.

8. Replace the upper arm to the swivel axle and tighten the retaining nut using a torque wrench set to read 60 lb ft.

9. Refit the front suspension system to the car as previously described in this chapter.

9. Modified upper support arm

A modified upper support arm is fitted to later models covered by this manual and differs from the original by having a Slipflex 'DX' bearing inserted in the inner end. The upper support arm fitted to manual steering cars is different to that fitted to power assisted steering. The identification marks are shown in Fig 13:8.

It is recommended that the type of upper support arm fitted is ascertained by seeing if the raised type identification marks are existant. If this proves to be the case it is strongly recommended that any bearing overhaul be left to the main agents as specialist equipment is required.

The castor angle for models fitted with power assisted or manual steering with a transverse rib on upper support arms and 'P' stamped on the steering arms and tie-rods (part No 11H1943 - grey painted identification) is $2^{\circ} \pm 1^{\circ}$ positive.

The castor angle for models fitted with manual steering and a longitudinal rib on the upper support arms and an 'M' stamped on the steering arms and tie-rods (part No. 11H1942 - black or zinc plated with red painted identification band at fork end) is 3° negative.

10. Ball joints - removal and replacement

To remove either the upper or lower support arm ball joint as shown in Fig. 13:8, it will be necessary to refer to the respective section dealing with the lower support arm or upper support arm to be found earlier in this chapter. Then knock back the lock washer tab using a screwdriver or small chisel. Using a ring spanner or socket carefully unscrew the ball joint assembly. Thoroughly clean the exterior and inspect the component for wear, which, if evident, means that a new assembly should be fitted.

Replacement requires care as the ball joint assembly position has to be adjusted using shims. Proceed as follows:

1. Gently screw in the ball joint less the lockwasher and shims until there is no end play between the ball and the sockets. Using a feeler gauge measure the gap between the housing and the swivel hub or upper arm.

2. Unscrew the ball joint assembly again and select shims to the thickness of the feeler gauge less the thickness of the lockwasher which is 0.036 inch. This will give pre-load to the bearing. Five thickness of shims are available these being 0.002 inch, 0.003 inch, 0.005 inch, 0.010 inch and 0.030 inch.

3. Lubricate the ball joint internal parts freely using only Dextragrease Super BP lubricant and reassemble, tightening with a torque wrench set to 60 lb. ft. (upper arm) or 45lb. ft. (lower arm). Using the side of a small chisel, tap up the locking washer on three flats ensuring that one of these is adjacent to the brake disc to secure the housing. Carefully slide the dust cover into position and double check that it is seating correctly to stop ingress of dirt.

4. Thereafter reassembly is the reverse procedure to removal except that a Nyloc locknut must be used, together with a special flat washer whose thickness is 0.160 inch on steel ball pins. The first type of ball pins, easily identifiable because of being copper plated, were secured by a nut and a spring washer and these should be replaced with a Nyloc nut and flat washer. The nut should be tightened using a torque wrench set to 45lb. ft.

11. Radius arms - removal, inspection and refitting

To enable a radius arm to be removed it is necessary for the hydrolastic system to be depressurized and this requires special equipment which most BLMC agents now possess. As the car will be very much lower it must be driven with extreme care avoiding rough road surfaces at a speed no greater than 30 miles per hour. The removal of the radius arm is now carried out as follows:

1. On the side of the car which is to be worked upon, remove the road wheel hub cap and slacken the wheel nuts. Chock both opposite side road wheels and raise the side of the car. Place firm stands one under the rear of the car and the other under the front side member.

2. Remove the road wheel and place to one side. Disconnect the brake flexible hose from the main hydrolastic line and plug both open ends to stop dirt ingress or fluid loss. Detach the handbrake cable from the rod positioned at the rear radius arm.

3. Disconnect the anti-roll bar if one has been fitted, depending on the year and model of car. Also disconnect the hydrolastic displacer hose and free the flexible hose from its retaining clip. Using a garage hydraulic jack or other form of jacking equipment take the weight of the suspension assembly and unscrew the four special bolts

securing the assembly to the body. Carefully lower the assembly and remove from the underside of the car. Take care it does not roll off the jack.

4. Unscrew the suspension bolt captive nut (1) Fig. 13:10 and remove together with the spring washer (2). Withdraw the radius arm to suspension member bolt (8). The radius arm may now be removed taking care to note the location of the distance piece (3) and collar (7).

5. Thoroughly wash all parts in paraffin and dry using a non-fluffy rag. It is important that unless new bearings are to be fitted the bearing cones should not be removed from the radius arm. The cones may be removed using an internal bearing puller.

6. The bearings should be washed in paraffin and thoroughly dried using a non-fluffy rag. Carefully examine the rollers for signs of chipping, pitting, cracking or overheating. Inspect the rollers for security in their cages and cracking of the cages especially at the thin sections. Finally examine the inner and outer cones for signs of chipping, pitting, cracking and ensure that they do not spin on their mountings. Any bearings that are suspect should be renewed. Once inspection has been completed immerse in a good quality mineral oil.

7. It is recommended that if new bearings are being fitted new shields (5) Fig. 13:10 are fitted if at all suspect. First fit the shields ensuring that they are the correct way round and press the bearing outer cones into the radius arms so that they are seating correctly in the radius arms, again ensure they are the right way round. Pack both bearings with a molybdenum disulphide grease and fit them into the radius arm taking care not to damage the bearing seals.

8. Push the fixed length spacer onto the outer end of the mounting tube, ensuring that the flat face of the spacer is flush and square with the end of the mounting tube. Ease the mounting tube through the bearings from the outside face and fit a spacer from the range available, preferably of the same original thickness, onto the inner end of the mounting tube.

9. Refit the assembly and tighten the nut finger-tight. Check that the spacer previously selected is not too

thick as this would lead to early bearing failure due to undue strain. This is done by measuring the torque required to rotate the shaft and should be in the range of between 5 to 10 lb. inch. If the torque reading is higher a thinner spacer is required whilst if the torque reading is less a thicker spacer should be fitted. From experience a thickness change of 0.003 inch gives a torque reading change of 5 lbs. inch. Nine special spacers are available ranging from 0.20 to 0.224 inch, in increments of 0.003 inch.

10. If a variable width spacer is being used care must be taken to ensure that the bearing is rotated whilst the variable width spacer is being fitted. It is also essential that the bearing inner race assembly is rotating with the shaft and NOT on it whilst the pre-load is measured.

11. Thereafter refitting is the reverse procedure to removal. For interest, the mounting bracket is secured to the cross-member by two set screws and to the body by two bolts with both spring and plain washers. These are accessible from the rear seat well panel. On earlier models the bracket was welded to the panel.

---

12. Front and rear displacer unit - removal

Before a displacer unit can be removed it is necessary to depressurize the hydrolastic system as described in section 11.

There are two methods of removing the front displacer unit but unfortunately both are a little involved. It is recommended that both procedures are studied and the best method of approach may be decided depending on workshop equipment available:

1(a) Disconnect the steering tie-rod from the steering lever and also the tie-rod from the lower support arm. Remove the drive shaft from the transmission unit and front hub assembly as described in Chapter 9, so giving more room to operate including the final withdrawal of the hydrolastic unit. Undo the nuts and bolts from the five mounting points holding the bracket to the valance and carefully draw the assembly forwards and away from

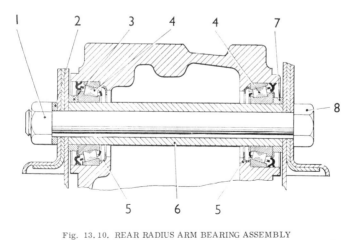

Fig. 13.10. REAR RADIUS ARM BEARING ASSEMBLY

No.	Description	No.	Description	No.	Description	No.	Description
1	Nut	4	Taper bearing with seal	6	Mounting tube	8	Bolt - radius arm to suspension member
2	Spring washer	5	Inner shield	7	Spacer		
3	Distance collar						

the valance to clear the displacer. Watch the flexible brake hose so that it is not damaged due to stretching. To stop any unnecessary strain on the suspension components it is recommended that it is supported on blocks under the wheel arch. Finally carefully withdraw the hydrolastic displacer unit.

2(b) Refer to the appropriate section in this chapter and remove the front suspension system. This will give easy access to the displacer unit which may now be removed, having first disconnected the displacer unit hose from the union mounted on the engine bulkhead.

For removal of the rear displacer:

3. Disconnect the joint between the brake main hydraulic pipe and the flexible hose, and also the handbrake cable from the backplate lever.

4. If an anti-roll bar is fitted to the rear suspension it should be removed completely to give better access. Slacken the clip and disconnect the hydrolastic displacer unit hose from the interconnection pipe.

5. Use a garage hydraulic jack or similar equipment to take the weight of the suspension unit, and undo the four special bolts that secure the suspension mounting member to the body and mounting bracket. Withdraw the complete assembly.

6. Firmly push the radius arm down out of the way of the displacer unit and press the piston inwards into the displacer unit so as to clear the spring loaded strut. Finally remove the displacer unit.

---

13. Front and rear displacer unit - replacement

Replacement of either a front or rear displacer unit is an exact reversal of the removal procedure. There has been a modification whereby up to body No. AS53787 and WS2775A an inner mounting tube was used but this has been discontinued and now the spring units are positioned in seatings. Fig. 13:11 shows how the seating ring and rear locating ring are positioned on the displacer unit before refitting to the car.

---

14. Hydrolastic suspension system valves and pipes

Should it be found necessary to fit a new Schrader valve into the valve block it is important that Loctite Grade A sealant is applied to the exposed threads once the valve has been screwed in two complete turns. Tighten the valve using a torque wrench set to read 10lb. ft. and then leave for at least 24 hours to enable the Loctite to cure.

It is recommended that when making a connection of the pipe, the end of the pipe is lubricated with Castor Oil so preventing the pipe binding or tightening.

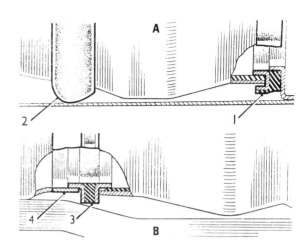

Fig. 13.11. SPRING UNITS WITH SEATING RINGS

No.	Description	No.	Description
A	Front assembly	B	Rear assembly
1	Seating ring	3	Seating ring - fits either way round
2	Anti-rattle sleeve	4	Locating ring

---

15. Steering - description

The rack and pinion type steering as shown in Fig. 13:12 is used on models covered by this manual except those fitted with power assisted steering. Positioned at each end of the rack is a ball joint which is attached to the inner end of the tie-rod. The ball joint and part of the tie-rod is enclosed in a rubber gaiter which is held in position by a clip at each end. It protects the ball joint and rack preventing road dust and dirt entering and causing premature wear.

The outer end of the tie-rod is threaded for adjustment and is attached to a ball joint assembly which in turn is connected to the steering arm.

Adjustment for end float may be made using shims. Pinion end play is adjusted by shims between the end cover and pinion housing, whilst backlash between the pinion and rack is controlled by shims between the cover plate yoke and the pinion housing.

---

16. Steering - routine maintenance

1. Lubrication of the rack and pinion during normal service operation is unnecessary as the lubricant is contained in the assembly by the rubber gaiters. However should a loss occur due to a leak from the rack housing or rubber gaiters then the correct amount of oil should

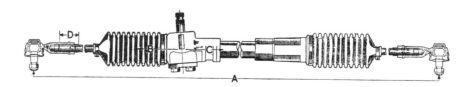

Fig. 13.12. THE STEERING RACK ASSEMBLY

Dimension 'A' - 49.62 ± 0.06 in.   Dimension 'B' - 3.28 in.   Dimension 'C' - 3.28 in.   D is the threaded length of tie-rod

be inserted using an oil can. Obviously before replenishment is carried out the source of the leak must be found and rectified.

2. To top up the oil in the rack and pinion steering assembly, remove the clip from the rubber gaiter on the right hand end of the steering rack housing and rotate the steering wheel until the rack is in the normal straight ahead position. Allow any remaining oil to seep out so that it is not overfilled. Using an oil can filled with the recommended grade of oil insert the nozzle into the end of the rack housing and refill with not more than 1/3rd pint of oil.

3. Reposition the gaiter and tighten the clip quickly to ensure minimum loss of oil and then move the steering wheel from lock to lock very slowly to distribute the oil in the housing.

4. If at any time the car is raised from the ground and the front wheels are clear and suspended do not use any excessive force or rapid movement when moving the wheels especially from one lock to the other, otherwise damage could occur to the steering mechanism.

17. Front wheel alignment

1. The front wheels are correctly aligned when they are turning in at the front 1/8 inch (3.2mm) as shown in Fig. 13:13. It is important that this measurement is taken on a centre line drawn horizontally and parallel to the ground through the centre line of the hub. The exact point should be in the centre of the side wall of the tyre and not on the wheel rim which could be distorted and give inaccurate readings.

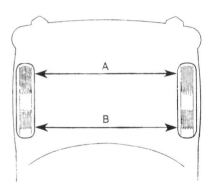

Fig. 13.13. Front wheel alignment. Dimension 'A' must be 1/8 in. less than dimension 'B'

2. The adjustment is effected by loosening the lock nut on each tie-rod ball joint, and also slackening the rubber gaiter clip holding it to the tie-rod, and turning both tie-rods equally until the adjustment is correct.

3. This is a job best left to your local BLMC dealer as accurate alignment requires the use of special equipment. If the wheels are not in alighment, tyre wear will be heavy and uneven, and the steering will be stiff and unresponsive.

18. Steering wheel - removal and replacement

1. To remove the steering wheel first disconnect the negative terminal (negative earth) from the battery. Depress and turn the horn push hub centre in an anti-clockwise direction. Lift away the centre.

2. With the front wheels in the straight ahead position make a particular note of the position of the spokes of the steering wheel and mark the hub of the steering wheel and column to ensure correct positioning upon refitting.

3. Using a socket or box spanner of the correct size slacken and remove the steering wheel nut. Remove the wheel by thumping the rear of the rim adjacent to the spokes with the palms of the hands which should loosen the hub splines from the column inner splines. Lift away the steering wheel.

4. Replacement is the reverse procedure to removal. Correctly align the two marks previously made to ensure correct positioning of the spokes. Refit the nut and tighten using a torque wrench set to 50 lb ft.

19. Rack and pinion steering gear - removal and replacement

1. Remove the two bolts securing the steering column coupling flange to the pinion flange. Slacken the right hand road wheel nuts for a right hand drive car (left hand road wheel nuts for a left hand drive car), jack up the front of the car and place on stands. Remove the road wheel. Chock the rear wheels and release the handbrake.

2. Extract the split pins and remove the locknuts securing the tie-rod ball joints. Using a universal ball joint separator or two hammers to shock release the taper, disconnect the ball joints. Remove the intermediate lever pivot bolt.

3. Remove the four bolts holding the steering rack assembly to the toeboard and ease the complete rack assembly forward to clear the pinion flange. Withdraw the assembly through the wing valance panel on the side from which the road wheel has been removed rotating it as necessary to clear the panel flange from the panel.

4. Refitting is the reverse procedure to removal but certain precautions must be taken to simplify the work. It is advisable to check the length of the two tie-rods and adjust as necessary until they are of exactly equal length. The tie-rod ball joints have nylon inserts which do not require lubrication. Should the rubber boots have become damaged or perished in service a complete new joint must be fitted. If the rubber boot has been damaged only during lifting out of the steering rack assembly through the valance, then the rubber boot only may be renewed. There should be no exception to this rule.

5. Before the steering rack assembly is finally fitted to the car it will facilitate installation if the rack is brought to its central position. This position is easily obtained by turning the pinion from one stop to the other and measuring the complete distance the rack has travelled at one end. The rack will be in its central position when it is moved back through half the measurement made.

In the central position the pinion flange must be at an angle of 20° (see Fig. 13:14) to the centre line of the rack. If the flange is not in this required position re-check the rack for its central position. Should this not correct the angle, remove the pinion flange pinch bolt nut and withdraw the pinch bolt. Reposition the pinion flange on the pinion splines by two splines in the required direction. Refit the pinch bolt and tighten the nut.

6. Carefully insert the rack assembly through the valance making sure the setting operation in paragraph 5 is not disturbed, locate and lightly tighten the four bolts holding the rack assembly to the toe-board.

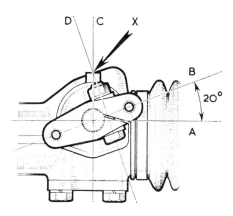

Fig. 13.14. CORRECT COUPLING FLANGE SET AT 20° TO THE CENTRE LINE OF THE RACK WITH THE RACK IN THE CENTRAL POSITION

No.	Description	No.	Description
A	Centre-line of pinion parallel to rack axis.	C	Centre-line of casting lug
B	Centre-line of coupling flange	D	Centre-line of pinch-bolt
		X	Point of intersection

7.   Slide the steering column assembly down so that the column coupling flange may be aligned and the two bolts inserted.   Tighten all bolts securely.

8.   Refit the pivot bolt to the intermediate lever and the tie-rod ball joints.   Fit new split pins.   Check and adjust wheel alignment.

---

20.   Rack and pinion steering gear - dismantling

It is not possible to make any adjustments to the rack and pinion steering gear unless it is removed from the car.   With it removed, it is recommended that it be dismantled and the whole unit examined before making any adjustments.   This will save having to remove the unit again later because of initial non-detection of wear. If wear is bad it is best to fit an exchange reconditioned unit.

(All numbers in brackets refer to Fig. 13:16).

1.   Hold the rack at the pinion body between soft faces fitted to the jaws of a vice.   Slacken the lock nuts (45) on the rack tie-rods and screw off the ball end assemblies (39) followed by the locknuts.

2.   Slacken the rubber boot clamps (38 and 37) on both ends of the two rubber boots on the rack housing and tie-rods and slide off the rubber boots (36).   Allow all lubricant to drain from the rack unit.

3.   Make a mark on the pinion coupling, the pinion and housing, once the rack has been set in the central position, so that the parts will be reassembled correctly relative to each other.   Remove the pinch bolt (22) and withdraw the flange (21).

4.   Remove the three damper cover plate holding screws (16) and lift away the cover plate (15), the joint washer (13) and the packing shims (14).   Place these shims to one side so that they can be replaced as a set upon reassembly.   Lift out the spring (12) and support yoke (11).

5.   Remove the three pinion end cover holding screws (29) and lift away the end cover (28), the joint washer (27) and shims (26).   Also lift away the outer thrust ring, ball cage, inner bearing ring (25) and finally withdraw

the pinion itself (18) from the rack housing.

6.   By tilting the pinion bearing assembly (25) carefully withdraw it from the housing followed by the thrust washer.   If an oil leak was evident from the pinion shaft oil seal (2) it should be removed and discarded.

7.   Using a pin punch, open the indentations in the locknut clear of the milled slots in the ball joint housing (51). Slacken the locknut (35) and unscrew the ball joint housing (34).   For this operation use BLMC tool 18G1030 or a 'C' spanner of suitable size.   This will release the tie-rod, ball seat and seat tension spring.   Repeat this operation on the other end of the rack.

8.   Very carefully withdraw the rack (9) from the pinion end of the housing so preventing the teeth damaging the bush in the other end of the housing.   Remove the bush retaining screw (8) (see also Fig. 13:15) and extract the bush (5) and its housing (6) from the rack housing.   Finally the top pinion ball cage (57) and shims (58) may now be removed.

NOTE: Two types of bushes were fitted.   On earlier models a felt bush was fitted and to remove this unscrew the securing self tapping screw two turns and, using a screwdriver, prise the felt bush up at the joint and then extract.

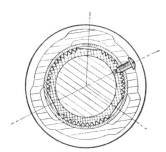

Fig. 13.15. Cross section through housing bush showing the retaining screw

---

21.   Rack and pinion steering gear - examination

---

1.   Thoroughly clean all parts with paraffin.   Carefully inspect the teeth on the rack and also the pinion for chipping, roughness, uneven wear, hollows or fractures.

2.   Carefully inspect the component parts of the inner ball joints for wear or ridging and renew as necessary.

3.   The outer track rod joints cannot be dismantled and if worn must be renewed as a complete assembly.   Examine the components parts of the damper and renew any that show signs of wear.   Pay particular attention to the various oil seals and as a precautionary measure it is always best to renew them.

4.   As it is difficult to refill the rack and pinion assembly with oil once it is fitted to the car, make sure that the rubber gaiters are sound before refitting them. If they are in the least bit torn or perished complete loss of oil could occur later and they must be renewed.

5.   If the steering gear is of the early type the felt bush in the end of the rack furthest from the pinion housing must be replaced with a plastic bush and a steel sleeved hub and spacer.

---

22.   Rack and pinion steering gear - reassembly

---

1.   Position a new rack bush and housing in the housing end opposite the pinion so that the self tapping screw hole is located between the two flats of the bush.

2.   Insert a metal rod into the bush so that it acts as a

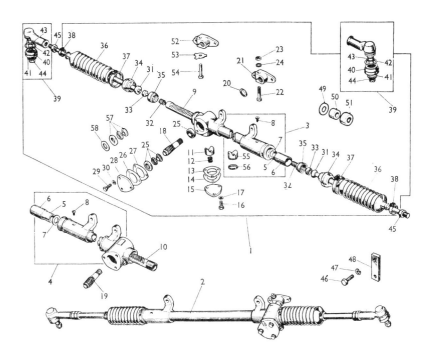

Fig. 13.16. EXPLODED VIEW OF STEERING RACK ASSEMBLY

No.	Description	No.	Description	No.	Description	No.	Description
1	Steering rack assembly - R.H.D.	16	Cover-plate bolt	31	Tie-rod	45	Ball socket locknut
2	Steering rack assembly - L.H.D.	17	Spring washer	32	Thrust spring	46	Screw - rack to body
3	Housing assembly - R.H.D.	18	Pinion - R.H.D.	33	Ball seat	47	Spring washer
4	Housing assembly - L.H.D.	19	Pinion - L.H.D.	34	Ball housing	48	Tapped block - rack to body
5	Felt bush	20	Oil seal	35	Lock - housing	49	Retainer) 2nd type
6	Bush housing	21	Pinion coupling	36	Rack seal	50	Bush - Polyvon) bearing
7	Backing disc	22	Bolt - coupling	37	Clip - inner seal	51	Housing) assembly
8	Retaining screw	23	Nut - coupling	38	Clip - outer seal	52	Pinion coupling)
9	Rack - R.H.D.	24	Spring washer - coupling	39	Ball socket assembly	53	Lock washer) 2nd type
10	Rack - L.H.D.	25	Ball cage	40	Boot	54	Bolt - 5/16 in.)
11	Rack support yoke*	26	End cover shim(s)	41	Ring - boot	55	Yoke) 2nd type
12	Spring*	27	Joint washer	42	Spring garter - boot	56	'O' ring oil seal) modified
13	Yoke cover joint washer	28	End cover	43	Retainer - boot	57	Ball cage) From 3.8 rack
14	Yoke cover shim(s)	29	Bolt - end cover	44	Slotted nut	58	Shims) assembly
15	Cover-plate yoke*	30	Spring washer				

*2nd type damper assembly illustrated

support preventing the bush distorting, and drill a hole 7/64 inch in diameter through the existing hole in the housing and then through the bush. Coat the threaded portion and under the head of the screw with a thick non setting oil resistant sealer and install it so securing the bush and spacer in the rack housing.

3. Upon dismantling the rack and pinion assembly, if the felt type bush was fitted, it must be replaced with the latest Polyvon type with its housing and spacer. In this case when tightening the self tapping screw ensure that it does not project into the internal bore of the bush.

If due to unavoidable circumstances a felt bush has to be fitted instead of the latest Polyvon type the steering rack assembly must be refilled with a S.A.E. 140EP oil.

4. Carefully position the top pinion bearing into the rack housing and slide the rack into its central position ensuring that the rack teeth do not damage the bush.

Refit the pinion taking care that the previously made marks on the pinion and housing align. Replace the lower pinion bearing.

5. It will now be necessary to preload the pinion bearing but two types of assemblies were fitted. Quick reference to Fig. 13:17 and Fig. 13:18 show the differences and when compared with the unit under reassembly, the applicable procedure should be followed.

6. On the first type to set the pinion bearing pre-load, fit the pinion end cover without the gasket and any shims that were there before. Tighten the three bolts until the cover is just held in position and by referring to Fig. 13:17 use feeler gauges to determine the clearance 'A' between the end cover and the housing. Once this has been found remove the end cover and select a new gasket and shims to the thickness of the feeler gauges used minus 0.001 to 0.003 inch to obtain the correct

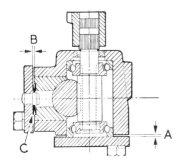

Fig. 13.17. CROSS SECTION THROUGH STEERING PINION AND
RACK DAMPER (FIRST TYPE)

No.	Description	No.	Description
A	Take a feeler gauge measurement and fit the pinion end cover with shims to the value of	B	to .003 in. (.02 to .07 mm)
			Measure the gap and fit shims
		C	Dished spring washers

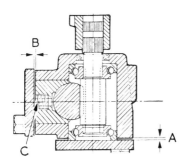

Fig. 13.18. CROSS SECTION THROUGH STEERING PINION AND
RACK DAMPER (SECOND TYPE)

No.	Description	No.	Description
A	Take a feeler gauge measurement and fit the pinion end cover with shims to the value of the measurement minus .001	B	to .003 in. (.02 to .07 mm)
			Measure the gap and fit shims
		C	Coil spring

pre-load. Three thicknesses of shims are available, 0.0024 inch, 0.005 inch and 0.010 inch. Coat both gasket surfaces with a sealant such as 'Wellseal' and reassemble.

7. On the second type to set the pinion bearing pre-load, fit the pinion end cover less a gasket but with the shims that were originally placed between the gasket and housing. Tighten the three bolts until the cover is just held in position and by referring to Fig. 13:18 use feeler gauges to determine the clearance 'A' between the end cover and the housing. Once this has been found remove the end cover and select a number of shims to produce a gap of a new joint washer thickness to which 0.001 to 0.003 inch should be added. Four thicknesses of shims are available, 0.005, 0.0075, 0.010 and 0.092 inch. Coat both gasket surfaces with a sealant such as 'Wellseal' and reassemble.

8. Continue reassembly of the unit by pressing in a new pinion oil seal until it fits flush with the top of the housing. Screw a new ball housing lock ring onto the rack end to the end of the threads and refit the seat springs, seat, tie-rod and the ball housing. Tighten up the assembly until the tie-rod is just pinched and then screw in the locking ring until it meets the ball housing. Double check that the tie-rod is still in the 'just pinched' condition and screw back the ball housing one eighth of a turn so allowing full movement of the tie-rod. Tighten up the locking ring with a torque wrench set to between 33 and 37 lb ft. using a BLMC service tool 18G1030. During this operation take care that the ball housing does not move otherwise the previously made adjustment will be lost. To check the adjustment just made, a torque of between 32 and 52lb in. on the end of the tie-rod will be required to produce movement. Lock up the ball housing by carefully punching the lips of the locking rings into the milled slots in the ball housing and rack. The lock ring must not fracture.

9. The rack damper adjustment must now be set but two types have been fitted. Quick reference to Fig. 13:17 and Fig. 13:18 show the differences and when compared with the unit under reassembly the applicable procedure should be followed.

10. On the first type damper adjustment is set by using a suitable preload gauge to check the torque required to rotate the pinion shaft before the damper is fitted. Make a note of the reading. Refit the damper yoke and spring less any shims that may have been previously fitted.

Fit the damper cover with a new gasket and tighten the three retaining bolts until it is just possible to rotate the pinion shaft with the bearing pre-load gauge set to 15 lb in. plus the torque reading obtained earlier. For this operation it is recommended that BLMC tool 18G207 plus the adaptor 18G207A be used.

11. Refer to Fig. 13:17 and measure the clearance 'B' between the damper cover plate and the rack housing using feeler gauges. Once this has been found remove the end cover and select shims to the thickness of the feeler gauges used. Three thicknesses of shims are available, 0.0025 inch, 0.005 inch and 0.010 inch. Coat the gasket faces with a sealant such as 'Wellseal' and reassemble. Finally check that the torque load necessary to start movement of the pinion after reassembly does not exceed 25 lb in.

12. On the second type damper adjustment is made by refitting the rack damper yoke with the spring and fitting the damper cover plate together with a new gasket, if fitted. Tighten the three retaining bolts until, by using feeler gauges 0.001 to 0.006 inch thick, there is a clearance of this amount between the damper cover plate and the yoke, with the rack in its central position. Rotate the pinion shaft $\frac{1}{2}$ a turn in each direction and recheck the clearance again using the feeler gauges. Remove the end cover plate and gasket, if fitted. Refer to Fig. 13:17 to determine which yoke is fitted to the unit under reassembly. If it is of the plain yoke type coat the faces of a new gasket with a sealant such as 'Wellseal' and refit the cover and gasket plus shims to the same thickness as the feeler gauge. However if the yoke is of the 'O' ring oil seal type fit a new 'O' ring oil seal to the yoke plus shims to the same thickness as the feeler gauge. Refit the cover.

13. Fit new rubber boots to the housing and tie-rods and tighten both the clips on the boot fitted to the end furthest from the pinion assembly, and the clip only on the second boot holding the boot to the rack housing. Release the rack and pinion assembly from the vice and place in a vertical position with the rubber boot unsecured end uppermost. Using an oil can filled with extreme pressure oil, insert the end of the can in between the gaiter and tie-rod and insert approximately 1/3rd of a pint of oil Fit and tighten the gaiter clip.

14. Return the rack and pinion assembly to the horizontal position in the vice and accurately centralize the rack. This position is easily obtained by turning the pinion from

one stop to the other stop and measuring the complete distance the rack has travelled at one end. The rack will be in its central position when it is moved back through half the measurement made. This should correspond to previously made marks unless a new pinion and rack has been fitted. With the rack centralized refit the flange coupling in its original position or if new parts have been fitted refer to Fig. 13:14 for its correct positioning.

15. Replace the locknuts and ball ends to the tie-rods. On early assemblies two locknuts were used for each ball end. In this case discard one locknut for each tie-rod until measurement 'D' shown in Fig. 13:12 is obtained. Lightly tighten the locknuts and refit the assembly to the car as described in Section 19.

23. Nylon-seated ball joints and steering levers

1. The ball joints fitted to the tie-rods have nylon seatings and therefore as they require no lubrication they are sealed by rubber boots for life. If a rubber boot has been damaged, fractured or perished, it is important that the complete ball end be renewed as road dust and dirt will have penetrated the joint thereby drastically shortening its service life. The exception to this is if the boot has been damaged whilst away from

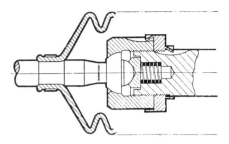

Fig. 13.19. Cross section through tie-rod balljoint.

the car, in which case it is permissible to fit a new rubber boot having first smeared the area around the joint with Dextragrease Super G.P. lubricant.

2. Two types of steering lever have been fitted since models covered by this manual were introduced.

3. The first (early) type of steering lever is attached to the swivel hub unit on a taper and positioned with a Woodruff key. It is secured by a locknut which also acts as a mounting for the brake flexible hose brackets.

4. If during a service operation the steering lever has

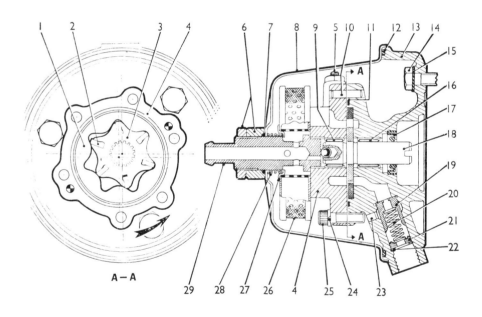

A—A

Fig. 13.20. CROSS SECTION THROUGH POWER ASSISTED STEERING PUMP

No.	Description	No.	Description	No.	Description	No.	Description
1	Annulus	9	Needle bearing - short	16	Needle bearings - long	23	Overspill) Flow control valve
2	Vane	10	Dowel	17	Oil seal	24	Spring washer
3	Hub	11	'O' ring seal - cover	18	Shaft assembly	25	Allen screw
4	Cover	12	'O' ring seal - reservoir	19	Plunger) Flow control valve	26	Filter
5	Pressure relief valve	13	Body	20	Spring)	27	Plate
6	Knurled nut and locknut*	14	Nut) Pump to adaptor	21	Abutment) Flow control	28	Spring
7	'O' ring seal	15	Seal washer)	22	Circlip) valve	29	Return union
8	Reservoir						

NOTES: AA. View of pumping members looking towards drive end. The hub must be assembled in the position shown
*Locknut not fitted on early pumps

been removed from the hub, it should be thoroughly cleaned and the tapered hole and keyway examined for ovality, movement, wear or distortion, and if a doubt exists a new steering lever should be fitted. Upon refitting always use a new copper Woodruff key and not as originally fitted, an all steel key. Lubricate the locknut and tighten using a torque wrench set to 85 lb ft.

5. The second (later) type of steering lever is attached to the swivel hub by two special bolts, the longer of which is placed on the lever side of the hub. Two levers are available one marked 'M' for normal steering and the other marked 'P' for use when a car is fitted with power assisted steering.

24. Power-assisted steering - description

With cars having the complete power unit in the front, the weight on the front wheels can be higher than that for a conventional car, so that a larger section tyre has to be used. These two points can raise the required steering wheel force to a higher than normal lever, unless a higher reduction ratio is used in the steering system. There is, of course, a limit to this as too low a geared steering system can be acceptable when parking the car but will necessitate large steering wheel movements for small direction changes. As an optional extra, power-assisted steering can be fitted during production of the models of cars covered by this manual, so that very simply the steering wheel can be turned with little effort. The system basically comprises an hydraulic pump and a special rack and pinion steering gear modified to operate under hydraulic pressure. Overhaul is not recommended to be within the scope of the Do-It-Yourself Motorist, as specialist knowledge as well as special tools are required. However there are certain jobs which can be attempted which are described in detail together with a description of how the system operates.

The special hydraulic pump as shown in Fig. 13:20 is fitted to the rear end of the dynamo and is of sufficient capacity to give power assistance with the engine at normal idling speed. The hydraulic pump passes fluid from the reservoir to a special control valve. This contains a spring loaded flow control valve to limit the flow of hydraulic fluid at high speed. The flow is limited by the fluid passing through an orifice causing a pressure drop across the orifice. When a pre-determined flow rate has been reached the flow control valve uncovers a bypass port and so allows excess fluid to return to the reservoir. As the flow increases more and more with increasing engine speed, the bypass port is opened even more, so resulting in a constant flow rate at the steering unit. This valve, although actuated by the rate of flow of hydraulic fluid, is not sensitive to pressure fluctuating and a special pressure relief valve is set to operate at about 1100 lb/sq inch, to control operating pressure.

A filter is situated in the hydraulic system so that all fluid returning from the steering unit is filtered automatically unless the filter is blocked due to lack of service, in which case a spring will operate the filter and unseat it so allowing the returning fluid to bypass it on its way back to the reservoir.

With the steering wheel in the straight ahead position, hydraulic fluid under pressure created by the pump enters the inlet port and returns to the reservoir without any pressure build up. This is shown in Fig. 13:22. If the steering wheel is turned slightly on either lock a reaction from the pinion in the steering unit moves the pinion housing so that via an operating rod, the control valve spool (3) is moved to direct fluid either to one side

of the steering unit rack or to the other side. Fluid from the steering unit flows back through the control valve to the pump.

When the steering wheel is released, the pressure will automatically balance causing the valve spool to centralise itself, and normal castor action of the front wheels will bring the steering wheel back to its straight ahead positions.

25. Power-assisted steering - maintenance

1. Maintenance of the power-assisted steering system is straightforward. The hydraulic fluid in the pump reservoir shown in Fig. 13:21 must be kept topped up to the level marked on the reservoir using only Automatic Transmission Fluid. It is important to check the level when the system is cold otherwise a false reading will be given. If the reservoir is empty do not run the engine otherwise the pump will be damaged.

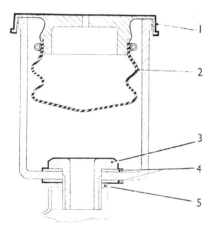

Fig. 13.21. THE PUMP RESERVOIR COMPONENT PARTS

No.	Description	No.	Description
1	Cap	4	Steel washers
2	Bellows	5	Fibre washer
3	Bolt - special		

2. The pump is driven by the dynamo, so it is important that the fan belt is always correctly adjusted, otherwise slippage will occur when the system is in operation.
3. From time to time examine the complete system for signs of leakage. Check that the hose connections are tight and the hoses free from oil or grease and show no signs of cracking.

26. Power steering pump - removal and refitting

1. Obtain a clean and dry container of sufficient capacity to accept hydraulic fluid from the reservoir and piping. Unscrew the outlet hose banjo from the pump and allow the hydraulic fluid to drain into the container.
2. Disconnect the fluid return hose at the pump union and blank off the ends of the hoses and the pump unions to prevent dirt entering into the system.
3. Remove the negative terminal from the battery and

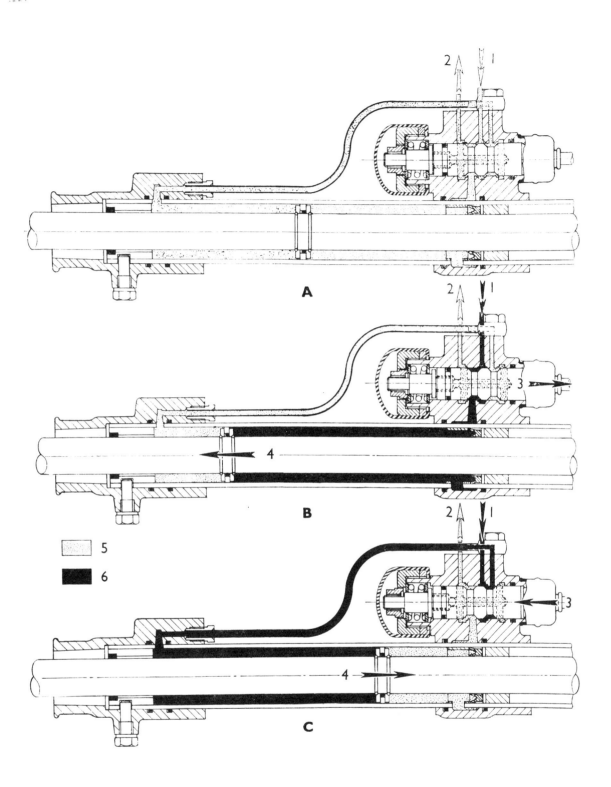

Fig. 13.22. POWER ASSISTED STEERING RACK POWER FLOW DIAGRAMS

NOTES: A. No steering effort applied - spool in neutral position, fluid flowing freely in open circuit.

B. Steering effort applied - spool moved to the left, pressure applied to left side of piston, turning right.

C. Steering effort applied - spool moved to the right, pressure supplied to right side of piston, turning left.

No.	Description	No.	Description	No.	Description	No.	Description
1	From pump	3	Spool movement	5	Fluid at low pressure	6	Fluid at high pressure
2	To resevoir	4	Rack movement				

disconnect the two leads from the back of the generator. Slacken the generator mounting bolts and push the generator towards the engine. Lift the drive belt from the pulley. Very carefully remove the two generator upper mounting bolts and the one lower mounting bolt, bearing in mind that the unit is considerably heavier due to the additional weight of the hydraulic pump on the back. Finally lift away the generator from the engine.

4. Refer to Fig. 13:20 and remove the locknut (6), (only fitted on later pumps) followed by the knurled nut and 'O' ring seal. Carefully lift away the pump reservoir.

5. So that the pump body may be correctly refitted to the generator commutator end bracket, mark the body and bracket. Unscrew the three nuts (14) securing the pump to the generator and lift away the pump. A flexible coupling is used to connect the drive from the generator to the pump end. This should be lifted from the back of the generator.

6. Refitting the pump is the reverse procedure to removal. Before mounting to the back of the generator, rotate the pump by hand to ensure that it is completely free and shows no sign of binding. When tightening the reservoir knurled nut tighten only by hand otherwise it will distort the metal casing and cause a fluid leak. Hold the knurled nut and tighten the locknut to it. The system will have to be bled, full instructions being given in the next section.

27. Bleeding the hydraulic system

1. It will always be necessary to bleed the hydraulic system when a hose has been disconnected or if the level in the reservoir has dropped and air drawn into the system. This operation must be done before the engine is restarted otherwise the pump could be damaged.

2. Turn the steering wheel until the front wheels are in the straight ahead position and leave them in this position throughout the complete operation. Disconnect the distributor cap side clips and remove the distributor cap from the distributor body. This is to stop the engine running. Switch on the ignition switch and operate the starter motor several times and at the same time fill up the reservoir with hydraulic fluid to the correct level.

3. Replace the distributor cap, start the engine and allow to run at idling speed. Turn the steering wheel from one lock to the opposite lock and at the same time continue topping up the reservoir. Obviously an assistant is required for this. This procedure should be continued until all frothing and bubbling ceases and the fluid level in the reservoir remains constant.

28. Steering column - removal and refitting

1. Disconnect the negative terminal from the battery and turn the steering wheel until the front wheels are in the straight ahead position. Leave them in this position if possible to ensure ease of refitting of the column.

2. Locate the wiring loom connectors under the parcel shelf and disconnect the connectors applicable to the steering column wiring.

3. Remove the four setscrews plus their spring washers which secure the clamping plates to the toe-board and draw both the upper and lower clamping plates as well as the bush up the column.

4. Remove the clamp bolt which secures the steering union pinion to the column followed by the two setscrews that hold the column clip and the abutment. Carefully

withdraw the column assembly making sure that the interior headlining is not damaged by the steering wheel or column switch.

5. Refitting is the reverse procedure to removal and providing the front wheels have not been moved the operation is straightforward. Otherwise first centralise the rack the procedure for this being given in Section 22 of this Chapter.

6. Locate the column assembly so that the clamping bolt and direction indicator switch is horizontal and gently engage the pinion splines. Ease the column down on the splines. Replace the column clip followed by positioning the two clamping plates and bush on the toe-board and refit the four setscrews and spring washers. Tighten the column clamp bolt with a torque wrench set to between 12 and 15 lb ft.

7. Refit the column clip and the clamping plates, and remake all electrical connections. Finally check that the column is correctly aligned with the pinion, otherwise this condition could cause a drag on the steering whilst on one or other lock, as well as lack of self centering action.

29. Rack and pinion power-assisted steering unit - removal and replacement

1. Release the steering column to pinion clamp bolt and also slacken off the outer steering column abutment clip set screws.

2. Check the rear wheels and slacken the right hand road wheel nuts (with a left hand car slacken the left hand road wheel nuts). Raise the front of the car and position on firm stands. Remove the road wheel.

3. Extract the split pins from the tie-rod ball joints and remove the locknuts. Use a universal ball joint separator or two hammers to shock release the ball

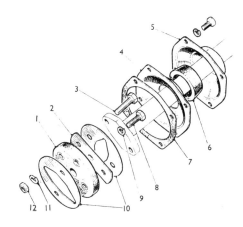

Fig. 13.23. EXPLODED VIEW OF STEERING COLUMN COUPLING

No.	Description	No.	Description
1	Coupling - steering column to rack	6	Bush
2	Earthing strip - dimple to column	7	Seal
3	Screw - coupling to column	8	Screw - coupling to rack
4	Clamp plate - lower	9	Spring washer
5	Clamp plate - upper	10	Coupling plates
		11	Spring washer
		12	Nut

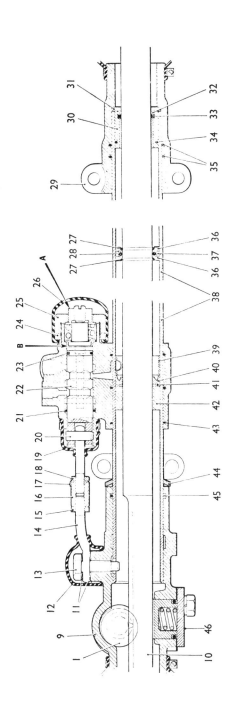

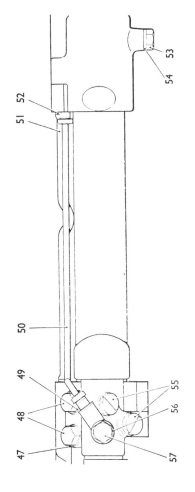

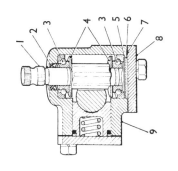

Fig. 13, 24. POWER ASSISTED STEERING RACK COMPONENT PARTS

No.	Description
1	Pinion
2	Oil seal – pinion
3	Bearings
4	Washers
5	Shims
6	Distance piece
7	Gasket
8	End cover
9	Pinion housing
10	Rack
11	Belleville washers and tab washer
12	Dust cover
13	Retaining bolt
14	Operating rod
15	Locknut – L. H. T.
16	Adjusting nut
17	Tab washer
18	Locknut
19	Dust cover

No.	Description
20	Dowel pin
21	'O' ring seal – large
22	Operating spool
23	'O' ring seal – small
24	Locknut
25	Retaining nut
26	Dust cover
27	Circlips
28	'O' ring oil seal
29	End housing
30	Bush
31	Backing washer
32	Anti-extrusion ring
33	Seal – Nu–lip
34	'O' ring seal
35	'O' ring seals
36	Backing washers
37	Piston ring
38	Valve body and rack tube assembly

No.	Description
39	Retainer
40	Seal
41	Anti-extrusion ring
42	Seal abutment
43	'O' ring seal
44	Dust excluder
45	'O' ring seal
46	Damper assembly
47	Washer
48	Locating pegs – valve body

No.	Description
49	Bonded washer
50	Dundy tube – fluid transfer
51	By-pass tube – rack oil
52	Seals
53	Locating peg – end housing
54	Bonded seal
55	Caps – inlet and outlet ports
56	Bonded seals
57	Banjo bolt

joint to steering arm tapers, and disconnect the ball joint.

4. Refer to Fig. 13:25 and note the location of the hydraulic hose banjo unions and hose positioning. Thoroughly clean the area around the banjo unions to ensure there is no possibility of dirt ingress. Place a container under the valve body to collect hydraulic fluid and remove the banjo bolts together with the joint washers. These must be discarded and new ones fitted upon reassembly. It should be noted that on steering units fitted to left hand drive vehicles there is a locating plate and a joint washer on either side and below each banjo union.

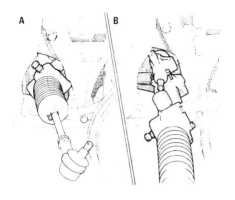

Fig. 13.26. METHOD OF REMOVING R.H.D. DRIVE RACK ASSEMBLY THROUGH VALANCE

No.	Description	No.	Description
A	Clearing the pinion		transfer pipe banjo
B	Clearing the valve body and		

6. Refitting the unit is the reverse sequence to removal. It will be necessary to centralise the rack, details of this operation being given in Section 22/14 of this chapter. Check that the column is correctly aligned with the pinion, otherwise this condition could cause a drag on the steering whilst on one or other lock, as well as lack of self centering action.

7. Bleed the hydraulic system, details of which are given in Section 27 of this chapter.

30. Rack and pinion power-assisted steering unit – overhaul

It is not recommended that this unit be overhauled by the Do-It-Yourself motorist as specialist knowledge and tools are required to complete a satisfactory repair. It is far better to allow the local BLMC Distributor to do this as he will be suitably equipped to do so.

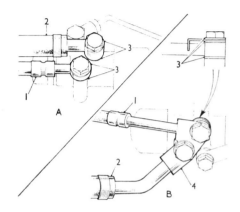

Fig. 13.25. POWER ASSISTED STEERING RACK BANJO CONNECTIONS

No.	Description	No.	Description
A	R.H. Drive	B	L.H. Drive
1	High pressure hose	3	Joint washers
2	Low pressure hose	4	Location plate

5. Remove the four set screws and spring washers that hold the steering unit to the toe board. It will be observed that there is a bracket in two parts at the valve end of the steering unit. Carefully withdraw the unit through the wing valance, turning it slightly to allow the pinion and valve body to clear as shown in Fig. 13:26.

SUSPENSION – DAMPERS – STEERING

FAULT FINDING CHART

Cause	Trouble	Remedy
SYMPTOM:	STEERING FEELS VAGUE, CAR WANDERS AND FLOATS AT SPEED	
General wear or damage	Tyre pressures uneven Dampers worn or require topping up Spring clips broken Steering gear ball joints badly worn Suspension geometry incorrect Steering mechanism free play excessive Front suspension and rear axle pick-up points out of alignment	Check pressures and adjust as necessary. Top up dampers, test, and replace if worn. Renew spring clips. Fit new ball joints. Check and rectify. Adjust or overhaul steering mechanism. Normally caused by poor repair work after a serious accident. Extensive rebuilding necessary.
SYMPTOM:	STIFF & HEAVY STEERING	
Lack of maintenance or accident damage	Tyre pressures too low No grease in king pins No oil in steering gear No grease in steering and suspension ball joints Front wheel toe-in incorrect Suspension geometry incorrect Steering gear incorrectly adjusted too tightly Steering column badly misaligned	Check pressures and inflate tyres. Clean king pin nipples and grease thoroughly. Top up steering gear. Clean nipples and grease thoroughly. Check and reset toe-in. Check and rectify. Check and readjust steering gear. Determine cause and rectify (Usually due to bad repair after severe accident damage and difficult to correct).
SYMPTOM:	WHEEL WOBBLE & VIBRATION	
General wear or damage	Wheel nuts loose Front wheels and tyres out of balance Steering ball joints badly worn Hub bearings badly worn Steering gear free play excessive Front springs loose, weak or broken	Check and tighten as necessary. Balance wheels and tyres and add weights as necessary. Replace steering gear ball joints. Remove and fit new hub bearings. Adjust and overhaul steering gear. Inspect and overhaul as necessary.

Chapter 14/Bodywork & Underframe

Contents

1. Bodywork and underframe - maintenance

1. The condition of your car's bodywork is of considerable importance as it is on this that the second hand value of the car will mainly depend. It is very much more difficult to repair neglected bodywork than to renew mechanical assemblies. The hidden portions of the body, such as the wheel arches, the underframe and the engine compartment are equally important, although obviously not requiring such frequent attention as the immediately visible paintwork.

2. Once a year or every 12,000 miles, it is a sound scheme to visit your local main agent and have the underside of the body steam cleaned. This will take about $1\frac{1}{2}$ hours and costs about £4. All traces of dirt and oil will be removed and the underside can then be inspected carefully for rust, damaged hydraulic pipes, frayed electrical wiring and similar maladies. The car should be greased on completion of this job.

3. At the same time the engine compartment should be cleaned in the same manner. If steam cleaning facilities are not available then brush 'Gunk' or a similar cleanser over the whole engine and engine compartment with a stiff paint brush, working it well in where there is an accumulation of oil and dirt. Do not paint the ignition system, and protect it with oily rags when the 'Gunk' is washed off. As the 'Gunk' is washed away it will take with it all traces of oil and dirt, leaving the engine looking clean and bright.

4. The wheel arches should be given particular attention as undersealing can easily come away here and stones and dirt thrown up from the road wheels can soon cause the paint to chip and flake, and so allow rust to set in. If rust is found, clean down to the bare metal

with wet and dry paper, paint on an anti-corrosive coating such as 'Kurust', or if preferred, red lead, and renew the paintwork and undercoating.

5. The bodywork should be washed once a week or when dirty. Thoroughly wet the car to soften the dirt and then wash the car down with a soft sponge and plenty of clean water. If the surplus dirt is not washed off very gently, in time it will wear the paint down as surely as wet and dry paper. It is best to use a hose if this is available. Give the car a final washdown and then dry with a soft chamois leather to prevent the formation of spots.

6. Spots of tar and grease thrown up from the road can be removed with a rag dampened with petrol.

7. Once every six months, or every three months if wished, give the bodywork and chromium trim a thoroughly good wax polish. If a chromium trim cleaner is used to remove rust on any of the car's plated parts remember that the cleaner also removes part of the chromium, so use sparingly.

2. Carpets and upholstery - maintenance

1. Remove the carpets and thoroughly vacuum clean the interior of the car every three months, or more frequently if necessary. Beat out carpets and shampoo them if they are very dirty.

2. If the headlining or upholstery is soiled apply an upholstery cleaner with a damp sponge and wipe off with a clean dry cloth.

3. Body - minor repairs

1. At some time during your ownership of your car it is likely that it will be bumped or scraped in a mild way, causing some slight damage to the body. Major damage must be repaired by your local BLMC agent, but there is no reason why you cannot successfully beat out, repair, and re-spray minor damage yourself. The essential items which the owner should gather together to ensure a really professional job are:
(a) A plastic filler such as Holts 'Cataloy'.
(b) Paint whose colour matches exactly that of the bodywork, either in a can for application by a spray gun, or in an aerosol can.
(c) Fine cutting paste.
(d) Medium and fine grade wet and dry paper.

2. Never use a metal hammer to knock out small dents as the blows tend to damage and distort the metal. Knock out the dent with a mallet or rawhide hammer and press on the underside of the dented surface a metal dolly or smooth wooden block roughly contoured to the normal shape of the damaged area.

3. After the worst of the damaged area has been knocked out, rub down the area with medium wet and dry paper and thoroughly clean away all traces of dirt.

4. The plastic filler comprises a paste and a hardener which must be thoroughly mixed together. Mix only a small portion at a time as the paste sets hard within five to fifteen minutes depending on the amount of hardener used.

5. Smooth on the filler with a knife or stiff plastic to the shape of the damaged portion and allow to thoroughly dry. A process which takes about six hours. After the filler has dried it is likely that it will have contracted slightly so spread on a second layer of filler if necessary.

6. Smooth down the filler with fine wet and dry paper wrapped round a suitable block of wood and continue until the whole area is perfectly smooth and it is impossible to feel where the filler joins the rest of the paintwork. Spray on from an aerosol can, or with a spray gun, an anti-rust undercoat, smooth down with wet and dry paper, and then spray on two coats of the final finishing using a circular motion. When thoroughly dry polish the whole area with a fine cutting paste to smooth the re-sprayed area into the remainder of the wing and to remove the small particles of spray paint which will have settled in the vicinity. This will leave the wing looking perfect with not a trace of the previous unsightly dent.

4. Body - major repairs

1. Because the body is built on the monocoque principle and is integral with the underframe, major damage must be repaired by competent mechanics with the necessary welding and hydraulic straightening equipment.

2. If the damage is serious it is vital that the bodyshell is in correct alignment, as otherwise the handling of the car will suffer and many other faults such as excessive tyre wear, and wear in the transmission and steering, may occur. The BLMC produce a special alignment jig and to ensure that all is correct a repaired car should be checked on this jig.

3. Alternatively, with the bodyshell jacked up off a level floor a series of measurement checks can be carried out to determine whether misalignment is present or not. Start by dropping a plumb line from the centre of each of the front suspension mounting bolt holes to the floor and mark the spot. Repeat this from the outside of the rear suspension support members. Carefully determine the centre line by scribing two arcs on the floor between AA and DD as shown in Fig 14:2.

5. Hinges and locks - maintenance

Once every six months or 6,000 miles the door, bonnet, and boot hinges should be oiled with a few drops of engine oil from an oil can. The door striker plates can be given a thin smear of grease to reduce wear and ensure free movement.

6. Front bumper (Austin and Morris models) - removal and replacement

1. Refer to Fig 14:1 and undo the nuts (7) that hold the support bracket (9) to the outer ends of the bumper bar. Lift away the nuts (7), spring washers (6) and flat washers (5).

2. Remove the bolts (2) that hold the overriders to the bumper bar and bracket and lift away the overrider, seating (1), spring washer (6), flat washers (5) and the overrider.

3. Remove the nuts (7) that secure the bumper bar to the mounting bracket and lift away the spring washers (6) and flat washers (5).

4. If it is wished to remove the bumper brackets these can be released from the body by removing the nuts (7), spring washer (6), flat washers (5) and bolts (20).

5. Replacement is a straightforward reversal of the removal sequence.

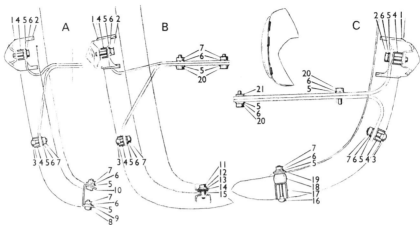

Fig. 14.1. FRONT AND REAR BUMPER BLADE MOUNTINGS

A. Front - Austin/Morris		B. Front - Wolseley		C. Rear	
No. Description	No. Description	No. Description	No. Description	No. Description	No. Description
1 Over-rider seating - 5 in. (127 mm) long	5 Flat washer		12 Spring washer		19 Flat washer - 1¼ in. (32mm) O.D.
2 Bolt -over-rider to mounting bar	6 Spring washer		13 Flat washer		20 Bolt - mounting bar to body
3 Special bolt - bumper bar to mounting bar	7 Nut		14 Grommet		21 Ferrule
	8 Special bolt bumper to bracket		15 Distance piece		Inset: Wolseley; buffer to over-rider fixing
4 Distance piece	9 Support bracket		16 Special bolt - long		
	10 Bolt - bracket to body		17 Distance piece		
	11 Bolt		18 Distance piece - rubber		

7. Front bumper (Wolseley models) - removal and replacement

1. Refer to Fig 14:2 B and remove the bolts (11) that secure the outer ends of the bumper bar to the body panel bracket and lift away the spring washer (12), flat washers (13), grommets (14) and distance pieces (15).
2. Refer to Section 6/2, 3, 4 and 5 as the sequence is identical to the Austin and Morris models.

8. Rear bumper (Austin and Morris models) - removal and replacement

1. Refer to Fig 14:2C, and undo the nuts (7) on the special bolts (16) and lift away the spring washers (6), flat washers (5), large diameter flat washers (19), rubber distance pieces (18) and the metal distance piece (17). Extract the bolts (16).
2. Remove the nuts (7) holding the bumper bar to the outer end of the bracket and lift away the spring washers (6), flat washers (5) and extract the special bolts (3) which will then release the metal distance pieces (4).
3. Remove the bolt (2) that holds the bumper bar to the inner part of the bracket and lift away the spring washer (6), flat washer (5) and metal distance piece (4). This bolt will also release the overrider.
4. Refitting is the reverse sequence to removal.

9. Rear bumper (Wolseley models) - removal and replacement

1. Disconnect the positive terminal from the battery.
2. Release the reverse lamp cable from its connector.

3. Refer to Section 8/1, 2 and 3 above as the sequence is identical to the Austin and Morris models.

10. Windscreen glass - removal and replacement

1. If you are unfortunate enough to have a windscreen shatter, fitting a replacement windscreen is one of the few jobs which the average owner is advised to leave to a professional mechanic. For the owner who wishes to do the job himself the following instructions are given:
2. Remove the wiper arms from their spindles using a screwdriver to lift the retaining clip from the spindle end and pull away.
3. Taking care not to damage the rubber surround, carefully prise up the end of the finishing strip from its channel in the rubber surround.
4. Move to the inside of the car and have an assistant outside the car ready to catch the glass as it is released. Push on the glass with the palms of the hands placed at one of the top corners. This is of course not applicable if the glass has not shattered. Remove the rubber surround from the glass or remains.
5. Now is the time to remove all pieces of glass if the screen has shattered. Use a vacuum cleaner to extract as much as possible. Switch on the heater boost motor and adjust the controls to 'screen defrost' but watch out for flying pieces of glass which might be blown out of the ducting.
6. Carefully inspect the rubber surround for signs of splitting or deterioration. Position the glass into the lower channel of the rubber surround commencing at one corner and carefully lift the lip of the rubber over the glass using a smooth flat ended tool.
7. With the rubber surround correctly positioned on

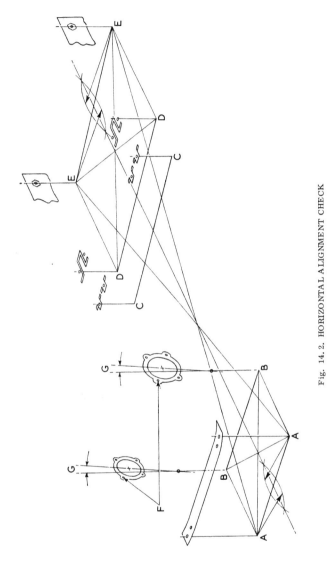

Fig. 14.2. HORIZONTAL ALIGNMENT CHECK

Code letter	Dimension	Location
A–A	27 9/32 in. (697.7 mm)	Tie-bar mounting hole centres
B–B	27¼ in. (697 mm)	Front suspension mounting, front hole (top)
C–C	46 1/8 in. (1171.6 mm)	Rear suspension mounting, front hole centres
D–D	47 5/16 in. (1201.7 mm)	Rear suspension mounting, rear hole centres
E–E	48 in. (1219 mm)	Bumper bar mountings
F	–	Centre of hole (horizontal check)
G–G		4° suspension mounting angle

205

the glass it is now necessary to insert a piece of cord about 16 ft long all round the outer channel in the rubber surround which fits over the windscreen aperture flange. The two free ends of the cord should finish at either top or bottom centre and overlap each other by about 1 ft.

8. Offer the screen up to the aperture and get an assistant to press the rubber surround hard against the body flange. Slowly pull one end of the cord moving round the windscreen so drawing the lip over the windscreen flange on the body.

9. It will now be necessary to fit the finishing strip for which BLMC tool No. 18G468B is necessary. This can probably be borrowed from the local agents. Thread the end of the finishing strip through the eye of the adaptor and under the roller. Push the eye of the tool into the finisher groove and hold the end of the finisher in position. Push the tool along the groove and seat using the roller. When negotiating a corner use a side to side action to stop tearing.

10. Refit the wiper arms and blades.

11. Door rattles - tracing and rectification

1. The commonest cause of door rattles is a misaligned, loose or worn striker plate but other causes may be:
(a) Loose door handles, window winder handles or door hinges.
(b) Loose, worn or misaligned door lock components.
(c) Loose or worn remote control mechanism.
2. It is quite possible for door rattles to be the result of a combination of the above faults so a careful examination must be made to determine the causes of the fault.
3. If the nose of the striker plate is worn and as a result the door rattles, renew it and adjust the plate as described later in this chapter.
4. If the nose of the door lock wedge is badly worn and the door rattles as a result, then fit a new lock as described later in this chapter.
5. Should the hinges be badly worn, then they must be renewed.

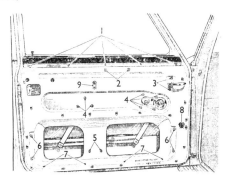

Fig. 14.3. DOOR LOCK AND WINDOW REGULATOR MOUNTING POINTS ON DOOR PANEL. (FRONT DOOR FITTED WITH THE EARLY INTERIOR LOCK HANDLE)

No.	Description	No.	Description
1	Screws - trim pad finisher	6	Companion box securing plugs
2	Door-pull securing plugs	7	Screw holes - low trim pad
3	Screw - door lock remote control	8	Screw - window channel
4	Screws - window regulator	9	Anti-rattle clip - remote control rod
5	Screws - window stop		

12. Door striker plate - removal, replacement and adjustment

1. If it is wished to renew a worn striker plate mark

its position on the door pillar so a new plate can be fitted in the same position.
2. To remove the plate simply undo the three Phillips screws which hold the plate in position. Replacement is equally straightforward.
3. To adjust the striker plate close the door and then push it hard against its sealing rubber. The door edge furthest from the hinges should move in approximately 3/32 inch.
4. Loosen the door striker plate screws and adjust the plate until the clearance is correct. Tighten the screws and check that the door closes properly, without lifting or dropping, and that on the road it does not rattle.

13. Door trim and interior handles - removal and replacement

1. Insert a steel blade behind the lock remote control escutcheon to release its spring clip from the handle assembly. Depress the window regulator escutcheon as far as it will go into the trim panel. Using a small diameter parallel pin punch, locate and carefully push out the retaining pin. Note the position of the handle in the glass fully raised position for correct refitting and lift away together with escutcheon.
2. If an arm rest is fitted remove its two No. 14 retaining screws and lift away. If a door pull handle is fitted remove its two No. 10 retaining screws and lift away.
3. Locate and remove the four Phillips head screws holding the lower trim pad and carefully lever the clips from the door panel plugs using a wide bladed screwdriver taking care not to damage the paintwork.
4. Use the wide bladed screwdriver again under the lower edge of the main trim panel and gently lever the edge from the door panel plugs. As before take care not to scratch the paintwork or damage the pad.
5. Unscrew the screws which hold the companion box to the door panel and lift away.
6. Refitting is the reverse procedure to removal. It

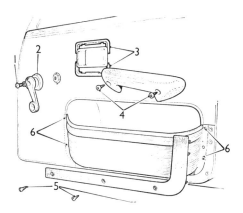

Fig. 14.4. INTERIOR DOOR HANDLE AND TRIM MOUNTING POINTS (LATER TYPE INTERIOR LOCK HANDLE)

No.	Description	No.	Description
1	Screw - window regulator handle	4	Screws - arm-rest
2	Escutcheon	5	Screws - lower trim pad
3	Bezel - remote control	6	Screws - door pocket

is advisable to grease all door lock moving parts before refitting the door trim. If a plastic cover was fitted to the inner door panel replace it or alternatively if the door cutouts were taped and these removed, tape over with new tape to act as a moisture seal.

7. The procedure for removing the trim panel is basically the same to that above. The operation is straightforward.

14. Door lock handles (exterior) - removal, replacement and adjustment

1. Close the window fully and by referring to Section 13 remove the door interior handles and trim.
2. Refer to Fig 14:5 and remove the two door handle retaining nuts (3) and spring washers.
3. Carefully pull on the handle and it should come away from the door panel. Note the two rubber pads on the handle mounting faces.
4. To adjust the handle offer up the handle together with rubber pads to the door panel and see if there is a clearance of 1/32 inch or more between the plunger bolt (4) and lock contact (6). If adjustment is required slacken the locknut (5) and move the plunger bolt (4) in or out as necessary until the clearance is at least 1/32 inch. Tighten the locknut.
5. Refitting the door handle is the reverse sequence to removal.

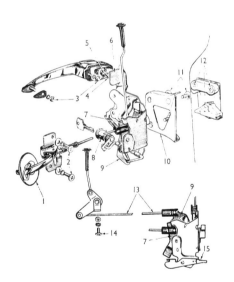

Fig. 14.5. FRONT AND REAR DOOR LOCK COMPONENT PARTS (EARLY)

No.	Description	No.	Description
1	Escutcheon	9	Locking lever
2	Screws -- remote control	10	Dovetail plate
3	Nuts - outside control	11	Dovetail securing screws
4	Plunger bolt	12	Striker plate securing screws
5	Locknut	13	Rear lock and remote control
6	Lock contact	14	Pivot screw
7	Lock operating lever	15	Safety catch
8	Twin-legged spring collar		

15. Door locks - removal and replacement

1. Close the window fully and by referring to Section 13 remove the door interior handles and trim.
2. Refer to Fig 14:5 and release the clip that connects the lock to the remote control rod. Also remove the door lock button (front locks only).
3. Disconnect the rear glass channel from its guide and move the channel to one side in the door panel.
4. Using a pencil outline the position of the dovetail plate (10) and unscrew the three retaining screws (11). Finally disconnect the lock assembly from the private lock actuation rod and lift the lock away from the access hole in the door.
5. Should it be necessary to remove the front door lock remote control system, hold the glass in the fully closed position using two pieces of tapered wood between the door and glass. Unscrew the seven screws that hold the regulator assembly and also the two screws that hold the remote control to the door panel. Position the regulator in the door to clear whilst pushing the control handle through its cut out and lift the assembly out through the cut out. Refitting is the reverse procedure to removal. It is desirable to be able to move the control handle 1/16 inch before it starts to operate the lock mechanism.
6. To remove the rear door lock remote control simply release the screw (14) securing the pivot assembly and lift away through the front most aperture in the door panel.
7. Thoroughly grease the moving components of a new lock and fit the unit in place ensuring that the lock contact (6) moves freely.
8. Insert the lock through the door access and engage the private lock actuating rod and hold in position ready for refitting the dovetail plate (10) and retaining screws.
9. Refit the three dovetail securing screws (11) and adjust to the original previously marked position.
10. Replace the rear glass channel and using a strong waterproof glue like Bostick, glue in its original location.
11. Reconnect the remote control rod to the lock lever using the special clip, and finally replace the door trim panel and interior handles.

16. Door glass regulators - removal and refitting

1. Remove the door trim and interior handles as described in Section 13.
2. With the door glass in its fully raised position use two pieces of tapered wood between the door and glass to hold the glass in this position.
3. Unscrew the seven screws that secure the regulator assembly to the door panel. Detach the regulator from the glass channel and contract the complete assembly to enable it to be drawn through the door panel cut outs. On the front doors use the larger cut out of the two.
4. Refitting is the reverse sequence to removal. Grease all moving parts well before re-assembling to the door.

17. Door - removal and refitting

1. Disconnect the door check pivot pin so that the door may be opened further. Take care that it does not open too far otherwise the panels could be dented by touching the wing panel (front or door pillar leading edge (rear).
2. Using a pencil, accurately mark the outline of the

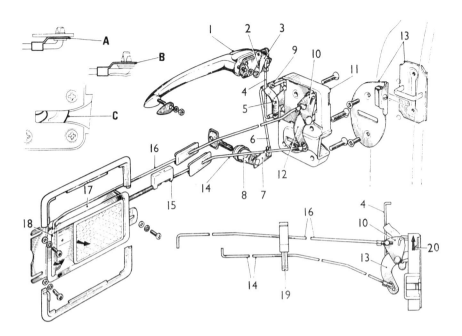

Fig. 14. 6. FRONT AND REAR DOOR LOCK COMPONENT PARTS (LATE)

No.	Description	No.	Description	No.	Description	No.	Description
1	Push-button	8	Twin-legged spring collar	14	Latch release rod (b)	20	Safety catch - children's
2	Plunger screw	9	Latch locking lever	15	Plastic clip	A	Bush assembly - clip rod side
3	Cranked push button arm	10	Locking quadrant	16	Lock control rod (a)	B	Bush assembly - clip other side
4	Push-button link (d)	11	Latch unit	17	Remote control unit	C	Latch disc - latched position
5	Contactor slide	12	Latch release lever	18	Safety locking latch		
6	Key-operated link (c)	13	Striker assembly	19	Anti-rattle clip		
7	Operating arm						

hinge to its mounting to assist refitting. It is desirable to have an assistant to take the weight of the door once the hinges have been released. Remove the screws holding the hinges to the door and lift away the complete door. For storage it is best to stand on an old blanket and allow to lean against a wall suitably padded at the top of the door to stop scratching the paint.

3. Refitting the door is the reverse sequence to removal. If after refitting, adjustment is necessary, it should be done at the hinges to give correct alignment, or the striker reset if the door either moves up or down on final closing.

___

18. Bonnet - removal and replacement

1. Open the bonnet and hold open using the bonnet stay. To set as a datum for refitting, mark the outline of the hinge position using a soft pencil.
2. With the assistance of a second person take the weight of the front of the bonnet and remove the screws securing the bonnet stay to the bonnet itself. Then remove the four bolts, spring and plain washers, holding the bonnet to the hinges and lift away the bonnet panel taking care not to scratch the top of the wings.
3. Lean the bonnet up against a wall suitably padded

to stop scratching the paint.
4. Should it be necessary to remove the hinges, disconnect the battery positive terminal and reach behind the fascia panel. Extract the split pin from the pivot pin holding the hinge to its bracket and carefully withdraw the pivot pin.
5. Refitting the bonnet is the reverse sequence to removal, any adjustment necessary can be made either at the hinges or bonnet catch.

___

19. Bonnet lock and safety catch - removal and refitting

1. Release the screw which secures the support to the bonnet lock platform and, on Wolseley models, also release the bonnet control cable at the trunnion.
2. Undo the two screws of the lock assembly and remove the screws together with spring and flat washers. NOTE: A trapped nut is used on the left hand side. Disconnect the return spring and lift away the complete lock assembly which also includes the locating cup.
3. Release the bonnet lock pin locknut and using a screwdriver in the screwdriver slot in the end of the bonnet lock pin, unscrew the pin and lift away together with the spring.
4. If it is necessary to remove the bonnet safety catch,

it is secured to the bonnet by three screws which should be removed together with the spring and plain washers so releasing the catch.

5. Refitting the lock and safety catch is the reverse sequence to removal. The catch and locking pin can be individually adjusted until the correct setting is obtained.

20. Boot lid – removal and replacement

1. It is recommended that an old blanket is placed under the top edge of the lid and spread over the wing panels to avoid scratching the paintwork during removal and refitting.
2. Locate and disconnect the number plate light cable snap connector situated against the right hand valance.
3. With the assistance of a second person support the weight of the lid and remove the set screws that secure the hinge brackets to the lid panel and carefully lift away the lid from the hinges.
4. Should it be necessary to remove the hinges from the body locate and remove the four set screws which secure the hinge assembly to the rear parcel shelf panel. Lift away the complete hinge assembly.
5. Refitting is the reverse sequence to removal and any adjustment required may be performed at the hinge to lid mounting.

21. Trunk lid – removal and replacement

1. To remove the locking device, release the four screws that hold the lock assembly to the lid and lift away the complete assembly. Carefully lift part of the sealing rubber surround and locate the two screws which hold the outer trunk lid handle to the lid. Unscrew the two outer and two inner positioned screws and lift away the handle.
2. Using a pair of circlip pliers or a screwdriver, carefully release the circlip (1), Fig 14:7, which secures the lock barrel and lift away the lock barrel together with the spring (3) and bearing washer (2).
3. The lock assembly is held to the trunk lid by four screws and these should be removed together with the spring washers. Plain washers are fitted over the two slotted holes.
4. Before removing the striker catch, mark the position carefully, using a soft pencil, to assist correct location upon refitting, and remove the two setscrews.
5. Refitting on all models is the reverse sequence to removal but some care is required to reset the latch. The latch push (11) must be set to the horizontal position and to the right when the lock is viewed from the key end with the key entry slot at the bottom. On early models it is important that the push lever securing nut (5) is checked for tightness. Then with the cut outs of the bearing washer (2) horizontal, slide this into position with the spring (3) and refit the circlip (1). Finally fit the handle and lock assembly and test the operation of the lock BEFORE closing the lid otherwise troubles could arise if the lid is closed and cannot be opened by normal means. The striker catch assembly can be adjusted to give easy closing action.

22. Rear quarter light – removal and refitting

It is not usual for the opening type of quarter light to have to be removed but should it be necessary proceed as follows:
1. Using the correct sized screwdriver carefully unscrew the screws which hold the catch to the rear panel.

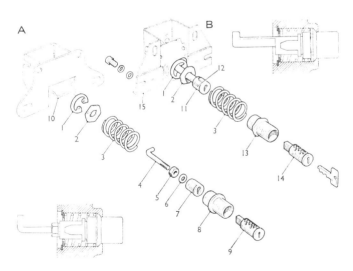

Fig. 14.7. TRUNK LID LOCK COMPONENT PARTS (EARLY 'A' AND LATE 'B')

No.	Description	No.	Description	No.	Description	No.	Description
1	Circlip	6	Lock washer	10	Lock assembly	14	Locking device
2	Bearing washer – push-button	7	Latch push	11	Latch push	15	Lock assembly
3	Return spring	8	Push-button	12	Bezel pin		Insets: Top view of lock assemblies in the locked position
4	Push lever	9	Locking device	13	Push-button		
5	Nut						

2. Gently ease the quarter light backwards and in an upwards direction so releasing the hinge tongues from the hinge rubbers. Lift away the complete assembly.

3. Refitting is the reverse sequence to removal. Take care when sliding the quarter light into position and lubricate well the hinge rubbers. Ensure that the hinge tongues enter their locations fully.

---

23. Parcel shelf - removal and replacement

A parcel shelf is fitted to Austin and Morris models covered by this manual and to remove the shelf proceed as follows:

1. Unscrew the screws which hold the steering column and hand brake brackets to the front rail of the parcel shelf (47), Fig 14:10. Disconnect the positive terminal from the battery for safety reasons and detach the steering column cables at their connectors which are located below the parcel shelf. Release the connectors from the parcel shelf. On later models covered by this manual it is also necessary to release the heater/fresh air unit control knobs followed by the bezel.

2. Release the parcel shelf support (29) and also the screws which secure the top of the parcel shelf. Carefully extract the board from its retaining clips taking care not to damage the board.

3. Undo the screws (28) which secure the rail (47) to the 'A' post brackets and lift away the screws together with spring and plain washers.

4. By careful manipulation first clear the side panels from the cold air vents and tip back, then pull the assembly towards the rear and withdraw the parcel shelf from the side furthest away from the steering column. Mind the interior roof liner, when lifting away the parcel shelf, to ensure that it is not damaged.

5. Refitting the parcel shelf is the reverse sequence to removal.

---

24. Instruments - removal and replacement

1. During some operations, for example when removing the fascia trim, it is necessary to first remove an individual instrument or the instrument panel. Details of how to do this are given below.

2. Wolseley models - For safety reasons disconnect the positive terminal from the battery. Locate and undo the screw situated at the bottom of the instrument panel.

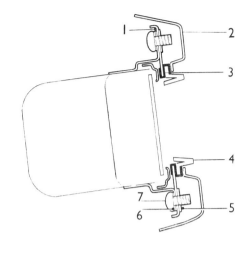

Fig. 14. 8. INSTRUMENT INSTALLATION

No.	Description	No.	Description
1	Instrument plate	5	Weld nut
2	Fascia panel	6	Internal lock washer
3	Packing	7	Screw
4	Instrument bezel		

Carefully pull the lower edge of this panel forwards and downwards so releasing the locating pegs at the top of the panel. Upon inspection it will be seen that both the 'three-in-one' instrument and the speedometer head are held in position by special fixing clamps with thumbscrews and shake proof washers which can be easily removed for individual instrument lead removal. The electric clock is retained by a bayonet type clip.

3. Refitting is the reverse sequence to removal. By referring to the wiring diagram applicable to Wolseley models in Chapter 12 the electrical connections can be correctly re-made if there is any doubt at all about their correct placement.

4. Austin and Morris models - For safety reasons disconnect the positive terminal from the battery. On later models covered by this manual with the second type of

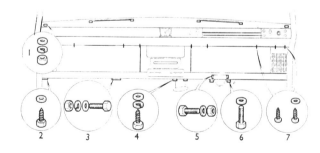

Fig. 14. 9. FASCIA ASSEMBLY FIXING POINTS (AUSTIN AND MORRIS)

No.	Description	No.	Description	No.	Description	No.	Description
1	Top cover to panel	3	Support to parcel rail	5	Reinforcement bracket to rail	7	Top cover and vents to panel
2	Parcel rail to 'A' post bracket	4	Hand brake bracket	6	Steering-column and choke		

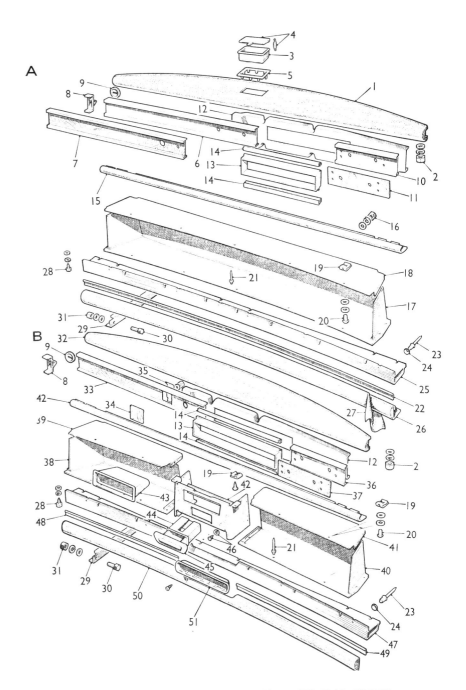

Fig. 14.10. FASCIA ASSEMBLIES COMPONENT PARTS (AUSTIN AND MORRIS)

A. First Type fitted from (C.N.) A17S-101A. M17S-101A/M.

B. Second Type fitted from (C.N.) A17S-56718A. M17S-11984A.

No.	Description	No.	Description	No.	Description	No.	Description
1	Top - cover fascia	15	Lower covering - fascia	28	Screw with spring and flat washer - rail to 'A' post bracket	39	Top - L.H.
2	Nut with spring and flat washer	16	Nut with spring and flat washers			40	Parcel shelf - R.H.
3	Ashtray assembly	17	Parcel shelf	29	Parcel shelf support R.H.	41	Top - R.H.
4	Lid and spring	18	Top	30	Screw	42	Fascia centre console
5	Bezel	19	Spring nut - 'U' type	31	Nut with spring and flat washer	43	Oddment box (or radio)
6	Panel finishers - long - Austin	20	Screw	32	Top cover	44	Ashtray case
7	Panel finishers - long - Morris	21	Pop rivet	33	Panel finisher - long	45	Ashtray tray
8	Clip finisher	22	Parcel shelf finisher	34	Clock aperture mask	46	Screw and spring washer
9	Retainer	23	Pop rivet - finisher to rail	35	Retainer - with nut and lock washer	47	Parcel shelf rail
10	Panel finisher - short	24	Cup washer	36	Panel finisher - short	48	Parcel shelf finisher - L.H.
11	Insert*	25	Parcel shelf rail	37	Insert	49	Parcel shelf finisher - R.H.
12	Instrument plate	26	Crash pad	38	Parcel shelf - L.H.	50	Crash pad
13	Instrument bezel	27	Crash pad cover - marked for heater or fresh-air unit			51	Bezel - heater or fresh-air unit controls
14	Packing - instrument to fascia panel						

*From (CN) A17S-56718A, M17S-101A/M

211

fascia fitted to the driver's side, the screws securing the top of the parcel shelf should be removed. Next remove the light switch retaining locknut and release the clips retaining the long fascia finisher from behind the fascia and carefully ease the finisher away.

5. The shorter fascia panel is held in position by the screen wiper switch and washer control locknuts and these should be removed next. A spring clip also holds the shorter fascia in position. Remove the warning light bulbs from the warning light units, undo the locknuts and carefully ease the finisher away. Disconnect the electrical wires from the panel light switch. Locate and remove the screws that secure the instrument plate, and push the complete assembly forwards with the lip downwards. This will allow the four securing screws to be removed from the panel and the instrument assembly may then be withdrawn.

6. Refitting is the reverse sequence to removal. By referring to the wiring diagram applicable to Austin and Morris models in Chapter 12 the electrical connections can be correctly re-made if there is any doubt at all about their correct placement.

25. Fascia trim top cover (Wolseley) - removal and replacement

1. Refer to the Section 24 and remove the fascia panel assembly so allowing easy access to the underside of the top panel. Then from under the top panel remove the six nuts with the spring and flat washers. Two will be found at the outside edges of the panel and the remaining four hold the demister nozzles. Carefully clear the studs from the top panel and lift away the complete cover.

2. Refitting is the reverse sequence to removal.

26. Fascia trim top cover (Austin and Morris) - removal and replacement

1. Release the instrument panel (see Section 24) Carefully push it forwards to clear. On earlier models covered by this manual withdraw the ashtray assembly. Then from under the top panel remove the six nuts with the spring and flat washers. Two will be found at the outside edges of the panel and the remaining four which hold the demister nozzles. Carefully clear the studs from the top panel and lift away the complete top cover.

2. Refitting is the reverse sequence to removal.

27. Crash pad lower covering (Wolseley) - removal and replacement

1. Refer to the Section 24 and remove the fascia panel assembly. Locate and remove the screws which secure the fascia board brackets to the parcel rails and lift the rail away, followed by the finisher. Undo the five nuts and lift away together with the spring and flat washers and carefully pull the crash pad from the rail.

2. Refitting is the reverse sequence to removal but take care that when fitting a new crash pad cover not to forget to centralize the heater and fresh air control markings.

28. Crash pad lower covering (Austin and Morris) - removal and replacement

1. On the first type fitted to earlier models covered by this manual remove the parcel rail finisher by drilling out the 'Pop' rivets. With the second type the control bezel must also be removed.

2. Refitting is the reverse sequence to removal but take care, that when fitting a new crash pad cover, not to forget to centralize the heater fresh air control markings.

29. Roof linings - removal and replacement

It is recommended that this operation be carried out by the local agents or a specialist motor car trim firm as, although apparently simple, practice is required, otherwise damage can result or an unsatisfactory fitting be obtained such as crinkling, tearing or distortion which will make the roof lining look untidy.

30. Heater - description

1. A combined fresh air heater and demister unit is fitted to all vehicles manufactured for the Home Market but is fitted as an optional extra to the Export models.

2. It is designed to heat and ventilate the car interior and to demist or defrost the windscreen depending on the control settings. The air supply to the interior may be at either the ambient temperature or heated by using water from the engine cooling system and passing it through a small radiator inside the heater unit. The air passes through the matrix of the heater radiator and is then directed either to the footwells or to the front screen by flap deflectors inside the heater and operated by the two sliding controls situated at the centre of the parcel rail. An electric fan is fitted onto the unit to boost the air flow at low car speeds.

31. Heater (Austin and Morris) - removal

1. Place a container having a capacity of at least 10 pints under the radiator drain plug. Unscrew the plug and allow the coolant to drain from the cooling system.

2. Disconnect the two rubber heater hoses from the unions on the bulkhead. It is recommended that if a compressed air line is available a gentle blast of air be applied to one of the hoses to force any water out of the heater radiator, so that upon removal there is less likelihood of rusty water damaging any trim.

3. Disconnect the positive terminal from the battery to act as a safeguard whilst separating the electrical connections.

4. Refer to Section 23 of this Chapter and remove the parcel shelf assembly. All the component parts being shown in Fig 14:9.

5. Locate and disconnect the electrical wiring going to the heater blower motor at the connector positioned on the right hand side of the heater unit casing.

6. Remove the four nuts together with spring and flat washers which secure the heater unit to the bulkhead panel. Place a folded blanket over the carpeting to absorb any water drips from the heater radiator. Tilt the unit towards the rear of the car and lift away from the steering column.

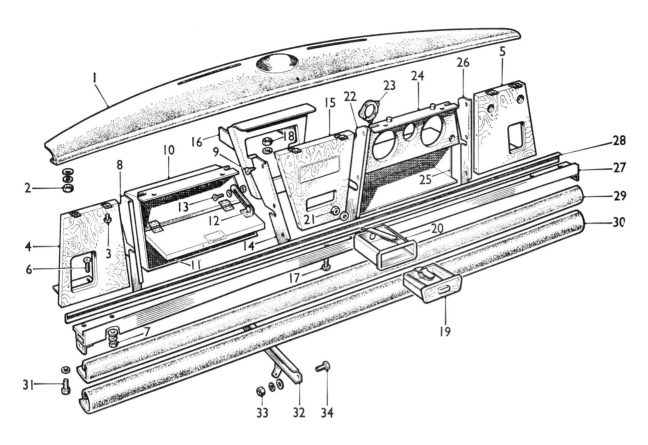

Fig. 14.11. FASCIA ASSEMBLY COMPONENT PARTS (WOLSELEY)

No.	Description	No.	Description	No.	Description	No.	Description
1	Top cover – fascia	10	Glovebox – passenger's		shers	28	Rail finisher
2	Nut with spring and flat washer	11	Lid	19	Ashtray	29	Crash pad
		12	Quadrant	20	Case	30	Crash pad cover
3	Screw – fascia to panel	13	Screw with plain washer and nut	21	Nut with washer	31	Screw – 'A' post bracket to rail
4	End board – passenger's			22	Finisher – glovebox	32	Parcel shelf support – with bonnet pull bracket
5	End board – driver's	14	Finisher – glovebox	23	Clock retainer		
6	Fascia to rail – screw	15	Centre board	24	Instrument board	33	Nut with spring and plain washer
7	Nut with spring and flat washer	16	Fascia centre panel	25	Glovebox – driver's		
		17	Screw – fascia panel	26	Finisher – glovebox	34	Screw
8	Finisher – glovebox	18	Nut with spring and flat washer	27	Parcel shelf rail		
9	Screw – finishers to board						

Fig. 14.12. FASCIA ASSEMBLY FIXING POINTS (WOLSELEY)

No.	Description	No.	Description	No.	Description	No.	Description
1	Parcel rail to 'A' post bracket	2	Support to parcel rail	4	Reinforcement bracket to rail	5	Steering column and choke
		3	Handbrake bracket			6	Top cover to panel

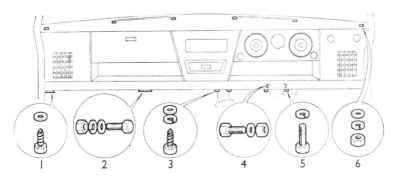

32. Heater (Wolseley) - removal

1. The procedure is basically identical to that for Austin and Morris models except that the fascia panel assembly must be removed for access to the heater unit.
2. Full details of this particular operation are given in Section 24 of the chapter.

33. Heater - refitting

1. Refitting the heater unit is the reverse sequence to removal. The heater duct drain pipes must hang down outside the front engine mounting and the heater pipes.

34. Heater matrix - removal, repair and replacement

1. With the heater unit removed from the car unscrew the screws which secure the front panel of the casing around the edge. Also undo the three screws across the centre of the casing followed by unscrewing the two bolts. Separate the cover from the heater casing and slide the heater matrix from the casing.
2. If there is a small water leak coming from the end panels or the edges of the matrix it may be possible to repair using an electric soldering iron. If the leak is at the centre of the matrix, repair is difficult and it is considered more economical to purchase a service exchange unit. Before refitting flush the matrix thoroughly in the reverse direction to normal coolant flow, to loosen any sediment.
3. Refitting the matrix is the reverse sequence to removal.

35. Heater boost motor - removal, repair and overhaul

1. The motor may be removed with the heater unit in position but obviously access is better with the unit removed. It the motor is to be removed with the unit in place do not forget to disconnect the battery before beginning work as a safety precaution.
2. To remove the motor, remove the motor retaining bolts at the rear of the heater unit and lift away the motor and support bracket.
3. If the motor operation is suspect, connect the leads to the battery taking care not to touch the rotating fan blades. Should the motor not operate it is recommended that it be taken to an automobile electrician for further testing and, if economical, repair, otherwise a new motor may be fitted. Ensure that the fan blade hub is mounted securely on the motor spindle.
4. Refitting is the reverse sequence to removal.

Index

Metric Conversion Table

Inches	Decimals	Millimetres	Inches	Millimetres
1/64	.015625	.3969	.001	.0254
1/32	.03125	.7937	.002	.0508
3/64	.046875	1.1906	.003	.0762
1/16	.0625	1.5875	.004	.1016
5/64	.078125	1.9844	.005	.1270
3/32	.09375	2.3812	.006	.1524
7/64	.109375	2.7781	.007	.1778
1/8	.125	3.1750	.008	.2032
9/64	.140625	3.5719	.009	.2286
5/32	.15625	3.9687	.01	.254
11/64	.171875	4.3656	.02	.508
3/16	.1875	4.7625	.03	.762
13/64	.203125	5.1594	.04	1.016
7/32	.21875	5.5562	.05	1.270
15/64	.234375	5.9531	.06	1.524
1/4	.25	6.3500	.07	1.778
17/64	.265625	6.7469	.08	2.032
9/32	.28125	7.1437	.09	2.286
19/64	.296875	7.5406	.1	2.54
5/16	.3125	7.9375	.2	5.08
21/64	.328125	8.3344	.3	7.62
11/32	.34375	8.7312	.4	10.16
23/64	.359375	9.1281	.5	12.70
3/8	.375	9.5250	.6	15.24
25/64	.390625	9.9219	.7	17.78
13/32	.40625	10.3187	.8	20.32
27/64	.421875	10.7156	.9	22.86
7/16	.4375	11.1125	1	25.4
29/64	.453125	11.5094	2	50.8
15/32	.46875	11.9062	3	76.2
31/64	.484375	12.3031	4	101.6
1/2	.5	12.7000	5	127.0
33/64	.515625	13.0969	6	152.4
17/32	.53125	13.4937	7	177.8
35/64	.546875	13.8906	8	203.2
9/16	.5625	14.2875	9	228.6
37/64	.578125	14.6844	10	254.0
19/32	.59375	15.0812	11	279.4
39/64	.609375	15.4781	12	304.8
5/8	.625	15.8750	13	330.2
41/64	.640625	16.2719	14	355.6
21/32	.65625	16.6687	15	381.0
43/64	.671875	17.0656	16	406.4
11/16	.6875	17.4625	17	431.8
45/64	.703125	17.8594	18	457.2
23/32	.71875	18.2562	19	482.6
47/64	.734375	18.6531	20	508.0
3/4	.75	19.0500	21	533.4
49/64	.765625	19.4469	22	558.8
25/32	.78125	19.8437	23	584.2
51/64	.796875	20.2406	24	609.6
13/16	.8125	20.6375	25	635.0
53/64	.828125	21.0344	26	660.4
27/32	.84375	21.4312	27	685.8
55/64	.859375	21.8281	28	711.2
7/8	.875	22.2250	29	736.6
57/64	.890625	22.6219	30	762.0
29/32	.90625	23.0187	31	787.4
59/64	.921875	23.4156	32	812.8
15/16	.9375	23.8125	33	838.2
61/64	.953125	24.2094	34	863.6
31/32	.96875	24.6062	35	889.0
63/64	.984375	25.0031	36	914.4

Printed by
Haynes Publishing Group
Sparkford Yeovil Somerset
England